DATE			
	JUN 1 0 1993		

The Dragons of Tiananmen

Studies in Comparative Religion
Frederick M. Denny, Editor

The Holy Book in Comparative Perspective
Edited by Frederick M. Denny and Rodney L. Taylor

Dr. Strangegod:
On the Symbolic Meaning of Nuclear Weapons
By Ira Chernus

Native American Religious Action:
A Performance Approach to Religion
By Sam Gill

The Confucian Way of Contemplation:
Okada Takehiko and the Tradition of Quiet-Sitting
By Rodney L. Taylor

Human Rights and the Conflict of Cultures:
Western and Islamic Perspectives on Religious Liberty
By David Little, John Kelsay, and Abdulaziz A. Sachedina

The Munshidin of Egypt:
Their World and Their Song
By Earle H. Waugh

The Buddhist Revival in Sri Lanka:
Religious Tradition, Reinterpretation and Response
By George D. Bond

A History of the Jews of Arabia:
From Ancient Times to Their Eclipse Under Islam
By Gordon Darnell Newby

Arjuna in the Mahabharata:
Where Krishna Is, There Is Victory
Ruth Cecily Katz

Ethics, Wealth, and Salvation:
A Study in Buddhist Social Ethics
Edited by Russell F. Sizemore and Donald K. Swearer

Ritual Criticism:
Case Studies in Its Practice, Essays on Its Theory
By Ronald L. Grimes

The Dragons of Tiananmen:
Beijing as a Sacred City
By Jeffrey F. Meyer

The Other Sides of Paradise:
Explorations into the Religious Meanings of Domestic Space in Islam
By Juan Eduardo Campo

The Dragons of Tiananmen:

Beijing as a Sacred City

Jeffrey F. Meyer

University of South Carolina Press

Copyright © 1991 University of South Carolina

Published in Columbia, South Carolina, by the
University of South Carolina Press

Manufactured in the United States of America

Library of Congress Cataloging-in-Publication Data

Meyer, Jeffrey F.
  The dragons of Tiananmen : Beijing as a sacred city / Jeffrey F.
Meyer.
    p.   cm. — (Studies in comparative religion)
  Includes bibliographical references (p.   ) and index.
  ISBN 0-87249-739-9 (hardback : acid-free)
  1. Sacred space—China—Peking.   2. China—Religion.   3. Peking
(China)—Religion.   I. Title.   II. Series: Studies in comparative
religion (Columbia, S.C.)
  BL1812.P45M49   1991
  299′.51235′0951156—dc20   90-29120

For Cathy, Elsa, Joel, Jonathan, and Julia

*Pékin est la dernier refuge de l'inconnu
et du merveilleux sur terre.*
—*Pierre Loti (1901)*

Contents

ILLUSTRATIONS

FIGURES

PLATES

Editor's Preface

The study of sacred space has been a prominent interest of historians of religion in this century. Although earlier scholars contributed important monographs on specific places and regions—Paul Mus's monumental *Barabudur* (1936) and A. J. Wensinck's compact *The Ideas of the Western Semites Concerning the Navel of the Earth* (1916) come to mind—it is Mircea Eliade who developed the study of sacred space into a major subdivision of comparative religion. Since Eliade's contributions, made in such works as *Patterns in Comparative Religion* (1958) and *The Sacred and the Profane: The Nature of Religion* (1959), published scholarship on sacred space has proliferated, ranging from studies of specific cases to comparative treatments.

Jeffrey Meyer's study of Beijing as a sacred city combines a concern for close focus on a specific major urban ceremonial center with an interest in comparative models and analyses. The universal appeal and authority of Beijing for traditional Chinese over many generations attests to its prestige. Meyer shows that, even today, a compelling if jumbled sacral character persists, even though China has had capitals other than Beijing in its long history.

A city can be sacralized by the laying out of its plan according to the cosmology of the region, thus uniting realm and ruler in a pattern of sacred kingship. This ancient pattern can be seen in the ancient Near East, in ancient Rome, in classical Mesoamerica, and other places, as well as China. The proper cosmic orientation in space, combined with the appropriate foundation lore, can start the process of transforming a new capital into what Meyer calls a "sacred city."

Yet there are urban ceremonial centers—Jerusalem, Mecca, and Banaras are good examples—that also possess religiously potent qualities unrelated to cosmic orientation, sacral kingship, or an intentional foundation ideology. Such centers are sacred in themselves, not because sacral power has been bestowed upon them but because they are already sacred places in essence. As Meyer says, "the very ground of the city is holy ground." Such a place Meyer calls a "holy city." "The sacred city has religious meaning because it is space organized according to a sacred model. The holy city has religious meaning because it simply *is* at a certain locus in the environment."

The distinction between sacred city and holy city has heuristic value, but Meyer is careful not to reify the two types or to claim exclusiveness for them as categories when examining specific cases. One of the main contributions of Meyer's combining of a focused historical perspective on Beijing with comparative analysis is a deeper appreciation of that great capital as possessing both cosmic and local sacrality in a complex and mutually reinforcing relationship. In the process, we gain a sense of what Beijing has meant not only to the rulers and elites—the sacred city aspect—but also to the common people, whose access to Beijing was characterized by factors that emerged from its intrinsic holiness.

Frederick M. Denny
Series Editor

Acknowledgments

I want to thank my publishers for the opportunity to revise this book thoroughly and the chance to see Beijing in a new way. Kevin Lynch, in *The Image of the City,* has wisely said: "We must consider not just the city as a thing in itself, but the city as being perceived by its inhabitants." When I first wrote this book, as my dissertation, I am afraid I was not able to take Lynch's advice. I had even written with sophomoric wisdom in the introduction, "we must pursue the question of symbolic meaning, but unless we also ask what the real city meant to all levels of society, this study will have missed its most important task." It was fortunate for me that my committee charitably overlooked the glaring omission of my dissertation's "most important task." Among the major changes in this revised version has been my effort to begin to see Beijing as "perceived by its inhabitants." To use the metaphor of the book's title, I had to try to see with the eyes of Tiananmen's dragons, looking not only inward toward the Forbidden City but outward toward the people's Beijing. I have found this to be a difficult though fascinating task, as the tapestry of the people's city is rich and cannot be comprehended in a single glance, or even a single book. I console myself with the saying that even a thousand *li* trip must begin with the first step. At least, I have made a start.

I wish finally to thank some of the many persons who have helped to make this book possible, foremost among them Joseph Kitagawa who first helped me find and refine this topic, and guided me over the academic hurdles toward my degree. I would also like to thank Wolfram Eberhard for his comments, corrections, and many invaluable suggestions; Anthony Yu and Paul Wheatley for reading the original version and giving me encouragement at a time when I needed it. In Beijing I had the help of two scholars who gave very generously of their time and knowledge: Chen Zhichao of the Chinese Academy of Social Sciences and Ge Zhaoguang of the Academy of Chinese Culture. In the U.S.A., my thanks go to Edward St. Clair for his professional encouragement and technical help over the years, and Liu Hong for technical and translation assistance. Finally I wish to thank Mircea Eliade. He read this book in its first incarnation years ago, and now has better things to do than read its second. Although he is not often quoted in this book, those who know his thought will find his influence throughout. With gratitude toward all these mentors and helpers, I take responsibility for whatever mistakes remain in this book and ask my colleagues to criticize, comment, and correct.

The Dragons of Tiananmen

Beijing,
An Idea in Stone

> . . . held fast by the people around him and the dead below
> him and the people to come, like a brick in a wall. He holds.

> —Paul Valéry

"Those passengers wishing to get off at Chaoyang Gate, please get ready now. . . ." The pleasant feminine voice of the tape recording warns subway passengers to prepare if they wish to get off at the next stop in the underground loop, which encircles the inner city of Beijing. Most of the names of the underground stations evoke memories of the city's history: "passengers wishing to get off at Dongzhi (East Upright) Gate . . . Anding (Peaceful Security) Gate . . . the Drum Tower . . . Xizhi (West Upright) Gate . . . Fucheng (Perfect Abundance) Gate . . . Xuanwu (Martial Valor) Gate . . . Qian (Front) Gate . . . Chongwen (Lofty Culture) Gate . . . Chaoyang (Facing Sun) Gate . . . please get ready now."[1] The actual gates are gone now, as are Beijing's massive walls. Only the names remain, faint echos from the imperial past. It is true that Qian Gate remains. Desheng (Victorious Virtue) Gate remains also, together with a small portion of the wall and tower at the southeast corner of the inner city. But that is all, and these immense gray relics stand alone now, without the support of encircling walls, like dinosaurs in a vast museum.

Beijing was an idea long before it was a city, an audacious idea that makes the pretensions of today's powerful nations look modest by comparison. It was an idea that gave shape and substance to the city and its surroundings, to the province in which it was located, to the whole of what we call China, and ultimately, to the entire world. It created a world, from center to circumference. It spoke, not in words, but in the language of architecture, mass, and space. The halls, large and small, the palaces, gardens, streets, walls, gates, altars, and temples of worship all combined together to make a remarkably clear statement.

What did they say? According to Chinese tradition, they said that this Beijing was the earthly termination of the axis of the universe, the center of the world, the pivot of the four quarters. We foreigners call it

China, the land of Ch'in (now written Qin), after the feudal state that eventually reunified the country twenty-two hundred years ago. They, the inhabitants, call it *Zhongguo*, the Central Kingdom, the middle land between the four seas. This concentric geography placed China at the center of the world, and Beijing, despite its northerly location, was at the center of China. Today we smile at such archaic pretensions. Yet the expression of this idea in stone was accomplished with absolute conviction, and its implications carried out with ritual exactitude over a span of nearly nine hundred years. The idea was so simple and compelling, so striking in its symmetry, that even if it were not true, one would *want* it to be true.

It was more than a political idea. It was a religious, transcendent concept, literally calling upon the heavens to witness its mandate, its divine support and sanction. It claimed that the ruler, ensconced on the dragon throne, was commissioned by heaven to rule China, pacify the outlying territories, and ultimately to set such a shining example of perfect government that the whole world would come to the foot of his throne and offer submission.

The ruler was therefore called the son of heaven. His rights and privileges were awesome, but his responsibilities were correspondingly heavy. Some of the occupants of the dragon throne may have cast a skeptical eye on such extravagant claims, but many believed them completely, and carried out their duties with agonized sincerity. Despite a fair number of imperial wastrels and scoundrels, the idea of Beijing lived beyond and above them. It was essentially a religious idea, and therefore survived its unworthy embodiments. Lesser ideas die when humans fail to carry them out, but the greatest ideas always have the ability to transcend such failures, at least for a time. They endure as a vision of what *ought* to be. Like shadows on the wall of Plato's cave, each Chinese capital was a momentary embodiment of the more real, but hidden, ideal. Of these shadows, Beijing was perhaps the most faithful and perfect.

This book is therefore far more the history of an idea than it is the history of a city. What I have done is to paint a composite portrait of Ming-Qing Beijing, since the city during that period of time remained fairly uniform, a basically unchanging expression of the ancient ideal. I hope this is valid. Although I note historic changes that occurred during that period of five hundred years, I am aiming more at the depiction of enduring characteristics than at an exact detailing of historic changes.

The city was an idea become visible in physical, architectural forms. Rarely has a translation from the medium of conceptual thought to the medium of urban form been made so faithfully as it was in the case of Beijing. Because its history is long, its historical documents readily available, and its monuments well preserved, it affords an excellent opportunity to study the phenomenon of the sacred city.

Traditional cities everywhere have something significant to tell us about the archaic concepts in the minds of those who planned, built, and lived in them. Our cities today also tell us much about the nature of contemporary civilization if we investigate them with understanding. The plan of any city is a code waiting to be deciphered, which can tell the astute interpreter much about present and previous inhabitants. As we build our cities, we are writing contemporary history, and in our own case this may prove to be embarrassing.

In truth our cities are a jumble, an uneasy alliance of many forces that compete for civic rights and urban space. Economic forces principally, but also social, political, religious, and various other parties have had a hand in the shaping of our cities. Which is to say, we are the citizens of a diverse, disjointed, and sometimes anarchic civilization. If traditional cities like Beijing were a clear statement, ours are the opposite. Twentieth-century writers like Eliot, Joyce, Rilke, Kafka, Proust, and Brecht have singled out the anxiety, isolation, apathy, and anomie characterizing urban life today. The "archetype" of city of the last two thousand years has come to an end, and "city" has become "cultural hieroglyph," a visual image still, but hard to read, undecipherable.[2] The forces often do not work in harmony.

Beijing today, too, is more and more a jumble of competing forces, and the shape of the ancient city is harder and harder to decipher. As the walls have come down, the gates degenerated into mere place names, the moats and lakes filled, the old meanings become more and more opaque. And the idea of socialism, even if it could have been translated into stone and superimposed upon the plan of the old city, is now increasingly uncertain of itself. The high-rise monuments to an experiment in capitalism poke their fingers up to create a new skyline for the city.

In a time of urban confusion, there is a temptation to nostalgia in a study like this, a longing for a simpler time of certainty and clarity when a city could make a unified statement, a clear expression of belief. Of course, there are few Chinese who would want the return of an emperor, just as few Europeans or Americans would wish for a time when the great cathedrals dominated the urban landscape, both figuratively and politically. Yet it is impossible not to envy imperial China, a civilization based on a simple and unified idea, just as it is hard not to long for an adolescent period when absolute certainties and utter conviction made sense of the puzzle of human life.

While absolutisms, both religious and political, had been challenged for centuries in Europe, China persisted in a monolithic religious/political concept right down to the early twentieth century. The idea of imperial China, sketched above, was so compelling that it took the exploitation, degradations, and humiliating defeats of the nineteenth century to cause the Chinese to finally question and ultimately reject it. And when they did, their rejection was abrupt and violent, with no transition, no constitutional monarchy, no experimentation with gradual change, nor attempts to save the forms of the millennia past. The revolution of 1911 overthrew the past suddenly, and when the dust had settled, Nanjing was the capital of republican China. The great monuments of Beijing were abandoned one by one, neglected, given over to other uses, here an army camp, there a factory or a school. The mortar crumbled, glazed tiles cracked and fell to the ground, grass and weeds sprouted in the courtyards of the Forbidden City. This neglect was partly because of hatred of the past, partly because of poverty, Japanese invasion, and war.

Then came the revolution of 1949, and Mao restored Beijing as the national capital. The monuments were belatedly reclaimed as museums and tourist attractions. Interrupted and set back by the Cultural Revolution (1966–1976), the work of restoration has been resumed today. History is being preserved with great zeal, but the connection between present and past has already been severed. There is no continuity, and the monuments of the emperor's city are only isolated pieces in an urban museum.

What was the essence of Beijing? It would be tempting to choose the Great Hall of Audience, which housed the impressive dragon throne, or perhaps the altar of heaven where the celestial ruler of the universe was worshiped. But that would be to judge Beijing only from the perspective of the ruler, not the people. The real essence of the city was its walls. "Wall" is what makes China, wall makes the city of Beijing, the Imperial City, the Forbidden City, and all subsidiary units down to country town, village, and private home. Give any Chinese some loose bricks and he will build a wall, a gate, and hire a gatekeeper to prevent the outsider from entering.

Walls are important to the Chinese because, over and above practical considerations (preventing thievery, resisting attack, and the like), the wall is the line clearly drawn between what is significant and what is insignificant, what is powerful and what is not powerful, who is kin and who is stranger, what is sacred and not sacred.[3] The Great Wall is the symbol of China par excellence. Traditionally it marked off civilization from barbarism; today it still marks off the "sacred land" (shenzhou) from the rest of the world. Walls of old Chinese cities were as much symbols as they were military stockades. The word for "city" in Chinese is "wall" (cheng), alerting us to the essence of what makes a city. The god or protective spirit of the city was the chenghuang, and his temple at the center of the city's spiritual "welfare system." At the bottom was the family or clan, and their home should, ideally, be surrounded by a wall, which marked off the most fundamental unit of Chinese society. It was not the individual who was accorded the protection of walled privacy. Within the walled compound there was very little privacy. It was the extended family itself that was sacrosanct, and clearly marked off from the rest of society.

Today walls are still a ubiquitous feature of the Chinese landscape. Even though a poor country, China lavishes an incredible amount of money on building walls where a non-Chinese would think them totally unnecessary. They are still much in favor in rural villages, and in the cities they now usually demarcate factories, businesses, schools, offices, and the other "work units" (danwei) of socialist society. The Chinese passion for walls reflects their passion for clarity in human relationships, signifying an individual's identity and place within society. The Marxist revolution has in no way diminished the Chinese love of a wall. It is only that they are now built in different places, and define different units of meaning.

The walls of Beijing began to come down soon after the revolution of 1911. The first rift was made when the Beijing to Hankou railroad was built in the late nineteenth century. The people objected, saying that Beijing was like a dragon and a break in the walls would create a wound in the dragon's body.[4] Since then all the walls have come down, and this factor more than any other signifies the death of the original idea of Beijing. A grand and historic city remains, but it is no longer sacred, for the lines of demarcation of the templum have been obliterated.

The wall is a feminine form, embracing, enclosing, securing, and protecting those within its compass. But there must be a way out. "We chisel out doors and windows; it is precisely in these empty spaces that we find the usefulness of the room."[5] Thus two functions are implied, exclusion and conjunction, at the place of the gate, where two realms meet. Qin Shihuang, the Unifier, remembered only one function, exclusion. His wall building and book burning served that same function. His book burning was not a momentary catharsis, like a Savonarola in Florence, but a permanent gesture like building the Great Wall. He closed off his subjects from access to the past, to individual conscience and the possibility of transcending the present, excluding the "poison" of subversive ideas as his wall was meant to shut out the barbarians.[6]

Besides serving the functions of exclusion and conjunction, the wall provides an image of what it means to be Chinese. The French poet Paul Valery understood this and wrote in 1895, when the great walls of Beijing were still in place:

Every man here feels that he is both son and father, among thousands and tens of thousands, and is aware of being held fast by the people around him and the dead below him and the people to come, like a brick in a wall. He holds. Every man knows that he is nothing apart from this composite earth, and outside the miraculous structure of his ancestors.[7]

A better metaphor of traditional Chinese self-understanding could hardly be imagined. The collectivist mentality of Marxism-Maoism, which guides Chinese ideology today, has only redrawn the lines, redefining significant units of society. The archaic concept of the city has been lost, but in the realm of Chinese imagination, "wall" still holds.

This book is a study in religious symbolism, a very complex set of symbols derived from many sources. But it is also the study of a real city where people lived, worked, played, married, produced children, got sick, and died. All had their own points of view: the emperor and his officials, Buddhist and Taoist priests and monks, military personnel and wealthy merchants, practitioners of geomancy, diviners and shamens, scholars, shopkeepers, peddlars, and laborers—ordinary men, women, and children. Each experienced the city in a different way. To give a complete picture of traditional Beijing, we must remember that it was both symbol and place, and to do it justice we must be aware of the many viewpoints, beliefs, and interests of those who lived there.

But despite the variety of standpoints, there was an underlying unity. Beijing was not the chaotic jumble of competing forces like so many of our cities today. I like to think of traditional Beijing as a tapestry, which is an exceedingly intricate artistic statement. A tapestry is a composite of many disparate elements and details, like a novel or a symphony, brought together in an artistic whole. Like all woven fabrics, it is unified by the underlying structure of warp and weft, two separate systems, which when woven together create the seamless cloth of the whole. Looked at from the wrong side, it can be a confusing pastiche of color and form. Looked at from the right side, its unity appears.

The warp of Beijing is the cosmic/astral system of symbols that identify it as the seat of government, the center of the earthly world, the place where the emperor ruled as the son of heaven. The warp, which is simply a pattern, can be strung anywhere, and we know that the Chinese capital has been built in many different cities throughout the course of history: in Changan, Luoyang, Kaifeng, Hangzhou, and elsewhere. The warp was simply space organized in a certain way. The weft of Beijing is place. It is reflected in the complex of popular beliefs that made it a sacred place, a unique spot on the face of the land where gods, spirits, and heroes visited, where unrepeatable events took place, where transcendent powers could be reached. The weft is specific and unique, it adds substance, color, and specificity to the whole fabric. I hope to show that despite complexity, variety, and rich detail, Beijing was a unified whole. It was of a piece.

NOTES

1. I will generally use the most recent Qing dynasty names for the gates and buildings of the city since these are most familiar to the modern reader. Most gates and buildings have had many name changes through the course of their long history.

2. Burton Pike, "The City as Cultural Hieroglyph," in Peter S. Hawkins, ed., *Civitas: Religious Interpretations of the City* (Atlanta: Scholars Press, 1986), esp. pp. 130–33.

3. Hwang Ming-chorng, "A Study of Urban Form in 18th-century Beijing" (MIT masters dissertation, February 1986), p. 78, admits that the walls of Beijing were more important for their symbolic and psychological meaning than their military usage.

4. Juliet Bredon, *Peking* (Shanghai: Kelly & Walsh, 1919), p. 36.

5. *Lao-tzu: Te-Tao Ching*, trans. Robert G. Henricks (New York: Ballentine Books, 1989), p. 208.

6. See the meditations of Jorge Luis Borges, *Other Inquisitions: 1937–1952*, trans. Ruth L. C. Simms (New York: Simon and Schuster, 1968), pp. 3–5, on the meaning of the first emperor's wall.

7. "The Yalu," *History and Politics*, vol. 10 of *The Collected Works of Paul Valery* (New York: Bollingen Pantheon Books, 1962), p. 374.

Chapter 1

The Chinese Capital
in Historical Perspective

. . . the wind custodian sings,
"I guard the fragrance of a thousand springs.
Draw near! Draw near!
Ten thousand yesterdays are gathered here."

—Yuan Mei

EARLY CHINESE CAPITALS

Beijing was the last capital of imperial China. After its eclipse during the first half of this century, it was reclaimed as national capital by the revolutionary leaders of New China. It is the last in a long series of capitals that go back thousands of years to the very beginnings of Chinese civilization in the valley of the Yellow River. In order to better understand Beijing, we must begin with a brief account of its predecessors, and examine the classical tradition of urban planning that shaped them. We can do this briefly, because a great deal of scholarly work has already been done on some of these earlier capitals. For the factual material, I will be simply summarizing this scholarship.[1]

"The Capital of Shang was full of order, the model for all parts of the Kingdom."[2] This reference to the earliest known historical dynasty, taken from the *Classic of Poetry*, already reveals in a cryptic way two of the embryonic aspects of the Chinese capital—a plan that has internal order and is paradigmatic for the surrounding domain. The *Pangang* section of the *Classic of History* contains the account of a Shang dynasty ruler who desired to transfer his capital to a new location. When he encountered some popular resistance, the king pointed out that the Shang capital had been moved five times already, each time resulting in renewal of the dynasty. "As from the stump of a felled tree there are sprouts and shoots, Heaven will perpetuate its decree in our favour in this new city; the great inheritance of the former kings will be continued and renewed, and tranquility will be secured to the four quarters [of the kingdom]."[3] This quote makes clear the traditional belief that the fate of the entire kingdom was somehow dependent upon the royal city and the quality of govern-

8

ment there. It also suggests that the transfer of the capital city to another site was not only possible, but potentially advantageous, an important concept that sets the sacred city in China apart from similar cities elsewhere.

Archaeological evidence for the Shang period (approximately 1700–1100 B.C.E.) is still fragmentary, but it confirms certain features mentioned in the texts above. Excavations at Anyang (between 1928 and 1937) and at Zhengzhou (since 1950) indicate that these places were probably the sites of two Shang capitals out of seven dynastic capitals attributed to the thirty Shang kings. The city at Zhengzhou (current provincial capital of Henan) is thought to be from the middle Shang period, possibly King Zhongding's capital at Ao, mentioned in the Han dynasty historical record, the *Shiji*. The city had substantial walls, was nearly rectangular in shape, and close to an exact north-south orientation.[4]

The capital at Anyang was late Shang, larger and grander than Zhengzhou. It covered an area of thirty to forty square kilometers, had symmetrically planned houses, some on platforms, multiple gates, a north-south orientation. Excavators believe that some of the foundations uncovered were a palace, ancestral hall, and ceremonial compound built to a preconceived plan.[5] Relating this information to later capitals, we may tentatively point out three important features in these Shang cities: (1) an apparent squareness or rectangularity in overall form and in the individual outline of particular buildings and clusters of buildings; (2) use of the pounded earth (*hang tu*) type raised platforms for all large structures, though whether these were originally residences, palaces, temples, or open altars is often open to debate; (3) cardinal orientation in overall planning and in individual structures.[6]

For the Zhou dynasty (1100–221 B.C.E.) we have some archaeological remains and a considerable body of literary evidence in the Chinese classics. There is a question of the reliability of these texts, however, for the classics we have today were edited during the Han period. While parts of these works are doubtlessly Zhou documents, it is not always clear what is authentic and what has been systematized to conform to outlooks current among Han Confucians. Still, the significant point is that these texts were the basis of all later Chinese understanding of the Zhou period, and that later city planning was based on them.

One ode from the *Classic of Poetry* describes the building of a capital city by the ancestors of the ancient line that would become the Zhou dynasty. It mentions the divination with tortoise shell before work could begin, recalls the careful and orderly planning for the new settlement, and tells of the building of four structures: the ancestral temple, the outer gate (of the palace), the gate of audience, and the great altar of the spirits of the land.[7] Another ode recounts how King Wu of the Zhou divined before settling in his new capital of Hao: "The tortoise-shell decided the site, and King Wu completed the city."[8]

The *Classic of History* records a change of capitals that occurred early in the Zhou dynasty under the guidance of the duke of Zhou. Divination was first performed in several localities around a place called Luo, not far from later Luoyang, and when favorable indications were given, the plan for the city was drawn up. The duke reported to the emperor that he had "made a great survey of this eastern region, hoping to found the place where he [the emperor] should become the intelligent sovereign of the people." The duke then offered two bulls as victims in the suburbs and on the following day, at the altar to the spirit of the land in the new city (the *she* altar), he sacrificed a bull, a ram, and a boar:

> Let the King come here as the vice-gerent of God (*Shang Ti*), and undertake [the duties of government] in this centre of the land. Tan (the duke of Zhou) said, "Now that this great city has been built, from henceforth he may be the mate of great heaven, and reverently sacrifice to [the spirits] above and beneath; from henceforth he may from this central spot administer successful government."[9]

The locus classicus for the foundation of the Chinese capital, however, is the *Zhouli* (Rituals of Zhou). Near the beginning of the book we find the statement that the sovereign alone constitutes the realm, determines the four sides, fixes the divisions within, traces the plan of the capital and the countryside. A commentary adds that the sovereign must determine the place of the ancestral temple, the place consecrated to the spirits of the soil and grain, the imperial palace, and the public market.[10] Specific procedures for laying out the capital are given in the section on the official duties of the *dasitou*, the "grand director of the masses." This official's duty is to determine the "center of the land" by the use of an instrument that Biot translates as the *tablette des mesures*, or gnomon. Precisely how this instrument is constructed and used is not clear from the text.

One commentary suggests that one moved from the borders of the land progressively toward the center and there set up the gnomon. A later commentary suggests the opposite, saying that the gnomon is used to determine the solstices and equinoxes as well as the borders of the land. It appears that one begins at the center, which is the place where the shadow of the sun at its height is one foot five-tenths as registered by the instrument. "This is the place where the heavens and the earth unite, where the four seasons are joined, where the wind and rain come together, where the two principles, male and female, are in harmony."[11] Although the exact

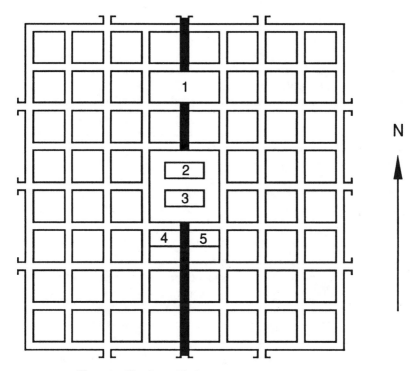

Illus. 1. Plan for an Ideal Capital, Based on the *Zhouli*.

nature of the Zhou gnomon is unclear, its symbolic function is unmistakable in the quote.

The final section of the *Zhouli*, a supplement called the *Kaogongji*, provides further specific directions for the layout of the capital, whether it be that of the king or the feudatory prince. The capital must be oriented, and to ensure that this is done properly, the builders are to set up a gnomon and examine the shadow of the rising and setting sun to determine east and west. At night they observe the pole star, and thus having obtained the four directions, they construct a city having nine *li* on a side, with each side having three gates.[12] Nine roads run north and south within the city, nine run east and west. The ruler's palace is to be situated in the center, the public market behind the palace area and to the north. In front of the palace complex, the hall of audience should be built. East of the audience hall is the ancestral temple, and west of it the altar of soil and grain[13] (see illustration 1).

Setting aside the question of whether these classical texts represent actual Zhou practice or are an expression of the Han Confucian synthesis, we are now in a position to summarize the major features of the layout of Chinese capitals that clearly emerge from these texts. *One*, preparatory divination, which was employed to determine both the proper time and place to lay the foundation for the capital. *Two*, orientation according to the four points of the compass. *Three*, cardinal axiality, that is to say, emphasis on the north-south line, with buildings built on this line or arranged symmetrically on opposite sides of it. *Four*, square form (which became rectangular in most later capitals) with twelve symmetrically placed gates. *Five*, concentricity, here seen in the central location of the palace within the royal city, which in turn was to be at the center of the land.[14] *Six*, location of the essential urban components: royal palace and audience hall, ancestral temple and altar to the spirits of the land and grain, the latter two paired on opposite sides of the north-south way that led from the royal residence in the center to the city's southern gate. *Seven*, a suburban altar or altars. *Eight*, a kind of embryonic zoning into governmental and commercial sections, sequestering the ruler in the center and placing the market to the north.[15]

Some of the features just given are not specific to capital cities. Divination, for example, was used before undertaking any great affair, such as a military expedition, performance of important religious rites, large architectural projects, and so forth. Many of the features also hold for feudal capitals (and in later times for administrative centers such as prefectures, subprefectures, counties—*fu*, *zhou*, and *xian* cities) as well, but in all of these cases the royal or imperial capital was taken as the model.

Archaeological evidence from the Zhou dynasty cannot, of course, support all these features, but it does reveal the following: walled cities that were mostly square or rectangular in shape; an orientation of the city enclosure and the ceremonial and palace structures guided by the four cardinal directions, with emphasis on the north-south axis; earthen platforms that served as the foundations of structures that were politically or ceremonially important; zoning of the city into the *tu* or *guo* section where the elite class lived and *pi* occupied by the ordinary folk (*min*) or the people of the field (*yeren*). Toward the end of the *Chunqiu* period (722–481 B.C.E.), a double wall began to appear, the inner one (*cheng*) enclosing the aristocratic residential, administrative, and ceremonial areas, the outer (*guo*) enclosing commercial and industrial quarters.[16]

What the references from the classics represent is an ideal of what the Chinese capital ought to be. Probably never actualized in Zhou times, it nevertheless exerted incalculable influence on later Chinese capitals (as also on Kyoto, Osaka, and Narashima in Japan; Hanoi and Hue in Vietnam). From Han times onward, one can study the great Chinese capitals in the light of these early prescriptions as an ideal to which they aspired. Sometimes, constrained by preexisting cities, they fell quite short, as in the cases of Song dynasty Kaifeng and Hangzhou. At other times they achieved nearly perfect conformity, as in Tang Changan and Ming-Qing Beijing.

IDEAL AND HISTORICAL REALITY

Very little is known about Xianyang, the capital of the unifier of China, Qin Shihuang. Far greater efforts have been applied to excavation of his burial mound than his capital. Xianyang's site is just to the north of Han Changan. The city straddled the Wei River, was square in form, and excavations show that the main palaces were in the northern portion of the city.[17] There is also a hint that there was astral symbolism in the structure of the Qin capital, for Sima Qian says that there was a covered or hidden way (*fudao*) leading from the *A Fang* palace to the city, across the Wei River. Sima Qian likens this arrangement to a group of stars equivalent to Cassiopeia, leading from the pole star to a constellation across the Milky Way.[18] While this information is quite sketchy, it does draw our attention to another element of the cosmology of the Chinese capital, the astral-terrestrial relationship, the correspondence of microcosm and macrocosm.[19] The builders were trying to create on the earth an image of the greater cosmos. I shall explore this type of symbolism more fully in regard to Beijing.

Han Changan was built on the ruins of Qin Xianyang. It was oriented along a north-south axis, but did not have the perfect square shape of canonical prescription. Its northwest and southwest corners were jagged due to the irregularity of the terrain, and its gates opened at irregular places along the wall, not in accord with the symmetrical plan given in the *Zhouli*. Furthermore, the houses of the people were mingled with governmental offices, and the palaces were not clustered in one compound, so zoning was not at all strict. The main palaces were in the north portion of the city, while markets were placed irregularly inside and outside city walls.

But according to an old Chinese source, there were in Han Changan eight main streets running north and south, nine running east and west, three palaces, nine office halls, three temples, twelve gates, sixteen bridges, and a moat thirty feet broad, twenty feet deep. Another source adds the information that there were thirty-two towers, twelve lakes, four earthen altars (presumably north, south, east, and west of the city), eighty-one main palace gates, and fourteen side gates.[20] In the absence of any supportive evidence, we must conclude that these are numbers that have symbolic and cosmological value, but are not historically accurate. This rationalizing tendency would suggest that attempts were made at a later date to *make* Han Changan fit a more regular pattern. This suspicion is supported by the fact that later Chinese began to find a model to explain the form of Changan other than that presented in the *Zhouli*, but still a cosmic one. They called it the "city of the dipper," claiming that its major palaces and other important loci (such as the northeast and southeast corners, the intersections of the major east-west road, and so forth) corresponded to the stars of the polar constellations Ursa Major and Ursa Minor.[21]

As a conjecture, it seems Han Changan was only moderately successful in realizing the classical norms for a royal capital. The question then quite naturally arises whether these norms were ignored or flouted by the early Han rulers, or, as a product of Han Confucianism, had simply not yet been systematically proposed. At this point I cannot answer the question conclusively, though one suspects the latter case. More important for the purpose of the present study is to note the later attempts to systematize Changan through the use of symbolic numbers and the existence of the popular appelation "city of the dipper." These features of symbolic proportion and celestial model, whatever their source, became important concepts as the idea of a perfect capital developed in later history.

Let us pass over the period of internal disruption between the third and sixth centuries and consider one of the two closest approximations to the ideal of a capital city, Sui dynasty (598–618 C.E.) Daxing and its successor Tang dynasty (618–905) Changan (now called Xian).[22] The new rulers used various methods of divination to determine when and where it would be best for the Sui to build their capital. One minister, we are told, consulted the esoteric diagram known as the river plan (*hetu*) and pronounced the time auspicious. Several ministers expatiated on the myriad signs that heaven and nature favored the new emperor. Others took oracles by the milfoil (the form of divinition used with the *Yijing*) and the tortoise; the astronomers took observations of the sun and stars. All these were made to ensure the correctness of the proposed site.[23]

As originally conceived by the Sui rulers, Daxing was a nearly perfect square with a gridwork of north-south and east-west streets that divided the city into one hundred units, each called a *li*. The east, west, and south walls each had three gates, though the north wall diverged slightly from the norm by having only two. Within the city enclosure and placed against the northern wall was the imperial city, the northern part of which was the *danei* or palace city, also called the *taijigong*. The *taimiao* or imperial ancestral temple was situated in the imperial city, to the east of the central axial way running south from the gate of the palace city. In a corresponding position on the west side of the axial way was the altar of the land, the *she*.[24]

Government offices were segregated from the dwellings of the people and there were two major markets, one near the eastern and the other near the western gate of the city. Although this zoning was sanctioned by the classical norms, its placement was not, for the markets should have been behind the imperial palaces, against the northern wall of the city. Centers for the imperial worship of heaven and for the spring plowing rite were located south of the city, just east of the great north-south thoroughfare.

The Tang emperors by and large completely followed the pattern for the city established by the Sui. However, they built two more palace complexes, one along the east end of the north wall of the city, called the *daminggong* (or the *dongnei*, "eastern within"), and another at the east gate of the city called the *xingqinggong* (or the *nannei*, "southern within"). While the original palace city along the northern wall of the imperial city continued to be considered as the most important palace complex, the emperors, from the time of Gaozong (650–684 C.E.) onward, began to use the *daminggong* as their residence.[25]

Thus with few deviations from the classical norms, the model of cosmic order was impressed upon the imperial capital of Changan. Nelson Wu, noting this striking regularity, says that there was only one flaw in the relentless rectangular planning and orientation of Tang Changan. According to a legend, there was a single old locust tree that was out of line, left over from the old landscape, because under it "the architect general had often sat to watch the progress of construction, and a special order from the emperor in honor of his meritorious official spared it from being felled." The author then goes on to remark that "except for this tree, the total superimposition of man's order on natural terrain was complete."[26]

It seems to me that the legend should be interpreted in the opposite direction. The order impressed on Changan is not an act of impressing the human order on the environment, but rather the cosmic order, a pattern derived from the motions and positions of the heavenly bodies, which, if realized on earth, would ensure the stability and permanence of capital, realm, and dynasty. The spared locust represents one small concession to human feeling, since it was allowed to remain in honor of a meritorious official.[27]

After the fall of the Tang, the site of Changan was never again to be chosen as national capital, but the architectural achievement demonstrated there was impressive. Because of its influence on all later Chinese capitals and on Japanese, Korean, and southeast Asian capitals, it became a legacy to all of Asia.

The story of later Chinese capitals through the Southern Song period is the story of adaptations to increasingly crowded and difficult terrain. We may summarize the situation very briefly. In certain respects Northern

Song (960–1126) Kaifeng and Southern Song (1127–1178) Hangzhou were able to be made to correspond to some of the inherited norms for the royal capital, but some geographical and demographic features made a close approximation impractical. The two cities were bounded by irregular watercourses and high lands and clogged with people, so the task of imposing the oriented square or rectangular grid pattern was too great and too expensive for the Song rulers. The imperial city of the Northern Song was rather small and placed in the southern part of Kaifeng, though it is said that the ancestral temple and altar to the spirit of the land were in proper position. The gates were not symmetrical, the streets not straight, and there were markets everywhere.[28]

There was, however, a suburban altar for the worship of heaven south of the city and an altar to the earth in the north, where the great solstitial sacrifices were performed, as well as altars to the sun and moon in the east and west suburbs, respectively, so the arrangement of ritual altars was at least complete.[29] During the reign of the last Northern Song emperor, Huizong, it appears that the aspiration arose to make Kaifeng more canonical. Describing the successive enlargements made during the course of the Song period, Soper concludes: "The resulting irregularity proved offensive, so that further additions were made to fill out something like a square. Unfortunately improvement came just in time to weaken the defenses till they could be easily overrun by the Jin Tartar raid of 1126; and the perfected Pien (an earlier name for Kaifeng) was burned down."[30]

In the city of Hangzhou, one can see the same struggle with an already existent, organically formed city, the gradual attempts to make it conform more closely with canonical norms. The essential components were there: the imperial palace compound, the ancestral temple, the altar to the spirit of the land, the altar of heaven, but their placement was irregular. In the end, Hangzhou proved unsatisfactory, its claims to cosmic form more an aspiration than a reality.[31]

BEIJING BEFORE THE MING

When the Ming took possession of Beijing in 1368 c.e., the city had already been a capital under three foreign dynasties, extending over a period of more than three centuries. These were the Khitan Tartar dynasty called Liao (907–1115), the Nuchen Tartar dynasty called Jin (1115–1260), and the Mongol Yuan (1260–1368). During the first of these periods, the city was rather limited in extent, perhaps just over half the size of the present "inner city."[32] Emperor Taizong of the Liao made it a "touring capital" (*xingdu*) in 937 and gave it the designation *Nanjing* or southern capital. At this time the population of the city and surrounding areas is estimated to have been approximately three hundred thousand. (The Liao had five capital cities, the main one called Shangjing, in the north.) The imperial area was located unsymmetrically in the southwest corner of the city. The walls, each having two gates, were built in 1012 and at that time the city was first called Yanjing by the Liao.[33] Although there were many Buddhist temples in Yanjing, the city was always of secondary importance to the Liao. The rulers therefore built no official altars of any kind there, and continued to perform their native forms of worship in their own principal capital of Shangjing. The name Yanjing, however, or Swallow Capital, endured and is still used today to refer to Beijing.

The Nuchen Jin entered Yanjing in 1122 c.e. They began an expansion and rebuilding program in the old Liao capital in 1151, more than doubling the size of the city. The name was changed in 1153 to Holy Capital (Shengdu) and immediately again to Middle Capital (Zhongdu), which was the official designation of the capital throughout the rest of the dynasty. The new capital was built on a magnificent scale, the outer wall supposedly 75 *li* in circumference. The imperial city, 27 *li* in circumference, was placed almost squarely in the center, in accord with the *Zhouli*. Although the Jin, like the Liao, kept up their native forms of worship, such as the worship of heaven, the sun, mountains, and other spirits,[34] they became ever more ardent to emulate Chinese dynasties in the form and grandeur of Zhongdu. Over the years they introduced a growing number of rituals based on Chinese traditions. The new city was constructed under the direction of a Chinese scholar named Zhang Hao, and he consciously based his plan on the classics as well as the Song capital at Kaifeng.[35]

Ironically, Zhongdu turned out to be more "correct" in many ways than the Song dynasty city whose culture the Jin sought to emulate. As we have seen, Zhongdu, oriented according to the four directions, was almost a perfect square shape. It had three gates in each of the east, south, and west walls, and four gates in the north. (The extra gate in the north wall exists because the Jin kept the old Liao wall, which already had two gates; their expansion to the east and west demanded a new gate in each part of the extended northern wall.) The imperial city enclosure was centrally located within the expanded capital.[36]

In 1153 c.e. Emperor Hailing transferred the spirit tablets of his ancestors to the newly named capital and two years later officially installed them in the *taimiao*. The traditional Chinese altars to the land and grain were completed in 1167 c.e. under his successor, the Dading emperor. The altar to the spirit of the land was square, about fifty *chi* broad and five high. The top was covered with the soil of five colors, symbolizing the five directions. In the soil was placed a white stone, half buried, its bottom somewhat larger than its top, giving it a bell-like shape. To the south of the altar was planted a chestnut tree, the species traditionally associated with the Zhou dynasty altar of the land.[37] There was a separate altar of grain a bit to the west, having the same form, but lacking any stone tablet. Following the Chinese practice, the times for worship at these altars were the mid-month of spring and autumn.

As we shall see in more detail later on, all these elements incorporated into the *shejitan* (as the altars were called when paired) were absolutely in accord with the ancient tradition. Why the Jin were so eager to build these altars and carry out the rituals so exactly is not difficult to understand. Chinese governmental rites were the prerogative of the emperor. Performing them in the proper setting was to claim authority, the mandate of heaven. Throughout Chinese history, it was often "barbarian" imitators, not the native Chinese dynasties, who were most correct in their observation of Chinese rites as well as the classical ideals of city planning. This holds true for the Northern Wei at Luoyang, the Jin and Yuan at Beijing, and also for the Qing. The notable exception would be the Sui-Tang dynasties at Changan, whose rules were trying to reassert Chinese political patterns after a period of disunity.

The Jin history shows us that the process of sinification went much further still. By 1194 C.E. the Jin had completed four suburban altars: the round, three-tiered altar of heaven in the suburb directly south of the main imperial gate; a square two-tiered altar of earth in the north; and altars to the sun and moon in the east and west suburbs, respectively, again in perfect accord with canonical prescription (and in imitation of Kaifeng).[38]

There were at least two forces at work here molding the Jin capital into a more perfect expression of the ancient traditions than most native dynasties had been able to achieve. First was the Jin desire to show themselves heirs to the Chinese imperial heritage. They had driven the Song out of northern China and now wished to rule all China and, in accordance with the theory of imperial ideology, the whole world. What better way to proclaim this intention than to build a capital fit for a son of heaven, the cosmic pivot who receives the mandate to universal rule? Second was the recurring tendency of Confucian literati to eventually accept the inevitable and serve the foreign ruler. The Jin had defeated the debilitated house of Song. If the Confucians could not have a native dynasty to serve, they might at least gradually form the barbarian into the native mold.

A small incident will serve to illustrate this process:

> Originally the Jin were without the worship of ancestors and ancestral temples, but after they had subjugated the Liao, the great officials they used to run the government were all native Chinese. These were constantly telling them that the Son of Heaven's filial

piety consisted in respect for ancestors, and that the essence of respect for ancestors consisted in building an Ancestral Temple. The Jin rulers then first began to have their eyes opened and consequently built the temple in the southeast corner of the city (their northern capital), which though correct in form was rather simple. But after Emperor Hailing moved to Yanjing, he built a complex in magnificent scale in the southern part of the city and called it the *Taimiao*.[39]

The Jin emperors also "had their eyes opened" in the case of their practice of sun worship. Native Jin worship of the sun apparently required that the ruler preside facing south. During the fifteenth year of Hailing, an officer noted that it would be fitting to honor the old Chinese custom and face east. The chronicle then adds laconically: "In the eighteenth year of his reign, the Emperor worshiped the sun in the Hall of Humane Government, for the first time facing east in the rite."[40]

The Mongols first entered Zhongdu in the tenth year of the reign of Taizu (Genghis Khan), which was 1215 C.E., but it was many years before the city began to assume its former importance. At first the old Jin capital was simply restored to use, but in 1267, under Yuan Shizu (Khubilai Khan), a new city was built to the northeast of the old capital and Shizu began to make it his royal capital. By 1272 its name was officially changed to Dadu (Great Capital), and from that time until the end of the Qing dynasty, over six hundred years later, it remained the capital of all China (save for a brief period in the early Ming).[41]

As noted earlier in discussing the Jin *mu* and *zi* city structure, the Mongols had a difficult time conquering Zhongdu, and by the time they overcame the Jin Tartars, the city was nearly destroyed. The new city of Dadu was built to the northeast of the site of old Zhongdu. For both of these reasons it has been assumed that the Yuan built their capital de novo. But G. N. Kates maintains that this conclusion is only partly true, since there was a Jin summer palace outside Zhongdu and to the north, which actually became the imperial residence in the Yuan period. Since this palace complex was spared in the general destruction of the siege, it was the logical place for Khubilai Khan to take as his residence while Dadu was being constructed.[42] This "temporary" palace later became permanent, an important feature of the later Mongol capital.

The city built by Khubilai was square in form, with a circuit of just over 60 *li*. It was oriented to the four directions and built on a north-south axis. The south, east, and west walls each had three gates, symmetrically placed. The north wall, however, like Tang Changan, had only two gates. The Imperial City was located in the center of Dadu, but a bit to the south. Inside it was the "great within" (*danei*) where the main imperial audience halls were located. Perhaps Khubilai foresaw the danger of the Mongols losing their nomadic vigor among the pleasures of urban life. It is said that when he built the *danei*, he had sand and desert grasses placed in the courtyards, so that his sons and grandsons would not forget their native traditions and their home in the northern steppes.[43]

To no avail. It did not take long for the sinification process to begin, and since the overall form of the city and the placement of its major components already fit comfortably into the traditional pattern, the change was not difficult. Unlike the Jin, however, the Yuan did not practice worship in the four suburbs, but worshiped heaven and earth, the mountains and rivers at a single altar complex to the south of the capital. At first, during the reign of Khubilai, it was performed at a temporary structure. It was not until 1305 that a permanent formal altar of heaven was built, quite likely just about on the site where the Ming-Qing altar stands today. The structure was round in form and three-tiered. The top level was about five *zhang* in diameter, the middle ten, and the bottom fifteen. Also in the complex were the usual auxiliary buildings: kitchen, storehouse, fasting hall, and so forth.

Although Khubilai Khan decreed the worship of the spirits of the land and grain in 1270, it was only 1293, just a year before his death, that he took steps to build a permanent altar. Like the Jin altar to the land, it used the five colored soils arranged according to the five directions, and had a stone tablet, though no chestnut tree is mentioned. There were separate *she* and *ji* altars and both were oriented toward the north.[44]

The imperial ancestral temple was begun in 1277, completed in 1280, and greatly expanded in 1323. In 1310, although the actual rites had been performed earlier, altars and centers were constructed for two other rituals hallowed by centuries-old Chinese tradition, the rite of spring plowing (to be performed by the emperor) and the rite of the silkworms (to be performed by the empress). These sites were built at the urging of a member of the Hanlin Academy, whose eloquence must have been considerable to overcome the natural disinterest of the pastoral Mongols in silkworms and farming.[45] Five years later the Yuan emperor was convinced by officials of the Board of Rites to build altars to the wind, rain, and thunder spirits.

But perhaps the sand and grass in the courtyards were not completely without effect. Though the city of Dadu finally received a truly Chinese impress, there were a number of features that deviated from the prescribed norms and many instances of imperial reluctance to accept traditional Chinese practices. It seems that the Yuan emperors never used the northern section of the *danei* for their living quarters. Their palaces of residence were in fact two complexes called the *xingshengdian* and *guangtiandian*, situated across a group of lakes to the west of the *danei*. If Kates is correct, this violation of the arrangement set for residential palace and audience halls in the *Zhouli* may have been partially a historical accident.

Nor were the locations of the *taimiao* and *shejitan* correct. They were not located on opposite sides of the grand imperial way south of the main palace gate, as was prescribed. The *taimiao* was located east of the imperial city near the *Jihua* eastern gate of Dadu. The *shejitan* was west of the imperial city between the *Pingze* and *Heyi* gates of the city. Although the Yuan built a large altar of heaven in the south suburbs, they personally worshiped there only four times in the one hundred years they were in power. The altar of silkworms, though built, was apparently never used.

In summary, then, we find a mixed picture in Yuan Dadu. Certainly in its orientation, axiality, gridlike regularity, and symmetry, Dadu was as canonical a capital as had existed in China, so that when the restoration-bent Ming rulers took over the city, they did little to change its general layout, though they did "correct" the positions of the *taimiao*, *shejitan*, and imperial residence. The Mongol accommodation to the Chinese system was somewhat less eager than that of the Nuchen Jin. Yuan history notes that as late as 1353 the "felt palaces" or yurts built for the use of Khubilai Khan still existed in Dadu.[46]

MING DYNASTY BEIJING

The first modifications in the form of Dadu were made in 1368 C.E., soon after the city had been conquered by Hongwu's victorious general Zhu Da. The city was rebuilt under a follower of Zhu Da, who, we are told, knew well the area and its people. The most striking change was the foreshortening of the northern portion of the Mongol city, supposedly because it made the city more defensible. Approximately the northern third of Dadu was excluded from the circuit of the new city wall, while the southern wall was somewhat extended. This foreshortening eliminated four Yuan gates: the northern gates in both the east and west walls, and the two in the north. Two new gates were then positioned in the new northern wall. Thus the Ming retained the "deviation" of only two northern gates and added another, reducing the gates in each of the east and west walls to two. For the rest of the city, including the position of the Imperial City and the *danei* (which now began to be called the Forbidden City), the old Yuan pattern was basically maintained.[47]

After much discussion and argumentation about where to establish his capital, Hongwu finally chose Nanjing. But in a decision fateful for the future history of Beijing, as well as China, he enfeoffed his fourth son Zhu Di as the prince of Yen in the old Yuan capital. Later, when Zhu Di had become the Yongle emperor, Li Zhigang and other members of the Board of Rites urged him to choose the seat of his old fief as the national capital, in order to give honor to the place that brought him to power. Yongle concurred with this request, making the official name Beijing (meaning northern capital) and designating it for the time being as a *xingzai* (traveling abode) or place of residence for the emperor when he was on tour.[48]

Thirteen years later the emperor ordered a thorough discussion of the question of rebuilding Beijing, in view of making it the official capital, the *jingshi*. All factors were discussed and the advisors pointed to its many advantages, economic, military, political, symbolic, and religious:

> The mountains and rivers make for Beijing's security, the water is sweet, the soil fertile, the people's customs are simple and pure, its produce rich. It is truly heaven's country (*tianguo*), a royal imperial capital. . . . In that year that you made the imperial tour, the four seas were brought together (i.e., the emperor united the whole world under his sway) and men's hearts were made to be in harmony. Auspicious omens have been multiplying, the good fortune (or blessing) of heaven has been renewed. Truly these are auspicious signs. The area is everyday more a hub of commerce. . . . Fighting men from all over the world are happily running here to offer their services. We consider this a time appointed by heaven and it is men's duty to comply with it. . . . We humbly beg you, in accord with the mind of heaven on high, and following the people's hopes here below, to give your imperial command to begin the work.[49]

Work was begun on Beijing in the fifteenth year of the reign of Yongle and announced complete in the eighteenth (1420). In that year the capital was transferred to Beijing, and the city was officially designated *jingshi* (the capital). Hongwu's old capital was simply called Nanjing, southern capital. On the occasion of the transfer, the emperor issued the following proclamation:

> Formerly, my imperial ancestor, the exalted Emperor Taizu, received heaven's glorious mandate and built his capital on the left bank of the *Jiang* River in order to lay the foundation for the country. Thereupon, I, in turn, received the empire, and in my loving care for this eternal country, have particular solicitude to make this city the northern capital. This site is strong and secure, the mountains and rivers protect it well, the ten thousand nations lie on its four sides. It is a place favored by sound reason, by the mind of heaven and by exact divination. And so, in imitation of ancient practice, and having consulted popular sentiment, I establish two capitals, set up the suburban altars, the altar of the land and the ancestral temple, construct the halls and palaces—in the former instance (Nanjing) to carry out the intent of the exalted former emperor Taizu, in the latter

instance (Beijing) to institute a norm for my sons and grandsons for ten thousand generations.[50]

Despite this portentous rhetoric, Beijing's place as undisputed capital of China was not assured until some years later. In 1425 c.e. the Hongxi emperor decreed that Beijing should revert to its *xingzai* status, but before he could carry out his plans to move the capital back to Nanjing, he died. In fact it was not until 1441 that the *xingzai* status was finally abolished and the *jingshi* title given in perpetuity, even though the real center of government had been in Beijing since the time of Yongle.[51]

We may say that the city plan and the cosmic symbolism of Beijing were established already in the reign of Yongle, and from that time until the twentieth century changed very little. There were some important changes made in the city during the reign of the Jiajing emperor (1522 to 1567), and we will be examining these more closely in the next chapter. However, the modifications were not really changes in the symbolism but rather clearer articulations of the cosmic meaning already present in the structure of the city. The ostensible motive for every change made by Jiajing was the desire to return to a more faithful imitation of the ancient norms.

The transition to Qing rule in the seventeenth century was not without its upheavals, but because the Manchu leaders were already completely familiar with Chinese tradition, they were able to carry on the imperial system in Beijing without interruption. They had established a system of Chinese imperial worship in Mukden (modern Shenyang) in 1636, using a square altar for the worship of earth and a round one for the worship of heaven. When Qing Shunzhi set up his capital in Beijing after Ming loyalists and Chinese rebels had been defeated, he simply abolished the Mukden altars and continued the worship in Beijing without a break.[52] Again, there was some large-scale building done during Qianlong's reign, but it was more a matter of amplification than essential change.

As rulers the early Qing emperors were far better administrators than their Ming predecessors. But because they were determined to be more authentically Chinese than their defeated Han opponents, they mostly copied traditional forms. They preserved and rebuilt the palaces, halls, and altars, but changed nothing substantially. In some cases, as in the rebuilding done under Qianlong, the architectural symbolism was made more accurate. In their development of Beijing as a sacred capital, the Qing emperors were excellent curators of the museum they had inherited, and we ought to be grateful to them for that.

Looking back over the history of the Chinese capital, it is obvious that no new *concepts* were added to the ideal beyond what had already been stipulated or at least mentioned in the Zhou and Han classics. The historical development is the story of more or less close approximations to the ancient ideal, with the Ming-Qing capital eventually coming closest to the norm. I shall now examine Beijing in more detail.

NOTES

1. I refer here to the archaeological assessments of Chang Kuang-chih, *The Archaeology of Ancient China* (New Haven: Yale University Press, 1968); Cheng Te-k'un, *Archaeology in China*, especially volumes 1–3, *Prehistoric China, Shang China, Chou China* (Cambridge: Heffer and Sons, 1959–); Paul Wheatley, *The Pivot of the Four Quarters* (Chicago: Aldine, 1971); various works by Arthur Wright, principally "Symbolism and Function: Reflections on Changan and Other Great Cities," *Journal of Asian Studies*, 24 (1964–65), 667–79, and "The Cosmology of the Chinese City," in G. William Skinner, *The City in Late Imperial China* (1977); Ho P'ing-ti, "Luoyang, A.D. 495–534: A Study of the Physical and Socio-Economic Planning of a Metropolitan Area," *Harvard Journal of Asian Studies*, 26 (1966), 52–101; and most recently, Nancy Shatzman Steinhardt, *Chinese Imperial City Planning* (Honolulu: University of Hawaii Press, 1990).

2. *Shih King*, trans. James Legge, in *The Shu King, The Religious Portions of the Shih King, The Hsiao King* (Clarendon Press, 1879), 3:313.

3. *Shu King*, p. 104.

4. An Chin-huai, "The Shang City at Cheng-chou and Related Problems," in Chang Kuang-chih, *Studies of Shang Archaeology* (New Haven: Yale University Press, 1986), pp. 15–48; see figure 9, p. 39.

5. Kwang-chih Chang, *Shang Civilization* (New Haven: Yale University Press, 1980), p. 132; Cheng Te-K'un, *Studies in Chinese Archaeology* (Hong Kong: Chinese University Press, 1982), p. 19.

6. Wheatley, *Pivot*, pp. 32–50.

7. *Shih King*, pp. 383–84.

8. Ibid., pp. 394–96.

9. *Shu King*, pp. 185–86. The same incident is recorded in the *Shiji*. See Edouard Chavannes (trans.), *Les Memoires Historiques de Se-ma Ts'ien* (Paris: Ernest Leroux, 1875). There is a Qing woodblock print of this famous scene in Joseph Needham, *Science and Civilization in China* (Cambridge: Cambridge University Press, 1971), 4, part 3, p. 83. The term "mate of heaven," *peitian*, will be explained more fully later.

10. Edouard Biot (trans.), *Le Tcheou-Li ou Rites des Tcheou* (Taibei: Cheng Wen, 1969), 1:1–2. First published, Paris: A l'imprimerie nationale, 1851. Hereafter cited as *Zhouli*.

11. Ibid., pp. 202–3. The odd measurement of the shadow at the center of the earth, one foot five-tenths, also causes problems of interpretation. Granet had noted in one place that Chinese political mystique always maintained that at noon on the day of mid-summer the gnomon would cast no shadow. He also refers to the myth of a marvelous tree set in the center of the perfect capital, uniting the nine sources of the underworld to the nine heavens, the foundations of the world to its zenith. It was called the *jianmu*, "upright tree." Standing perfectly upright under this tree at noon, one would cast no shadow (Marcel Granet, *La Pensée Chinoise* [Paris: Albin Michel, 1968, first published 1934], p. 268). Needham, *Science*, vol. 3, has an extended discussion of the Chinese gnomon, pp. 284ff. By the time of the Qing dynasty, it was common knowledge among the educated that China was not the geographic center of the world. The Qing editors of the *Zhouli* (the edition used by Biot) acknowledged this fact, but distinguished two meanings of "middle," one of form and one of climate. The equator is obviously too hot, the poles too cold for the highest development of human life, so China is after all the *climatic* center of the world. This may appear to be superficial casuistry,

but to do justice to the Qing commentators, we have to realize that they were not speaking in terms of human comfort but of the place where the *principles* of heat and cold, movement and repose, and the five phases were in proper balance according to yin and yang. As we shall see, these principles, which may truly be considered cosmic, were of immense importance in the organization of the capital city. See the discussion of changes in Qing cosmological views in John B. Henderson, *The Development and Decline of Chinese Cosmology* (New York: Columbia University Press, 1984).

12. The Chinese measure called *li* is 500 meters. To avoid the confusion of continually translating into English equivalents, I will use the Chinese measures of length. The *zhang* is about 3.3 meters. The *chi* is one-tenth of a *zhang*, the *cun* is one-tenth of a *chi*, and a *fen* one-tenth of a *cun*. No other terms are necessary. It seems to me that it will aid clear exposition to retain the Chinese names, since for the purpose of this study the proportions and numerical symbolism are most important, not the actual measurable length.

13. The prestige of this scheme of the capital plan is hard to overemphasize. It was reproduced and discussed countless times in later Chinese history, becoming the "ideal" of capital building, most closely approximated in Tang Changan and Ming/Qing Beijing. One can see renderings of the plan in the *Zhouli*, 2:557; Needham, *Science*,4, part 3, p. 6. A Ming diagram of this plan may be found in the Ming encyclopedia of Wang Qi, the *Sancai tuhui* (Taibei: Cheng wen chubanshe, 1970; first published, 1607), 3:1017.

14. The same concentric structure is envisioned in the *Zhouli*, 1:204–6, in the *Classic of History*, and the *Shiji* of Sima Qian. See Chavannes, *Memoires Historiques*, 1:147.

15. Rome has always provided one of the closest parallels to China in its early religion and town planning, with its four steps in the foundation of an urban center: *inauguratio*, the consultation of the gods through *augures* to determine suitability of time and place; *limitatio*, fixing the boundaries of the town through various ritual practices, a step accomplished in China by the placement of walls; *orientatio*, determining the direction and conjunction of *cardo*, the north-south line, and *decumanus*, the east-west line; *consecratio*, placing the town under the protection of the gods, which finds its Chinese parallel in the erection of the ancestral temple and the altar of the land. See E. A. Gutkind, *Urban Development in Southern Europe: Italy and Greece*, in *International History of City Development* (New York: Free Press, 1967), 4:52.

16. See summary in Chang Kuang-chih, *The Archaeology of China*, pp. 305–11; also Wheatley, *Pivot*, pp. 184–85.

17. Archaeological work at Xianyang is briefly reviewed in Li Xueqin, *Eastern Zhou and Qin Civilizations*, trans. K. C. Chang (New Haven: Yale University Press, 1985), pp. 230ff; see map p. 231.

18. See references in Willets, *Chinese Art* (New York: Braziller, 1958), 2:665; Wheatley, *Pivot*, p. 442; Osvald Siren, *The Imperial Palaces of Beijing* (Paris: Librarie Nationale d'art et d'histoire, G. van Oest, 1926), 1:5. The relevant passage in the *Shiji* is found in Chavannes, *Memoires Historiques*, 2:138.

19. Wheatley, *Pivot*, pp. 436ff.

20. Quoted in Lan Mengbo, *Xian* (Taibei: Zhengzhong shuju, 1970; first published, 1957), p. 27.

21. Wheatley, *Pivot*, p. 443, has a chart showing the imposition of the two constellations on a map of the city of Changan. See also Lan Mengbo, *Xian*, p. 27, and Nelson Wu, *Chinese and Indian Architecture* (New York: Braziller, 1963), p. 37.

22. I may mention that Ho P'ing-ti, "Loyang," pp. 52–102, maintains that the source for the Sui and Tang capitals was Luoyang of the Northern Wei (c.e. 386–534). The author claims that one of the innovations of Luoyang was its "embryonic separate palace unit" in contrast to Han Changan, where the intermingling of government offices, residence, stores, and markets required that palace groups be linked by overpasses and underpasses (p. 77). Further special features were axiality and generally strict zoning. A major thoroughfare ran

from the east to the west gate, passing south of the palace city. A north-south axial way began at this point running south (see map 3, opposite p. 95). The zoning principle was based on legally defined social groups, divided according to social class, which reflected the rigidities of social structure in medieval China (pp. 79ff). While it may be true that Northern Wei Luoyang is the first city for which we have proof that such features were incorporated, the idea of a separate palace unit, axiality, and zoning were already a part of the classical heritage and in fact are strongly suggested by the archaeological evidence I have summarized earlier, as features of Shang and Zhou capitals.

23. Wright, "Symbolism and Function," p. 669.

24. The *general* placement was in accord with the norms of the *Zhouli*, but there was a slight but highly significant deviation. The ancestral temple and the altar of the land were each one building away from actually fronting on the axial way. The complex of buildings fronting on the north-south way were Taoist and Buddhist temples. It was during the Tang period that China was most cosmopolitan, most open, and religiously pluralistic. Buddhism and Taoism both had their moments of great influence in imperial circles and for a time it seemed possible that Buddhism in particular might become the new imperial ideology. This "high tide" of Buddhism is neatly symbolized by the more prominent place of its temple complex, a confirmation of the truism that architecture and city planning reflect the fundamental ideas of the culture that produces them.

25. Lan Mengbo, *Xian*, pp. 65ff., and Wright, "Symbolism," p. 672.

26. Nelson Wu, *Chinese*, p. 38.

27. My understanding of this legend reflects a more general question about Dr. Wu's overall interpretation of Chinese architecture and city planning, which he understands as a humanistic statement reflecting the "city of man," as opposed to the Indian "city of the gods." I certainly agree that Indian cities represent a more transcendental or "otherworldly" conception of religion expressed in urban architecture. But the Chinese model is still clearly religious. In fact, the classical prescriptions of Indian city planning as recorded in the *Silpa Sastras* are almost identical with those of the *Zhouli* (see below, chapter 5), and it is the pilgrimage cities that show the greatest difference. Both Indian and Chinese traditions are a clear attempt to sacralize their cities by the use of religious models of planning.

28. Arthur F. Wright, "The Cosmology of the Chinese City," unpublished paper prepared for the Research Conference on Urban Society in Traditional China, Wentworth-by-the-Sea, New Hampshire (August 31–September 7, 1968), p. 50.

29. Werner Eichhorn, "Die Wiedereinrichtung der Staatsreligion in Anfang der Sung-Zeit," *Monumenta Serica*, 23 (1964), 238–48.

30. In Laurence Sickman and Alexander Soper, *The Art and Architecture of China* (3rd ed.; Harmondsworth: Penguin Books, 1968; 1st ed. published, 1965), p. 255.

31. Wright, "The Cosmology of the Chinese City," pp. 52–57. According to Jacques Gernet, the altar of heaven in Hangzhou was itself elaborately proportioned according to the traditional cosmic numerical symbolism, which we will later see perfected in the Ming and Qing altar of heaven at Beijing. See his *Daily Life in China on the Eve of the Mongol Invasion 1250–1276* (New York: Macmillan, 1962), pp. 200ff.

32. See the superimposed maps of Liao, Jin, Yuan, and Ming-Qing Beijing in Beipingshi Zhengfu, *Jiudu wenwu lue* (Taibei: Guoli gugong bowuyuan, 1971; first published, Beiping, 1935), part 1, p. 2. See also map 2 in G. Bouillard, "Note succinte sur l'histoire du territoire de Beijing," *Bulletin of the Museum of Far Eastern Antiquities*, 1 (1929), 39–60. The maps that most accurately record Beijing's evolution throughout history may be found in Hou Renzhi, ed., *Beijing lishi dituji* (Beijing: Beijing chubanshe, 1988); for the three foreign dynasties, see pp. 21–28. All the cities on the site were oriented to the four cardinal directions.

33. Zhu Yicun et al. (Qin Ding), *Rixia jiuwen kao* (40 vols.; Taibei: Guangwen shuzhu, 1968), VIII (29), 2. Citations of this work will be given in this fashion: Roman numeral = the volume number of the 1968 soft-bound edition; the next number = the original chapter

number (160 in all); and page. This is the most important source for the history of Beijing. It was first published in 1688 by Zhu Yicun under the title *Rixia jiuwen* and at that point already contained supplements by the author's son Zhu Kuntian. In 1774 Qianlong had the work reprinted under imperial auspices (*qin ding*) and its scope was greatly expanded under the direction of Ying Lian and others. Fortunately the Qing editors use symbols to inform the reader whether the material in the 1774 edition was the work of Zhu Yicun, Zhu Kuntian, or their own additions. This work is the major authority for all later histories of Beijing. The most recent and comprehensive bibliography on Beijing has been published and edited by Wang Canchi, *Beijing shidi fenwu shulu* (Beijing: Beijing chubanshe, 1985).

34. *Rixia jiuwen kao*, VIII (29), 14, 16; Ling Shun-sheng, "Beiping ti fengshan wenhua," *Bulletin of the Institute of Ethnology Academia Sinica*, 16 (Autumn 1963), 5.

35. Hwang Ming-chorng, "Study," p. 21, map p. 22.

36. Hou Renzhi, *Beijing*, after map 24; *Jiudu wenwu lue*, part 1, pp. 1–2, describes a unique feature of Zhongdu. Apparently the imperial city was also called "mother" (*mu*) and there were four partially independent walled units on each of the four sides called "sons" (*zi*). During siege, arms could be rushed from the center to whichever front most needed help, and this arrangement was said to have long delayed the Mongol capture of the city. As far as I know this plan, if accurately described, is unique in the history of Chinese capital building. The arrangement is not verified by the map in Hou Renzhi, but it is shown in Hwang Ming-chorng, p. 22. Other than this feature, however, Jin Zhongdu was a conscious approximation of the ideal Chinese capital, one of the most successful in Chinese history.

37. *Rixia jiuwen kao*, VIII (29), 8, 26–27; Ling, "Beiping," p. 6. Each of the three early dynasties, Xia, Shang, and Zhou, is said to have had a particular species of tree that it planted at the altar of the land. The Xia used the pine, the Shang the cypress, and the Zhou the chestnut. See *Zhouli*, 1:193–94.

38. Ling, "Beiping," p. 6. The Jin also built three altars of lesser importance that reflected traditional imperial worship, altars to the spirits of the wind, rain, and the bringer of male offspring—the last always a matter of great imperial concern.

39. *Rixia jiuwen kao*, VIII (29), 8–9.

40. Ibid., p. 14.

41. Zhu Xie, *Yuandu gongdian tukao* (Shanghai: Shangwu yinshuguan, 1936), p. 8; Ling, p. 8.

42. G. N. Kates, "A New Date for the Origins of the Forbidden City," *Harvard Journal of Asian Studies*, 7 (1942–43), 201.

43. Zhu Xie, *Yuandu*, p. 26; *Rixia jiuwen kao*, VIII (30), 12.

44. Ling, "Beiping," p. 11. Hwang Ming-chorng gives an extensive chronology of the stages in the construction of Dadu, p. 27.

45. Zhu Xie, *Yuandu*, p. 52; Ling, "Beiping," p. 12. The *Rixia jiuwen kao*, VIII (30), 24, has an account of a kind of "practice" plowing field in an imperial park near *Houzai* gate (the north-central gate of the *danei*) as though the Mongol emperors needed practice in the agrarian arts, lest they reveal themselves inept at the actual spring plowing ceremony. (See chapter 2, below, for the background and history of the plowing and silkworm rites.)

46. Kates, "New Date," p. 200.

47. *Rixia jiuwen kao*, II (4), 15–16; *Jiudu wenwu lue*, part 1, p. 13.

48. Edward Lewis Farmer, "The Dual Capital System of the Early Ming Dynasty" (Ph. D. dissertation, Harvard University, 1968), p. 253. Farmer's dissertation has now been published as *Early Ming Government: The Evolution of Dual Capitals* (Cambridge: Harvard University East Asian Research Center, 1976); this citation, pp. 114ff. In a sense, wherever the emperor was, was the center of the empire, even if he was away from the capital. Thus the rationale for the traveling capital, the *xingzai*. But certain functions, such as the great sacrifice to heaven and earth, could be done *only* in the *jingshi*, the official national capital.

49. *Ming Chengzu shilu*, quoted in *Rixia jiuwen kao*, II (4), 18, parentheses mine. I should like to call the reader's attention to the interpenetration of secular and sacred in the motives given by Yongle's advisors. It would be a mistake to emphasize one at the expense of the other, yet the "profane" reasons suggested—military, commercial, etc.—are taken together as a sign of heaven's will. Many modern historians of China have the tendency of discount all reference to auspicious signs, omens, heaven's will, as purely rhetorical or outright deception, proposing secular motives as the *real* factors. But I think this type of interpretation is to read our contemporary bias into the context of traditional China.

50. Qu Xuanying, *Beiping shibiao zhangpian* (Taibei: Guting shushi, 1969; first published, Beiping, 1933), p. 95. Passage is again from the Ming *Veritable Records*, and is also quoted in *Rixia jiuwen kao*, II (4), 19. Note the proclamation's mention of the three essential elements for a royal city (palace-halls, *shejitan*, *taimiao*), its centrality in relation of the rest of the world, and the inclusion of the suburban altar.

51. Ibid., p. 107, and Farmer, "System," p. 163.

52. Ling, "Beiping," p. 40. The author points out that the Manchus also maintained their own native forms of worship and built numerous temples and other structures in Beijing to accommodate them, side by side with the Chinese rites.

Chapter 2

The Geometry of
the Universe

But I am constant as the northern star,
Of whose true-fix'd and resting quality
There is no fellow in the firmament.
The skies are painted with unnumber'd sparks,
They are all fire and every one doth shine,
But there's but one in all doth hold his place;
So in the world, 'tis furnish'd well with men . . .
Yet in the number I do know but one
That unassailable, holds on his rank,
Unshaked of motion, and that I am he.

—Shakespeare, *Julius Caesar*, II, 1

Most of the symbolism used in the architecture and planning of Beijing comes from two sources, the classic of divination, called the *Yijing*, and the yin yang, five-phase (*wuxing*) "philosophy." I put the word in quotes because philosophy often implies a sophisticated conceptual framework, the possession of an educated elite. Yin yang, five-phase, thought is, to the contrary, a system of belief whose general principles are known to nearly everyone, even the uneducated. It is a total Chinese worldview, elements of which go back to most ancient times, even though the complete framework may not have been given a systematic expression until the Han period.

Recent studies have indicated that many of the familiar patterns of Chinese thought and belief can be found in recognizable prototype already in bronze age Shang China.[1] Ideas of binary opposition and complementarity, later connected with yin yang thought and Taoism, were already present at that time. A more confident, secularized, and skeptical approach, later identified with Confucianism, was also present in embryonic form. We shall see much evidence of both of these conceptual views at work in the shaping of Beijing, themselves harmonized into a convincing synthesis that endured through many centuries.

This worldview was expressed in various parts of the classics, such as the *Hongfan* and *Yueling* sections of the *Liji*, in professed works of the Han

Confucian synthesis, in the *Huainanzi*, *Bohutong*, and other writings of the Taoist school. But it was also expressed in the rituals of religious Taoism and on a popular level in countless customs, rites, and beliefs native to the Chinese people, whose origin and early history may never be known.

I presume that most readers will be conversant with the main features of the yin yang, five-phases, worldview. I will not therefore attempt to summarize all its features, but mention only those that have a direct bearing on this study. The beginning of things is seen as "the limitless" (*wuji*). This negative expression does not mean a vacuity, but rather the opposite, an ultimate reality that transcends all words and concepts. That same reality, when considered positively, is called "supreme ultimate" (*taiji*). The *taiji* too is beyond conceptual expression. Another word that came to be used for this reality was *Dao*, an immanent reality present everywhere. This supreme reality becomes manifested in the world when it divides into two cosmic principles, yin and yang. These complementary forces give birth to the dualities embodied in all existent things, light/darkness, male/female, warm/cold, dry/moist, and the like. Through the interaction of these forces, the myriad things of the visible universe are produced.

This cosmogonic explanation is, of course, not particularly important in popular beliefs, but yin and yang, as the expression of the observable bipolarity in nature, were well known to all. They formed the framework of thought out of which Chinese persons, from literati to commoner, understood the world. Through the continual interaction of these two principles, change took place, season followed season, cold succeeded heat and then warmth returned again, day and night followed one another in orderly succession.

During the philosophical ferment of the late Zhou period, the yin and yang worldview became closely associated with what some called the five-phases (*wu xing*) philosophy.[2] Though they may originally have been the systems of two different philosophical schools, their viewpoints were so compatible that they later came to be considered a single school. What is certain is that their thought became so pervasive in Han Confucian thinking, especially under the influence of the philosopher Tong Zhongshu, that they were an essential part of imperial ideology from that time forward. A neo-Confucian source describes the close relationship between the two:

The *Wuji* gives birth to the *Taiji*.
[The *Taiji*] moves and gives birth to *Yang*.
Rests, and gives birth to *Yin*.
Yang shifts, *Yin* unites,

Then is born water, fire, wood, metal, and earth.
The *Five Breaths* make things flourish in their proper order;
The four seasons progress according to them.[3]

The five phases—water, fire, wood, metal, and earth—like yin and yang, are metaphysical principles that express themselves in nearly every aspect of the human and nonhuman universe. Eventually an elaborate, comprehensive, inclusive system of correspondences was built up by which one could classify time, space, numbers, the human body, heavenly bodies, temperaments, foods, and so forth.[4] For example, corresponding to the five elements just listed were five directions (north, east, south, west, and central), five colors (black, green, red, white, and yellow), five numbers (6, 8, 7, 9, and 5), five seasons (winter, spring, summer, fall, and a kind of intercalary period in the summer). Like yin and yang, these principles were not static, but succeeded one another relentlessly, causing the process of change.

For intellectuals, the yin yang, five-phase, worldview was indeed a philosophy, a way to comprehend and therefore in some measure control the universe. For ordinary people it was a way of life, providing orientation, telling them when to do things, how to arrange their living space, how to plan graves, how to practice their religion, and many other aspects of daily living.

As we shall see in detail in this chapter, yin yang, five-phase, thinking was expressed consistently in the architecture and planning of the city of Beijing. This is true both in terms of the total structure and of individual units within the whole, such as the palace groups, the altars and altar complexes, and the temples. In giving expression to these principles, the Chinese planners were following a tradition that told them how to conform with cosmic order and to embody it in the things they built. To go against that order was unthinkable, while to conform to it in every possible detail was a means of embodying in human structures the power and permanence of that order. To use a homey metaphor, it was to go with, not against, "the grain" of the cosmos.

AN OVERVIEW OF THE STRUCTURE OF BEIJING

If we look at a map of Qing dynasty Beijing, we see what appears to be a square above, or just seated into, a rectangle. Perhaps the feature most likely to strike the eye is the impression of a regular geometry. The city as a whole is perfectly oriented to the four cardinal directions according to the ancient prescriptions of Chinese architecture and city planning. Major and most minor streets run north-south and east-west[5] (see illustration 2).

The next impression one gets would probably be that of con-

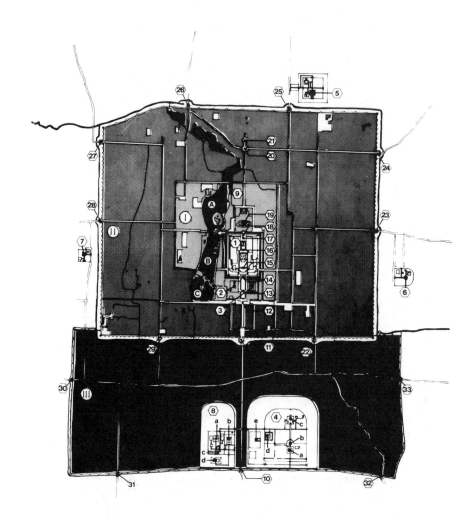

Illus. 2. Map of Qing Dynasty Beijing

The Concentric cities
  I.   The Imperial City
  II. The Inner City (Manchu City or Tartar City)
  III. The Outer City (Chinese City)

The "Three Seas" of the Imperial Park
A. North Sea (*Beihai*)
B. Middle Sea (*Zhonghai*)
C. South Sea (*Nanhai*)

The Ritual Sites of Beijing
  1. The Forbidden City (see detailed map, p. 51)
  2. The Altar of Land and Grain (*Shejitan*)
  3. The Imperial Ancestral Temple (*Taimiao*)
  4. The Altar of Heaven (*Tiantan*)
      a. the Altar of Heaven
      b. the House of the Imperial Firmament (*Huangqiongyu*)
      c. the Temple of Heaven or Hall of the Yearly Harvest Prayer (*Qiniandian*)
      d. the Hall of Abstinence (*Zhaigong*)
      e. the Liturgical Music Academy (*Shenyueshu*)
  5. The Altar of Earth (*Ditan*) or Altar of the Square Watery Place (*Fangzetan*)
  6. The Altar of the Sun (*Ritan*)
  7. The Altar of the Moon (*Yuetan*)
  8. The Altar of Agriculture or Altar of the First Farmer (*Xiannongtan*)
      a. the Hall of the Great Year Star (Jupiter) (*Taisuidian*)
      b. the Hall of Abstinence (*Zhaigong*)
      c. the field for the Ritual Spring Plowing
      d. the Altar to the Spirits of Heaven and Earth (*Shenzhitan*)
  9. The Altar of the First Silkworm (*Xiancantan*)

The Structures of the Axial Way
  10. Eternal Foundation Gate (*Yongdingmen*)
  11. Central Yang Gate (*Zhengyangmen*), popularly called Front Gate (*Qianmen*)
  12. Heavenly Peace Gate (*Tiananmen*)
  13. Short Gate (*Duanmen*)
  14. Meridian Gate (*Wumen*)
  15. Supreme Peace Gate (*Taihemen*)
  16. Heavenly Brightness Gate (*Qianqingmen*)
  17. Imperial Garden
  18. Martial Spirit Gate (*Shenwumen*)
  19. Bright Prospect Hill (*Jingshan*), also called "The Coal Hill"
  20. The Drum Tower
  21. The Bell Tower

The Outer Gates of the Tartar City
  22. Reverence Culture Gate (*Chongwenmen*)
  23. Facing Sun Gate (*Chaoyangmen*)
  24. East Upright Gate (*Dongzhimen*)
  25. Peace Established Gate (*Andingmen*)
  26. Virtue Victorious Gate (*Deshengmen*)
  27. West Upright Gate (*Xizhimen*)
  28. Abundant Accomplishment Gate (*Fuchengmen*)
  29. Proclaim Martial Valor Gate (*Xuanwumen*)

The Outer Gates of the Chinese City
  30. Extensive Tranquility Gate (*Guangningmen*)
  31. Right Peace Gate (*Youanmen*)
  32. Left Peace Gate (*Zuoanmen*)
  33. Broad Channel Gate (*Guangqumen*)

centricity. First, there are the outer walls enclosing the city itself; within, near the center, is another walled enclosure, square except for the south-west corner, which marks the limits of what is called the Imperial City; which in turn surrounds another walled compound called the Forbidden City, the seat of imperial government and home of the emperor. Finally, in the center of the Forbidden City is a group of three halls built on a three-tiered platform, which is the true center of the whole ensemble. In these halls the most important acts of imperial government were performed. The halls could almost be called "temples," because of the ritualistic nature of Chinese governance. "The great business of state was worship and weapons (*si* and *rong*)"—that is, the offering of sacrifices to the spirits and ancestors, and military defense.[6] The emperor was both ruler and high priest in the civil religion of imperial China.

The next impression one might get from viewing a map of the city would be that of cardinal axiality. There appears to be a center line running north and south through the center of the three cities mentioned above, with balanced structures on both sides of this line creating strong patterns of symmetry.

The only apparent flaw in all this geometrical perfection is the existence of the rectangular "Chinese" city, the walled south part of traditional Beijing, shorter in its north-south dimension than the main city but longer in its east-west dimension, and including within its territory the altar of heaven and agriculture.[7] Actually, according to the original Ming conception of the city, an outer wall was supposed to surround the entire inner city. But although Xu Da ordered his subordinate Ye Gouchen to plan it, it was never done. Had the plan been realized, there would have been an even more impressive series of enclosures, the outer city, inner city, Imperial City, Forbidden City, and finally the compound of the "three halls."

In 1550, because of a Mongol attack, the project of building an outer wall around the entire city was again raised for discussion. The ministers quoted the precedents we have already seen in the Zhou classical literature, urging the emperor to build an outer wall (*guo*) to enclose the suburban altars and protect the people who dwelt beyond the primary city walls (*cheng*). Impressed as always by an appeal to ancient authority, Jiajing was persuaded to begin the construction. He ordered the proper geomantic studies to be made and the divinatory experts picked an auspicious day on which to initiate the project. Unfortunately, the work proved more difficult than had been anticipated and funds were insufficient. Hence, after the southern wall had been completed, the extremities were brought north and curved around to meet the southeast and southwest corners of the existing city walls, and the area thus enclosed became the outer or

Chinese city.[8] "Chinese city" was a term of the Qing dynasty, which issued regulations to prevent Han Chinese from living in the inner city, which then came to be called the "Manchu city." The resulting odd form was what gave Beijing the name "hat city."

We have already seen how the features of concentric structure, orientation, cardinal axiality, and square or rectangular form accord with classical prescriptions and how they were realized or approximated by Chinese capitals down to the time of Beijing. We must now consider how these features were a conscious imitation of the structure of the cosmos itself. The Chinese observed the brilliance and impressive regularities of the heavenly realm, the movements of the sun, moon, planets, and stars, the passage of the seasons, the alternation of day and night. They wished to participate in the power of this order, and believed that by imitating it, they could secure the continuity of imperial government. If this order could be realized on earth, then the harmony and permanence of the celestial sphere might be brought into the domain of the son of heaven, which was the whole earth. "Under heaven, there is no land that does not belong to the son of heaven."

It was natural, therefore, that the Chinese should desire to have the capital of the son of heaven imitate the capital of Shangdi, the emperor of heaven in the stars. In writing the introduction to the section on the halls and palaces of the imperial and forbidden cities, the Qing editors of the *Rixia jiuwen kao* make an explicit reference to this aspiration. They addressed the Qianlong emperor:

> Your subjects respectfully maintain: Of old, those who established the realm first raised in lofty proportion the altar of the land and the ancestral temple, erected the system of palaces and courts, so that they would imitate the stars and poles, encompass and control the upper and lower world, to promote reverence and respect, to spread the truth of the Chinese way (*hua*), and render permanent its foundation.[9]

The Chinese capital was first and foremost the home of the emperor, the ruler and pivot of the terrestrial order, as Shangdi (emperor on high) or Tian (heaven) was the ruler of the celestial world. These two orders were not separated, but intimately related, and the point of communication and interaction was the person of the emperor. Over the centuries the view developed that as the earthly order ought to be a mirror image of the heavenly, so the capital of the son of heaven ought to imitate the capital of Shangdi in the firmament. And as Shangdi ruled over all heaven, so his vice-regent ruled not just a country, but every land "under heaven."

Beijing and the other Chinese imperial seats were not the capitals of "China," but of the whole world.

In order to study this symbolism in more detail, we must look briefly at traditional Chinese concepts of astronomy, which as Needham has shown, had already been developed at a very early period in history. The heavenly geography (or "uranography," as Schlegel calls it) reveals strong concentric and axial imagery. The celestial capital was located in the "center" of the heavens, the area of the polar constellations, and the pole star itself, Polaris, has the name *tianhuang dadi*, "great emperor of the heavens." "The pole star was thus the fundamental basis of Chinese astronomy. It was connected with a background of microcosmic-macrocosmic thinking. The celestial pole corresponded to the position of the emperor on earth, around whom the vast system of the bureaucratic state naturally and spontaneously revolved."[10] The stars and constellations in the area of this central enclosure have names that describe a celestial capital city, with its office buildings, palaces, temples, altars, walls, gates, and other sites of importance. There are, for example, star groups that represent the imperial field plowed by the emperor in the spring rite,[11] the site of the spring audience, the apartments of the imperial princes in the eastern part of the palace, the interior palace, the palace of the empress and the royal concubines, the imperial granaries, the altar of the land and grain, the ancestral temple.[12]

Not surprisingly, the polar region is conceived by the Chinese to be a walled compound called the "purple protected enclosure" (which explains the full name for Beijing's palace city: "Purple Forbidden City"), purple being a regal color.[13] The name of the stars in the enclosure reveal the fact that they are members of the imperial entourage: the great and lesser ministers, the great and lesser counselors, the great and lesser military guards. The enclosure itself is composed of two "wings" or "hedges," not unlike Bernini's embracing colonade in the Vatican. Their southern terminal stars are called *Zuoshu* and *Youshu*, the left and right pivots. At the summer solstice, when the tail of the great bear points south, the left pivot is found in the east, the right pivot in the west. At the winter solstice the placement is reversed. In a year's time, a complete circuit has been made and the enclosure thus described is what is called the purple protected enclosure[14] (see illustration 3).

In certain accounts of the symbolism of Beijing's Forbidden City, it is suggested that Taiyi, or Shangdi, the supreme emperor, rules from this heavenly enclosure just as the son of heaven rules from the Forbidden City.[15] The name is translated by Schlegel as *Premier du ciel* or *l'Archi-primière*. One Chinese source says quite directly that Taiyi is another name

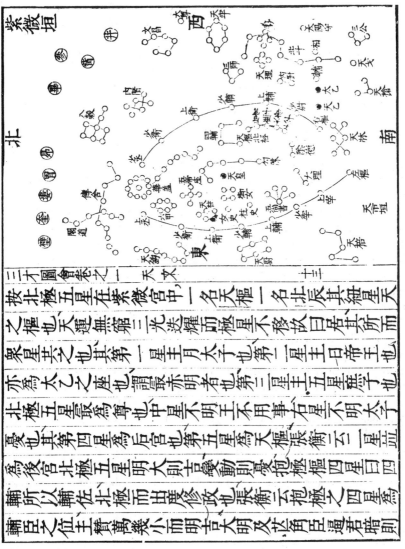

紫微垣

北

南

東

西

按北極五星在紫微宮中一名天樞一名北辰其紐星天之樞也天運無窮三光迭耀而極星不移故曰居其所而衆星拱之也第一星主月太子也第二星主日帝王也亦為太乙之座取其最赤明者也第三星主五星庶子也第一星不明主不用事第二星不明太子憂第三星不明庶子憂第四星為後宮北極五星明大則吉變動則蔑勤則修政也又為天樞璇璣玉衡云抱北極之四星曰四輔所以輔佐北極而出度授政以輔臣之位主斗斟酌元氣役使萬神幾小而明吉大明吉變大明及角臣逼君暗則

Illus. 3.　The Purple Protected Enclosure.　Source: *Sancai tuhui*

for the sovereign of the heavens, the most venerable of all heavenly divinities.[16] De Saussure also notes the complete parallelism between heavenly and earthly capitals, and calls the sovereign of heaven Taiyi, Tianyi (the "ace" of heaven), and Shangdi, so there is no doubt as to the identity of this supreme spirit.

What did puzzle me when I first read this material is the fact that the stars labeled *Taiyi* and *Tianyi* are pictured *outside* the purple hidden enclosure in the star maps of the Song and Ming dynasties. The solution to the problem lies in the fact that these two stars were pole stars in more ancient times, and thus formerly within the enclosure.[17] But by Song and Ming times, the pole star had become the same as we have today, the last star of the handle of Ursa Minor, the Little Dipper. This "recent" pole star is called by the Chinese *tianhuang dadi*, great emperor of the imperial heavens, so although the stars have changed, the nature of the symbolism has not.

The names of the stars in the vicinity of the pole star continue the imagery of the imperial court and the royal family: there are stars with the appellations imperial prince, sons of imperial concubines, maids in waiting, the four "supports" (referring to the intimate ministers of the sovereign), the imperial daughters, the guard, the secretaries, censors, grand judges, the officer of audience, three tutors of the imperial princes, the prime minister, parents of the emperor, imperial kitchens, and so forth. All these stars are found within the purple protected enclosure.[18]

Besides the enclosure just described, there are two others that have particular prestige in traditional Chinese astronomy. One can see them clearly indicated in the star maps of the Ming and Qing periods.[19] The first of these is called *taiweiyuan*, the great hidden enclosure, and although its position is not polar, it also symbolizes the imperial court for historical reasons. This enclosure included by association the constellation *yi* (one of the well-known twenty-eight constellation groups called "habitations"), which rose in the last month of summer and therefore became connected with the grand audience of feudatories supposed to have taken place during that month in the Zhou dynasty.[20] (As always, Zhou patterns became paradigmatic for later dynasties.) Again the stars have such appellations as counselors, ministers, advisors and the like, and the enclosure has the additional name "court of the heavenly capital." Three stars in the group have the names of gates, *zuoyimen*, *youyimen* (right and left lateral gates), and *duanmen* (short gate), all three of which are names given to gates in the Imperial City of Ming and Qing Beijing.

The third enclosure is called *tianshiyuan*, enclosure of the heavenly market. Within we find again a certain amount of imperial symbolism in the nomenclature of the stars, but this enclosure really refers to the historical situation of king and feudatories of the Zhou dynasty, for the twenty-two stars that compose it have been given the names of the large and small feudal domains of that period. Each of these states was thought to have an astral referent and star, which governed its fate. One of these states was Yan, the territory of Beijing, but I will postpone a discussion of this relationship until a later chapter, because it implies symbolism of a different kind than we are examining in this chapter.

Besides the parallelism between heavenly and earthly capitals, two other aspects of Chinese space conceptions deserve comment. Statically speaking, space, whether celestial or terrestrial, is organized from the point where *cardo*, the north-south axis, intersects *decumanus*, the east-west axis. This is the center, the fixed point in the turning world, the locus of the imperial throne. Power is concentrated at this point and, as one moves from center to periphery, the power "thins." Ranged about the throne are the great ministers and officials, and the dynastic family dwelling in the capital. Further out in ever-decreasing positions of power and importance are the governors and subjects of the surrounding territories, and finally the tributary and barbarian states.[21] The emperor ruled from the center, just as the pole star/heavenly sovereign ruled from his fixed position in the sky while all the other stars circled about him.

This was the ancient model of perfect government, supported by Confucians and Taoists alike. As Confucius said: "He who rules by moral force (*te*) is like the pole star which remains in its place while all the lesser stars do homage to it."[22] This type of imagery was often used as a conventional way of speaking about or addressing the emperor. The Qing editors of *Rixia jiuwen kao*, for example, began their flattering address to the Qianlong emperor by referring to him as the pole star.[23]

Dynamically speaking, the concentricity of the Chinese space conception becomes centripetal. The sovereign, ruling by exercise of virtue from his inner court, maintaining the cosmic order from his throne at the center of space, draws all toward himself. Confucius put it most memorably: "Govern the people by regulations, keep order among them by chastisements, and they will flee from you and lose all self respect. Govern them by moral force, keep order among them by ritual, and they will come to you of their own accord."[24] Should the imperial rule be ideal, not only would China be tranquil and secure, even the barbarians would flock to the central kingdom to seek the benefits of the Chinese way.

The Chinese have been quite consistent in their concentric conception of space. The heavenly enclosures just described were round because heaven itself is round, while the earthly enclosures were square or rectangular to imitate the earth. As the ancient cosmological belief maintained: *tian yuan, di fang*, "heaven is round, the earth is square." The pairing of these two geometric forms therefore created a model of the universe, a true *imago mundi*. The square and circle motif was often evoked in Chinese literature, art, architecture, and city planning. We have just seen it in the contrast between the square earthly and round heavenly capitals. We will meet it again in the forms of the altars of heaven and earth, in the architecture of the so-called Temple of Heaven, in the Hall of the Imperial Firmament, and in the motifs of square and circle employed in the "lantern ceiling" of many imperial halls.[25] Sometimes the forms are separate, as at the altars of heaven and earth, sometimes in conjunction forming a kind of mandala, as in the lantern ceilings. Round and square were the binary components of Chinese cosmic symbolism, yin and yang again in one of their most important guises.

The north-south axiality impressed so strongly on the plan of Beijing and other great Chinese capitals sets the Chinese apart from other classical civilizations where north-south and east-west axiality were equally important. There are two major reasons for the Chinese stress on the *cardo*. Because the central region of the heavens was actually north in relation to the earthly kingdom, it was evident that Shangdi ruled the cosmos "facing south," where he sits enthroned looking toward the human world. The line projected south from the pole star, the *cardo*, intersected the *decumanus* at the center of the world. The north-south line was far more emphatic because it was the "line of dominion." As Willetts notes, the north-south axis of the capital was the celestial meridian writ small; the emperor's palace corresponds to the pole star, from which Taiyi rules and views the world of humankind to the south. In imitation of him, the son of heaven takes the corresponding position.[26]

Cardinal axiality has had a long history in China, as archeology and literature both testify. "The Master said, Among those that 'ruled by inactivity,' surely Shun may be counted. For what action did he take? He merely placed himself gravely and reverently with his face due south; that was all."[27] Certain imperial rituals made dramatic use of this axial symbolism. At the New Years festival or on the emperor's birthday, officials and citizens assembled at the same hour in the capital and in all the cities and villages to kneel before his altars throughout the empire and offer their homage, looking north toward him, the son of heaven.[28] Seated on his dragon throne, the emperor faced south at audiences and all occasions of state, as well as for most sacrificial rites. But at the greatest of his rites, such as the worship of heaven at the winter solstice, or at the sacrifices to his ancestors, the emperor faced north to acknowledge his position of subordination to Shangdi and his forebears.

It was at this point that axial symbolism came together with another symbol system called *fengshui* (literally, wind and water, usually translated as geomancy). Actually, all important cities, temples, graves, and private homes, especially in north China, were ideally oriented toward the south. Yin yang and five-phase thinking, among the central concepts of geomancy, required that a person or building's "back" be toward the north to ward off harmful (too much yin) influences. The doors, conversely, should open toward the south from which come healthful yang emanations. As a result, the ancient prescription of having a square capital with three gates facing each direction was early abandoned (or perhaps *never* accepted) by Chinese planners, not because they flouted principle but because they must have felt that more important considerations superseded the textbookish idealizations of the *Zhouli*. Planners did not carry the north-south axis all the way to a northern central gate because that would have given direct access to baleful yin influences from the north. Han and Tang Changan had the imperial city "backed" against the northern wall, and Yuan and Ming Beijing simply eliminated a northern central gate altogether.[29]

Fengshui was the Chinese system for determining the location and form of a particular structure, temple, home, store, or grave. We do not know when *fengshui* first became organized into a system (Feuchtwang suggests the Tang dynasty), but it is clear that its component principles are derived from yin yang, five-phase thinking. In reading accounts of the history and description of Beijing, one frequently finds *fengshui* cited as the reason for a certain feature of the city. De Groot, for example, claims that Beijing is in perfect accord with the principles of geomancy:

> Peking is protected on the North-west by the Kinshan or Golden Hills, which represent the Tiger and ensure its prosperity, together with that of the whole Empire and the reigning dynasty. These hills contain the sources of a felicitous watercourse called the Yuh-ho or "Jade River," which enters Beijing on the North-west and flows through the grounds at the back of the Imperial Palace, then accumulates its beneficial influences in three large reservoirs or lakes on the west side, and finally flows past the entire front of the inner Palace, where it bears the name of The Golden Water. . . . Its course therefore perfectly accords with the principles which are valid for grave brooks and grave tanks.[30]

We are also told that the northwest corner of Beijing's inner city is slightly irregular because of *fengshui*, and that the gates and towers of the city were no more than 99 feet high because good spirits soar through the air at 100 feet and they must be allowed unhindered passage. Conversely, we read that in the 1930s, when one of Beijing's gates was destroyed by fire, the authorities, in a panic, quickly rebuilt it, not so much for fear of night incursions but because of the danger of evil spirits that the precise height and position of the structure prevented from flying straight into the city.[31]

Legendary material contains many references to aspects of Beijing's geomantic situation: in building a military camp for the Manchu bannermen in the Kangxi period, in modifying the influences on a village that would later become the Yiheyuan, building a reflecting wall at the great enlightenment temple, all during the Qianlong period.[32]

Since we are trying to understand the symbolism of the city, we must seriously consider the question of whether geomancy represents a competing set of symbols that were more important than the classical prescriptions of the *Zhouli* in planning and building Beijing. This is a rather complex issue, which I have dealt with more fully elsewhere, but I should like to summarize my conclusions here.[33]

Although I have encountered countless scattered statements about this or that feature of Beijing's *fengshui*, I know of only P'eng's comprehensive interpretation of the city's geomancy.[34] Unfortunately, the author does not give any indication of Chinese sources for his analysis, but he is able to provide a geomantic explanation for many of the city's most important monuments, especially its gates, towers, hills, pagodas, and watercourses.

Let me give the bare essence of P'eng's analysis. He begins with a description of Beijing's topographical situation, lying on a plain, and "protected" by the mountains to the west, north, and east. This arc-shaped protective barrier, together with the watercourse running from the northwest to the south of the city, provide a rather ideal arrangement according to *fengshui* principles. I myself was somewhat skeptical of this because topographical maps of Beijing give the impression that the mountains are mostly concentrated in the northwest. And certainly, I thought, the city-mountain relationship would not be clear to the naked eye of the ordinary observer. But I was wrong. I recall one autumn night in Beijing, when a sudden cold front blew in from the north and brought to the city a rare interval of crystal clear air. The next morning I looked north out of my hotel window and saw the semicircle of "protecting mountains" stretching all the way from west to north to east, a perfect arc.

This siting of Beijing to the south of the mountains gives it its *kan* position in the famous *luoshu* diagram, an ancient arrangement of the eight trigrams attributed to the Zhou dynastic founder, King Wen (see illustration 4). Having established this crucial relationship, all the rest of P'eng's geomantic analysis flows from it. According to the traditional interpretation of the *luoshu*, there are lucky and unlucky directions. Next the five-phase theory is brought into the analysis: earth, metal, water, wood, and fire. These relate to each other in either productive or destructive ways.

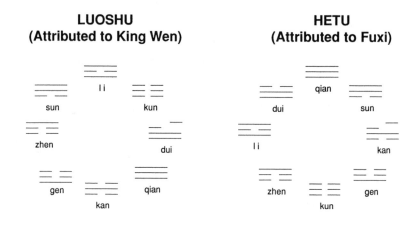

Illus. 4. Luoshu and Hetu diagrams.

Each of the main features (we might call them "power points") of Beijing's topography and landscape are assigned to one of the five elements. Rivers and lakes belong to the phase water; gardens, schools, clock towers are fire; temples and palaces wood; walls and streets earth, and so forth. The geomancer must make sure that all these elements are in a productive rather than a destructive relationship:

All the southern gates of Peking on the north-south axial way are in the dangerous *li* position in relation to the *kan* city. Various modifications must be introduced into the urban scheme in order to rectify the problem. Between *Qianmen* (*li*, "fire") and the central city (*kan*, "water") the wood element must be inserted, which is accomplished by building a tower (wood) above the gate, thus regaining a productive series of relationships (water—wood—fire). Within the Forbidden City the same relationship of water and fire exists, so between *Wumen*, or Meridian Gate, which is its major entrance, and the Inner City, runs the Golden Waters (a canal), which destroys "fire" and thus protects the nuclear city.[35]

The possible geomantic "power points" appear to be not only innumerable but their relationships extremely complicated. While one could imagine dealing with all of them in relationship to a single site like a grave, it becomes impossible to do so when we are dealing with an entire city. Without further examination of this expanding net of complexities, let me simply summarize my conclusions about the *fengshui* of Beijing:

1) While one may speak of the *fengshui* of a grave, a house, a temple, or some other single site, when the term is applied to an entire city, it is used metaphorically. The possible points of reference are simply too many, and there is no way to determine priorities as to which of these points of reference are most important.

2) There are too many potential symbolic referents in *fengshui* itself to make a systematic analysis possible. To give a partial list, there are the trigrams and hexagrams in both *luoshu* (posterior heavens) and *hetu* (prior heavens) arrangements, the ten stems and twelve branches, the sexagenary characters, the five phases, yin and yang, the twenty-four directions, the planets, the constellations, the twenty-eight habitations (*su*), the four seasons, eight directions, the symbolic animals, colors, the twenty-four half-month periods, and so forth. All these symbolic factors can be seen on the faces of the larger geomantic "compasses" (*luopan*).

3) Although not a comprehensive system, *fengshui* nevertheless is a significant factor in Beijing. Once we accept the fact that geomancy is not so much a tool of urban planning as it is a method of *analysis*, then we can affirm that it too is a way of understanding the city, its history and destiny. For the geomantic expert (the *fengshuixiansheng* or *kanyujia*), Beijing was seen with different eyes than those of the ordinary person. It was the relationships of these features, together with the overall siting of Beijing in its macroenvironment (hills, watercourses, etc.), that created the fate and destiny of the city.

Fengshui is religious language, a tool for naming the mystery, for dealing with cosmic forces that may bring threat, problem, danger, luck, good fortune, or prosperity. If the city suffered a reversal, such as famine, drought, rebellion, or military attack, the *fengshui* expert offered a possible way of explaining it and dealing with it. What Victor Turner pointed out with regard to Ndembu ritual also applies here. It is the hidden that is dangerous and harmful. To name the inauspicious condition is halfway to removing it. To embody the evil in a symbol is a big step toward remedying it.[36] This was the function of the geomancer and his worldview must therefore be accepted as an alternate and valid way of interpreting the meaning of Beijing.

The reason that no "authentic" geomantic interpretation of Beijing can be found also has another reason, the "marginal" status of its practitioners. Geomancers were not members of the Confucian literati class and therefore did not receive the "approval" of the molders of Chinese tradition, although privately many officials (and emperors) were in fact engaged in *fengshui* and other occult practices. Geomancers belonged neither to the upper class nor to the ordinary people, yet their services were used by both.[37] Their traditions were basically oral and their body of knowledge passed from person to person without benefit of extensive literature. Their methods of interpretation were highly individualistic, indeterminate, and intuitive, as the following quote brings out:

> [What] life breath [is] cannot be conveyed in words, but only recognized by the eye. If you can recognize life breath, then you need not recognize the stars [shapes], nor analyze the branches and trunks, nor investigate the site conditions, nor distinguish the eminences and waters, yet when you pick a site for someone, it will always be right—how is this? It is because all the multifarious methods were devised for no other purpose than to seek out life breath; when life breath is found, there is no longer the least need to discuss the methods.[38]

With a Zenlike simplicity (when you've caught the fish, throw away the net!), the geomancer throws out all the complicated factors listed above.

One final point needs to be made about Beijing's geomancy. The principles that governed it are the symbols of cosmic thinking we have already seen in analyzing the form of Beijing: the trigrams of the *Yijing*, yin jang, and the five-phase worldview. Feuchtwang and de Groot note that there were two main schools of geomancy, the Fujian school, which specialized in topographical analysis, and the Jiangxi school, which emphasized cosmological factors. Yet in both schools, the geomantic compass is used as a sort of model of the universe by which the features of heaven and earth can be brought into relation with a given site. The basic metaphysic on which the geomancer works—"a universe pulsing between *Yin* and *Yang*, permeated by *Qi* (matter-energy), moved back and forth by the Five Agents of Water, Fire, Wood, Metal, and Earth—is the metaphysic of scholardom, . . . but the geomancer puts his metaphysic to common use."[39]

INTERSECTIONS AND EXCLUSIONS: THE NUCLEAR CITY OF BEIJING

Within the confines of the Beijing created by the Ming emperors were buildings and sites of many sorts: palaces, audience halls, bureaus, official quarters, stores, temples, homes, altars, parks, and so forth. Since this is a study in religious symbolism, we must choose for consideration from among these sites only those that express the essential structure, occupy key positions in the articulation of the son of heaven's city as world capital.[40] Following the classic description in the *Zhouli*, I will first describe what might be called the "nuclear city": the imperial palaces, the altar of the spirits of land and grain (*shejitan*), and the imperial ancestral temple (*taimiao*). In the next chapter I will examine the suburban altars, with particular emphasis on the altar of heaven.

The Imperial Palaces

Let us begin our journey through Beijing at the southern gate, *Yongdingmen*, following a course that would have been impossible in traditional times.[41] (Refer to map, p. 32.) In fact, no one, with the exception of the emperor (who would have had no reason to do so) could have traversed the entire axial way, from its southern terminus at *Yongdingmen* to the bell tower at the northern terminus. Yet, to understand the significance of Beijing, this imaginary pilgrimage must be made.

Passing through *Yongdingmen* we find ourselves in the outer or Chinese city. To the right as we walk north is the wall of the immense altar of heaven complex, and to the left the smaller, but still extensive, compound of religious structures called the altar of the first farmer (or altar of agriculture). These sites will be considered in the next chapter. Continuing north on the axial way the distance of about three kilometers, we come to the major gate to the inner city, called Central Yang Gate (*Zhengyangmen*) but popularly called simply Front Gate (*Qianmen*). Here we enter the old city of Beijing through a gate built originally in the Yongle period, and pass by what in imperial times were very important offices and bureaus, including the Board of Rites, on the right. Today this whole area has been cleared to create the vast space that forms the central square of Beijing, with the mausoleum of Mao Zedong in the center and the great Hall of the People on the left.

Continuing on ahead for about eight hundred meters we come to the massive gate called the gate of heavenly peace (*Tiananmen*). This is the formal entrance to the next walled enclosure, the Imperial City, which was restricted to ministers, officials, staff, and members of the imperial family. The Gate of Heavenly Peace was a Ming structure, originally called *Chengtian* Gate, from the phrase *chengtianhu:* receiving prosperity from heaven. The gate was remodeled during the Qing Shunzhi reign (1644–62 C.E.) and called by its present name.

It was only at particular times and under very restricted circumstances that persons other than the emperor might use the gate, and he used it chiefly for ceremonial purposes. At the winter and summer solstices, when the emperor went to worship heaven and earth, his entourage issued forth from this gate. Whenever the army was dispatched, the emperor performed a ceremony here, including worship of the spirit of the road. Most important, great imperial proclamations were promulgated at this gate during Ming and Qing times. On such occasions, the emperor stood on the platform built over the gate. His official decree was read in its entirety to the assembled military and civil officials bowed below him, then lowered from the platform in the mouth of a gilded wooden pheasant and received below on a special wooden plate by a member of the Board of

Rites. Then it was copied by a board secretary, and promulgated. This ceremony showed, says one source, "the supreme respect given the emperor's authority and that there was no spiritual authority higher than his"[42] (see illustration 5).

Tiananmen was therefore the symbolic point of contact between the emperor and his people, so it was no accident that the revolutionary leaders in 1949 chose this place to proclaim the new republic. There is a very ancient legend that highlights the pivotal nature of this famous gate. Outside and inside the gate were pairs of high ornamental pillars, on top of which were carved images of protective beasts, a type of dragon (*huo*). The two dragons on the outer pillars looked south; those inside the gate looked north toward the Forbidden City. Carved or tiled dragons of this type are often found on the eaves of important buildings. When the emperor was away on a journey, the beasts positioned outside the gate were believed to admonish him: "Oh ruler, do not continue to travel about for so long a time, return quickly and take hold of the reins of government yourself! Our eyes watch in expectation of your return." Inside the gate, the eyes of the dragons look north, and when the emperor spends too long in the pleasures of the inner court, they warn him: "Oh ruler, do not stay in your halls and palaces, come forth and see the sufferings and difficulties of your people."[43] This simple legend, set at the highly symbolic point of contact between the ruler and his subjects, is a perfect expression of the dual roles of the son of heaven, a summary of the people's expectations of what a good emperor should be.

Walking north, we next pass through *Duanmen*, or Short Gate. On the right are the walls of the imperial ancestral temple, on the left the walls of the altar of land and grain. Ahead is the most massive gate in all Beijing, *Wumen*, or Meridian Gate. It is "U" shaped, its side wings reaching south to embrace the entering visitor. It has five portals in the central section. Only the emperor could use the center portal, and the empress once in her lifetime, on the occasion of the imperial wedding.

Meridian Gate is the entrance to the Forbidden City, the final and most impressive barrier between the "outside" and the more powerful and sacred "inside" (see illustration 6). Various ceremonies were carried out at the gate, including the flogging of officials and bureaucrats as legal punishments. As *Tiananmen* is the meeting point between emperor and people, *Wumen* is the place of contact between emperor and his host of ministers and officials.

Just inside the gate are two other lateral gates, and at one of these a famous incident occurred in the reign of Jiajing. Trying to give his own parents imperial status, the emperor aroused the opposition of many of his officials. On August 14, 1524, officials prostrated themselves outside the

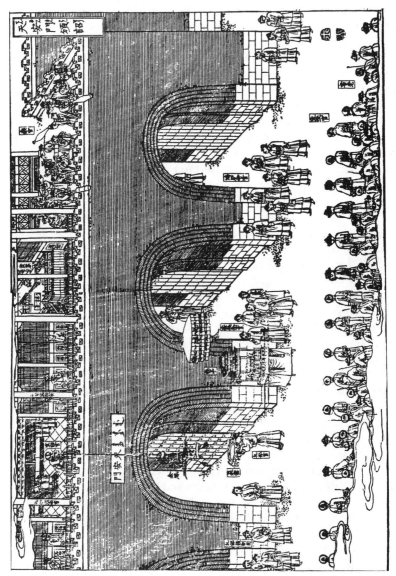

Illus. 5. *Tiananmen*, the Gate of Heavenly Peace. Lowering the Golden Pheasant. Source: *Tangtu mingsheng tubui*

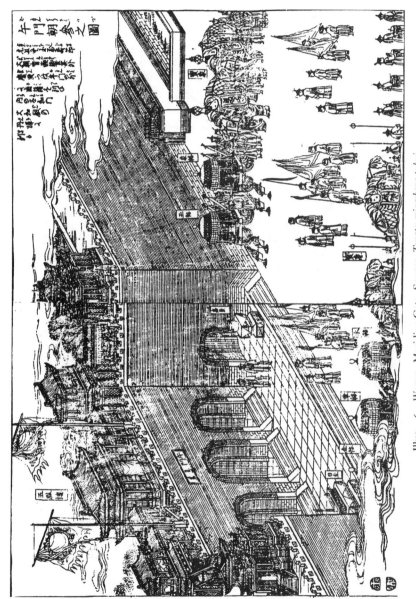

Illus. 6. *Wumen*, Meridian Gate. Source: *Tangtu mingsheng tubui*

east lateral gate and raised their voices in lamentation. Angrily Jiajing ordered them to disperse and when his repeated orders failed to stop them, he had 134 imprisoned and flogged brutally at Meridian Gate. Seventeen died as a result of their beatings.[44]

Just north of the gate are the five marble bridges spanning the Golden River, a canal that follows a meandering route through the Forbidden City. A map will show that it is an errant form in an otherwise totally geometrical enclosure. The presence of the canal and its course are determined by the requirements of geomancy.

Continuing north across the Golden River and a broad courtyard, we pass through yet another gate, *Taihemen*, the Gate of Supreme Harmony, and this takes us finally to the "three halls" (*sandian*), which were the real center of Beijing (see illustration 7). It was said in the ancient classics that the son of heaven ought to rule from the "three courts," and this innermost enclosure seems to be a literal rendering of this prescription.[45]

There are three palace halls sited on a high, three-leveled "I" shaped platform. The most important building was the first, the Hall of Supreme Harmony (*Taihedian*). It was a part of the original Ming plan for the city, and was rebuilt many times thereafter.[46] This building was the true throne hall of the Ming and Qing emperors, where they presided over the *dachao*, the grand audiences, the most important being New Year, the winter solstice, and the emperor's birthday.[47]

The purpose of the grand audience was ceremonial and ritualistic, demonstrating the emperor's sublime authority. On the great ceremonial occasions, the position of all participants was fixed by ancient symbolism, the emperor on the dragon throne, and all officials in their properly assigned places. The military officials stood on the west side of the courtyard facing east, the civil officials on the east side facing west. The officials of both ranks had particular stones set in the surface of the courtyard on which to stand. The vestments of the military were decorated with animals that faced left on their garments, those of the civil ministers were decorated with birds that faced to the officials' right. When all had assumed their proper stations, the birds and animals all faced the dragon throne, the center of the Chinese natural and social order.[48] Thus the highest ranked were to the north, and the east had priority over the west, a clear expression of hierarchy through spatial symbolism.

One can imagine the impressiveness of this ritual order at the great audiences, an order expressive of the cosmic and hierarchical worldview of the Chinese.[49] As Hucker remarked, "Anyone who works extensively with Ming documents . . . cannot avoid the conclusion that proper government in the Ming view was largely a matter of performing proper rituals."[50] It was after just such a grand audience some fifteen hundred years before the

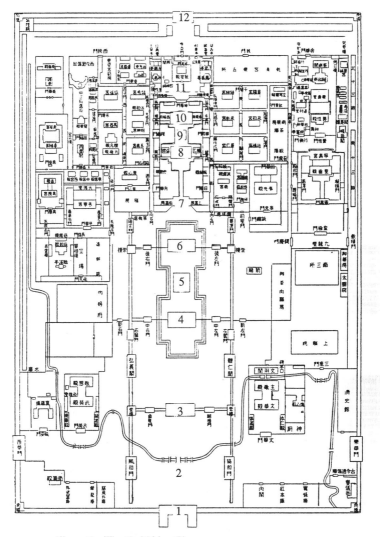

Illus. 7. The Forbidden City.

1. Meridian Gate (*Wumen*)
2. Golden River
3. Gate of Supreme Harmony (*Taihemen*)
4. Hall of Supreme Harmony (*Taihedian*)
5. Hall of Middle Harmony (*Zhonghedian*)
6. Hall of Protecting Harmony (*Baohedian*)
7. Heavenly Brightness Gate (*Qianqingmen*)
8. Palace of Heavenly Brightness (*Qianqinqgong*)
9. Hall of Peaceful Unity (*Jiaotaidian*)
10. Palace of Earthly Tranquility (*Kunninggong*)
11. Imperial Garden
12. Martial Spirit Gate (*Shenwumen*)

Ming period that Han Gaozu, the erstwhile peasant general who ruled China as the first Han emperor, exclaimed: "I know only now the exalted status of the Ruler of Man"[51] (see illustration 8).

The grand audience is described as follows. Very early in the morning, as the drum is struck once, the civil and military officials assemble outside the Meridian Gate, take their assigned places and wait in solemn silence. The drum sounds twice, an official from the Board of Rites leads them to the courtyard of the *Taihedian*, and they take their places according to the nine ranks (as described above). At this time the emperor is resting in the *Zhonghedian*. When the drum sounds three times, the emperor, to musical accompaniment, enters the hall and ascends the dragon throne. There he sits, high above everyone else, while the smoke of incense curls toward the ceiling, creating an awe-inspiring atmosphere. A large whip is then cracked three times at the foot of the throne, in a powerful and daunting manner. Afterward, to the *wansui* music, the multitude of ministers come and perform obeisance. When the music is finished, then the specific content of the grand audience is presented (New Year, emperor's birthday, etc.). At the end, again to the accompaniment of music, the military and civil officials once more make obeisance, and the shouts of "ten thousand years, ten thousand years, ten thousand times ten thousand years" carry throughout the vaults of the immense hall. The emperor returns to the palace and the grand audience is officially over. With over three thousand persons performing the ritual, with the precious ritual vessels displayed in front of the hall, this is a most powerful, solemn, and extraordinary ceremony. This sort of atmosphere makes clear the dictum: "Under the azure heaven, all is bestowed on one single person; within the sacred borders, all is bestowed on [his] ministers and people."[52]

Theoretically, the Hall of Supreme Harmony was also the place where the ordinary audience (*changchao*) should be held. This was the audience at which the daily business of the governing of China should be carried out. Here the emperor would hear reports, memorials to the throne, criticisms, make decisions, and generally keep in touch with his ministers and officials. Dynastic regulations varied: the Han were supposed to have an ordinary audience every five days, the Tang every day, the Ming about every third or fourth day. In point of fact, many emperors ignored them. The late Ming rulers were very negligent. Between 1471 to 1497, under the reign of two emperors, there was not a single audience. Jiajing met with his ministers regularly for the first three years of his entire reign (1522–1566) but for the last forty-two years saw his chief ministers only once! The early Qing rulers, on the other hand, were very zealous and energetic about regular audiences and personal rule. It seems that in the Qing dynasty the *changchao* was "lifted" in status to a more ceremonial

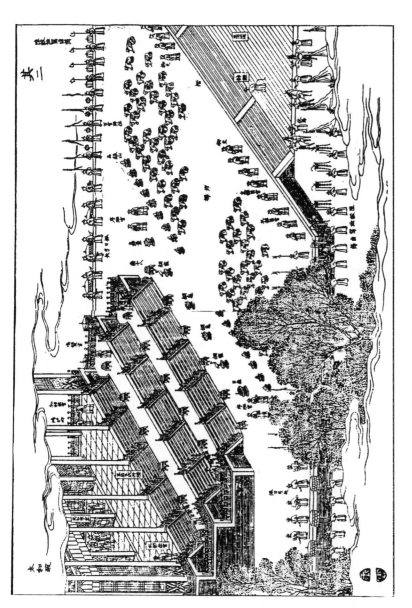

Illus. 8. A Ceremony at *Taihedian*, the Hall of Supreme Harmony. Source: *Tangtu mingsheng tuhui*

function and the ordinary business meeting of emperor and officials was called *yumen* (emperor's gate), from Kangxi's habit of having the business audience at his palace gate (described below) each morning.[53]

Edkins remarks in one place that "there was never in China any notion of local sanctity in buildings. All the reverence attached to a palace is on account of the emperor, the brother of the sun and moon, and his ancestors."[54] While untrue as a general statement, Edkins's insight illuminates a particular feature of Chinese imperial religion. The Hall of Supreme Harmony is in fact not *specifically* sacred. That is to say, it is not sacred *because* it is on this specific piece of ground, but because it is an important *part* of the total scheme of the Chinese capital. This fact helps explain the apparently contradictory statement of Bredon, that the Hall of Supreme Harmony was considered so sacred that no woman, not even the redoubtable empress dowager Cixi, ever dared set foot there.[55] The dowager did not hesitate to exercise total power and in fact completely control imperial government. But she did not dare to assume the emperor's ceremonial and symbolic functions, and that is why she did not take the dragon throne in the great hall of audience. This fact makes clear what it is that the ritual signifies. It makes a claim to total authority. Performing the rituals is what legitimates the assumption of power, and Cixi found it more prudent to go on exercising power without making such a claim.

Behind the Hall of Supreme Harmony is a smaller building, whose name was changed a number of times during the Ming, but was called the Hall of Middle Harmony (*Zhonghedian*) in the Qing dynasty. Speiser offers an unusual interpretation of the Hall of Middle Harmony, calling it the true center of the city of Beijing. He notes the imperial throne in the hall, and above it the so-called lantern ceiling, an effect created by the use of timbers forming successively an octagon, two squares, and a circle as one rises toward the pinnacle. In the center was a carved dragon in whose mouth was a pearl. "The lantern ceiling was called the 'Window to Heaven'—no more than a symbolic aperture that allowed the power of Heaven to enter in the shape of a dragon."[56] As pointed out earlier, the superimposition of square and circle suggested the total cosmos and symbolized the enthronement of the emperor at the center of the world. The dragon and pearl (moon) are traditional yin yang symbols. Above the throne was a placard reading *wu-wei* (nonaction), the code phrase that described the ideal of imperial government. The author concludes: "Thus the small hall, situated between the two big halls where the events of the empire are accorded their ceremonial 'correspondence,' becomes the true focal point of the 'Purple Forbidden City' . . . in which the Son of Heaven alone as the fixed pole harmonizes earthly with cosmic events."[57]

While I accept the author's analysis of the architectural motifs, I find no evidence in any Chinese source to suggest that the Hall of Middle Harmony was so important. It was the place where the emperor, prior to important sacrifices, inspected the *zhuban* (written prayers to be burned and sent to the spirits at the time of sacrifice), and where implements and vessels used in the spring plowing ritual were kept.[58] The same dragon throne under the lantern ceiling was a motif found in other buildings in the Forbidden City, such as the *Jiaotaidian* (see below). And of course the dragon throne in the *Taihedian* is larger and more impressive. I believe that Speiser's misunderstanding lies in mistaking a diagramatic centrality, which the Hall of Middle Harmony has, for a focal point or culmination of meaning, which the hall does not have.

The third of the three halls is called the Hall of Protecting Harmony (*Baohedian*). It was a large building conceived in relation to, and balancing, the Hall of Supreme Harmony to the north. During the Qing dynasty it was the place where the emperor entertained representatives of border states tributary to China and where he received successful candidates in the imperial exams and members of the Hanlin Academy. Banquets were also held here for imperial princes and their families, and for high-ranking ministers.[59]

Behind *Baohedian*, leading from the top of the three-tiered platform down to the level of the courtyard, was the largest "cloud-dragon" stairway in the Forbidden City. It was a single piece of white marble carved with the lovely pattern of clouds and dragons (yin and yang), over 16 meters long, 3.7 meters wide, 1.7 meters thick, and weighing 250 tons. It was brought from the mountain quarry to Beijing, more than 50 kilometers, in the winter, by flooding the road ahead of it, letting the water freeze, and then sliding the marble slab. It required twenty thousand laborers 28 days to accomplish this task.

This slab of marble, like all the others in the Forbidden City, had a ritual and symbolic purpose. No one but the emperor was allowed to walk upon it, so like the central portal of the city's gates, it was an indication of royal privilege. Near the end of Bertolucci's film *The Last Emperor*, as Puyi walks up the steps to his old throne hall, *Taihedian*, he looks at the dragon-cloud ramp, which has been roped off so that tourists will not walk on it. In a small act of defiance, or perhaps nostalgia, he steps across the rope onto the ramp, a wonderful metaphoric action whose significance most viewers will miss.

North of the three halls one passes through the Heavenly Brightness (*Qianqing*) Gate. This portal marks another transition into a very different sort of sacred space, from the public realm of the official audience halls and grand ceremony to the private realm of the palaces of the imperial family or inner court. The arrangement of public and private, south and north, is, of course, in complete accord with the canons of the *Zhouli*. The main palaces of the inner court were built in the early Ming period as a mirror image of the three halls on a slightly smaller scale. Again there is the "I" shaped, three-tiered platform, and the group of three buildings (see again illustration 7).

The purpose of these three palaces is, however, totally different. We have now left the public and entered the private realm, and their spatial arrangement is exactly like that in a private home. In theory the privacy of the inner court was strict during the Qing. Except for officials "on duty," or persons summoned by the emperor, even the high ministers and impe-rial princes of the royal family were forbidden to enter. The government of the last five hundred years of imperial rule can be seen as a pull and tug between the forces of the inner and outer courts, the eunuchs and the ministers, as they sought influence over the emperor. Traditional histories all blame the eunuchs for every disaster that befell Chinese government, but we must recall that these traditional histories were written by the "outer court."

In the early Qing period, the emperors held the ordinary audience just at the liminal place between these two realms, the *Qianqing* Gate. Kangxi (1661–1722) was especially conscientious about personally holding audience every morning, rain and wind, heat or cold notwithstanding. He changed the place for the audience to the *Qianqing* Gate, which was much more convenient than going each day to *Taihedian*. "I always attend care-fully to the details. . . . The emperor's work is of great importance . . . so I attend to all matters, whether they are great or small. Even if it is just one character wrong in a memorial, I always correct it before forwarding it. Not to neglect anything, that is my nature."[60]

The names of the three palaces of the inner court were *Qianqing*, *Jiaotai*, and *Kunning*. Given in the Ming period, their names were never changed, although the usage of the buildings changed. The Ming em-perors took the *Qianqinggong*, Palace of Heavenly Brightness, as their official residence; Shunzhi, the first Qing emperor, followed this practice. But later the building was used as a throne hall where certain government affairs were transacted and where the emperor received congratulations and gave banquets on particular occasions. Qianlong is said to have invited some ordinary people (*renmin*) to a banquet held there on the fiftieth anniversary of his ascending the throne.[61]

The small building behind the emperor's quarters was called the *Jiaotaidian*. The building was originally a throne hall for the empress, and her symbols of the phoenix and full moon are apparent in its decorative motifs. Furthermore, all the paraphernalia for her only sacrifice, to the goddess of the silkworms, was kept in this hall. Later in the Qing period, the Qianlong emperor used this hall as a storage place for the imperial jade seals.[62]

The third palace was the official residence of the empress during the Ming dynasty. Its name, *Kunninggong*, means Palace of Earthly Tranquility. The Qing also used the building as the place for imperial weddings and it was here that they held some of the most important rites of their native Manchu religion.[63]

The names of the three buildings of the inner court, just briefly described, represent a kind of culmination of traditional symbolism—natural, social, cosmic. The images are taken directly from China's most comprehensive repository of symbolism, the *Yijing*. The key words in the building titles are *qian*, *kun*, and *tai*. *Qian*, "creativity," is the first of the sixty-four hexagrams and encompasses all the accompanying qualities of brightness, daylight, pure yang, maleness, heaven, south, summarizing all that the emperor is supposed to stand for. *Kun*, "receptivity," is the second hexagram: darkness, night, pure yin, femaleness, earth, north. In the *hetu* diagram of the prior heavens they are perfect opposites, but in the world of experience—the posterior heaven—they are never pure but must be joined together in proper proportions to produce harmonious conditions. *Tai*, "peacefulness," is the eleventh hexagram, and in the *Jiaotai* hall the two opposites are brought together. *Jiao* means a coming together, a union in mutual love and affection, and *tai* is the tranquility that results from this harmony. But we should not think of this harmony in primarily personal terms of the love between emperor and empress. The image refers to harmony at every level, from the cosmic world of the two ultimate forces, to the social, interpersonal, and individual biological level of the human body.

The *tai* hexagram is a combination of the *qian* and *kun* trigrams brought together in the proper relationship: "Heaven and earth unite: the image of PEACE. Thus the ruler divides and completes the course of heaven and earth; he furthers and regulates the gifts of heaven and earth, and so aids the people." The commentary adds, "Heaven and earth are in contact and combine their influences, producing a time of universal flowering and prosperity."[64]

The symbolic names embodied in the titles of the three buildings of the inner court "express through the ages the most beautiful of imperial aspirations," so the names of these three palaces were never changed.[65] Though the names of nearly every other hall, palace, office, and gate of the Forbidden City were changed many times during the course of the Ming and Qing dynasties, the names of these palaces remained the same for over five hundred years.

Behind the Palace of Earthly Tranquility to the north one passes through a gate into the imperial garden, another important transition. Here we leave the world of regularity, symmetry, and hierarchy, and pass into the realm of nature, where human beings, even the emperor, must stand in reverence. I will discuss the significance of Beijing's imperial gardens later.

Finally, we exit the Forbidden City at the Martial Spirit Gate (*Shenwumen*). This gate was said to be for the exclusive use of the empress, as the Meridian Gate at the south end of the Forbidden City was for the use of the emperor. Whether this theoretical restriction was actually observed I do not know, but it is another expression of the symbolism of balance of which we have already had so many examples.

North of *Shenwu* Gate is the Bright Prospect Imperial Park, also called the Coal Hill, because coal for heating the Forbidden City was stored there during the winter. The hill was formed at the beginning of the Ming period with the soil excavated from the moats around the Forbidden City, and was an important aspect of Beijing's *fengshui*. The park interrupts the axial way, which resumes north of it. *Dianmen*, the Gate of Earthly Peace, marks the border of the Imperial City, and is obviously named to contrast with *Tiananmen*, the southern gate. Outside the gate, the axial way continues to the Drum Tower and the Bell Tower in the northern portion of the city. There it ends, for as we have already seen, there is no gate in the center of the northern wall.

The true center of Beijing is the three halls, the *sandian*, yet a dramatic architectural climax is lacking in the overall plan. There is no monumental form to overawe the observer. The Forbidden City had no conception of an *omphalos*, no well or passage to the underworld, no linga, pillar, tree, or temple to the gods, which might serve to mark the focal point of the city. Yet there is no question that Beijing was conceived as the center of the world. The horizontal passage I have described is strongly axial, but there is no climactic center. We cannot even call the Hall of Supreme Harmony a "climax," for behind it the movement flows in a gradual diminuendo as one leaves successively the Forbidden City, the Imperial City, and the Inner City. In Needham's happy phrase, this plan has no place for the "bathos of anticlimax."[66]

In interpreting the sacral significance of the Forbidden City, its halls and palaces, I would like to consider three points. The first is the fact that the halls and palaces are themselves models of the universe. As Granet remarks, the edifice itself in China is less important than the terrace that supports it and the roof that covers it—the former a figure of earth, the latter of heaven. In certain buildings, such as the two found in the altar of heaven, the imagery was made explicit by the use of a round roof. Between the roof and terrace is the airy section of screens, dividers, and pillars, but rarely the heaviness of thick walls (the hall of abstinence in the altar of heaven is an exception). The pillars symbolize the mountains or supports of the sky, variously numbered as four or eight in Chinese mythology.

The myth of Nuwa, sister of legendary Emperor Fuxi and successor to the throne, tells of her struggle with a rebel named Gonggong. Enraged at his inability to overcome her, the violent Gonggong fled to a mountain where the bases of the eight columns supporting the vault of heaven rested. Grasping one column he shook it violently until it collapsed, taking with it part of the vault and causing tumultuous wind and rain to descend on the earth. Then Nuwa melted stones of the five colors to repair the heavens and she cut off the feet of the celestial tortoise to set upright the four extremities of the earth.[67]

The frequent use of the celestial turtle as a base for the major columns that support imperial halls and palaces confirms the imagery of the columns.[68] Boerschmann sees the same cosmic imagery in the form of the Forbidden City itself, interpreting the four corner towers as symbolic as well as military structures. He maintains that they find their counterpart in the walled battlements of the temples in the sacred mountains, which themselves "present a conception of the universe."[69] While I cannot verify Boerschmann's interpretation, it represents at least another possible articulation of the omnipresent cosmic expression found in Beijing.

The second and much more significant point is to call the reader's attention to the grand orchestration of yin yang, five-phase thinking in the arrangement of the Forbidden City. There is first the alternation of the official and residential portions of the city, as the *Zhouli* prescribed, with the larger and more important group of three in the south and the smaller and less significant group in the north. Within the individual ternary group the same alternation is maintained, the larger and more important *Taihedian* to the south, the *Baohedian* to the north. In the residential section, the emperor's palace, the *Qianqinggong*, is to the south, the *Kunninggong* of the empress to the north. The large Meridian Gate used by the emperor is the south central gate of the Forbidden City, the smaller Martial Spirit Gate used by the empress is the north central gate. One could carry the analysis to more detailed lengths, and at every step meet the dialectic of yin yang, emperor-empress, north-south, male-female.

Besides the north-south dialectic, there are also symmetries of east and west in the Forbidden City. The civil officials must enter by *Donghua* Gate from the east when they come to the palace city on government business. The military officials enter by *Xihua* Gate from the west. When they take their positions at the great audiences, as we have already seen, they have the same directional positions. In the Ming period the important Hall of Military Valor was in the southwest corner of the Forbidden City, the Hall of Flourishing Culture in the southeast.

The civil-cultural complex fits into the yang pattern of symbols and thus was connected with the east, the sun, day, and the like, while military fits in the yin complex and was accorded its position in the west. Like the north-south arrangement, this one also implied a hierarchy, for the civil officials were given a position of preeminence, as east was "higher" than west and accorded more prestige. We shall see a great deal more of this type directional symbolism as we examine the placement of altars and of their individual arrangements.

The third and final point has to do with the position of the emperor. Despite the clear evidence of yin yang, five-phase thinking on the Forbidden City, there is still a certain opaqueness to the religious or sacral significance of the city. This opacity stems, I believe, from a more fundamental ambiguity about the religious meaning of the Chinese imperial system, and the specific type of sacrality it embodies. Some authors speak of a "civil ritual," implying that the conceptions and practices of the Chinese government were basically secular-political, though covered by a veneer of elaborate ritual and etiquette. Marxist critics often contend that the entire imperial ideology, especially the mandate of heaven concept, was merely a subterfuge to gain power and manipulate the people. There are historical reasons for these essentially secular interpretations of imperial politics, but this is not the place to attempt to trace them. I take the position that the Chinese imperial ideology was fundamentally a religious conception, that the emperor was in fact a "sacred king" par excellence, and that the capital built to house him was a cosmic "sacred city."[70]

The opacity I referred to has its source in the fact that *everything* done by the emperor had a sacral flavor to it, and this sort of universalizing can lead to the opposite perception, that *nothing* he does is sacred. Ritual logic seems to dictate that the greater the sacred power involved, the greater the regulations and prohibitions that surround it. The elaborate ceremonies performed by the emperor in the audience halls were not different in kind but only in degree from the whole host of formalities required at every moment of his day. Whether he held the grand or ordinary audiences, studied the classics with his scholar-tutors, ate meals, went to visit someone, or called for wife or concubine to sleep with him, he was hedged in by the most complex set of rules and ritual behavior to safeguard and express his exalted status.[71]

In regard to sleeping partners, for example, the *Zhouli* stipulated that there be one empress, three consorts, nine spouses, twenty-seven concubines, and eighty-one assistant concubines, each group having an alloted time of the month to cohabit with the emperor, with the empress given one night each month nearest the full moon when the yin principle was most potent. "A corps of secretarial ladies kept the records of the emperor's cohabitations with the brushes dipped in imperial vermillion. The proper order of these proceedings in the imperial bed chamber was believed essential to the larger order and well being of the empire."[72] The ritualization of all life's details emphasizes the sacred status of the emperor and shows that the real center of the Forbidden City is not a place but a person, the emperor himself.

Roland Barthes, reflecting on the nature of the Japanese capital, has remarked that Western cities are "in accord with the very movement of Western metaphysics, for which every center is the site of truth, the center of our cities is always *full:* a marked site, it is here that the values of civilization are gathered and condensed." Tokyo, in contrast, offers a precious paradox, "it does possess a center, but this center is empty. The entire city turns around a site both forbidden and indifferent, . . . inhabited by an emperor who is never seen, which is to say, literally, by no one knows who."[73]

One could say that his description applies equally well to Beijing, and that the shape of the city is in perfect accord with the movement of Oriental metaphysics, for which every center, as the site of truth, is perfectly *empty.* Beyond all the superficial comparisons between Orient and Occident, a most fundamental difference is the Oriental view that true reality is empty (*kong*), true thinking is "nonthinking" (*wu xin*), true action is "nonaction" (*wu wei*), and true power is concealed. These paradoxes are obviously true of the metaphysics of Taoism and Buddhism, but traces of this tendency glimmer even in humanistic and practical Confucianism: "Heaven does not speak, yet the four seasons run their course thereby, the hundred creatures, each after its kind, are born thereby. Heaven does no speaking."[74]

As the most effective word is unspoken, so Beijing's architecture of concealment enhances even more powerfully the sacred presence within. Instead of overwhelming the viewer with vertical monuments, the Forbidden City hides in order to impress. One can never forget the power of the emptiness at the center because one is forever forbidden to see it:

> Let us take as our comparison the wall around a building. My own wall reaches only to the level of a man's shoulder. And it is easy enough to peep over it and see the good points of the house on the other side. But our Master's [Confucius's] wall rises many times a man's height, and no one who is not let in by the gate can know the beauty and wealth of the palace that, with its ancestral temple, its hundred ministrants, lies hidden within.[75]

John Ruskin's dictum, that a great nation writes its autobiography most clearly in the book of its art, is verified in the architecture of the Chinese capital. The walled center of Beijing, the emptiness concealed, gives evidence of a deep intellectual commitment to paradox as the way to ontology. This unique spatial conception, to paraphrase Giedion, gives insight into the Chinese attitude toward the cosmos, toward nature, and toward its most enduring values.[76]

The Altars to the Spirits of Land and Grain (*Shejitan*)

The second of the three essential components of a capital city is the altar (or altars) to the spirits of land and grain. The history of this altar is extremely long, and perhaps, for that very reason, unclear in many of its particulars. Although it is impossible to answer all the questions one must have regarding the identity of the spirits involved, we will first look at the historical development of their altars in Beijing and then assess how the Ming ritual experts understood their meaning.

We have already noted the fact that the first *sheji* altars in Beijing were built by the Nuchen Jin in the twelfth century. Although no actual remains of an actual Yuan *sheji* altar have been found, its location is reported to have been west of the imperial city just north of the *Wanan* Buddhist temple. Literary sources allege that it was built at the instance of a certain minister named Zui in 1293, as part of the movement toward a city structure and ritual practice more in keeping with Chinese practice. In form and function, it was traditional.[77] There were twin altars to the *she* and *ji* at the southern end of the forty *mou* (roughly between six- and seven-acre complex), each one five *chi* high and five *chang* square, the *she* altar to the east, the *ji* to the west. The soil covering the *she* altar was, as usual, of five colors representing the five directions: blue-green (*qing*), red, white, black, and yellow. The accounts do not make clear exactly how the soils were arranged on the altar in the Yuan. Directionally, the east was blue-green, the south red, the west white, the north black, and the center yellow, according to the five phase conception. Some texts suggest that the soil was mounded in the center, specifying that "ordinary soil" should be placed in the center and covered with yellow soil. The *ji* altar, however, was covered with yellow soil only.

The stone marker was placed in the southern part of the *she*, facing (inclined toward?) the north. It was white in color, five *chi* long, two in diameter, though narrowing at the top to form a bell-like shape. The bottom half was buried in the ground. No such stone was placed in the soil of the *ji* altar. A pine tree (identified with the Xia dynasty) marked the southern end of each of the two altars. At the time of the sacrifice, four spirit tablets were used. The two receiving chief worship were, of course,

Fig. 1. *Shejitan* **Spirit Tablets**

the *she* and *ji* spirits, while the two being worshiped as accompanying spirits were called *Hou Tu* and *Hou Ji*.[78] At the time of the sacrifice, the spirit tablets of these four would have been placed on the altars in the arrangement shown in figure 1 (the arrows indicate which direction the tablet faced). I have chosen to describe the Yuan *sheji* altars at some length because their form and use, with a few minor deviations, also hold true for the Ming and Qing dynasties.

As I mentioned in chapter 1, the *sheji* altars are referred to frequently in the classics. One chapter of the *Zhouli* stipulates that a certain official, called the *dasitou*, was to set up the enclosure consecrated to the spirits of the land and grains. The commentary on the text discusses the identity of the two spirits involved, saying that the *she* is the spirit of the locality or of the five kinds of work attributed to the diverse types of land. Qu Long, a minister under one of the legendary emperors, became assimilated to this spirit after his death because of his service to the people as land superintendant, and was called Hou Tu. The *ji* spirit is called *supérieur de la culture*, or "millet" since that was the first type of grain to be cultivated. The minister of grain under the Emperor Yao first taught the people how to sow and reap, so after his death he was assimilated to the *ji* spirit and designated as Hou Ji, Prince Millet.[79]

The classics are in accord on the placement of the altar of the spirits of land and grain outside the southern gate of the palace complex, west and opposite the ancestral temple, but inside the southern gate of the city.[80] What continued to remain unclear to later Chinese was the identity of the two spirits and whether they should be worshiped at a single or double altar.

The beginning of Ming rule over China saw the emergence of a restorationist outlook, and so the Hongwu emperor made every effort to have his capital Nanjing satisfy all the prescriptions of the classical tradition. The emperor and his officials were disturbed that the ancient worship of these spirits had been neglected so long during the Yuan period of rule. Even though an altar had finally been built for their worship, it had not been used frequently. The emperor called for a thorough discussion of the rite, and it is from the discussions that took place in the early years of the founding of the dynasty by the Ming ritual experts that we may learn something of the history and importance of *sheji* worship, as well as its ambiguities.[81]

At the beginning of the dynasty, there was in Nanjing a double altar to the *she* and *ji* spirits, surrounded by a single wall—the same arrangement as we have seen used by the Yuan at Dadu. But by the eleventh year of his reign, the emperor began to have doubts about this system, and called for a discussion by the Board of Rites, which offered the following summary of theories regarding the *she* and *ji*. The theories fall roughly into two categories: they are the spirits of either men or of earth and grain.

The first party of discussants refer to the explanation we have already mentioned, that the spirits were originally the ministers of land and grain under the ancient emperors and thus the spirits of deified men. The second party said that in worshiping the *she* and *ji* spirits the emperor actually worships the spirits of the five types of land and the five kinds of grain. Quoting a number of authoritative sources, they pointed out that land and grain must "go together." Without land, grain cannot grow; without grain, land has nothing to produce. The second party, therefore, in favoring the theory that the two were spirits of earth and grain, concluded that because of the intimate natural connection, the two should be worshiped at a single altar. Impressed by this logic, Hong Wu built a new single altar for the *sheji* spirits at the prescribed place southwest of the Meridian Gate in Nanjing, and in the eleventh year of his reign first began to worship there. He gave the order that the altars of *she* and *ji* in the hierarchy of administrative centers follow the single altar system as established in the capital. Then, without any reason being given, the *Ming History* says that the two-altar system was reinstituted two years later.[82]

In the eighteenth year of the Yongle reign, when the emperor decided to move his capital to Beijing, he immediately established a single *sheji* altar in its canonized position southwest of the Meridian Gate, thus correcting the Yuan misplacement. The emperor went back to the original Hongwu order, a single altar for the worship of the two spirits. This system became standard for the rest of the Ming and the whole of the Qing period.

The only innovation in the worship of *she* and *ji* came during the Jiajing reign. The emperor took a great interest in all aspects of the imperial ritual system, principally with a view to promoting the cause of his natural father, whom he wished to raise to imperial status. He became more knowledgeable in the baroque intricacies of liturgy than any other Ming or Qing emperor, with the possible exception of Qianlong. Jiajing noticed that the ancient system of offering equivalent worship to Hou Tu and Hou Ji at the sacrifice to the *she* and *ji* spirits had been abandoned by the Hongxi period (1425–26 C.E.) and in their place the spirit tablets of Taizu and Taizong, the Hongwu and Yongle emperors, had been substituted. The emperor doubted the authenticity of this change. He berated the Board of Rites and urged its members to observe the ancient norms, returning the tablets of the two Ming founders to the ancestral temple.[83] But imperial ancestors are not lightly demoted. Jiajing then established a whole new complex in the park to the west of the Forbidden City, a double altar within a single enclosure, which he called an "imperial" *sheji* altar, but only after another argument with the Board of Rites.

The ritualists had at first called the new altar a *tugutan* (earth and grain altar), but the emperor objected that although the words were different, the meaning was exactly the same as the *shejitan*. An official explained that they could not call it a royal *sheji* because that word (royal = *wang* or king) referred exclusively to the sovereign in the Zhou dynasty. As a result, the designation "imperial *sheji*" was agreed upon, and the altar was presumably a place where Jiajing could continue to "associate" (*pei*) the spirits of Hongwu and Yongle while Hou Tu and Hou Ji could assume their rightful places at the ordinary altar to land and grain.[84] But, as happened with a number of Jiajing's innovations, his successor abolished the worship at the imperial *sheji* as superfluous, so the altar was used only about thirty years in all.

As noted above, the Qing simply followed the Ming system of imperial worship and used the Ming *sheji* altar (see illustration 9). There were some new buildings added to the altar complex in the Qian Long period, but the form of the altar and the type of worship remained the same.[85] A few details are further clarified by the descriptions of the altar and its worship in Qing ritual texts. They state, for example, that the walls surrounding the altar were of a permanent color, according to the color of the appropriate direction, while the five-colored soil was spread upon the top of the altar in the proper pattern the day before the ceremony took place. We are also told that the stone was completely buried and covered with a piece of wood when not in use at the rite.

Today in Beijing, the *she* altar has been nicely restored and lies within Zhongshan (Sun Yat Sen) Park. The surface is flat, the altar square, and the colored soils are arranged as in figure 2. A sign just outside the enclosure tells the visitor that the colors of the soils symbolize that "under the whole of heaven, there is no soil that does not belong to the ruler." It also interprets the stone, which is called the "*she* ruler stone," or the "mountains and rivers stone," stating that it symbolized the emperor's title, "The mountains and rivers everlasting firmness."

We are now left with the question of the meaning of the *sheji* altar and its worship in the context of imperial ideology. Since its origins are unknown, various interpretations have been given, including chthonic worship, tree worship, stone or phallic worship, and so forth. All are

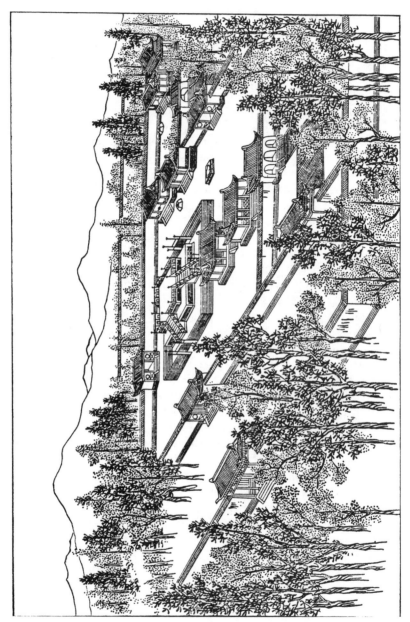

Illus. 9. *Shejitan*, the Altar of Land and Grain. Source: *Tangtu mingsheng tuhui*

Fig. 2. Patterns of Soils on the *Sheji* Altar

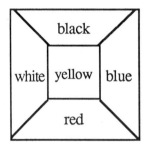

possibilities, but by the time we are considering, when the Ming dynasty ruled in Beijing, the meaning of the mound, stone, and tree, and the identity of the spirits, was as much a mystery to the experts of the Board of Rites as it is to us today.

Ling Shunsheng has published an article bringing together a large number of ancient texts dealing with the various *she* altars in antiquity, and has assessed the many theories about their meaning proposed by Western, Japanese, and Chinese scholars. The author concludes that because of the varied types of worship connected with the *she* in the ancient texts, it was in antiquity simply a designation for a communal altar, an open mound used for the worship of any number of earthly and heavenly spirits. The spirits of land and grain became the sole deities worshiped at this type of altar only after imperial times.[86]

Let us leave aside the question of origins and primitive meaning, and concentrate on the meaning of the *sheji* in the Ming dynasty. We may begin by dismissing the possibility that the *she*, the spirit of the land, was in any sense interchangeable with the cosmic principle earth (correlative of heaven). If it had been, there would certainly have been a question raised as to its superfluity, since the Ming already worshiped "sovereign earth," at first in conjunction with heaven at the south suburban altar and later at its own altar north of the city. Such a question never arose. Particularly during the reign of Longqing, Jiajing's successor, when the latter's ritual "excesses" were cut back drastically, there was never any suggestion made that the worship at the *she* and the worship of sovereign earth at the north altar were in any sense duplications.[87]

I believe that we can at least be certain that three aspects in the nature of the worship of the *sheji* spirits were clear to Ming-Qing ritual experts. First, these spirits were in some sense genii loci, divinities of particular places; second, they embodied or represented the societal group over which they presided; and third, they were connected with the fruitfulness of the land. These spirits were limited in their jurisdiction. The *she* and *ji* of the imperial altars would seem to have power over the whole realm. Yet it appears that their influence "thinned" as one moved away from the imperial capital, since every city within the administrative structure of the empire had a *sheji* altar to the spirits particularly responsible for the smaller territories to which they were attached, the prefectures, subprefectures, and counties (*fu, zhou, xian*).[88]

In ancient times, part of the enfeoffment ceremony included the sovereign giving a clump of soil from his *she* altar to the enfeoffed. The clump was taken from the side of the altar corresponding to the direction of his fief, and the soil then became the nucleus for the local *she* of the enfeoffed. It is interesting to note that the practice was completely reversed by Ming times, when soil of the five colors was brought from the provinces of the empire to make the imperial *she* altar. This reversal implies a change in meaning and might be due to the influence of five-phase thinking in Han times.[89] Whether centripetal or centrifugal, the *she* altar is obviously a way of dealing with the relationship of center and periphery, the centralization of authority in imperial government.

We may also see the connection of the *sheji* altar with the fruitfulness of the land. Each dynasty followed the ancient practice of worshiping at the altar in the middle month of the spring and fall seasons, the times of planting and harvest. The practice of planting a tree at the altar site seems also connected with vegetal fertility.

The old practice of covering but not destroying the *she* of a fallen dynasty well illustrates the three points I have suggested. The spirit of the land of the former people must be imprisoned, out of fear and respect, but will not be allowed to become fruitful in the land. Covering the spirit allows a continuation of his existence in a shadowy sort of way, but without the influence of sun and rain, he will be ineffective. An interesting detail found in the Qing worship of the *sheji* (and perhaps used in earlier dynasties) may be a vestige of this belief. During the time of worship there were two men with poles posted at the east and west sides of the altar to keep birds from flying over the altar and blocking the heavenly influences in any way.[90]

The Imperial Ancestral Temple (*Taimiao*)

The third essential element of the capital city was the *taimiao*, the temple where the spirits of the imperial ancestors were worshiped. In a superficial sense, the meaning and usage of the ancestral temple is clear and straightforward, at least compared to the *sheji*. But I think we have to acknowledge that during much of Chinese tradition, the worship of ancestors was a profound and mysterious act. This point of view may be hard for non-Chinese to comprehend. During the sixteenth and seventeenth centuries, when Roman Catholic missionaries began to evangelize China, their judgment was that ancestral worship was not "religious," but simply a ceremony of remembering. Though the missionaries were supported by some Chinese in this viewpoint, the traditional attitude is much closer to the view expressed by Confucius. When asked for an explanation of the ancestral sacrifice, he replied: "'I do not know. Anyone who knew the explanation could deal with all things under Heaven as easily as I lay this here;' and he laid his finger upon the palm of his hand."[91] Taking my cue from the master, I will not try to penetrate the deeper meaning of the ancestral sacrifice, but confine my remarks to some historical considerations of form, usage, and symbolism of the *taimiao* in Ming and Qing Beijing.

I have already mentioned that the Jin and Yuan dynasties somewhat belatedly established ancestral temples because of the persistent urgings of the Confucian ministers who knew well that one had neither true son of heaven nor universal empire without it. The first Ming emperor established a *taimiao* in Nanjing at the prescribed location southeast of the gate to the palace city and opposite the *sheji* altars.[92] When Yongle moved his capital to Beijing, one of his first acts was to have the *taimiao* built at the proper place, as it had been at Nanjing. The Yongle *taimiao* contained a main central building with two subsidiary buildings flanking it on either side. Behind it was the *qin*, a kind of repository for the spirit tablets, or better, an apartment where the ancestors "rested" when they were not in the temple at times of worship.[93] Just as the emperor had his private realm behind and north of the public audience hall, the *qin* was the dwelling place or palace where the ancestors stayed when not having audience at the times of public ritual.

In the eleventh year of the Jiajing reign, the Ming dynastic ancestral temple in Nanjing burned down. This gave an official named Liao Taonan an opportunity to urge the emperor to build nine separate temples within the precinct of the *taimiao*, so that each imperial ancestor would have his own building. Up to this time Jiajing had been maneuvering to elevate his father to a position of equality with the other emperors of the Ming line. Already in the third year of his reign (1524) he had tried to have a temple built for his father inside the *taimiao* complex, but the Board of Rites refused, allowing him as a compromise to build a temple *adjacent* to it. At issue was the fact that Jiajing was not the natural son of his predecessor Zhengde, but his first cousin. The imperium fell to him because Zhengde died without male heir. Many of Jiajing's ritual innovations and his struggles with the Board of Rites stemmed from his wish to give imperial honors to his father, whereas tradition required that they be reserved for his imperial "father," Zhengde.

Now the fire in Nanjing gave him an opportunity to end official ancestral rites there and bring them to Beijing where he could supervise them more closely. Naturally he assented to Liao's suggestion, seeing it as an opportunity to give his natural father imperial honors. Gradually, through a series of maneuvers he succeeded in having his natural father accorded imperial status, but he was still unsatisfied. Even though the elaborate new temple complex was completed in 1535 c.e., on the site of the old Yongle *taimiao*, his father's temple still remained separate.

Six years later, on April 30, 1541, eight of the nine new buildings burned to the ground in a fire that broke out during a severe thunderstorm. Curiously, only his father's remained untouched by the conflagration. Jiajing then rebuilt the temple compound according to the old formula of one large temple with separate aulae or fanes for each of the imperial ancestors, and into it he placed the spirit tablet of his natural father. This temple was later restored and rebuilt, but its form was essentially preserved down to the present century[94] (illustration 10). Today it is the Working People's Cultural Palace, used mostly for various kinds of exhibitions.

What is perhaps most significant in the *taimiao* of the Ming and Qing dynasties is their complete consistency with the classic prescriptions as to location, arrangements within the temple, and the general congruence with the spatial conceptions embodied in the layout of the city of Beijing as a whole. We find again the directional symbolism characteristic of the yin yang, five-phase worldview. The ancestral temple of the son of heaven, say the classics, should embrace seven fanes, three on the left and three on the right, while that of the most ancient ancestor should be in the center, facing south. The ancestral temple of the Zhou had the arrangement shown in figure 3.

When the question of establishing a *taimiao* came up in the first year of the reign of the Ming founder, his Board of Rites immediately brought up the Zhou practice of the seven fanes as the ideal. But as one can see from a reading of the changes of Ming ancestral worship in the *Ming shi*, nine fanes were often used in later periods. The nine temples of Jiajing, however, were so arranged that seven of them were placed in the classical formation, while the separate one to honor the emperor's natural father was north of the main temple (which housed the dynastic founder, Hongwu) and another to the great emperors of the past called the *wenhuang shimiao* built northeast of the main temple.

Because of the intense conflict between Jiajing and his high ministers,

太
廟

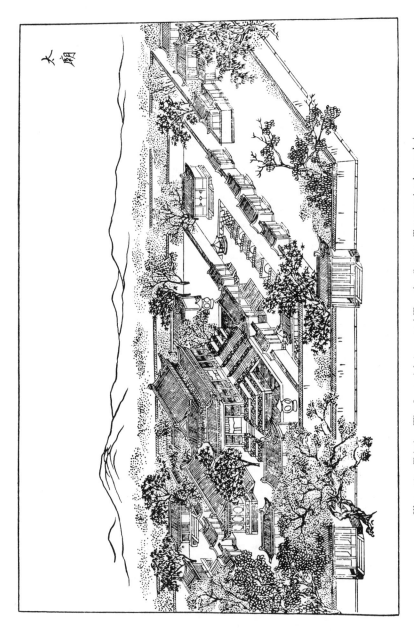

Illus. 10. *Taimiao*, The Imperial Ancestral Temple. Source: *Tangtu mingsheng tubui.*

Fig. 3. *Taimiao* **of Zhou Dynasty**

Great Ancestor

King Wen	——————————	King Wu
Great-Grandfather	——————————	Great-Great-Grandfather
Father	——————————	Grandfather

Main Gate   north

Explanation: Main gate of entry at the south. At the center of the north end, facing south, is the most ancient ancestor of the Zhou dynasty, the founding emperors Wu and Wen (Taizu and Taizong), and finally the four emperors preceding the currently reigning monarch. Father never follows son on the same side. At the back of each fane was a *qin*, where the spirit tablets were kept. The series of ancestors on the east side of the temple had a special designation, *chao*, while the group on the west was called *mu*. The spirit tablet in each fane faced south.[95]

the ongoing struggle was called "the great ritual controversy." It is difficult today to comprehend why this controversy was so heated, why the factions battled so bitterly, and why so many officials were willing to literally put their lives on the line. The controversy shows at least two things: one, that the question of ancestral worship was so important that it penetrated to the level of the participants' ultimate commitments; and two, that as had happened so many times in the past, there were Chinese officials willing to oppose the emperor and become "martyrs" to their moral concern.[96]

The *Ming shi* does not give the list of emperors ensconced in the separate temples, but after the single-temple separate-fane system was restored, the arrangement was as follows:[97]

Taizu (Hongwu)

Jenzong (Hongxi)	Taizong (Yongle)
Yingzong (Zhengtong)	Xuanzong (Xuande)
Xiaozong (Hongzhi)	Xianzong (Chenghua)
Wuzong (Zhengde)	Ruizong (Jiajing's father)

During the Jiajing reign, Yongle's temple name was changed to Chengzu, suggesting that he was a "second founder" of the dynasty. Jiajing liked this idea because it gave him precedent to claim that his father's line, separate from the ordinary line of succession, could be considered a new beginning as well. This not only allowed him to insert his father into the imperial succession, but as the chart above shows, place him "above" Zhengde.

The *taimiao* of the end of the Qing dynasty included all the noted ancestors beginning with Nurhachi and his son, who built Manchu power, and who were honored as Taizu and Taizong. The arrangement was as follows:[98]

Taizu (Nurhachi)

Shizu (Shunzhi)	Taizong (Huang Taiji)
Shizong (Yongcheng)	Shengzu (Kangxi)
Renzong (Jiaqing)	Gaozong (Qianlong)
Wenzong (Xianfeng)	Xuanzong (Daoguang)
Dezong (Guangxu)	Muzong (Tongzhi)

The arrangement shown here would have been the order of precedence in the Qing ancestral temple during the reign of the last emperor, Xuantong, who later became a pawn of the Japanese in their plan to set up a puppet kingdom in Manchuria, and finally citizen Puyi after the revolution of 1949.

One can see in all vagaries above a consistancy in the location of the *taimiao* and of the order within the temple itself. In fact, the schemas shown above repeat in miniature the time-honored positions of the capital city and of its model, the heavenly capital. The ruler, most honored personage, is placed in the center north, facing south. The interior of his fane follows the pattern of the Forbidden City: his audience hall or throne to the front (south), his *qin* or residence to the rear.

The same arrangement is found in the subsidiary fanes. Even though their entrance gates face west (on the *chao* side) and east (on the *mu* side), their spirit tablets face south within the fane. The primacy is given to the eastern side, with Taizong, the secondary dynastic founder, always in the first fane on the east (corresponding to yang, civil official, *chao*, left side), while the last and most recent ancestor is placed on the west side nearest the gate of the temple complex (corresponding to yin, military official, *mu*, right side). Thus the same principles that govern the structure of the city also govern the arrangement of the *taimiao*.

NOTES

1. David N. Keightley, "Shang Divination and Metaphysics," *Philosophy East and West*, 38, no. 4 (October 1988), esp. 385–89.

2. *Wuxing* has been most often translated as "five elements." The consensus now is to use the word "phase" instead, which I like because it conveys the dynamic nature of the concept.

3. Translation of this text from Michael R. Saso, *Taoism and the Rite of Cosmic Renewal* (Pullman: Washington State University Press, 1972), p. 11. I have changed his Wade-Giles transliteration to the pinyin system, which I am using. Good summaries of the yin yang, five-phase philosophy may be found in Fung Yu-lan, *A History of Chinese Philosophy*, trans. Derk Bodde (London: Allen & Unwin, 1952–53), 1:159; William Theodore de Bary, ed., *Sources of Chinese Tradition* (New York: Columbia University Press, 1964), 1:198–210.

4. See de Bary, *Sources*, 1:199, for an extensive table of correspondences.

5. Qi Rushan, *Beiping* (Taibei: Zhengzhung shuqu, 1971; first published, 1957), pp. 25–26, says that the regularity of orientation of streets is so perfect that no one ever gives directions with the terms left and right, but always north, south, east, or west. One of the best purchases I made before going to Beijing was a small compass. I never got lost.

6. Yan Chongnian, *Gudu Beijing* (Beijing: Chaohua chubanshe, 1987), p. 175.

7. Detailed maps of Beijing may be found in *Jiudu wenwu lue* and Shao Yuechong and Lu Qieqing, *Xiuzhen Beiping fenqu* (Shanghai: Fuxing youti xueshe, 1948), in which the city is presented in separate maps, section by section. Recently an invaluable book has been published by Hou Renzhi (cited above), containing maps of the city from the time it was the Liao capital until it became *Beiping* under the nationalists in the twentieth century. Based on the best scholarship available, this book provides the clearest understanding of the historical evolution of Beijing.

8. *Jiudu wenwu lue*, part 1, p. 8; Qu Xuanying, *Beiping*, pp. 149–50. There is evidence that in the Zhou period the inner wall or *cheng* had a ceremonial and administrative purpose: to enclose the enclave containing the three essential elements of the city—altar of land, ancestral temple, and royal palace—while the outer wall or *guo* was primarily military in purpose. The two walls were not always built simultaneously, though the inner wall was of the essence. It appears that in peaceful times only the *cheng* was built, while the *quo* was added under threat of invasion. See Wheatley, *Pivot*, pp. 186–87. In the Jiajing period, participants in the discussion were aware of the ancient practice, but their advocacy of the double wall stressed its protective purpose. As the influential minister Xia Yen said: "The ancient practice was thus: if one had an inner wall (*cheng*), one should also have an outer wall (*kuo*), the inner wall to protect the people, the outer wall to protect the inner wall."

9. *Rixia jiuwen kao*, III (9), 1.

10. Needham, *Science*, 3:230.

11. Gustave Schegel, *Uranographie Chinoise* (Taibei: Chengwen Publishing Co., 1967; first published, Leyden: E. J. Brill, 1875), pp. 89–90.

12. Ibid., pp. 93ff., 103–4, 155, 337, 521, 575.

13. See a discussion of this symbolism in Florence Ayscough, "Notes on the Symbolism of the Purple Forbidden City," *Journal of the North China Branch of the Royal Asiatic Society*, 52 (1921), 51–78. A Song dynasty map of the same enclosure is reproduced in Leopold de Saussure, *Les Origines de L'Astronomie Chinoise* (Taibei: Chengwen Publishing Co., 1967; first published, Paris: Maisonneuve Frères, 1930), p. 510. Schlegel, *Uranographie*, 1:506ff., gives the individual names of the stars of the enclosure and an explanation of the location in reference to Western astronomical terms.

14. Needham, *Science*, 3:259–60.

15. William Willets, *Foundations of Chinese Art* (New York: McGraw-Hill, 1965), p. 336.

16. Quoted in Schlegel, *Uranographie*, 1:507.

17. De Saussure, *Origines*, p. 171, n. 2, and p. 172, n. 1. The author provides a diagram on p. 383, which indicates the successive pole stars from about 4000 B.C.E. to 3000 C.E.

18. Schlegel, *Uranographie*, 1:523–34.

19. *Sancai tuhui*, 1:20.

20. The reference may be found in the *Zhouli*, 1:58.

21. Viewing this from another perspective, we may note that certain criminal punishments were graded as progressively more serious the farther the offender was banished from the capital. There is also a suggestion of moral rather than cosmic centrality in the words of Ming Taizu in 1383: "The capital is the pinnacle of virtue. Its residents should be foremost in the empire in the practice of proper behavior and the reverence of the good" (Farmer, "System," pp. 250, 269).

22. Arthur Waley, trans., *The Analects of Confucius* (New York: Vintage, 1968; first published, New York: Hillary, 1964), p. 88.

23. I (1), 3.

24. Waley, *Analects*, p. 88.

25. A few more examples of the paired square-circle motif: the form of the Ming Tang, the hall proper to royal rule, which I shall discuss in the next chapter, the turtle, symbol of the emperor, whose carapace is round above, square below. See Granet, *Pensée*, p. 147. The body of the imperial cart was square, the canopy-umbrella above it round. See *Zhouli*, 2:488, and picture on opposite page. The bronze mirrors, so popular in the Han period, superimposed the square and circle in their design. See Schuyler Cammann, "Chinese Mirrors and Chinese Civilization," *Archaeology*, 2, no. 3 (Autumn 1949), 114–20.

26. Willetts, *Foundations*, p. 366.

27. Waley, *Analects*, p. 193.

28. Ernst Boerschmann, "Chinese Architecture and Its Relation to Chinese Culture," *Annual Report of the Smithsonian Institution* (1911), pp. 539–67.

29. Cf. Bouillard, "Note succinct sus l'histoire du territoire de Beijing." *Bulletin of the Museum of Far Eastern Antiquities*, 1 (1929), 39–60, referring to the building of Beijing by Yongle: "Le futur empereur transforma aussi l'enceinte de la ville en s'inspirant des principes du vieux feng-shui chinois; laporte du milieu du mur Nord fut supprimée et, les deus portes Nord-est et Nord-ouest qui restaient furent reprochées. De plus il fallait in écran protecteur au Nord du Nouveau Palais pour le préservée des influx pernicieux qui pénétrent toujours par le Nord."

30. J. J. M. de Groot, *The Religious System of China* (Taibei: Cheng Wen, 1969; first published, Leyden: E. J. Brill, 1892), 3:950. See also Andrew L. March, "An Appreciation of Chinese Geomancy," *Journal of Asian Studies*, 27 (February 1968), 253–67; and M. Freedman, "Geomancy," *Proceedings of the Royal Anthropological Institute of Great Britain and Ireland*, 1968 Presidential Address, pp. 5–15. The most complete study of Chinese geomancy available is that of Stephan D. R. Feuchtwang, *An Anthropological Analysis of Chinese Geomancy* (Vientiane: Vithagna Press, 1974), an M.A. thesis done under Freedman.

31. See Qi Rushan, *Beiping*, p. 25; Juliet Bredon, *Beijing: A Historical and Intimate Description of Its Chief Places of Interest* (Shanghai: Kelly & Walsh, 1931), p. 29; Nigel Cameron and Brian Brake, *Peking* (New York: Harper and Row, 1965), p. 4.

32. Zhang Baozhang and Peng Zheyu, eds., *Beijing qingdai chuanshuo* (Beijing: Chunfeng wenyi chubanshe, 1984), pp. 51, 55, 70.

33. Jeffrey F. Meyer, "*Fengshui* of the Chinese City," *History of Religions*, vol. 18, no. 2 (November 1978).

34. P'eng Tso-chih, "Chinesischer Stadtbau unter besonderer Berüchsichtigung der Stadt Peking," *Gesellschaft für Natur and Volkerkunde Ostasiens, Nachrichten*, 89/90 (1961), 5–80.

35. Meyer, "*Fengshui*," p. 145. I have changed the Wade-Giles system of romanization originally used in this quote to the pinyin system, to harmonize with the usage in this book.

36. *The Ritual Process* (Chicago: Aldine, 1969), pp. 25–26.

37. Freedman, "Geomancy," p. 9.

38. Yeh T'ai, *Ti li ta ch'eng*, quoted in Andrew L. March, "Appreciation," pp. 253–67.

39. Ibid., pp. 9–10. See de Groot, *System*, plate 26, opposite p. 958 of vol. 3, for an illustration of a typical geomantic compass; also Feuchtwang, *Analysis*, p. 255.

40. Certain buildings of religious importance must be eliminated, because they are not a part of imperial religion and therefore not *structurally* important in the plan of Beijing. Although they were very important in the religious lives of the people, the hundreds of Taoist and Buddhist temples of Beijing are not a structural part of the urban plan, and their placement was not rationalized according to the ancient norms. One can read accounts of

various Ming emperors attempting to bring elements of Taoist or Buddhist worship into the imperial precincts, only to be strenuously criticized by Confucian officials. In one instance, when the emperor was urged by a eunuch to hold Taoist *Jiao* and *Zhai* rites, the Board of Rites objected that this contravened ancestral practice, and added: "it is not fitting to hold such rites *within the Forbidden City*" (*Rixia jiuwen kao*, X [35], 12ff.; emphasis mine). And even though Han Confucianism formed the imperial ideology, the worship of Confucius was not itself a part of it, for the sage's temple was located at a nonstructural site in the northeast part of the city.

41. In describing the gates and palaces of the city, I will use the names current in the Qing dynasty, as the names most familiar to modern readers. In fact the names of almost all the gates and palaces have been changed more than once through the reigns of three dynasties, Yuan, Ming, and Qing. The names were carefully chosen and "naming" was considered very important by traditional Chinese. The Qing, for example, wishing to stress the stability and peace that their dynasty had brought to China after the turbulence of the late Ming, chose gate and palace names using words like *he* (peace), *ding* (stability), *an* (tranquility).

42. Yan Chongnian, *Gudu Beijing*, p. 104. See the accounts in Chen Hongian, *Gudu fengwu* (Taibei: Chengchung shuzhu, 1970), pp. 151–52; Ji Chaozi, *Jiujing xiaoji* (Taibei: Guting shushi, 1969), p. 87; *Rixia jiuwen kao*, IX (33), 5.

43. Yan Chongnian, *Gudu Beijing*, p. 104. There are currently two pairs of *huo*. Early photos indicate that formerly there may have been only one inner and one outer *huo*.

44. L. Carrington Goodrich and Chaoying Fang, eds., *Dictionary of Ming Biography* (New York: Columbia University Press, 1976), p. 316; hereafter cited as *DMB*. Yan Chongnian, *Gudu Beijing*, p. 104.

45. Soper, *Art*, p. 287.

46. A summary of the names, history, and usage of the *Sandian*, together with the three residential palaces I will study, may be found in Shao Xing and Yu Qichang, *Gudu bianqian jilue* (Taibei: Guting shushi, 1969), pp. 23–32. English accounts may be found in Bredon, *Beijing*, pp. 86ff.; Siren, *Walls*, pp. 10ff. (illustrated by some excellent photographs), and Ayscough, "Notes on the Symbolism," pp. 66ff.

47. *Rixia jiuwen kao*, IX (34), 7.

48. There is a good description of imperial audiences and a discussion of their "confirmative" and "transformative" functions in Christian Jochim, "The Imperial Audience Ceremonies of the Ch'ing Dynasty," *Journal of Chinese Religions Bulletin*, no. 7 (Fall 1979), 88–103.

49. Described in Qi Rushan, *Beiping*, p. 67.

50. Charles O. Hucker, *The Traditional Chinese State in Ming Times (1368–1644)* (Tucson: University of Arizona Press, 1961), p. 68. The author adds that 75 of 228 chapters of the vast Ming Administrative Procedures Code are devoted to ritual.

51. Quoted in Wu, *Chinese*, p. 31.

52. Yan Chongnian, *Gudu Beijing*, p. 108.

53. Jochim, "Ceremonies," p. 90.

54. Joseph Edkins, *Chinese Architecture* (Shanghai: Kelly & Walsh, 1890), p. 4.

55. Bredon, *Peking*, p. 86.

56. Werner Speiser, *Oriental Architecture in Color* (New York: Viking, 1965), p. 432. See a photograph of this palace ceiling in *Jiudu wenwu lue*, II, 3. Rolf Stein, "Architecture et Pensée religieuse en Extrême-Orient," *Arts Asiatiques*, 4 (1957), fasc. 3, 77ff., traces the lantern ceiling with pearl and dragon motif back to most ancient Chinese architectural traditions where each home had an aperture in the ceiling called the *tianjing*, well of heaven. The suggestion would be that the later lantern ceiling motif was a metaphor for communication with heaven. However, I believe that by the Ming-Qing dynasties the motif had become a stock feature of imperial architecture, with little thought given to its "original" meaning.

57. Speiser, *Architecture*, p. 435.

58. The *Rixia jiuwen kao*, III (12), 2, notes that in Qing times, prior to the three great irrperial festivals of New Years, winter solstice, and the emperor's birthday, there was a preparatory ceremony in the Hall of Middle Harmony, attended by the emperor and a number of officials.

59. Ibid., p. 3.

60. Jonathan D. Spence, *Emperor of China: Self-portrait of K'ang-hsi* (New York: Alfred A. Knopf, 1974), p. 147.

61. *Gudu bianqian jilue*, pp. 29–30; Yan Chongnian, *Gudu Beijing*, p. 114.

62. *Gudu bianqian jilue*, p. 30; Bredon, *Peking*, p. 86; Chen Hongnian, *Gudu fengwu*, p. 144.

63. *Gudu bianqian jilue*, pp. 30–31; Ling, "Beiping," pp. 38–39.

64. *The I Ching*, trans. Richard Wilhelm (Princeton: Princeton University Press, 1967, 3rd ed.), p. 49.

65. Yan Chongnian, *Gudu Beijing*, p. 111.

66. Needham, *Science*, vol. 4, part 3, p. 77.

67. E. T. C. Werner, *A Dictionary of Chinese Mythology* (New York: Julian Press, 1969; first published, Shanghai: Kelly & Walsh, 1932), pp. 334–35.

68. See Granet, *Pensée*, pp. 149, 285; the discussion of the eight "nipples" on Han bronze mirrors, which the author interprets as the eight pillars or mountains that support the heavenly canopy, in Schuyler Cammann, "The 'TLV' Pattern on Cosmic Mirrors of the Han Dynasty," *Journal of the American Oriental Society*, 68 (1948), 164.

69. Boerschmann, *Architecture*, p. 556.

70. Despite some extravagances in the development of the "sacred king" concept from the time of Frazer, it has now been successively refined to the point where it has become a useful category in the study of religions. For an assessment of this development, see Carl M. Edsman, "Zum sakralen Königtum in der Forschung der letzten hundert Jahre," *Studies in the History of Religions*, 4 (1959), 3–17. See a summary of the Chinese material in D. Howard Smith, "Divine Kingship in China," *Numen*, 4 (1957), 171–203.

71. See *Rixia jiuwen kao*, III (12), 3ff., for a description of the complicated rite that took place when the emperor went to study with his tutors (Qing period). Qi Ru-shan, *Beiping*, pp. 18–20, describes the formalities of the imperial meals, calling for sleeping partners, etc. Reading these accounts, one can immediately understand why so many emperors liked to excape the Forbidden City for the more informal atmosphere of the residences in various parks or the summer palace.

72. Daniel Boorstin, *The Discoverers* (New York: Random House, 1983), p. 76. The *Zhouli* prescriptions were of course idealized. Some emperors had far more concubines in their harems than the numbers suggested.

73. Roland Barthes, *Empire of Signs*, trans. Richard Howard (New York: Hill and Wang, 1982), p. 30.

74. Waley, *Analects*, p. 214.

75. Ibid., p. 229.

76. Sigfried Giedion, *The Eternal Present: The Beginnings of Architecture* (Washington, D.C.: Bollingen Pantheon Books, 1964), pp. 495–96.

77. Information on the Yuan *sheji* may be found in Zhu Xie, *Mingqing*, pp. 53–55; for location, see map 27–28 in Hou Renzhi, *Beijing*.

78. The Chinese term for this association of spirits with the main spirits to be worshiped at a certain ceremony is *pei*, "to accompany," or "to associate." It means that the emperor accorded high honor to a spirit or human ancestor by associating him with a god or divine figure at the time of sacrifice. The classic case is found in the *Xiaojing* (p. 476) where Confucius describes how the duke of Zhou, while sacrificing to Shangdi at the suburban altar, associated with him the Zhou ancestor Hou Ji, thus bringing great honor to the Zhou dynastic line.

79. *Zhouli*, I, 193. See another discussion of these two personages in Chavannes, *Memoires Historiques*, 1:80, 184. Bernard Karlgren, in "Legends and Cults in Ancient China," *Bulletin of the Museum of Far Eastern Antiquities*, 18 (1946), 240, shows how the Chinese practice of associating spirits at the time of sacrifice (*pei*) developed out of strong ancestral traditions. Families of the nobility, desiring to enhance their prestige, developed the practice of adopting spirits into their family cults. Thus a venerable ancestor, Hou Tu, would have originally been associated with the *she* spirit. Eventually the latter would have been worshiped under the name Hou Tu and effectively incorporated into the family ancestral cult.

80. *Liji*, II, 206; *Zhouli*, I,441; II, 556. There was, however, mention of more than one type. *Liji*, II, 206, says that the king erected an altar to the spirit of the land, called the *taishe*, for all the people, and one for himself, called the *wangshe*.

81. Except as otherwise noted, the following discussion is taken from Zhang Tingyu et al., *Ming shi*, vols. 46–50 of *Ershiwu shi* (Taibei: Yiwen Yinshuguan, 1956), 46:522–24.

82. See diagrams of the *sheji* altars in the Hong Wu period in *Sancai tuhui*, 3:1031–41.

83. *Ming Shi*, 46:523; *Chunmingmeng yulu*, quoted in Ling, "Beiping," p. 30.

84. Presumably the authority for Jiajing's additional altar came from the statement of the *Liji* mentioned in footnote 80 above, but the text of the *Ming shi* does not expressly say so.

85. See a photo of the altar as it looked in the republican period in *Jiudu wenwu lue*, IV, 1.

86. Ling Shunsheng, "Zhongguo gudai sheji yuanliu," *Bulletin of the Institute of Ethnology, Academia Sinica*, 17 (Spring 1964), 1–44. Although the author takes a questionable "diffusionist" position in the article, it is still an excellent textual source for the study of the ancient *she*. The best work in a Western language is Edouard Chavannes, *Le dieu du sol*, appendix to *Le Tai Chan* (Paris: Ernest Leroux, 1910).

87. This is not to say that there was no ambiguity during the period of the formation of the classics. A text such as the *Liji*, I, 424–26, leaves room for uncertainty, as do many of the texts quoted in the article by Ling (see previous note). Chavannes, *Le dieu du sol*, pp. 520–25, considers the cult of sovereign earth, the counterpart of heaven, as a practice that developed much later than the worship of the *she*, arising sometime during the Han dynasty.

88. *Ming shi*, XLVI, 522. The text notes five such levels of *sheji* altars: imperial, *wang, fu, zhou, xian*, but the *wang sheji* was just a historical relic. There had been no such altar since the Zhou period. The three lower levels were determined in the eighteenth year of the Hongwu reign, when the emperor decreed that every town of 100 or more families establish one.

89. Ibid., p. 523; *Rixia jiuwen kao*, III (10), 1.

90. Li Hongzhang et al. (Guangxu), *Shuntianfu zhi* (Taibei: Wenhai chubanshe, 1965; first published, 1885), 1:315. This extensive work is a history of the prefecture of Shuntian, the administrative division including Beijing. Though it contains much useful material, it is heavily dependent on the *Rixia jiuwen kao* and *Chunmingmeng yulu*.

91. *Analects*, p. 96.

92. See *Sancai tuhui*, 3:1034, for map of its placement in the city, and p. 1038 for a diagram of the temple complex in Nanjing.

93. *Rixia jiuwen kao*, IX (33), 5–6.

94. Frederick W. Mote and Denis Twitchett, *The Cambridge History of China*, Vol. 7, *The Ming Dynasty, 1368–1644*, part 1 (Cambridge University Press, 1988), pp. 457–61; Xu Daoling, *Beiping miaoyu tongjian* (Beiping: Guoli Beiping yenjiuyuan, 1936), 1:83. See also *Rixia jiuwen kao*, IX (33), 5–6,and Qu Xuanying, *Beiping*, pp. 141–46.

95. *Liji*, I, 223–24.

96. See the summary and reflections in Carney T. Fisher, "The Great Ritual Controversy in the Age of Ming Shih-tsung," *Society for the Study of Chinese Religions Bulletin*, no. 7 (Fall 1979), 71–87.

97. *Ming shi*, XLVI, 544–45. See Ming family tree in *Sancai tuhui*, II, 612.

98. *Jiudu wenwu lue*, III, 11–12.

Chapter 3

"Heaven Is Round, Earth Is Square": The Suburban Altars of Beijing

> He who is the sovereign has Heaven for his father and Earth for his mother—there is no reason to worship them separately.
>
> —Ming Taizu (Hongwu), 1378

As we leave the nuclear city and proceed south to examine the altar of heaven, we do more than traverse geographical space. We enter into an entirely different realm, appropriately symbolized by crossing the Heavenly Bridge (the name of the district adjoining the Altar of Heaven Park in contemporary Beijing). Here we leave the realm of the square, the form of the city and of the enclosures, platforms and buildings within it, where rectangular regularity and gridwork planning suggest hierarchy, control, balanced and measured relationships. The new realm is signaled by the predominance in the altar of heaven complex of the symbol of the circle. This geometric form is paradoxically the image of the formless. Although expressed as a two-dimensional plane figure, the circle really means the sphere, and even a boundless sphere, "whose center is everywhere and circumference is nowhere."[1] It suggests the heavenly, the infinite, undefined, the open, the divine, the nonrational, unpredictable, unknowable, undisclosed, and unfinished. It is not disorder, but the matrix and precondition of ordered existence that transcends every human notion of order.

No lines can divide it, not even the primordial axis. "An axis is perhaps the first human manifestation, it is the means of every human act. The toddling child moves along an axis, the man striving in the tempest of life traces for himself an axis. The axis is the regulator of architecture. To establish order is to begin to work."[2] The circle, in contrast, points to the trans-human, and is therefore untouched by any sort of definition. The realm of the square is bisected and defined by lines of all sorts, creating the nine continents of the universe, the nine divisions of the empire drawn by the sage king Yu, the intersecting streets of the city. The realm of the circle suggests the divine, the realm of the spirit called Shangdi, emperor on high, or as the ordinary people called him Laotian Huangdi, the ancient heavenly emperor, or even more popularly, old man heaven.

79

The immense complex, called by metonomy the altar of heaven, was the "temple" dedicated to this chief heavenly spirit, the highest god worshiped by the emperors, together with the other heavenly spirits—the sun and moon, the stars and planets, winds, rains, thunder. It included the altar of heaven itself, the temples, platforms, slaughter houses and kitchens (for preparing sacrifices), the palace of fasting, and all the other places necessary for the proper execution of the most important of all imperial rituals (see illustration 11).

In this complex is found the Chinese expression of a worldwide phenomenon, specifically religious architecture that invites comparison with that of Egypt, Mesopotamia, India, southeast Asia, Mesoamerica, and the other great centers of classic civilization. I will begin, however, with a detailed study of the Chinese expression, saving comparisons for a later chapter.

ALTAR OF HEAVEN COMPLEX

The *shejitan*, the *taimiao*, the audience halls and palaces, were the essence of the Chinese capital city. All important decisions and projects were announced at the altar of land and grain and at the ancestral temple before they were initiated. Before the emperor undertook a military campaign, he offered prayers at these places, and after a successful battle, gave thanksgiving there. Sacrifices were also offered regularly at the time of planting and harvest. Yet these were not the most sacred places in the capital, as the following statement of the Board of Rites makes clear: "Heaven and Earth are worthy of the highest reverence, then comes the ancestors, and after them the Spirits of Land and Grain."[3] Because of this primacy of rank, and because the cosmic symbolism is carried out in such exquisite detail there, I will examine the altar of heaven complex with particular care.

As illustration 11 shows, the huge altar of heaven complex has three focuses: the round, three-tiered altar of heaven to the south; a single-eaved round building called the House of the Imperial Firmament (*Huangqiongyu*) in the center; and a triple-eaved temple built on a three-tiered platform in the north called by a number of puzzling names: *Qigutan* (altar of prayer for grain), *Qiniandian* (hall of yearly harvest prayer), *Dasidian* (great worship hall), and popularly, by Westerners, the Temple of Heaven. Like Beijing as a whole, these three elements are connected by an axial way, with the altar complex itself perfectly oriented to the four cardinal directions. Besides these main structures, there are other buildings and areas shown on the map. I will discuss the most important of these as well.

Understanding the religious symbols and meaning of the altar of heaven is not an easy task. I will first have to begin with a review of what

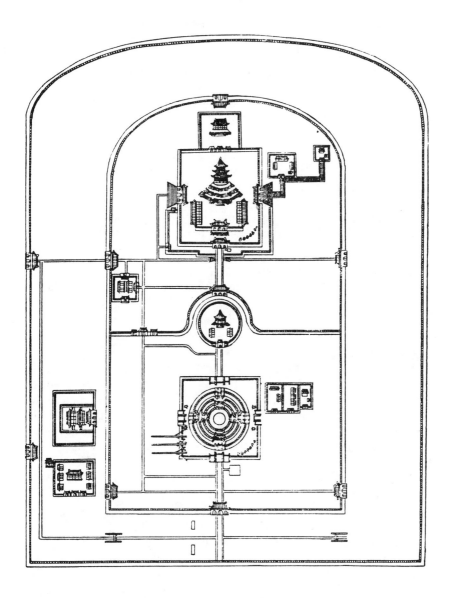

Illus. 11. *Tiantan*, the Altar of Heaven Compound. Source: *Da Qing huidian*

the classics have to say, then study the original Ming order of sacrifice to heaven at Nanjing before examining the development of the complex at Beijing.

The ancient classics were full of references to the suburban sacrifices of the son of heaven, for it was through these most prestigious ritual acts that he both established his right to rule the world and carried out his responsibilities as universal sovereign:

> When thus at the felicitous spot (chosen for their capitals) they presented their offerings to God in the suburb and announced to Heaven . . . , the phoenix descended, and tortoises and dragons made their appearance. When they presented their offerings to God in the suburb the winds and rains were duly regulated, and the cold and heat came each in its proper time, so that the sage (king) had only to stand with his face to the south, and order prevailed all under the sky.[4]

The approved spot for this sacrifice was "in the southern suburb;—the place most open to the brightness and warmth (of the heavenly influence)."[5] The spirit to whom the sacrifice was offered was called heaven or Shangdi in the classics, although sometimes heaven and earth were mentioned together, and sometimes the sense of the passage in question is collective, meaning the spirits of heaven and earth.[6] The spirits of heaven include preeminently Shangdi, then the spirits of the sun, moon, stars, and planets, wind, rain, thunder. The spirits of earth included sovereign earth, the mountains, rivers, seas. Because of a lack of consistency in the classics, certain ambiguous interpretations arose that had repercussions in the controversies and ritual changes of the Ming period. I will deal with these ambiguities as they arise in the historical development of the altar of heaven.

The Ming founder, Hongwu, began his system of suburban sacrifice in Nanjing with a type of ritual that I shall hereafter call "discrete." That is to say, he worshiped the spirits *separately*, heaven in the southern suburb at the winter solstice, the earth in the northern suburb at the summer solstice, "because of the relationship of yin and yang," as the *Ming shi* puts it. The winter solstice was, of course, the time that the yang principle (the sun, light, warmth) passed its nadir and was about to return, while the summer solstice was the time when yang was spent and the yin principle began its ascent.

But in the tenth year of his reign, Hongwu, seriously worried by bad weather that was threatening China's agriculture, made a far-reaching change in the system of worship. The sources say that the "wind, rain, cold, and heat were frequently not in harmony (*fudiao*)," various calamities

The Golden River Canal and Meridian Gate.

The ornamental pillar with dragon, just outside Tiananmen.

The triple–eaved "temple of heaven," (*Qiniandian*) as it exists today, on a three-tiered platform.

The 72–bay arcade, looking toward the "temple of heaven."

A gate in the altar of heaven complex, with patterns of 81 decorative nails in each door.

Northwest corner tower overlooking the moat of the Forbidden City.

The bell tower, northern terminus of Beijing's axial way.

Detail of ornamental pillar.

occurred including the burning of some important buildings in the capital.[7] The emperor attributed the problems to something improper in the system of imperial worship, and said: "He who is the sovereign has Heaven for his father and Earth for his mother—there is no reason to worship them separately." So he decreed that henceforth the conjoint worship of heaven and earth at the same altar would be the rule, "a pattern for all times."

Actually, the system of conjoint worship itself was not really an innovation. The Board of Rites had reviewed Chinese history ten years earlier at the beginning of the Hongwu reign and found a very mixed tradition. Generally speaking, it reported, during the more than one thousand years from the Han through the Tang dynasties, all but four emperors practiced conjoint worship of heaven and earth at a south suburban altar called the *yuanqiu* (round mound). Two Northern Song emperors, Zhezong and Huizong, sometimes practiced discrete worship, but during the Southern Song conjoint worship was again the rule.[8] Some of the later Yuan emperors practiced conjoint worship and some merely worshiped heaven alone at the south suburb.

As is obvious, the historical research was inconclusive. Despite this long history of precedent for conjoint worship, the members of the Board of Rites finally recommended discrete worship to the emperor. The reason they alleged was that it conformed with "ancient practice." By this they meant to express their conviction that the rulers of the Zhou and earlier dynasties had practiced discrete worship. Their earlier recommendation therefore was part of the Ming restorationist outlook. In point of fact, the sources adduced by the board in support of their position, the *Zhouli*, *Shujing*, and *Liji*, were far from clear on the subject.

Conjoint worship itself was not new therefore, but what did fly in the face of thousands of years of Chinese tradition was Hong Wu's decision to build a great worship hall (*Dasidian*) in which this worship was to take place. To put a roof over the altar where the spirits of heaven were to be worshiped was indeed an innovation, for its prescribed place was an open mound, the *yuanqiu*. Hongwu's system was later called "completely unorthodox ritual" (*feili zhili*), but because of the prestige of the Ming founder, the new system remained in effect for almost one hundred fifty years. When the capital was transferred to Beijing, Yongle built a great worship hall in the south suburb in imitation of the building in Nanjing, and there practiced the conjoint worship of heaven and earth under one roof.[9]

Predictably, it was during the reign of Jiajing that the question of conjoint and discrete worship came up for discussion. Again, it was because of his desire to find ways to legitimate an imperial status for his natural father that aroused his avid interest in liturgical questions. He wanted to associate his father with the great spirits of heaven and earth at the time of sacrifice, so he called for a discussion of whether or not to reinstate discrete worship.

The commission called by the emperor to consider the question did not endorse his plan, so he had a divination performed before Hongwu's spirit tablet to obtain the Ming founder's approbation. He failed to get it. Later Jiajing formed a second commission to restudy his plan, but again the group did not endorse it, and a second divination proved that Hongwu had not changed his mind either.

Finally the emperor called for an expression of opinion by all members of the Board of Rites, which resulted in a stormy debate. All parties involved claimed to find historical precedent for their viewpoints, but they were unable to achieve a consensus. Failing that, the discussants presented a memorial to the emperor, which included a breakdown of the officials' positions. Eighty-two officials straightforwardly advocated discrete worship. Eighty-four others also approved discrete worship in principle, but said they wanted to weigh carefully "existing laws"—they shrank from an abrupt rejection of the ritual system the Ming founder had decreed and by this time had one hundred and fifty years of tradition behind it. Twenty-six others also accepted discrete worship but wanted to use an altar already in existence, the altar of mountains and rivers (just to the west of the altar of heaven, across the axial way). These either felt that a new altar would be too expensive or thought an altar north of the city was unsanctioned by classical precedent. Thus there were a total of 192 men advocating, or at least not adamantly opposed to, discrete worship. Another 206 ritual experts advocated continuing the system of conjoint worship, but stopped short of saying that discrete worship was false or wrong. Finally another 198 officials refused to take a position on one side or the other.

Jiajing was a very willful emperor, a quality he had shown from the tender age of fourteen, when he had first ascended the dragon throne. He ultimately got his way by biding his time, playing off one group of officials against another, and dogged persistence. In the present case, the vacillations of the ritual experts gave Jiajing all the latitude he needed. He arrested Huo Tao who refused to go along with his plan, promoted Xia Yen who supported his idea of having four suburban altars, and brushed aside the suggestion that the current great worship hall and altar of mountains and rivers be used for the new ritual. Then he decreed the construction of a round altar in the south suburb and a square altar in the north, both open to the sky.[10] This was the arrangement used for the rest of the Ming and the whole of the Qing.

The prolonged and heated discussions of conjoint versus discrete worship make clear the importance of the issue to the ritual experts of the

Ming period. Even Zhu Yicun, author of our major source on Beijing, expresses amazement at the breadth of the discussion and number of participants.[11] There is no question about the fervor and conviction on both sides of the controversy. But I do not believe that they implied any substantial change in the cosmic symbolism. Rather, the system of discrete worship with its new altars simply expanded and made more explicit the same symbols we have discovered elsewhere in imperial Beijing: the trigrams and hexagrams of the *Yijing*, the yin and yang polarities, and the elements of the five-phase thought world. As we shall see, the suburban altars, especially the altar of heaven, employed these symbols to create replicas of the cosmos. I begin by examining the Hongwu great worship hall, which provided the model imitated by Yongle in Beijing.

The arrangement of the spirit tablets in the great worship hall reveals the same patterns of symbolic thinking that guided the planning of the *taimiao* and Beijing as a whole. The chief spirits of heaven and earth (the cosmic principles) have been assigned places at the center of the north end of the complex, facing south. The sun (yang principle) is placed in the position of next prestige in the east, while the moon (yin principle) is opposite it on the west. Then come the stars and planets. The other spirits of heaven (Jupiter, wind, rain) and spirits of earth (the five mountains, five peaks, four seas, marshes, and rivers) are placed in shrines east, west, and south of the shrine. An attempt is made to have them in their proper positions but, of course, the spirits of the north sea, mountains, and peaks cannot actually usurp the northern place of honor of heaven and earth. The structure of this arrangement is completely traditional and consistent with all we have previously examined; see Figure 4.

Fig. 4. Hongwu *Dasidian*[12]

	Heaven-Earth		
North Sea	Moon	Sun	North Peak
West Peak			North Mountain
West Mountain	Stars	Stars	East Peak
West Sea			East Mountain
			East Sea
Middle Peak		Jupiter	
Middle Mountain		Kings-Emperors	
Wind-Rain		Mountains-Rivers	north
South Peak		Earth-Heaven Spirits	
South Sea		Four Marshes	

In the effort to understand the meaning of the northernmost building of the central three of the altar of heaven complex, we have begun historically, seeing that the building may be traced back to the "unorthodox" great worship hall of Taizu. When Jiajing decreed the change from conjoint to discrete worship in 1530, he built a new round altar south of the old great worship hall and changed the form of the latter, naming it the *Qigutan*, the altar of prayer for the harvest. In 1542 C.E. the emperor razed the old building, rebuilt it, and again changed the name to *Daxiangdian*, Hall of Great Sacrifice. The new name was quite significant, for the same appellation had been used in ancient times to describe the worship that took place in the so-called *Mingtang*. By this act the emperor was articulating a connection that had always existed in the minds of the Ming ritualists: that this building, whatever its current name, was equivalent to a *Mingtang*.

The round altar in the south and the great hall of worship in the north of the complex have their roots in two basic places for worship in ancient China. One was a place out in the suburbs or countryside, open to the sky. One variation of this suburban type called for the building of a mound and was called *tan*, which we now translate as "altar." A second variation required the scraping away of earth to form a flat place, also open to the sky. This was called a *shan*. Originally the *tan* may have been used for the worship of heaven and celestial spirits, while the *shan* was employed for earth and its spirits. During the course of time, however, the *tan* form became prevalent, and contrasted to another type of sacred place that was roofed over. Heaven and earth were worshiped outside; the spirits of men and ghosts were to be worshiped inside.[13]

By the time of the Song, Yuan, and Ming dynasties, the designation *Mingtang* had assumed a very broad meaning, referring to the second type of sacred place of worship, "inside" worship, so that the *Dasidian* and its successors were considered a *Mingtang*. Originally, however, the term had a much more specific meaning, referring to a royal hall to be used only by a universal sovereign, whose architectural features expressed in every detail his role as cosmic ruler. Mencius, Confucius's greatest disciple, was asked by a certain feudal lord whether to dismantle his *Mingtang*. No, said the sage, for this is the building *proper to royalty.*[14] The idea of such a building exercised a fascination over the minds of many Chinese sovereigns, and from the Han through the Tang period, many dreamed of building a *Mingtang* to enhance their prestige or confirm their legitimacy.[15]

As a matter of fact no "authentic" plan for the building has ever been found, though many believed that in ancient China such a building existed. The *Mingtang* is best looked upon as a product of the Han synthesis, an idealization that allowed the "telescoping" of the emperor's cosmic role, as ruler of space and time, into the form of a building, while his role was dramatically expressed or acted out in the various activities he was supposed to perform there. The richest source of classical references to the *Mingtang* was the *Yueling* (monthly commands) section of the *Liji*. The Qianlong edition of this classic has a diagram of the *Mingtang*, which is reproduced in Legge's translation, clearly showing how the building is a true microcosm.[16]

The *Yueling* is a compendium of the yin yang and five-phase thought. For each month of the year, the sovereign is to dwell in a different apartment of the *Mingtang*. Each season is assigned a location corresponding to the four points of the compass (and center), a color, an appropriate activity, a type of sacrifice, a number, a taste, and a smell. The system of correspondences is elaborate and complex, but its purpose is to guide the sovereign in his duty to regulate or "tune" the times, seasons, directions in a universal harmony. There are also prohibitions that have the same purpose. They reveal an intense effort to make every activity in the human world harominize with the total order of the cosmos, for acts done "out of season" may have a destructive effect in the world.

The universal sovereign leads the world in harmonizing the human and cosmic orders:

> If, in this last month of spring, the governmental proceedings proper to winter were observed, cold airs would constantly be prevailing; all plants and trees would decay; and in the states there would be great terrors. If those proper to summer were observed, many of the people would suffer from pestilential diseases; the seasonable rains would not fall; and no produce would be derived from the mountains and heights; if those proper to autumn were observed, the sky would be full of moisture and gloom; excessive rains would fall early; and warlike movements would be everywhere arising.[17]

As Soothill observes, "the Ming Tang is the oldest known expression of the Chinese discovery that man dwells in a cosmos. It is a symbol of the conviction that law dominates the universe, that man's prime duty is to accord with that law, and that for its harmonious working, man's part is essential."[18]

As an expression of cosmic symbolism, the *Mingtang* is simply a more concentrated expression of the same symbolism we find in the overall structure of Beijing. But there is another element implied in the classics, one that became more frequently connected with the usage of the building as time went on. This was the idea that the Ming Tang was the preeminent site for worshiping ancestors as correlates of heaven. The classical authority for this development in the *Xiaojing* was already quoted in chapter

2. It was this quotation that the Board of Rites had in mind when it composed a memorial during the Jiajing period in response to the question, whether the emperor could honor his natural father Ruizong as the correlate of heaven.

After asserting that the ancient dynasties all had their own form of *Mingtang* in which Shangdi was worshiped, they claimed that the Zhou system was most complete. During the course of the year the Zhou sovereigns sacrificed at the round altar at the winter solstice, prayed for grain during the first month of spring, held the rain sacrifice during the first month of summer, and the rite of the *Mingtang* during the last month of autumn. The purpose of both the round altar and the *Mingtang* is the worship of heaven. Today, they continued, the *Dasidian* north of the round altar corresponds to the ancient *Mingtang*. Quoting the *Shijing* and the *Zuochuan*: the ten thousand creatures receive their forms from Shangdi, just as humans receive their forms from their parents. Thus, when autumn sacrifice is offered to Shangdi in the *Mingtang*, the imperial ancestors are honored as correlates, at the time (autumn) when all things have achieved their perfected form.[19]

The view that the *Dasidian* was indeed a *Mingtang* was reasserted at the time of the conjoint-discrete worship controversy. The discrete worship party quoted Song neo-Confucian Zhuxi to support their position that when one sacrifices on an open altar, it is considered the worship of heaven, while sacrifice under a roof is considered the worship of imperial ancestors. How, they asked, could the present practice of worshiping under a roof in the *Dasidian* be considered true worship of heaven? The conjoint worship party countered with the assertion that the *Dasidian* was, in fact, the three-tiered round altar with a temple (*shi*, roofed building) on top. The top structure was really a *Mingtang*, while the bottom was none other than the round altar. By this casuistic turn they were able to maintain that *both* types of worship could be performed there.[20]

In an article analyzing the worship in the *Mingtang*, particularly as it developed during the Song dynasty, a Chinese scholar asserts that there was a parallel development of *Mingtang* worship and imperial despotic growth during the Song. He says that in the early Song there was a simple worship of heaven alone on the open suburban altar south of Kaifeng. As time went on the importance of the *Mingtang* (or roofed) worship increased, and finally the older form of outdoor worship was almost completely neglected. The effect of moving indoors the sacrifice to heaven and honoring the imperial ancestors as correlates was to "familyize" heaven. That is to say, worship of heaven under a roof had the effect of reducing Shangdi to the level of an ancestor, while at the same time elevating the emperor's own status.[21]

A study of the form and numerical symbolism embodied in the great worship hall shows that is as indeed meant to be a kind of *Mingtang*. I have already given a diagram of the arrangement of the shrines it contained. While detailed descriptions of the earlier version are lacking, we do know a great deal about the building that was built in the Ming and lasted until near the end of the Qing, when it was destroyed by fire. The base of the building was a three-tiered platform, the lower 25 *zhang* in diameter, the second 23, and the top 21. There were three flights of steps on the north and south sides of the building, one each on the east and west. The building on top of the platform was three-eaved. There were four central pillars forming a square in the center of the building. Outside this was an inner circuit of twelve pillars, and finally an outer circuit of the same number of pillars. There were nine windows and three doors (the north lacking a door).[22] Besides the obvious use of yang or "heavenly" numbers, which are the odd series (preeminently three and nine), there are four pillars representing the four seasons, the inner twelve pillars representing the months and the outer twelve the signs of the solar zodiac. Taken together, the twenty-eight pillars equal the number of the constellations of the Chinese lunar "habitations" (*su*).[23] The round roof above the square formed by the four central pillars also recalled the round roof and square base of the *Mingtang*.

As I have already said, there is no authentic description of the ancient *Mingtang*, yet all the classical descriptions reveal a building similar in form and symbol to the great worship hall. The Han dynasty *Mingtang* of the usurper Wang Mang (9–23 C.E.) was said to be:

A two-storeyed fane with double eaves, having eight apertures and nine chambers, compass drawn like the Heavens and squared off like the Earth; telling of the season and conforming to the cardinal directions. Various other sources give the following description of other numerical aspects: eight windows for the eight winds, four other apertures for the four seasons, nine apartments for the traditional nine provinces of the empire, twelve halls for the twelve months, thirty-six doors for the number of ten-day periods in the year.[24]

We also have the account of a Tang dynasty planner who proposed to build a *Mingtang* to compete with Buddhist pagodas, which because of their height were dominating the landscape of Changan. His plan called for a twelve-story structure to symbolize the twelve months of the year.[25]

I have now traced the evolution of the northern building in the altar of heaven complex through the Jiajing period. Beginning as the *Dasidian* in the early Ming, it became known as the *Qigutan* (altar of prayer for grain) after Jiajing established the discrete worship system and built the round altar to the south. In 1531 the emperor first had the spring and autumn rite of prayer for grain held at the *Qigutan*. Eleven years later he demolished and rebuilt the building, calling it the *Daxiangdian* (great sacrifice hall), in an effort to imitate the ancient *Mingtang* more explicitly. However, this building and the rites performed in it gradually became less and less important to Jiajing, and during the reign of his successor Longqing, the sacrifices there were abolished as redundant, since they seemed to have the same purposes as the sacrifice at the altar of agriculture.[26]

The Qing dynasty again changed the name of the building. It was officially designated the *Qiniandian* (hall of yearly prayer), and there, on the first day of the year, the emperor went to pray for peace and for a good harvest. At the time of worship, the spirit tablet of Shangdi was placed in the center of the hall, facing south. Honored as his correlates were the Qing dynastic ancestors and former emperor, with their spirit tablets flanking Shangdi, facing east and west. The building that one can see today in Beijing was erected during the Guangxu reign after the previous structure burned down in 1889, but it failed to achieve the magnificence of the earlier hall.[27]

The history of the building just discussed is long and complex. It is no wonder that there is confusion in the minds of many as to its use and purpose. Sometime in the late Qing it acquired yet another name when Western visitors began calling it the Temple of Heaven. Trying to explain why this appellation is a misnomer, the authors of a book on Beijing assert that the *Qiniandian* "was never regarded by the Chinese as an important building, because it had nothing whatever to do with the worship of Heaven. In this hall prayers were said for a propitious year, and especially for a bountiful harvest."[28] An understandable error. But while it was not an important place in the scheme of late Ming and Qing imperial rites, it had once been, as we have seen, the chief place of worship where the most important of all rituals were carried out, the sacrifice to heaven and earth.

Between the building whose history we have just discussed and the actual altar of heaven was a smaller round structure called the House of the Imperial Firmament (*Huangqiongyu*). It was built at the same time as the altar of heaven and was originally called the *Taishendian*—Hall of Great Spirits), when the Jiajing emperor decreed the change to discrete worship. Again the "heavenly" or yang members are exclusively used in the proportions of the building. The platform is nine *chi* high, five *zhang*, nine *chi*, nine *cun* in diameter. There are three stairways ascending the north and south sides of the platform, each having nine steps. Like the small central buildings between the audience halls and the residential palaces in the Forbidden City, this hall was of secondary importance. It was the repository of the spirit tablets of Shangdi and the imperial ancestors at the time of the sacrifices in the altar of heaven complex.[29] In appearance and architectural style it is much like the Hall of Yearly Prayer, but its roof is only single-eaved.

As we have already noted, the original altar of heaven was built by the Jiajing emperor in 1530. Details of the original altar are scant, but we know enough to assert that the Qing altar of heaven, which I will describe below in detail, was a close approximation of it. We read that the Jiajing altar was three-tiered, each level paved with bricks in patterns that used the yang numbers 1, 9, 7, and 5. There were four stairs, one at each of the cardinal directions, and each had nine steps. There is a disagreement among the sources as to the overall measurements of the altar, but it seems to have been smaller than the later Qing altar.[30] At the time of worship, the spirit tablets were arranged as shown in figure 5.

Until the time of the Qianlong emperor, the Qing dynasty made very few changes at the altar of heaven. But then Qianlong undertook an extensive restoration project and charged the planners "to preserve the numbers five and nine" in the structure.[31] The enlarged altar is the one that still exists today in Beijing. Few other examples of monumental

Fig. 5. Spirit Tablets at the Ming Altar of Heaven

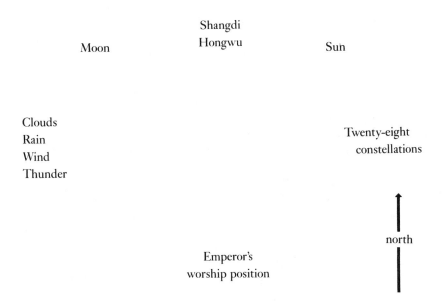

architecture in the world can compare with the altar of heaven in its consistent use of symbolic numbers. The form of the altar is, of course, round to imitate the heavens. The numbers used in the elements of the total structure are the yang odd series, especially 5 and 9. There are three levels: the highest is nine *zhang* in diameter (one nine); the second level is fifteen *zhang* in diameter (three times five); the third is twenty-one *zhang* (three times seven). The basic unit of measure used was the older *chi* measure (called the *ying-zao chi*). This older unit was employed for symbolic reasons—it was eight *cun*, one *fen* in length, a combination suggesting eighty-one or nine times nine.

The pattern formed in the stone pavement on the surface of each of the three levels was also calculated to continue the repetition of nines. There is a single large round stone in the center (This too is an echo stone, and the major entertainment for tourists is to stand on the center stone, clap, and listen for the echo.) Surrounding it is a circle of nine stones, the second circle has eighteen stones, and so forth, until one reaches the ninth circle, the outer rim of the highest level of the altar, which has eighty-one stones. The first circle of stones on the second level has ninety stones, and each circle continues to increase by multiples of nine until the outer rim of the lowest level is reached, which has 243 stones, or twenty-seven times nine (see illustration 12).

There is a stone balustrade around each of the three tiers, formed of rectangular slabs of white marble separated by marble pillars. These too were meant to express the numerical symbolism. A Qing document, reporting on the rebuilding of the altar under Qianlong, points out that the Ming builders did not quite get it right, but that now all shortcomings have been corrected. There are 72 pillars and posts around the first (highest) level, 108 around the second, and 180 around the third. The total then is 360, which is the heavenly number of totality (*yingzhou tianshu*).[32]

A Chinese guidebook to the altar of heaven admits that this claim of numerical perfection has been repeated in many books since the time of Qianlong, but that there is a discrepancy. There are actually 19 posts and slabs in each quarter of the top level, making a total of 76. The same discrepancy exists on each of the two lower levels, so the total is not 360. Even Homer nods. This discrepancy aside, the rest of the numerical symbolism reflects perfectly the yang proportions, even down to the gold nails that decorate the doors of the various wooden gates in the complex. Each has nine vertical and nine horizontal rows, eighty-one nails in all.[33]

Nine is the Chinese lucky number, the number with more prestige than any other. It is the numerical value given to the unbroken or yang line in the hexagrams of the *Yijing*. The festival of double nines is also called double yang. Yet, as Granet points out, all numbers are *rubriques emblém-*

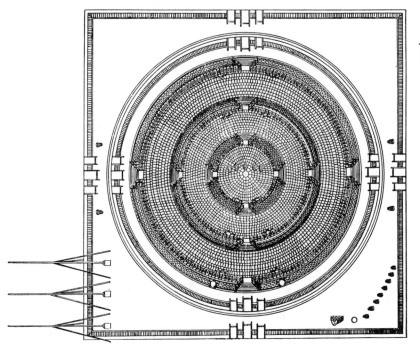

圓丘壇圖

Illus. 12. Stone Patterns on the Altar of Heaven. Source: *Da Qing huidan*

atiques. Numbers can be interchanged, their use in symbolic situations depending more on their "quality" than quantity. Certain numbers of different quantity may have approximately the same meaning, such as the numbers in the series 3, 9, 27, 81 (which we have seen employed in the building of the altar of heaven and in the ideal number in the emperor's harem) or the series 8, 16, 32, 64 (which we will see used at the altar of earth). While nine is the preeminent *yang* number, others in the odd series can be used with little or no change in meaning.

Numbers also have what Granet calls a *fonction protocolaire*. By this he means that they serve to indicate a hierarchy or order. The number five is frequently used to indicate him who reigns over time and space, according to the thinking of the five-phase school. The central number is five and it rules over the four directions, a configuration observable in the famous diagrams *luoshu* and *hetu*, the magic squares and the floor plan of certain plans for the *Mingtang*.³⁴ How conscious Ming and Qing planners were of the ancient web of symbolism surrounding these numbers is, of course, debatable. The sources point out only that one series of numbers is "heavenly," the other "earthly."

Besides the numerical symbols, a glance at the overall plan of the altar of heaven complex reveals constant repetition of the square and circle, even in the overall shape as defined by the walls, which are rounded on "top" (north) and squared at the "bottom" (south). The three-tiered altar is surrounded first by a round wall, then a square wall. The Hall of Yearly Prayer combines the square and circle pattern, as did the audience halls of the Forbidden City. This conjunction of these two geometric forms here, the square-circle mandala, indicates clearly that this is the sacred place where the emperor functions as mediator between heaven and earth. His ritual station is exactly where the two realms come together.

The map of the altar of heaven complex also shows that there are other sites and structures contained within the compass of the walls. I will look at some of the most important of them.

Joining the three components of the Hall for Yearly Prayer, the House of the Imperial Firmament, and the altar of heaven is a broad axial way, approximately 360 meters long, called the Vermillion Platform Bridge. Conceptually it was divided into three "lanes," with the center way for the spirits (*shendao*), the east way for the emperor (*yudao*), and the west way for the princes and ministers (*wangdao*). It not only connects the three major monuments of the altar of heaven, it *leads* the visitor from the south to the north. Beginning at the altar of heaven at about one meter high, it rises gradually to a height of three meters at the Hall for Yearly Prayer. Yongle is supposed to have exclaimed, when the project had been completed: "This is truly a road that leads to Heaven!"³⁵ While the direction of the

Vermillion Platform Bridge fit well into the Yongle plan for worship, it was less fitting after Jiajing made the altar of heaven into the most important worship site.

Just east of the Hall for Yearly Prayer are two other buildings important in imperial sacrifice, the slaughterhouse for the sacrificial animals and the "spirit kitchen," where animals were cleaned and prepared for the ceremonies. The two are joined to the main hall by a remarkably beautiful arcade, called the "72 bay arcade" (the word "bay" refers to the space between the pillars). It was first built under Yongle, when it had 75 bays, then changed to 72 in the Qianlong restoration, to conform better to the symbolic number. Each of the 72 bays is like a separate "house," open on the south side, having a plaster wall and decorative window on its north side, and of course covered in its whole length by a tiled roof.

On the night previous to the sacrifice, the animal victims were brought in a solemn procession along this corridor. There were wooden lamps placed periodically along the way, which created an eerie alternation of darkness and flickering light. That, together with the lugubrious task of transporting the hundreds of dead animals, must have caused the corridor to be named the place of "the 72 earthly malignant spirits." And with this there was again the inevitable complimentarity, for thinking of the 36 pillars of the Hall for Yearly Prayer, they spoke of "the 36 heavenly auspicious star spirits" above.

As the map reveals, there was a separate slaughterhouse and spirit kitchen for the altar of heaven, just to its east. According to the *Collected Rituals of the Qing Dynasty*, some 280 cooks were required to prepare the hundreds of animals required for the sacrifices. Previous to being cooked, the animals were killed, skinned, and cleaned by 80 butchers in what must have been the world's most elegant slaughterhouse. Each had its own specialization (cows, pigs, etc.) and had to follow a set of complex and cumbersome rules handed down through the centuries.

An enormous number of animals was required for the yearly round of imperial sacrifices, and these beasts were brought from every province of China. They had to meet stringent specifications as to color, form, and a perfect state of health. During the Ming dynasty there were stables in the southwest part of the altar of heaven complex where most of these animals were kept. Ledgers have been preserved with lists of the quantities of hay and grain for feeding and the amounts of money expended. One list gives an estimate of the number of animals required for the entire round of imperial sacrifices during the period of one year: 204 cows, 806 sheep, 109 goats, 979 pigs, 214 deer, 216 rabbits.[36]

Another important part of the altar of heaven complex was the *zhaigong*, or hall of abstinence. This was built like a miniature Forbidden

City in the west central part of the compound. It was surrounded by a moat (now dry) and wall, with public hall to the front, private palace behind, a bell tower, and four corner towers to recall those of the Forbidden City. While these features in the Forbidden City may have had some practical usage, here in the hall of abstinence they were solely symbolic.

It was important for the emperor to have the proper frame of mind for his most important ritual duties, and so he was required to come to this place and abstain from various things for the day previous to the imperial sacrifices. The rules were very strict: no alcohol, no eating of meat, no indulging in sex, no entertainment, no seeing of the sick, observing mourning, or attending to criminal punishments. He must be humble and reverential, quieting his heart, meditating and trying to eliminate all coarse or common thoughts.[37] In other words, the practice of abstinence called for the emperor to live for a day in a manner exactly the opposite of his normal life, to create in his mind a sense of sacred time just as he now occupied sacred space. Ideally, isolated in the guarded precincts of the hall of abstinence, the emperor experienced time differently. Qianlong, in the *zhaigong*, wrote the following poem, which well captures his experience of a different sense of the passage of time:

> I sit at leisure,
> hearing the glorious chimes and the wind in the pines without;
> I sit at leisure,
> examining the shadow on the sundial within.[38]

In the ancient tradition, abstinence was the most sacred sort of behavior. As in other respects, the better emperors took this obligation seriously, the others did not. Hongwu was so conscientious that he had the Board of Rites cast a bronze statue of "the admonisher," to remind him of the seriousness of his obligations. The hall of abstinence today still has, on the platform of the main hall, a small pavilion where this bronze image was placed.[39]

During the Qing period, a number of rituals were performed each year at the altar of heaven. There were prayers for the harvest on New Years day, prayers for rain at the beginning of summer, and formal announcements made here on various other important occasions: the accession of the emperor, appointment of the empress, the heir apparent, and so forth. And there were minor rites on the first and fifteenth of every month with burning of incense before the spirit tablets in the Hall for Yearly Prayer and the House of the Imperial Firmament. But the most important and awesome by far was the liturgy for the worship of heaven at the winter solstice.

Let us look at the events leading up to this ritual and the order of ceremony on the day itself. Preparations began some two months ahead of time. Soldiers, workers, and carpenters would be sent to clean, sweep, and repair. A liturgical calendar was drawn up in the ninth month for the entire following year, rather like the *Ordo Rituum* of the Roman Catholic Church, which determines the entire liturgical calendar for the year.

Five days previous to the winter solstice, officials were dispatched to inspect the sacrificial animals. Four days beforehand, the hall of abstinence was made ready for the emperor. On the third day before, abstinence was officially declared, urging not only the emperor but all officials to a serious and conscientious attitude. There was then a changing of clothes, and from that time on a solemn attitude was required in the Forbidden City. (The actual fast took place either at the altar of heaven or in the Forbidden City. Later Qing emperors preferred the latter.)

On the second day previous to the rite, all documents and ritual utensils were prepared. The day before was filled with activity. The documents and utensils, jade instruments, fabrics, incense, and the like, were brought to the emperor for inspection. The emperor went to the ancestral temple to make an announcement of the rite to his forebears. During the afternoon, the grand procession would leave the Forbidden City, passing through each of the various gates on the way south. The street was leveled, potholes filled, and water sprinkled on the surface to reduce dust. The people were not permitted to watch this procession. Blue cloths were hung over windows along the way to block their view. If, by chance, persons were unable to get away in time as the processions passed, they must turn their back, under pain of death.

When the emperor went to the Hall for Yearly Prayer, he entered by the west gate; if to the altar of heaven, by the south gate. There he dismounted and walked to the House of the Imperial Firmament, where he made obeisance to Shangdi and his own ancestors, offering incense and doing the ninefold kowtow. He inspected the offerings and ritual implements again, then retired to the hall of abstinence.

On the day itself, the official called the *taichangsi* came one and three-quarters of an hour before sunrise to summon the emperor, who left the hall of abstinence and went to the altar, where the spirit tablets had been arranged under blue tents in their proper places. The nine stages of the actual ceremony were as follows:

1. The emperor goes to his place on the south quadrant of the second level of the altar (see illustration 13, which shows the places of all ministers involved in the sacrifice.) The animals are burned in the stove and offered to Shangdi and the other spirits. Music plays. The emperor makes obeisance and offers incense before each of the spirits, then returns to his place after performing the solemn kowtow.

2. Offering of the jades and silks to the spirits.

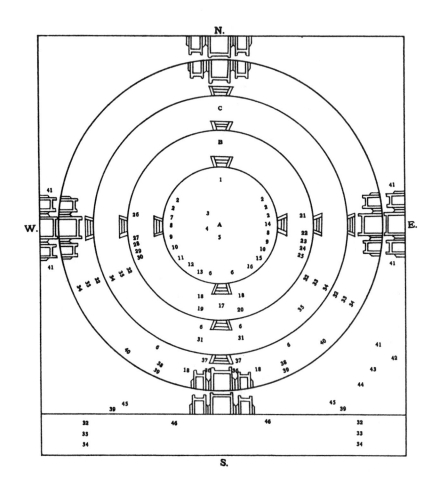

Illus. 13.   Liturgical Positions for Worship at the Altar of Heaven. Source: John Ross, *The Religion of China*. No. 17 is the position of the emperor.

3. Offering of the *zu* (a sacrificial utensil containing meat).

4. First presentation rite. The military (*wu*) dance is performed. The emperor offers the *jue* (wine container) to Shangdi. All music stops as the prayer documents are read, while the emperor prostrates himself. Then the music resumes as the emperor offers wine at the other spirit shrines.

5. Second presentation rite. Exactly as the previous rite, except that the cultural (*wen*) dance is performed.

6. Third presentation rite. Again to the accompaniment of music and dance,[40] the emperor presents offering of wine and meat.

7. The food and wine offerings are removed.

8. Sending off the spirits. To the sound of music, the emperor performs the kowtow to bid farewell to the spirits. Ministers take the offerings, prayer documents, silks, incense, food, and drink, and deposit them in the roaring flames of the sacrificial furnace. The emperor watches this ceremony from a platform nearby.

9. After the offerings have been consumed, the rite is concluded. The emperor walks to the south gate, remounts his palanquin, and returns to the Forbidden City in a procession like the one on the previous day. Now Shangdi has received the worship of the son of heaven and he will send down his blessings to the world.

ALTAR OF EARTH

Just outside *Anding* Gate, the eastern gate of Beijing's northern wall, was the altar of earth. Its position, shape, and symbolism are in every way calculated to emphasize its correlation with the altar of heaven. The yin or even-number series is used as relentlessly here as the yang numbers are at the altar in the south. In fact, the striking features of this altar are those that manifest a total complementarity with the altar of heaven: the location, the form, numbers, the colors, the spirits worshiped, and the placement of spirit tablets at the time of sacrifice. If we ask the source of this perfect complimentarity, the answer lies in the same Chinese cosmological views we have already encountered numerous times.

The classical precedents for building this altar and for the worship that took place here, however, are not very clear. The texts are often ambiguous, particularly in regard to the cosmic spirit known in later times as "sovereign earth." At times the references clearly identify heaven as male, earth as female, but often enough there are no sexual designations whatever. Earth is undoubtedly a cosmic principle, but its nature is quite shadowy, and in the end one feels that its "personality" is known only in opposition to that of heaven, as though it could not stand on its own.

Ming ritual writings mention the use of a number of designations in the classics to signify "sovereign earth." In ancient times, the Board of

Rites pointed out on one occasion, various terms were used when speaking of the sacrifice to *Di* (earth): *Dizhi* (spirit or spirits of earth), *Houtu* (empress earth), and even *She*. However, the scholars asserted, all terms refer to the same spirit, the counterpart (*tui*) of heaven.[41] While the board's conclusion is quite debatable, it at least expresses a prevalent Ming view. The very vagueness revealed in the statements issued by the Board of Rites shows why the altar of earth never attained the importance of the altar of heaven. Not only was the spirit's personality more ambiguous, but the subsidiary spirits worshiped at the altar of earth—the mountains, seas, and rivers—received sacrifices at altars elsewhere.

Beijing did not have an altar of earth in the early Ming period. Its construction in the north suburb of the city in 1530 was the outcome of the conjoint-discrete worship controversy. The altar was originally called the *Fangzetan*, which can be literally translated as the altar of the square watery place. The name reveals the Chinese conception of earth as very different from our own. We generally think of "earth" as dry land, terra firma, the opposite of water. But for the Chinese, sovereign earth was first conceived as the chthonic spirit that ruled over the entire sublunary region, as opposed to heaven or Shangdi, who ruled the celestial world. They conceived earth as square, because it was surrounded by the four seas, a watery region crisscrossed by rivers, dotted with marshes, and frequently inundated by rains. In the midst of this watery instability were the religiously and mythologically important mountains, the "pillars of support," which gave earth its foundation and security. So just as heaven was sometimes individual and sometimes collective, sovereign earth too was often conceived in conjunction with the spirits of the seas, rivers, and mountains. Although Jiajing later changed the name of the altar to the simple *Ditan* (altar of earth), the older name for the altar is a much clearer expression of the conception behind it.

Once more we know better the details of the Qing altar of earth, but the following brief description of the Ming altar makes clear that it was the model for the later altar. The original Jiajing altar was square in form, a two-level platform with the first tier six *zhang*, six *chi* square, and six *chi* high. The sources also add that the paving of the stones on the surface of the altar made use of the yin numbers 6 and 8. The principal color of the tiled surfaces, the sides of the altar, and the walls of the two square enclosures was yellow. In five-phase thought, yellow was the color of the earth, the center, just as blue was the contrasting color used in the roof tiles at the altar of heaven. There were four stairways, one at each of the cardinal directions, and each had eight steps. The square altar was completely surrounded by a small "moat," crossed by four footbridges at the base of each of the four stairs. The moat was eight *chi*, six *cun* wide, and six *chi* deep. Just as the round House of the Imperial Firmament housed the spirit tablets of heaven and the imperial ancestors previous to the winter solstice sacrifice, so there was a square Hall of Imperial Earth at this site where the tablets of earth and the ancestors were housed previous to the summer solstice sacrifice.[42]

The arrangement of the spirit tablets on the altar of earth at the time of sacrifice is shown in figure 6.[43]

Sources record a large-scale remodeling under Qing emperors Yongzheng and Qianlong, which added greatly to the scope of the altar of earth. This statement is either an example of dynastic boasting or refers to

Fig. 6. Altar of Earth Spirit Tablets

The four rivers		The four seas

The five *chen* (mountains)

The five *yu* (peaks)
Three other mountains

Taizu

Sovereign earth

north

an extension of the ambitus of the altar complex or of the addition of subsidiary buildings within it, for the Qing description of the altar itself gives exactly the same dimensions, the same tile colors, and the same numerical symbolism.[44] Nevertheless we do have some additional details about the Qing altar, which serve to further emphasize correlation with the altar of heaven.

At the center of the top platform was a square composed of 36 large stones, and surrounding it were successively larger circuits of stones, the first having 36, the second 44, and so forth. Each circuit increased by eight stones until the eighth circuit was reached, the last one at edge of the upper tier began with 100 stones and increased by eights until there were 156 stones in the eighth row, which formed the outer perimeter[45] (see illustration 14).

The arrangement of the spirit tablets at time of worship was approximately the same as the one I have shown for the Ming period. But instead of offering worship to just one ancestor, Taizu, the Qing had five, and they added another set of five mountains. The yellow color motif was carried out not only in the tiles, but in many other facets of the sacrificial rite. The jade ritual objects, the vessels, the vestments worn, and so forth, were all yellow. At the time of worship, sacrifices to earth were buried in the ground, in contrast to those offered to heaven at the southern round altar, which were burned. The order of the ritual performed at the altar of earth at the summer solstice was very similar to that done at the altar of heaven, but there were eight parts instead of nine.

Today the basic altar of earth has been beautifully restored, standing within *Ditan* Park. In the hall to the south of the altar are all the spirit tablets used at the time of sacrifice, with sovereign earth in the primary position. In front of this tablet, lined up three on each side, are the spirit tablets of six Qing rulers, from Shunzhi to Qianlong, and including the two earlier Manchu founders. Behind these, arranged in two rows on each side of the hall, are twenty-three other tablets: the four seas, the four great rivers of China (Yangtze, Yellow, Huai, Ji), and three sets of five sacred mountains.

Outside again, on the lower tier of the altar are four stone bases made to hold the mountains and river spirit tablets at the time of sacrifice. These are imitations; the authentic Qing stone bases have now been taken inside the hall for protection from the weather. Each is carved with mountains or rivers, depending upon which tablets they hold. In 1984 a yellow tile slab was unearthed. Originally it was one of those paving the Jiajing altar, and is kept inside the building.

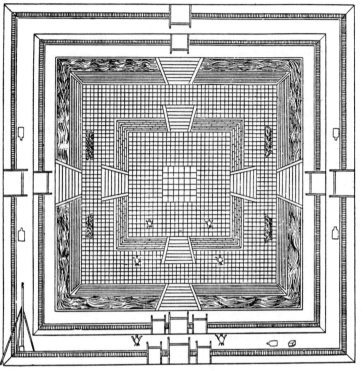

方澤壇圖

Illus. 14. *Fangzetan* or *Ditan*, the Altar of Earth. Source: *Da Qing huidian*

ALTAR OF AGRICULTURE

The old complex called the altar of agriculture is one of the casualties of twentieth-century China. The area is now filled with schools, factories, apartment buildings, and sports fields, and the old altars and temples have either been torn down or are in a sad state of disrepair. So far only the temple of *Taisui* (great year star, the planet Jupiter), which was the largest building in the complex, is being restored.

The term "altar of agriculture" is one that grew popular during Qing times to designate, by metonymy, the large enclosure opposite the altar of heaven, on the west side of the north-south axis of Beijing (see illustration 15). The complex was first completed in the eighteenth year of Yongle (1420), modeled on the one built by Hongwu at Nanjing and having the same name, the altar of mountains and rivers (*shanchuantan*). Within this enclosure Yongle also built the *xiannongtan*, the altar dedicated to the first farmer. In the Jiajing reign (1532), the emperor added to the complex twin altars to the spirits of heaven and earth, and an enclosure for the worship of *Taisui*, the great year star. After these additions had been completed, the complex remained the same through the Qing period. Because of obvious redundancies, I will examine certain parts of the altar complex only briefly, concentrating on the most important rite performed there, the spring plowing ritual.

The worship of mountains and rivers is an ancient practice in China, canonized by frequent injunctions in the classics. There is, for example, a passage in the *Liji* that describes the imperial tour of inspection, made every five years, during the course of which the emperor visited the four quarters of his domain. In each section he offered a sacrifice on the top of a sacred mountain in the second month of each of the four seasons, announcing to heaven his arrival and sacrificing to the hills and streams.[46] Sacrifices to the mountains and rivers never ceased in imperial China; what varied was the importance placed upon them. Always accorded at least subsidiary worship, they sometimes received sacrifices at altars of their own. Hongwu and Yongle both constructed enclosures specifically for their worship, and although Jiajing abolished the altar by name, he soon built twin altars where these same spirits were worshiped, the altars of the spirits of heaven and of earth.

As the name suggests, these twin altars contained shrines to a large host of spirits. Among the heavenly spirits were the spirits of the clouds, rain, wind, and thunder, while those of earth included many mountains, the four rivers, four seas, together with the hills and streams of *Zhili*, the area surrounding Beijing. Certain years were determined when the emperor himself would offer sacrifice, while at other times an official would be deputed. But during the Longqing (Jiajing's successor) reign an official

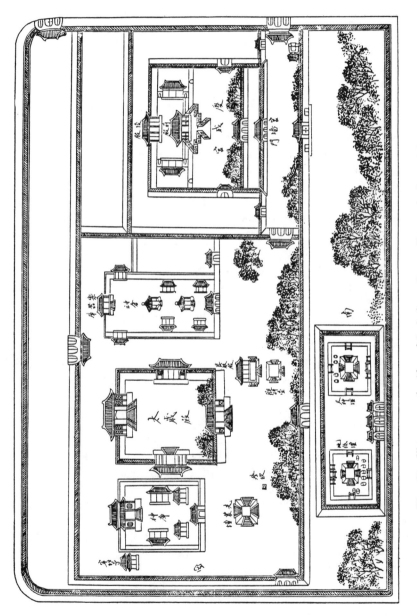

Illus. 15. *Xiannongtan*, the Altar of Agriculture. Source: *Tangtu mingsheng tuhui*

memorialized to the effect that since the spirits already received sacrifice, along with heaven and earth, at the solstitial ceremonies, to continue their worship at the special altars was a mere repetition. The emperor agreed and abolished the sacrifices.

The configuration of the two altars is in complete conformity with the principles we have already seen applied in the case of the altars of heaven and earth. These two lesser altars were placed opposite each other, east and west, within a single walled enclosure. The altar of the heavenly spirits was oriented to the south, with its spirit shrines on the north side of the altar facing south. The altar of the earthly spirits was oriented to the north, with its spirit shrines on the south side facing north, though some subsidiary shrines were placed east and west. The measurements of the heavenly spirits altar were done in multiples of 5 and 9, while that of the earthly spirits was done in 6, 4, 10.[47]

The other building complex added by Jiajing at the old mountains and rivers enclosure was the temple to *Taisui*, together with some subsidiary buildings dedicated to the spirits of other astral phenomena. There had been some discussion of the worship of *Taisui* early in the Ming period. A yin-yang expert urged the importance of this powerful spirit, and Hongwu decreed his worship in the main hall of the mountains and rivers complex, as we have seen. During the Jiajing discussion of the worship of *Taisui*, the ritualists had to admit that there was nothing in the classics to guide them in the proper manner of worship, and that even as recently as the Tang and Song dynasties there was nothing written on the subject. The Yuan performed the worship, but only on extraordinary occasions, so there was no record of an ordinary rite available.

However, *Taisui* was considered by the Ming Chinese to be an important and powerful spirit governing the passage of time. This may have been partly due to the great increase in astronomical knowledge at the time. They knew that his planet moved through one of the twelve constellations of the astrological zodiac each year, and that in the course of twelve years he made the circuit of the heavens. This twelve-year period was called "the great year" or *taisui*, and thus his name.[48] Because there was no model to follow, Jiajing's advisors suggested that his altar be built on the order of the *shejitan*, but slightly smaller. He followed this suggestion, and built a large temple to Jupiter in the north-central part of the enclosure. The Ming was the first Chinese dynasty to establish an altar and offer regular worship to the great year spirit.[49]

The most important site in the altar of agriculture complex, which eventually gave its name to the whole enclosure, was the altar of the first farmer and the field for the emperor's rite of spring plowing. Unlike the worship of Jupiter, this ceremony had its basis in the clear directive of the

Yueling section of the *Liji*, which lists it as a ritual to be performed in the first month of the spring:

> In this month the son of Heaven on the first *hsin* day prays to God for a good year; and afterwards, the day of the first conjunction of the sun and moon having been chosen, with the handle and share of the plough in the carriage, placed between the man-at-arms who is its third occupant and the driver, he conducts his three ducal ministers, his nine high ministers, the feudal princes and his great officers, all with their own hands to plough the field of God. The son of Heaven turns up three furrows, each of the ducal ministers five, and the other ministers and feudal princes nine. When they return, he takes in his hand a cup in the great chamber, all the others being in attendance on him and the Great officers and says, "Drink this cup of comfort after your toil."[50]

Though the canonical precedent was clear, the meaning of the rite, the identity of the personage *Xiannong*, and the conjunction of his worship with the plowing rite in the spring was not. In the review of the subject by the Board of Rites, an official in the Hongwu period noted a confusion between the royal *she* and the plowing field. Although the first farmer (*Xiannong* or *Shennong*) is regularly identified with the legendary emperor who followed Fuxi—namely, *Yandi*—a Tang dynasty commentator said that he was the same as the *she* spirit, while a Song commentator said that they were absolutely distinct.[51]

Like the *sheji* rites, the ceremony of spring plowing was carried out at the lower administrative units of the empire, the *fu*, *zhou*, and *xian*, by the officials who presided there. While it is clear that the *sheji* rite and the spring plowing had the same general purpose—namely, the fertility of the land and a successful harvest—they were apparently never viewed as redundant. The first mention of worshiping Xiannong on the same day as the plowing rite comes from the Han dynasty, and this practice was followed all the way through the Song. Zhenghe, a Northern Song emperor, had underlings carry out the two rites, but the ancient tradition of the emperor performing the ceremonies in person was restored during the Southern Song. The Yuan, probably because of their pastoral background, always sent Chinese officials to carry out the rite, but from the Ming period on, the spring plowing and worship of the first farmer were among the emperor's most important ritual obligations.

During the *Hongzhi* period (1488–1506), the following rite was determined for the spring ceremony. Officials participating were bound by the *zhi* fast (external fast, abstinence, sexual prohibition, etc., as opposed to *san* or internal fast). An official of *Shuntianfu* (the prefecture in which

Beijing was located) made presentation of the plow and plowshare, and the various grains to be planted, which were inspected and returned by officials of the interior court. The imperial retinue awaited the son of heaven outside the Meridian Gate on the day of the ceremony, and the entourage moved south down the axial way to the altar of agriculture, amid the sound of music and drums. Donning his vestments at a hall built for that purpose, the emperor proceeded to the altar of Xiannong, where he again changed into sacrificial garments. After the sacrifices were concluded, he revested in his original garments.

An official then led the emperor to the site of the plowing, where he stood facing south. The imperial princes and lower-ranking personages then took their assigned places. An official of the Board of Population, facing north, made obeisance and presented the plow and plowshare to the emperor. An official of the prefecture, also facing north, presented the whip. The emperor then grasped the plow and three times plowed a furrow back and forth. After he finished, the ministers reverently received back the equipment and all returned to their places.

The prefectural governors then came forth with green boxes of seed, which they sowed and covered in the furrows the emperor had made, and from this point on the latter merely observed the ceremony from a platform constructed for that purpose. The imperial princes plowed five furrows back and forth, and the ministers plowed nine furrows. After the work was completed, the *fu* and *xian* governors led a group of aged men forward to pay their homage. Then they led forward three ranks of farmers, ten in a rank, to pay homage, and afterward this group of thirty "professionals" would complete the plowing of the field. Subsequently congratulations were offered to the emperor and there was a grand banquet for all participants. At the conclusion of the feast, the emperor returned to the forbidden city to the music of pipes and drums, and the participant farmers were rewarded for their labors with a bolt of cloth.

The Qing dynasty continued to emphasize the rite of plowing, and the form of the ritual they used was the same as the Ming rite just described, almost down to the smallest details[52] (see illustration 16). And as often was the case, the Qing emperors tried to outdo the Ming in their scrupulous observance. According to one account, the notorious debauchee Emperor Xianfeng (1851–1862) plowed four furrows in a burst of fervor "to show added reverence."[53] The farmers must have been impressed.

ALTAR OF SILKWORMS

The ceremony of the silkworms is a rite complementary to the spring plowing rite in many of its particulars. It was never as important as the

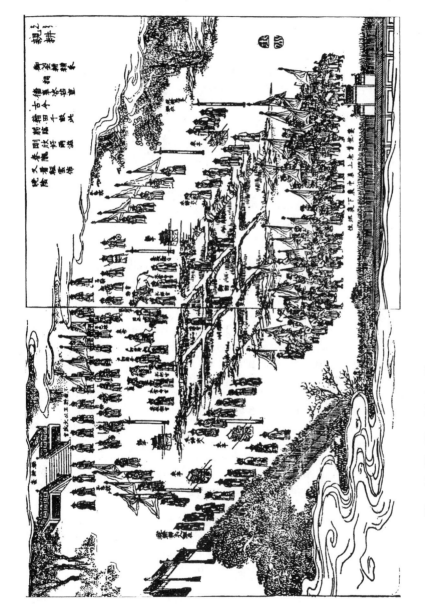

Illus. 16. The Rite of Spring Plowing: Source: *Tangtu mingsheng tubui*

latter ritual, but its history is long and it quite clearly reveals the same dualism we have already seen in all aspects of imperial worship. Again we find a clear precedent in the classics:

> In this month orders are given to the foresters throughout the country not to allow the cutting down of the mulberry trees and the silk-worm oaks. About these the cooing doves clap their wings, and the crested birds light on them. The trays and baskets with the stands (for the worms and cocoons) are got ready. The queen, after vigil and fasting, goes in person to the eastern fields to work on the mulberry trees. She orders the wives and younger women (of the palace) not to wear their ornamental dresses, and to suspend their women's-work, thus stimulating them to attend to their business with the worms. When this has been completed, she apportions the cocoons, weighs out (afterwards) the silk, on which they go to work, to supply the robes for the solstitial and other great religious services, and for use in the ancestral temple.[54]

The *Yueling* section of this classic, from which this quote was taken, established the proper time for the rite as the third month of the spring. A Ming source claimed the wife of the Yellow Emperor, Xilingshi, first performed this rite, and that there is evidence of its observance in every dynasty from the Zhou to the Song. The author then briefly described the usages in various dynasties: Zhou, Han, Wei, Jin, Northern Qi, Sui, Tang, and Song. His purpose was to show that there was a weight of tradition behind this ceremony and the emperor ought to reestablish it.[55]

Apparently there was a desire to reinstitute the rite in the later Ming even though it had been ignored by the Yuan and early Ming rulers. When one of Jiajing's advisors urged him to build an altar of the first silkworm (*xiancantan*) north of the city, the emperor readily agreed, announcing: "Of old, the son of heaven personally plowed, the empress personally performed the silkworm rite to stimulate and encourage the world. This year I will myself perform the rite of Xiannong; the empress will perform the silkworm rite."[56]

The following rite was submitted by the Board of Rites to the emperor. After an auspicious day has been chosen, officials of *Shuntianfu* send a group of "silkworm mothers" (*canmu*—women in charge of the work of silk-making) to the altar. Previous to the ceremony, the empress must fast three days in the company of her servants. The ritual vessels and equipment (hooks, baskets, mulberry seeds, etc.) are presented to the empress much as the corresponding agricultural tools were presented to the emperor before the plowing rite. On the appointed day, the empress was met by the entourage at the Palace of Earthly Tranquility and all progressed to the place of the ceremony.

The details of this procession, the arrival at the altar, the changing of vestments, the personnel involved, almost exactly paralleled the rite at the altar of agriculture. After an initial summoning of the spirits, the empress took her place on the altar for plucking mulberry leaves, where she faced east. The officials made obeisance, presented her with the hook and basket, and then the empress stripped the mulberry leaves from the trees three times, returning to her place to observe the rest of the ceremony. The imperial princesses and other chosen women then stripped the trees five times, while others of a lower rank did the same nine times.[57] The leaves were taken to the *canmu* who cut them up. Finally, the leaves were fed to the silkworms and the signal for the end of the rite was given. Afterward, the customary congratulations were offered and there was a banquet for the participants.

Some time later, after the silkworms had accomplished their part of the work, the silk-making process was completed and the material was used to fashion vestments for the various imperial sacrifices, just as the grain harvested from the imperial plowing field was used as a food offering in those sacrifices. The Qing continued the silkworm rite on the site in the West Park using a ritual quite similar to the one I have just described[58] (see illustration 17). The enclosure for the altar of silkworms still exists. It is in the northeast corner of *Beihai* Park and inside is a kindergarten, not open to the public. But the old lock and dam, with fresh running water, can still be found, reminding the visitor of the importance of the washing done in the ritual.

The meaning of these twin rites of spring plowing and silkworm ceremony is certainly rooted in the ancient belief that the sacred ruler was mediator between the cosmic powers and the natural world. According to this belief, the quality of imperial rule had a definite impact on the success of farming and sericulture, on the fertility of the land, and the harmonious balance of sun and rain. We have evidence that the better emperors took this function quite seriously.[59] However, it seems that the direct connection between these rites and the sacral function of the sovereign was no longer present, for later texts consistently use the phrase "encourage and stimulate the people's labors," as the rationale for performing the rites. However that expression is interpreted, one wonders how the people were to be encouraged, since they were not allowed to witness the rite.

On the other hand we know that even the earliest references to these ceremonies in the classics are already rationalized. That is to say, they are the product of the Han synthesis, when the original meaning of many ritual practices had already been lost, or was no longer believed.

Perhaps we may come closer to the original meaning by examining a legend about a *shenshu*, a spirit tree, said to have been planted by the Yongle emperor in the enclosure of the *taimiao*. During a visit to the ancestral temple, the emperor noted that most of the trees in the enclosure were dying. No sooner had the new sapling, planted by imperial hands, taken root, then all the other trees recovered and have continued to thrive ever since.[60] Here there is no question of stimulation and encouragement through imitation, but a kind of direct mysterious efficacy emanating from the power of the sacred ruler. Of course, by Ming and Qing times the officials may not have believed in this kind of efficacy. All that we can say with certitude is that they had a general awareness that it was their role to harmonize the seasons and the weather, and the emperor and his officials were chiefly responsible if the earth did not produce its bounty.

ALTARS OF THE SUN AND MOON

I will conclude this chapter with a brief account of the altars that complete the symbolism of the four directions for the city of Beijing, the altar of the sun in the eastern suburb and the altar of the moon in the west. The question running through the history of Chinese imperial worship of sun and moon was similar to that regarding the worship of sovereign earth. Should there be separate altars for their sole worship or should they simply receive correlate worship at the suburban sacrifice to heaven?[61] Early in the Hongwu period, a report emanating from the Board of Rites noted that both forms had been practiced in Chinese history. During the Qin and Han dynasties there is literary evidence for the worship of the sun and moon, but it is not clear whether they had separate altars. The Tang and Song dynasties did have separate altars to the east and west of the capital, but the Yuan did not. The board then went on the urge worshiping the sun at the vernal equinox at a specially constructed altar outside the east gate of the city, the moon at the autumnal equinox at an altar outside the western gate. It emphasized that these rites were certainly important because they are well documented in the classics, then added a second reason. Heaven and earth are due the highest respect, the sun and moon next. At the vernal equinox, the yang breath is dominant; at the autumnal equinox, yin is dominant. Worshiping them separately at these times of the year "would achieve the proper balance of yin and yang." The emperor agreed.

The later fortunes of these two altars followed the course of the conjoint-discrete worship controversy. After Hongu abolished discrete worship, the sacrifices to sun and moon became less important. In his twenty-first year (1388), "because *Da Ming* and *Ye Ming* [appellations for the sun and moon, respectively] already received correlate worship," he abolished the special rites at the altars of sun and moon.[62] Yongle followed the founder's worship system in Beijing, and again it was only when Jiajing restored discrete worship that the altars were built there.

Illus. 17.   The Altar of Silkworms. Source: *Tangtu mingsheng tubui*

The altar of the sun was built outside the *Chaoyang* Gate in 1530. It was an altar of one level, surrounded by a round wall, and it faced west. It was five *chang* square, five *chi*, nine *cun* high, and in its measurements generally used yang numbers, though not as comprehensively as the altar of heaven. The altar was faced with red brick, the color of yang and the east. The Qing went through a brief period of worshiping the sun and moon at the altar of heaven, then changed to discrete worship and used the Jiajing altars. They must have remodeled them to some degree, since the collected rituals of the dynasty say that the brick facing used at the altar was gold colored. But the red color was preserved in the jades used, the cloth offerings, utensils, and vestments. The time of worship was 5–7 A.M. All these details are obviously the product of yin yang, five-phase concepts[63] (see illustration 18).

Today the altar of the sun is a part of *Ritan* Park, which is located in area of the foreign embassies, a very pleasant part of Beijing with tree-shaded streets. The altar and its walled enclosure have been recently restored, with handsome bright red tiling facing the round encircling wall. Just outside the west gate to the altar is a sign that tells the visitor that the altar of the sun was destroyed by the Red Guards during the Cultural Revolution, then rebuilt according to its original Ming form in 1984.

The altar of the moon was built outside *Fucheng* Gate to the west of Beijing's inner city. It was of one level, but surrounded by a square wall. The altar platform was four *zhang* square, four *chi*, six *cun* high, and generally showed the yin numbers in its measurements. The altar was oriented to the east and was faced in white tile. The time of worship was 5–7 P.M. In the Jiajing period the emperor was supposed to worship in person once every two years at the altar of the sun and once every three at the altar of the moon. In the years when he did not worship personally, the emperor deputed a *wen* (civil) official to represent him in offering sacrifice to the sun, and a *wu* (military) official to offer sacrifice to the moon.

During the Qing dynasty, the emperors followed the Jiajing system in the liturgy. At the moon altar sacrifice, the spirit tablet faced east and correlate worship was offered to the twenty-eight constellations, the five planets, and all the stars, whose tablets faced south. The brick facing was also changed to gold here, but the color of vestments, vessels, jades, and so forth was white, the color of the west[64] (see illustration 19).

Today there is a *Yuetan* (altar of the moon) Park, but the old altar itself is gone. The three arched gates that led into the altar compound have been bricked up. Inside the walled enclosure, in the place of the altar, is a new nocturnal object of worship, a television tower.

There are, of course, many other altars and temples in and around Beijing, but those I have just examined are certainly the most important

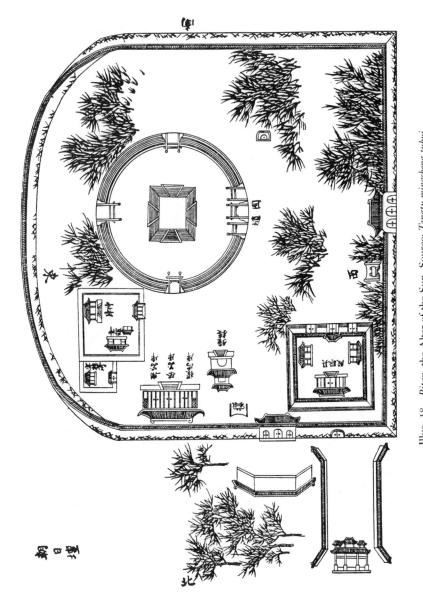

Illus. 18. *Ritan*, the Altar of the Sun. Source: *Tangtu mingsheng tuhui*

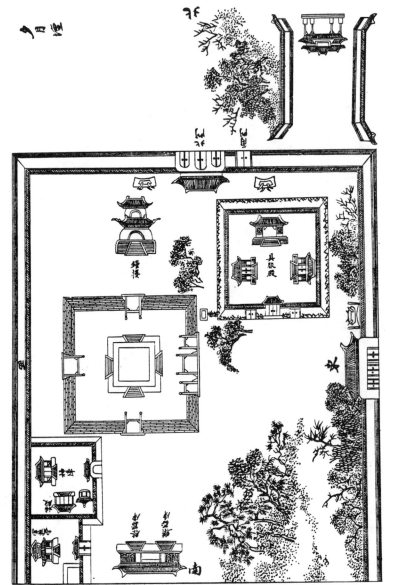

Illus. 19. *Yuetan*, the Altar of the Moon. Source: *Tangtu mingsheng tuhui*

sites used for the elaborate system of imperial worship. The rituals performed at them had a confirmatory and efficacious function. They confirmed the status of the "one man," the son of heaven, who alone could be the high priest to offer sacrifices to the heavenly and earthly powers. Each time he performed the rites, his exalted status was reaffirmed.

The performing of these rituals at the various suburban altars was the clearest expression of the emperor's religious function, enabling him to make his mind consonant with heaven and earth. "The Order of the divine ruler consists in this, that his heart is always the same as that of Heaven and earth. That is the reason he can do things here, while the 'small man' can accomplish nothing."[65] His ritual actions were truly "liturgies," that is, work done or acts performed for the common good. The emperor worshiped heaven and the other spirits not simply because they deserved to be praised but because their powers had to be channeled from the other world to this world, to bless, enrich, and strengthen the Central Kingdom. Performing these rituals sincerely and faithfully, harmonizing the powers of the cosmos, the emperor would continue to enjoy the mandate of heaven.

Four emperors must be given particular credit for giving Beijing the form it has even today: Hongwu, the Ming founder who set so many precedents in Nanjing, which would later be imitated in Beijing; Yongle the executor, who gave the ancient city plan its classical expression in the building of his new capital; Qianlong, who rebuilt and perfected so many halls, palaces, and altars that had fallen into disrepair; and finally Jiajing, who despite his dubious motives, perhaps most perfectly carried out Yongle's supposed command to the builders of his capital: "seek harmony with the Universe and obey the Laws of Space and Direction."[66]

NOTES

1. See Borge's tracing of this concept in Western history, "Pascal's Sphere," *Other Inquisitions*, pp. 6ff.

2. Le Corbusier, *Towards a New Architecture*, trans. Frederich Etchells (New York: Prager, 1963), p. 173.

3. *Ming shi*, XLVI, 523. The greater importance of the ancestral temple over the altar of land and grain is clearly indicated by the easterly placement of the former.

4. *Liji*, I, 410. "God" is Legge's translation of Shangdi.

5. Ibid., p. 427.

6. E.g., ibid., pp. 116, 185, 186, 225; II, 203.

7. *Ming shi*, XLVI, 513; *Chunmingmeng yulu*, quoted in Ling, "Beiping," p. 15.

8. A good summary of these early Ming events and the Song precedents is given in Yun-yi Ho, "Ritual Aspects of the Founding of the Ming Dynasty 1368–1398," *Society for the Study of Chinese Religions Bulletin*, no. 7 (Fall 1979), 58–67. Ho sees Hongwu's ritual maneuvers as an

attempt to reconcile his dual role as a perserver of old traditions, while at the same time founding new dynastic institutions.

9. *Ming shi*, XLVI, 513–14; Ling, "Beiping," pp. 16–17.

10. *Ming shi*, XLVI, 514–15; *DMB*, p. 458.

11. *Rixia jiuwen kao*, XVI (57), 5.

12. From a diagram in Ling, "Beiping," p. 16. See the verbal description of the same building in *Rixia jiuwen kao*, XVI (58), 1. I translate *zhen* as mountains and *yu* as peaks to distinguish these two sets of five mountains whose spirits were worshiped in imperial China. The mountains (here *shan*) and rivers shrine, center of the southeast group, is quite small because there was a large altar complex dedicated to them elsewhere in Nanjing and later in Beijing. We can presume that the arrangement reproduced here is approximately the same as in Yongle's Great Worship Hall in Beijing.

13. Ling, "Beiping," pp. 1–2.

14. W. A. C. H. Dobson, trans., *Mencius* (Toronto: University of Toronto Press, 1963), p. 19.

15. Not surprisingly, the sovereigns with the most doubtful credentials to rule were most avid in their desires to have a *Mingtang*. Two of the best known attempts are those of Wang Mang and Empress Wu. The best historical treatment of the *Mingtang* I know of is in Soper, *Art*, pp. 212–15, 226–39, passim. Granet (*Pensée Chinoise*) has the most comprehensive discussion of the cosmic symbolism involved. See his index, p. 558, for numerous citations. Other valuable treatments are Henri Maspero, *Mélanges chinois et bouddhiques, 1948–51*, pp. 1–71, and Wm. Ed. Soothill, *The Hall of Light* (London: Butterworth, 1951), though the last takes the quest for the historical *Mingtang* much too seriously.

16. *Liji*, I, 252. See p. 58 of the same book, and Granet, *Pensée*, pp. 150–51, for different conceptions of the structure of the building.

17. Granet, *Pensée*, pp. 266–67.

18. Soothill, *Hall*, p. 68.

19. *Ming shi*, XLVI, 517–18.

20. Ibid., p. 514.

21. Liu Tzu-chien, "Fengshan wenhua yu Songdai mingtang jitian," *Bulletin of the Institute of Ethnology, Academia Sinica*, no. 18 (Autumn 1964), 45–57. In general, I do not find the author's conclusions completely compelling. He implies (p. 45) that the change to indoor worship was related to the whole movement toward despotism "of the last thousand years." As we have seen, the change to outdoor worship at the four suburban altars under Jiajing was not accompanied by any reduction of despotic behavior on the part of the emperor.

22. Descriptions in Ling, "Peiping," p. 48; Chen Hongnian, p. 158; *Rixia jiuwen kao*, XVI (58), 1–2, and Speiser, *Architecture*, p. 442.

23. For the Chinese solar zodiac, see Schlegel, *Uranographie*, 1:557ff.; for the lunar habitations, ibid., pp. 583ff.

24. Soper, *Art*, p. 226.

25. Wright, "Symbolism and Function," p. 674.

26. *Ming shi*, XLVI, 518–19; *Rixia jiuwen kao*, XVI (58), 1. The sacrifices of spring and autumn were, however, reestablished briefly during the reign of the last Ming emperor, Chongzhen.

27. See the photo, *Jiudu wenwu lue*, III, 4, and compare the drawings, pp. 43 and 49, in Ling, "Beiping." While Yongle had the assistance of mountain spirits in bringing great timbers to Beijing for the building of its great halls (see this legend in the following chapter), the logs for the Guangxu *Qiniandian* had to be brought from Oregon. So diminished were the fortunes of the son of heaven!

28. L. C. Arlington and W. Lewisohn, *In Search of Old Peking* (Peking: Henry Vetch, 1935), p. 109. On the whole, this is a valuable introduction to Beijing. Though the sources of the authors' information are rarely given, it has many good maps and the reproductions of Chinese prints of various sites around the city are very worthwhile.

29. Ling, "Peiping," p. 45; *Jiudu wenwu lue*, III, 2, photo p. 3; Chen Hongnian, *Gudu fengwu*, p. 159. The last source relates some interesting acoustical phenomena in the area around the House of the Imperial Firmament, which is due to the absolute geometrical regularity in the construction of the altar of heaven complex. The concave wall behind the Hall of the Imperial Firmament carried the human voice, even though a whisper, with perfect clarity from one end to the other. There are what the author calls "echo stones" on the front (south) steps of the building. If a person claps once on the first step, he hears one echo; if on the second step, he hears two echos; if on the third, three echoes.

30. Ling, "Peiping," pp. 25–26; *Rixia jiuwen kao* XVI (57), 6–7.

31. Ling, "Peiping," p. 40; *Rixia jiuwen kao*, XVI (57), 11. The Qing altar of heaven may be seen in fig. 19, Ling, "Peiping," p. 47, and photograph, *Jiudu wenwu lue*, III, 3; detail of pavement and balustrade, p. 4.

32. *Da Qing huidian shili*, quoted in Wang Chengyong, ed., *Tiantan* (Beijing: Beijing luyou chubanshe, 1987), pp. 30–31.

33. Ling, "Peiping," pp. 44, 47–48. Mention of the discrepancy is in Wang Chengyong, *Tiantan*, p. 31.

34. Granet, *Pensée*, pp. 127–28, 148–52. The author attributes the Chinese preference for odd numbers to the need to have the elements, seasons, directions, etc., ranged around the one in the center, the sovereign ruler. John Major gives an excellent description of nonary cosmography in "The Five Phases, Magic Squares and Schematic Cosmography," in Henry Rosemont, Jr., *Explorations in Early Chinese Cosmology* (Chico, Calif.: Scholars Press, 1984), pp. 133–66.

35. Jia Qunnuo, Wang Chengyong, *Tiantan jingwu chuanshuo* (Beijing: Zhongguo minjian wenyi chubanshe, 1987), p. 37. The structure is called a "bridge" because there is a tunnel under it, for leading the animals from the stables in the southwest area to the slaughterhouse east of the Hall for Yearly Prayers.

36. Details about the animals, their preparation and use, may be found in Wang Chengyong, *Tiantan*, pp. 24–25, 42–45.

37. Ibid., pp. 35–39.

38. Ibid., p. 39.

39. Ibid., p. 36.

40. The persons performing the music and dancing for the rites were trained at the *Shenyueshu*, the Academy of Liturgical Music, which was located on the west side of the altar of heaven complex. See Wang Chengyong, *Tiantan*, p. 39ff.

41. *Ming shi*, LXVI, 513.

42. *Chunmingmeng yulu*, quoted in *Rixia jiuwen kao*, XXVIII (107), 15–16.

43. Ibid.

44. *Da Qing huidian*, as quoted in Ling, "Peiping," p. 50.

45. Ibid., p. 53.

46. *Liji*, I, 216–18; for other examples, see pp. 116, 225, 365–86; II, 203; also Chavannes, *Memoires Historiques*, 1:60, and Bredon, *Peking*, p. 34.

47. Though the sacrifices were abolished, the altars were left standing. See photo, *Chiudu wenwu lue*, III, 8.

48. Ibid. Cf. Schlegel, *Uranographie*, 1:614ff.

49. *Ming shi*, XLVI, 530–31; illustration in Ling, "Peiping," p. 33. An illuminating

discussion of the history and significance of *Taisui* may be found in Hou Ching-lang, "The Chinese Belief in Baleful Stars," in Holmes Welch and Anna Seidel, *Facets of Taoism: Essays in Chinese Religion* (New Haven: Yale University Press, 1979), pp. 193–228.

50. *Liji*, I, 255; another reference in II, 222.

51. *Ming shi*, XLVI, 525. Most of the following information is taken from this source.

52. The Qing rite is found in *Jiudu wenwu lue*, III, 7.

53. Zhi Chaozi, *Jiujing xiaoji*, p. 91.

54. *Liji*, I, 265; another reference in II, 223.

55. *Sancai tuhui*, III, 1017–18. Along with the text are drawings of the buildings where the worms are kept and cocoons processed, and of the altar of the spirit of the first silkworm.

56. *Ming shi*, XLVI, 526. There was a controversy over a suitable site. The altar was first begun according to the most approved tradition, at a place north of Beijing. But this location had two disadvantages. The ritual procession route there was quite long and might overtax the empress. Furthermore, there was no ready source of water for the cocoon washing. After construction had already begun, the emperor finally agreed to change the site to an island in West Park in the imperial city, where the complex was completed and remained through the Qing dynasty.

57. I have not been able to discover when the numerical parallel originated. It is evident that the agriculture rite has been used as a model, but one might have expected stripping the trees two, four, and six times, since nothing is specified in the *Liji*.

58. See *Jiudu wenwu lue*, III, 9, for text and a photograph of the altar; cf. also Ling, "Peiping," p. 66.

59. See the *Qibao* section, *Ming shi*, XLVI, 528, which clearly describes the role of the emperor as mediator and his responsibility in case of calamity. The same section describes some of the penetential acts performed by Hongwu to regain heaven's favor and reestablish harmony after a long period of disastrous weather threatened China's agriculture.

60. Arlington and Lewisohn, *Old Peking*, p. 62. There is a story, similar in some respects, of a Ming empress planting a bo tree in the palace courtyard, found in *Rixia jiuwen kao*, IX (34), 22.

61. *Liji*, II, 215ff., seems to leave room for both ideas, subsidiary worship at the altar of heaven and separate worship in the eastern and western suburbs.

62. *Ming shi*, XLVI, 524.

63. *Da Qing huidian* and *Chunmingmeng yulu*, quoted in *Rixia jiuwen kao*, XXIV (88), 22ff.

64. *Ibid.*, XXVI (96), 1ff; and Ling, "Peiping," pp. 29, 54–56. See figures 24, 25, 26, 27 on pp. 55–59 for drawings of the altars of sun and moon.

65. *Taipingjing*, quoted in Wolfgang Bauer, *China and the Search for Happiness*, trans. Michael Shaw (New York: Seabury, 1976), p. 124.

66. Bredon, *Peking*, p. 81.

Chapter 4

The Weft of the Fabric:
Beijing in Myth and Legend

. . . tell me, if you know
. . . why the glassy lights,
The lights in the fishing boats at anchor there,
As the night descended, tilting the air,
Mastered the night and portioned out the sea.

—Wallace Stevens, "The Idea of Order at Key West"

The material presented in this chapter is quite different from what we have considered until now. Although it begins with semiofficial "historical" sources, most of what follows is taken from myths and legends, which were originally oral, and often hard to place chronologically since they were written down at a much later period of time. Furthermore, most come not from the official or gentry class but are the lore of ordinary people. As I try to analyze Beijing, these stories are important because they throw an entirely different light on the religious significance of the city. They reveal a structure of sacrality quite in contrast with the astral-cosmic symbolism I have been examining until now. I will save a methodical analysis of this alternate structure, which I call "local sacrality," until the end of the chapter.

Earlier chapters have made occasional reference to a few of the myths and legends preserved in the quasi-official sources for the history of Beijing. The astral-cosmic symbolism is one mythic structure, of course, but the stories I will now consider present a different mythic pattern, an alternative way of understanding the religious meaning of traditional Beijing. In this chapter I will be looking at two types of literary sources, which I will refer to as myth and legend. A great deal of sophisticated analysis has been applied to these terms, but I will be using them with this simple distinction in mind: "myth" refers to very ancient foundational stories— that is, stories that tell us of origins and foundational events, of the significance of the site on which Beijing is built and why such a place was chosen. By "legends" I refer to stories that appear to be of more recent origin in the Ming and Qing dynasties. They tell of some specific feature of the city and of persons who built it, and of the gods, spirits, or heroic figures who helped them.[1]

The legends have a character all their own. What they lack in elegance of style, they more than make up for in vividness. They are strong on narrative, and always specific and very concrete as to locale. They often show a sense of humor, earthiness, occasionally irreverence, and sometimes a surprising familiarity in naming the great beings whom they are supposed to hold in great awe and respect, the emperor and Shangdi. In content, they range from the trivial to the profound.

In a very real sense, the myths and legends are just as valuable as more sober historical accounts of the city, because they give us a precious insight into how the masses of ordinary folk experienced Beijing, how its monuments, temples, walls, and towers came to be important in their everyday lives. A few of the best of them reveal an understanding of human nature that transcends the particularities of time, race, and culture.

On the other hand, these stories sometimes are surprising in that they also reveal an unexpected historical accuracy. The emperors whom history tells us are the most important in the building and renovation of Beijing (Yongle, Jiajing, Qianlong) are precisely the ones most often featured in these popular accounts. The legends give us the weft of the tapestry of the Chinese capital: the substance, color, and specificity that make Beijing different from all other past or potential capitals of China.

A PLACE IN THE STARS

The first chapter of the voluminous sourcebook on Beijing, the *Rixia jiuwen kao*, is appropriately entitled "Stars and Earth." Traditional Chinese believed that a very close relationship existed between heaven and earth, and that the forms of things made on this earth should imitate the models already given in the heavens. We have already examined the belief that the Chinese capital should be a replica of the polar capital where Shangdi ruled over the universe. But besides this generic pattern for the capital city, there was also a *specific* place in the stars that referred to Beijing alone. This was because in ancient China they believed that each part of the Chinese empire corresponded to a star or group of stars in the heavens.[2]

The Chinese term used to describe the fact that there is an order in the heavens with its mirror image on earth is *fenye*. It can be literally translated as "dividing the wastes," but the freer translation "finding an order in the chaos" perhaps better expresses the meaning. The words "order" and "chaos" alert us to the mythic dimensions of this concept, for most creation stories from every culture are in one way or another a description of how order emerged from a primordial chaos. The Chinese perceived in the heavens, demarcated by the stars, a given order that could then be applied on earth. Probably the best known myth of *fenye* describes how Yu the Great, successor to the sage emperors Yao and Shun, accomplished this ordering when he traced the divisions of the nine traditional provinces of China on the face of the land.

Seeking to give order to what appears potentially chaotic is a quintessentially human act. It is also a religious act, and nearly every cosmogonic myth in every culture describes the process of the creation of, or discovery of, the order without which human life would be impossible. Even today, when science tells us that the "order" of the stars is illusory and without basis in reality, we cling to our constellations.

The Chinese interest in *fenye* was, however, more practical than theoretical or esthetic. They looked for any abnormal occurrences in the heavens to have repercussions on earth. Falling stars in a certain region, eclipses, movements of the planets, stars that appeared brighter or dimmer in a particular section of the heavens had meaning for the corresponding areas on earth. Astral phenomena were predictive of terrestrial events. It was important to identify any given locale's place in the stars, then omens could be identified and interpreted. Although the *fenye* of Yu the Great was most famous, other systems also existed. Because all of them offered potential help in understanding the fate of Beijing, the editors of the *Rixia* do not attempt to determine which is more correct, but relate all methods. Perhaps the accumulation of so many references to the great stars that govern Beijing adds in their eyes to the glory of the capital.

The first method mentioned is the traditional division of the land into nine provinces. The *Zhou Li* has a section stating that a certain officer, the *baozhangshi*, has as his duty to observe the heavenly bodies and earthly conditions to determine the blessings and misfortunes that have been made known to the world. He is to assign constellations to each of the nine regions according to the divisions of the empire. Each division will then have a distinct constellation in which the rulers may observe the extraordinary omens that have significance for their own territories.[3] Illustration 20 shows a Ming encyclopedia conception of this method.

Next the editors present a group of scattered references to stars that are said to govern the area of Beijing. The locale is called *Yan* in the texts, after the name of the feudal state that occupied the territory in Zhou times, or *Youzhou*, a prefectural name given to the area at the time of the sage emperor Shun. One of the stars named as controlling *Yan*'s fate is the sixth star of the Big Dipper. The constellation, the authors add, is sometimes called the Imperial Chariot, because it revolves around the center of the heavens and controls the four quarters. Another source claims that the fifth star of the Central Palace constellation rules the fate of *Yan*, while a third says that it is ruled by the eighth star of the Jade Regulator group.

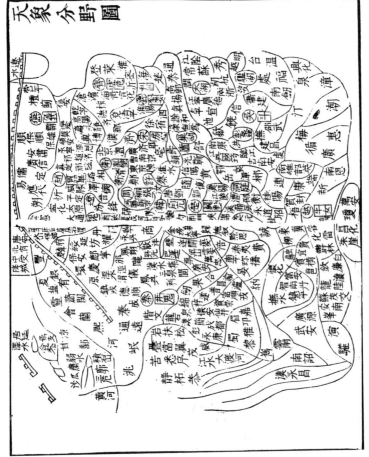

Illus. 20. *Fenyeh*, Ming dynasty map showing the division of the Central Kingdom according to the constellations. Beijing's position is in the upper right-hand corner, just below the Great Wall. The *yan* constellation is within a circle, the *wei* and *ji* constellations are within the square just below it. Source: *Sancai tubui*

More numerous sources point out that the constellation called the Heavenly Market Enclosure has a star called *Yan*, which is the true governor of Beijing. This claim provides us an opportunity to illustrate the difference in the logic of the two structures of sacrality, cosmic and local. As we have seen in chapter 1, the Purple Hidden Enclosure constellation was the model for Chinese capitals generally. Whether the capital be Beijing, Changan, or Loyang, however, *all* have their heavenly model in the Purple Hidden Enclosure. But in the source we are discussing, the star *Yan* of the Heavenly Market Enclosure is seen as the model for Beijing and Beijing alone. On the other hand, the assignment of Beijing to the star *Yan* does not give it any particular preeminence as a potential site for a capital, since each of the feudal states had its corresponding star in the same constellation.

Another method of *fenye* places Beijing in relation to the constellations *wei* and *ji*. These are two constellations of the twenty-eight *su* (dwellings, habitations), which encompass the entire heavens. These twenty-eight star groups are the main elements of Chinese astronomy. They were called dwellings because they were seen as the background against which the sun, moon, and planet's movements could be calculated. These "moving" bodies seemed to "dwell" in the *su* a certain period of time, just as Western astrology might speak of the moon or a planet residing in a zodiac constellation for a certain period of time.[4]

The twenty-eight dwellings were placed into four groups of seven: the first seven were called the Azure Dragon and identified with the east and spring, the second seven were called the Black Warrior (north, winter), the third group was called the Red Bird (south, summer), the fourth the White Tiger (west, autumn). The constellations of Beijing, *wei* and *ji*, were two of the seven belonging to the Azure Dragon.[5]

The authors then cite another method of *fenye* in which the heavens are divided into twelve *ci* (again meaning a habitation). The twelve *ci* correspond to the Western zodiac (Capricorn, Aquarius, Pisces, Aries, etc.). Unlike the twenty-eight habitations (*su*), each of the twelve is the same size, exactly thirty degrees, all of them making up the 360 degrees of the heavenly circuit. Some of the *ci* therefore include three of the *su*, others only two, the *su* being irregular in size. The *ci* to which Bejing is assigned is called *ximu* (our Sagittarius) and it includes *wei* and *ji*[6] (see illustration 21).

Finally, Beijing is related to the heavens in terms suggested by the yin yang and five-phase thinking. It is said to be under the influence of yin and the planet Mercury, governed by the element water and the color black, all because of its northern location. It is for the same reason considered to be under the patronage of the Black Emperor, a reference to the Han dynasty theory of five heavenly emperors.

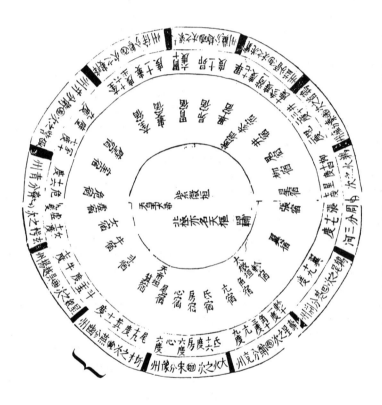

Illus. 21. Circumpolar *fenyeb*. The inner circle contains the polar constellations, the next circle the 28 habitations (*su*), the outer ring the 12 dwellings (*ci*). Beijing's segment is upper left, as indicated in the chart. Source: *Sancai tuhui*

All this sounds rather complicated, and did in fact provide for observers a number of celestial areas possibly affecting the fate of Beijing. Here are some examples of how this knowledge was used and interpreted. The *History of the Later Han Dynasty* records a spectacular display of falling stars in 36 C.E., during the Jianwu reign. The passage says that the phenomenon had the "appearance of the movement of common people," and notes that three years later the emperor moved more than sixty thousand people to protect the border against bandits. This verified the earlier omen, for the falling stars had been seen in the part of the heavens corresponding to Beijing. Another quotes the appearance of the planet Venus in the constellations *wei* and *ji* in the year 304 C.E. The following month of the same year a man named Wang killed the governor of Youzhou. Later in the same dynastic period there was a fall of stars near *ji* and soon followed a terrible slaughter near *Yan* (the blood fell "like rain," says the account) when a man named Mu Rong set himself up as emperor. Later, another source says, lucky stars appeared in *wei* and *ji*, when Mu Rong restored *Yan*. All these events, the editors indicate, "are the verification of *Yan's fenye*."[7]

All of the above occurences are important events in the history of Beijing, and all were predicted by astral signs that show the value of the various systems of *fenye*. Still, there is nothing in any of this material that would elevate the location of Beijing to the status of sacred capital. Similar omens and events could be found in the records of many areas in China. To discover the reason for Beijing's preeminent place, we must go to the second chapter of the *Rixia*.

A MYTH OF THE FOUNDATION: HUANGDI BUILT HIS CAPITAL AT YAN

In the second chapter, the editors take up the "history" of Beijing, and present material that establishes the city's local sacrality and makes an implicit claim that Beijing is uniquely qualified to be the imperial capital. The editors begin their history with Huangdi, the Yellow Emperor, continue with the sage emperors Yao, Shun, and Yu, then trace significant events through the Xia, Yin (Shang), Zhou, and all succeeding dynasties. But the emphasis during the early period is on the great occurrences during the reign of the Yellow Emperor. At that time an important battle took place that may be interpreted as a foundational event, for after it was over, Chinese civilization as we know it was established. It is a myth that has different and even contradictory versions, but in its general form is similar to battle-foundational stories of other cultures, such as the Babylonian Marduk-Taimat myth of the *Enuma Elish* or that of Leviathan-Yahweh mentioned cryptically in the Bible.

It is difficult to forge the details of this myth into a consistent narrative, and the authors of the *Rixia* again use their "catalogue" method, reporting all versions, only at the end making some attempt to resolve the contradictions among them. But the protagonist of the myth is clear. He is Huangdi, the Yellow Emperor, who is the first sovereign treated at length in the paradigmatic history of Sima Qian, and the Chinese culture-hero par excellence.[8] The identity of the antagonist is less clear. In some texts he is called Shen Nong (or Yandi), the ruler traditionally listed as preceding the Yellow Emperor. In most texts, however, he is given the name Chi You. The battle took place at Zholu, near the capital of the Yellow Emperor, the site that later became Beijing. (Zholu is now the name of a small town a few miles to the southwest of Beijing.)

The battle is portrayed in various ways. True to the historicizing tendency of most Chinese official writing, the event can be represented drably as a mere dynastic changeover: "The Yellow Emperor levied troops and led the feudal lords to do battle with Chi You at the waste of Zholu. He seized and slew Chi You and the feudal lords honored him as the Son of Heaven, replacing the dynasty of Shen Nong."[9]

Other sources are much more colorful and give us a clearer picture of the mythic proportions of the battle. One relates that the Yellow Emperor trained bears, leopards, and tigers to fight with him against Chi You. Another tells of how Chi You was able to call forth a dense fog during the battle, which threw the Yellow Emperor's troops into confusion. To counter this tactic, Huangdi made a marvelous chariot called the *zhinanche*, or "compass chariot." This miraculous vehicle enabled the Yellow Emperor and his troops to recover their sense of direction and defeat the enemy, Chi You himself falling under the wheels of the chariot.

Our account then goes on to give further information about Chi You from other sources. Among his troops were eighty-one of his own brothers who had the bodies of beasts but spoke like humans. They had bronze skulls and iron foreheads, and for their food ate gravel and stones. They had terrifying weapons of all sorts, which they brandished to frighten the people of the world. One source describes Chi You as a flying beast with fleshy wings, and another says that he had horns on his head with which to butt and gore his opponents. We are told that, like Proteus of Greek and Mahisa of Hindu mythology, he can change form at will. He has the body of a man and the legs of an ox, with four eyes and six arms. He can command the wind, rain, and fog. Finally, a source called the "History of Extraordinary Narrations" claims that the bronze and iron bones, which are continually being excavated in the area of Zholu, are really the bones of Chi You.

The texts available describe the battle between the Yellow Emperor and Chi You in various ways, but taken together they portray an event of monumental importance. Some assert that the two combatants fought over seventy times without a victory for either, others say one hundred times. Taoist authors emphasized the plight of the Yellow Emperor and tell of how Taoist spirits came to his aid, lifting the significance of the conflict to cosmic proportions. The Queen Mother of the West (Xiwangmu) commanded her pupil Yuannu to instruct him in the knowledge of certain miraculous musical notes, which he might use to defeat his enemy. Taiyi offered him miraculous means of escape (*dunjia*), together with other tricks, talismans, and amulets "thanks to which he defeated Chi You." The *dunjia* (literally, "escape armor") is a phrase often appearing in Taoist writings and popular fiction, and refers to the magic body of concealment, the ability to travel invisibly. Other sources add to the list of miraculous devices used by the hero a horn that sounded like the cry of a dragon, and magical songs for each day of a ten-day battle.

We need not spend much time on the final part of chapter 2 in the *Rixia*. There the authors puzzle over the identity of Chi You, testing various explanations. He is either Emperor Shen Nong, or a man commissioned by him. Others say he was simply a commoner who coveted the throne, or a spirit, or a collectivity—the rebellious feudal lords. But these "explanations," instead of telling us anything about Chi You, are evidence of the historicizing tradition in Chinese scholarship. We should not let this obscure the fact that the myth seems to be telling the story of the transition from chaos to order, from barbarism to civilization. We may see in the description of a bestial Chi You and followers a way of emphasizing the lawless chaotic condition that existed before the advent of Chinese culture and civilization (and the danger of lapsing back into that terrible condition if Chinese culture were threatened). This interpretation seems more plausible when we realize that Chi You has traditionally been identified by the Chinese with the invading northern "barbarians," the nomadic tribes that from ancient times have been the most feared and potent threat to the security of Chinese civilization.

The Yellow Emperor, on the other hand, is the great culture-hero. By his victory over Chi You, he lays the foundation for the Chinese way. This identity is even clearer if we add to his victory over Chi You the accomplishments attributed to him by the historian Sima Qian. The Yellow Emperor is said to have had supernatural powers from his birth, including the ability to speak in an adult manner. To serve the people he pierced mountains, opened roads, planted the hundred kinds of grain, herbs, and trees. He promoted the development of birds, quadrupeds, insects, reptiles, and established everywhere the order of sun, moon, and stars. He regulated the use of water, fire, and wood. In short he brought true human culture and civilization to the Chinese people.[10] A glance at his portrait in the Ming dynasty encyclopedia makes this quite clear. He is a person of culture, while his two imperial predecessors, Fuxi and Shen Nong, are semibestial in appearance (see illustration 22). Huangdi's importance in Chinese tradition is considerable. "Whether he is presented as a eu-hemerized or deified figure, Huang Ti appears as a symbol of the center and of the beginning of society and of the universe."[11]

This myth of the Yellow Emperor is without a doubt the most important narrative in establishing a local sacrality for Beijing. The cosmic symbolism of the capital is reinforced by the mythic centralizing character of the Yellow Emperor. His cycle of myths gives Beijing preeminence over any other city in China as the most fitting site for a national capital. Beijing becomes the very symbol of civilized life and ordered existence, for it was there that the Yellow Emperor first established the Chinese way.

The rest of Beijing's history is rather lackluster until it actually became the national capital. We are told that the sage emperor Yao stationed a man there named He Shu. At the time of sage emperor Shun the area offered its allegiance, was redistricted, and given the historic name Youzhou. Next follows a discussion of the names of the territory from the time of Yu the Great down to the Zhou dynasty when king Wu enfeoffed the territory to the duke of Zhao and it was given the equally historic name Yan. Finally, the area's name changes are carefully catalogued from that time down to the period when it became one of the capitals of the Liao dynasty. In none of this long sweep of history is Beijing of any great political importance. But at the beginning of the next chapter of the *Rixia*, as if to make sure that the essential point of the previous chapter has not been missed, the authors begin: "The Yellow Emperor built his capital at Yan."[12]

THE SHAPE OF BEIJING AND ITS MONUMENTS

We have already seen one answer to the question of the origin of Beijing's city plan. Its form is a careful execution of the prescriptions of the classics, especially the *Zhouli*, and in these cosmic patterns reside the city's claim to be a perfect capital. Now we shall look at different answers to the question of Beijing's form, derived from more popular perspectives. Some of these accounts have a mythic quality, such as the story of Nezha, others are more legendary. But in either case, they point to a different source of sacrality, not derived from a cosmic pattern, but from unique mythic events in the city.

If we ask in more detail how local sacrality is created, we find that it is because of the unique visitation of a divine personage, or the presence of an object such as a well, rock, tree, or temple that has special religious significance, or because the place was the scene of some sort of miraculous event. Usually, in the case of important sacred places, it is because of the

Illus. 22. The Yellow Emperor, shown in the lower left corner. The Yellow Emperor's family tree is given in the upper right corner, leading to the sage emperors, the Shang and Zhou kings. Source: *Sancai tuhui*

combination of all three of these factors. To use the term of Mircea Eliade, some sort of "hierophany" has taken place.

In this section I want to examine some legends of Beijing telling of miraculous events that occurred at particular places in and around the city. These stories tell us why Beijing is unique, why it has its specific form, and how the immortals and spirits helped in the design of its form and features.

Perhaps the best-known legend of Beijing is that which gave it the name *Nezha cheng*, the city of Nezha. According to one version of the legend, Zhu Di (later to become Emperor Yongle) was sent by the Ming founder Hongwu to be prince of Yan on the site of the former Mongol capital Dadu. This much is historically accurate. But before he left Nanjing, a "Taoist priest" named Liu Bowen gave him a sealed packet that was to be opened "in time of trouble." On arriving at the ruins of Khubilai Khan's old capital of Dadu, Zhu Di became disconsolate at the sight of the desolation before his eyes, and immediately opened the packet. Inside was a paper that said: "When you reach Beipingfu [a district name for the area] you must build a city there and name it Nezha city." On the back of the paper was a plan for the future city, which was to be carefully followed.[13]

Nezha is one of the most popular figures of Chinese romance, appearing in *The Pilgrimage to the West* and the *Canonization of the Gods*. He was the product of a miraculous conception and birth, and grew to gigantic size, having three heads, nine eyes, and eight hands. His life was full of marvelous deeds and adventures, not always exemplary, but he was consistently saved from the wrath of the gods by the intercession of a Taoist priest named Taiyi Zhenren. The climax of his life occurred when he slew himself to save the lives of his parents from four dragons that had seized them because of a murder that Nezha himself had committed. He later appeared to his mother in a dream and asked her to build a shrine to him on a mountain where he might be reincarnated. After some setbacks caused by his father, the Taoist priest brought Nezha back to life out of "two water lily stalks and three lotus leaves," which he had spread on the ground in human form.[14]

According to another more elaborate version of the legend, when Yongle decided to build Beijing as his capital, he sent a man to survey the situation. The man returned in distress, saying that the place was called Youzhou of the Bitter Waters, a desolate location that lacked even potable water.[15] The emperor finally found two volunteers among his generals who thought they could plan and build the city, one named Liu Bowen and the other Yao Guangxiao.[16] The two men despised one another, however, so they took up residence in the eastern and western parts of the city. They agreed to work independently on the plan and to meet in ten days to compare results.

The next day, when Liu Bowen went forth to inspect the site, he found himself preceded by a small boy. When Liu walked quickly, the boy also walked quickly, and when he slowed his pace, so did the boy. Try as he might he could not overtake the boy, but heard him saying over and over again: "If you follow my appearance in your plan, wouldn't it be exactly right?" Yao Guangxiao, on his part, had the same experience, preceded by the same young boy. The two "generals" perceived that the lad was wearing a strange type of red jacket. When the wind blew it gave the appearance of having eight sleeves, and both recognized that this was the "eight-armed Nezha." When the rivals met on the appointed day, they were astonished to find that their plans embodied the identical eight-armed form. Thus was revealed the miraculously sanctioned plan for the city of Beijing.[17]

The version just recounted gives a fairly simple explanation of what it means that Beijing reflects the form of Nezha. Yongding Gate is his head, its flanking gates east and west his ears, the two wells at the gate his eyes. His eight arms include the east and west gates of the southern wall of the outer city, together with the three gates on the west side of the city and the three gates on the east. The two northern gates are his legs. The great axial way from south to north is his alimentary canal, while the Imperial City contains his five viscera: heart, liver, lungs, stomach, and kidneys. The larger and smaller streets that crisscross Beijing with such regularity are his ribs. Arlington and Lewisohn give an even more detailed set of thirty-three points of correspondence in their account of Beijing.[18] However, the meaning of the story is clear in both versions. The plan of Beijing is not arbitrary, nor just the result of human skill, but is given miraculously through the intervention of a divine being.

There was a folk belief current in the late Qing period that explains Beijing's form as the imitation of the form of a dragon. At this time the Chinese were being pressured by the Western powers to modernize Beijing. They particularly wanted to have part of the southern wall of the city torn down to allow the Beijing-Hankou railroad to pass through. But the Chinese resisted. They said that Beijing had the form of a dragon, the central gate his mouth, the flanking gates his eyes, and so forth. When the rift in the wall was finally made, the people said that the dragon's body had been wounded and the blood of the dragon (the wealth of the city) would ooze out.[19]

These legends of Beijing remind us of the desire of *homo religiosus* to have divine models as guarantees for the security and stability of life on earth. But there are differences among them. The astral patterns and the classical designs of the Zhouli and the dragon form provide *general* plans, which can be imitated anywhere. These models are similar to ancient Hindu beliefs that their royal cities should imitate the form of the god

Purusha. Because connected with the appearance of a specific divine person, the form of Nezha is unique to Beijing. The former models are expressions of cosmic sacrality, the latter expressions of local sacrality.

More official Chinese writings rarely preserve much of the legendary material. However, there is a category of signs called auspicious omens, which is given great attention in historical accounts. We have already indicated how important were the astral omens. The *Shuntianfu zhi* relates that in the fourth year of Yongle, the emperor wished to rebuild the devastated old Yuan capital of Dadu. He sent high officials separately into the various provinces of China to look for trees large enough to build great palaces and audience halls. The man sent to Sichuan, named Song Li, found a number of giant timbers that would serve perfectly as the pillars in the halls and palaces the emperor wished to build. By a miracle, he reported, all the fine logs floated by themselves, in the period of one night, down through the valley all the way to the Yangtze River. When this news was brought to Yongle, he thought it was the work of spirits and named the mountain where the timbers had been found *Shenmushan*, mountain of the spirit trees. He then dispatched an official there to offer sacrifices.[20]

In the fifteenth year of Yongle, after he had moved the capital to Beijing, official records note that the palaces and halls had auspicious clouds floating over them, and the Golden River that flowed through the Forbidden City froze into "pagoda shaped mounds." Furthermore, some bright clouds later revealed a colorful spherical form that was like the sun hovering over the emperor's throne. These and other signs were taken as heavenly portents of the virtue of the emperor and the wisdom of his decision to build his capital at Beijing.[21]

It is hard to know whether these auspicious signs were taken seriously or whether they were just conventionalized genres to eulogize the emperors. The Kangxi emperor once said:

> I've never let people talk on about supernatural influences of the kind that have been recorded in the Histories: lucky stars, auspicious clouds, unicorns, and phoenixes, *chih* grass and suchlike blessings, or burning pearls and jade in the front of the palace, or heavenly books sent down to manifest Heaven's will. Those are empty words, and I don't presume so far. I just go on each day in an ordinary way, and concentrate on ruling properly.[22]

Returning to the popular accounts, we notice that many of Beijing's legends are about its water supply. Situated on the dry north China plain, Beijing has always had trouble obtaining an adequate supply of good tasting water. Werner records a simple version of a legend that tells of a terrible drought that occurred soon after the city of Nezha had been built.

Zhu Di found in the miraculous packet given to him by Liu Bowen another paper that revealed the source of the problem. Two dragons, disguised as an old man and woman, had carried off all Beijing's water in two baskets. Zhu Di rode off toward the west in pursuit of the dragons, pierced their baskets with a spear, and the water that gushed forth became a well that has provided Beijing its water down to the present day.[23]

Another version is more mythic in structure, beginning with a description of the Beijing locale as a large mass of bitter-tasting water. All the people were forced to live in the mountains to the northwest where they led a wretchedly poor existence, while the mass of waters was inhabited by a dragon king and his family. It was at this time that the area was called Youzhou of the Bitter Waters. Then one day there came a young man named Nezha who fought with the dragon king and his son for 99,811 days. Finally, Nezha captured the dragon king and his wife, and put the rest of the family to flight. After the battle was over, the waters subsided and dry land began to appear. Nezha imprisoned the two dragons in a large pool over which he built a large pagoda. Then Beijing began to be called simply Youzhou, and the people began to build houses and dwell there.[24]

The legend then continues with material similar to that we have just recounted, but considerably expanded. The dragon king was defeated, but now his son and wife watched with envy as the area continued to prosper, and when he heard that Beijing was about to be built, he became angry and planned to disrupt the effort. Taking their son and daughter, the two dragons, disguised as an old couple, entered the city with a vegetable vendor's cart. Their children drank lustily, the son swallowing all the city's sweet water and the daughter all the bitter water. Immediately they changed their form to that of water baskets, while the old couple pushed their cart out the western gate and headed for their home in the hills.

At this time, says the legend, Liu Bowen was the general in charge of Beijing. Informed of the strange old couple leaving the city, he guessed what had happened and asked for a volunteer to pursue the dragons and regain the water. A young man named Gao Liang accepted the challenge. He encountered many obstacles in his search for the dragons and had adventures at bridges, crossroads, and other sites that still exist today. Finally he overtook them and thrust his spear into the water basket that was the daughter, producing the water that has fed Beijing ever since. But the son escaped and slithered into a lake in the northwest hills, which explains why Beijing's waters even today are mostly bitter.[25]

The rest of the legends we will examine all tell of a particular place or a specific monument of Beijing that still exists and is thought to be important because of a famous person or spirit who has performed a miraculous deed at the place. There is the legend of Yongle and the spirit tree (*shen shu*) in the Imperial Ancestral Temple, mentioned in the previous chapter. It is said that whenever a subsequent emperor passed by this tree, he descended from his sedan chair and made three bows to the tree. Most of the legends of Beijing, however, do not deal with the great worship sites of the imperial religion, but with the structures familiar in the day-to-day life of the ordinary people: gates and bridges that marked transition points in their daily journeys, pagodas and temples where they worshiped, wells that provided their water, and the bell and drum towers that signaled the passage of hours of their days and nights. An important exception is the altar of heaven and its legends, which we will examine below. But generally it was not the sites where the son of heaven worshiped (and which were supposedly off limits to common people), but the ordinary landmarks of their everyday lives that excited their interest and imagination.

Such ordinary sites become significant, as I have suggested, by becoming connected with a god, spirit, or extraordinary personage of the past, places where some miraculous event had occurred. One of the most frequently encountered spirits in the Beijing legends is Lu Ban, whom Werner calls the "God of Carpenters and President of the Celestial Ministry of Public Works." From the baggage of his official titles one can already see that he is a figure from popular legend who has been coopted into the "official system." Historically speaking, it cannot be shown that such a person actually existed, but according to the traditions he was extremely skilled in all crafts relating to architecture, and it was just in the Yongle reign that he received the title of grand master, sustainer of the empire.[26] It is obviously no accident that he became the subject of so many legends relating to the building of Beijing.

The Lu Ban stories follow a general pattern. There is some difficult architectural or engineering feat to be performed at the behest of a cantankerous emperor (probably Yongle). The workmen must meet a certain deadline for the project or the emperor will have their heads. They despair of finding the solution until someone, usually an old man, presents an idea in cryptic form, shows an odd object, or makes a mysterious statement that solves the problem. After the project has been successfully completed, the old man disappears and the workers realize that it was Lu Ban who helped them out of their difficulty.[27]

Let us take the legend of the cricket vendor's basket as an example. When Yongle decided Beijing would be his capital, he sent a trusted minister to the site with orders to build the Forbidden City. At its four corners, rising majestically above the great moat, should be built towers of definite specifications. They must be nine beam (*liang*), eighteen post (*zhu*), seventy-two column (*tiao*) structures. Should the minister fail to carry out these difficult orders with absolute precision, the son of heaven will have his head! Predictably the minister was unable to conceive of a plan for the towers that would satisfy the complicated instructions, so he merely passed on the same command and the same threat to the ordinary workmen. The men sat idly for many days trying to figure out a plan that would appease the imperial demands, as the deadline drew perilously near. Finally, just as their time was used up, an old cricket vendor happened on the scene. His small reed cages were cleverly constructed to the exact specifications made for the four corner towers. After they had finished building the towers, the cricket seller disappeared, but they realized that he was none other than Lu Ban.[28]

There are many other legends in the Jin Shoushen collection. Dragons are often figures in the stories connected with bridges and pools around Beijing. There are stories of Liu Bowen, of Yue Fei, of bridges, wells, temples, lakes, and the famous bell and drum towers. All of them have strong similarities. They deal with a place set apart from its surroundings because of the presence of a sacred person (or one who later becomes divinized), a god or spirit. Miraculous events take place there, and boons are "given" from above. The form of Beijing is given by the immortal Nezha, the form of the towers is given by Lu Ban, victory at Xinbei Bridge is given by Yue Fei, and so forth. Even the seemingly random placement of Beijing's wells is a "system" whose pattern is given by an old man (the guise of an immortal) miraculously.[29]

One of the most striking legends is the "Maiden of the Bronze Cast Bell," in which workers are attempting to cast the huge bell for the Bell Tower at the terminus of the axial way in the northern section of Beijing. As usual, the workmen are under a threat of death by the emperor if they should fail. Mysteriously they are unable to cast the bell successfully until a young maiden, the daughter of the foreman, falls into the molten metal. This accident provides the necessary ingredient, allowing the casting to succeed. More important, the young woman has saved the lives of the workers. The bell is still at the tower, the legend says, and the maiden is honored as a patron spirit by the people who live in the vicinity.

LEGENDS OF THE ALTAR OF HEAVEN

It may seem strange that the altar of heaven, which was forbidden territory to ordinary people, should be the subject of so many legends and stories, some of which show familiarity with rather small details of its architecture. Even though they were not supposed to go inside the vast grounds of the altar of heaven, the people knew that it was the most important site of imperial worship. It may be that the prohibition itself stimulated the popular imagination and increased the sense of importance of the rites that were performed there. But closer to the truth, I think, is that the people often *did* get inside the grounds, or knew someone who did. I will explain my reasons for thinking this after relating some of the legends.

There is a legend of the origin of the altar of heaven that shows some of the elements of humor, earthiness, and irreverence that I mentioned earlier in this chapter. Just as it was impossible for people to believe that the placement and form of Beijing as a whole was random or accidental, they also felt that the place and shape of the altar of heaven was "given" from above. According to one legend, after Yongle established his capital at Beijing, the area suffered a series of progressively more severe years of drought. The people became extremely worried and began reviling "old man heaven" (Laotianye—the popular way of referring to Shangdi, the God of heaven). Yongle came to the realization he was at fault for not properly sacrificing to heaven. Laotianye appeared to him in a dream, looking like "a big fellow whose body was red all over," and instructed him that the empress must perform the prayers for rain.

The god left before answering a very important question in the mind of the emperor. *Where* should the empress pray for rain? The question may seem rather insignificant, but points out how localized the legends are. Each of them shows a great concern for the specificity of place. Soon a mysterious old man appeared in court who said: "The son of heaven is considered yang. Left is the yang way, right the yin." Based on these cryptic words, Yongle's ministers then suggested that the place to pray should be south of the city (the yang direction) and to the left (east), and the emperor agreed. Then the *fengshui* experts were brought in to determine the exact site and they discovered a "lump" on the surface of the earth to the southeast of the city. It was "as hard as porcelain," a sign that this was the precise location of the rain prayers.

At first the empress treated her responsibility lightly, considering this duty no more than a pleasant outing to the countryside. A full day passed, her stomach began to growl, and she became impatient to return to the comforts of the palace. But Yongle had told her that she might not come back until it rained. Finally the evening of the third day arrived. Her mouth was so dry, the legend says, that she could not even spit and her stomach rumbled loudly. The emperor was by this time worried about his consort and decided to go to the altar site himself. At the very moment of his arrival, the sky darkened and the rain fell in torrents. Then Yongle decided that he could not put the empress through this ordeal every year, and on a sudden inspiration, determined to build the altar of heaven on this very spot. Every year thereafter he would go there to worship heaven and pray for harvest, so that heaven would protect and bless the land, and the five grains would be bountiful.[30]

Aside from the origin of the altar of heaven, there are many stories and legends about sites, buildings, and architectural details of the whole complex. There is, for example, a Lu Ban story to explain the origin of the present three-tiered Temple of Heaven. Emperor Jiajing, according to the story, was unhappy with the Temple of Heaven that had been build by Yongle. He wanted to be able to stand in the temple and gaze up at the twenty-eight *su* (astral habitations), the thirty-six heavenly stars (*tiangang*), and looking down see the twenty-four periods of the year that guide the people's agricultural activities. If the master builder cannot build a temple to such specifications, he will be beheaded!

The master builder was convinced that he would fail in such a task. Contemplating suicide, he went to a tavern and drank himself into a stupor. Just at that moment, an old man entered the tavern wearing shabby clothing spattered with mud. The old fellow ordered a bowl of rice, which he gobbled down, then ordered a second and a third. Then he began to complain that the rice was insipid and called three times for salt. Finally the master builder staggered off to get some salt, but when he returned the old man was gone. But on his table were stacked upside down the three empty rice bowls, and propping them up were chopsticks set in a very complicated arrangement that the builder immediately realized was the model he could use to build the Temple of Heaven. Then he knew that this was a miraculous appearance of Lu Ban. The legend then goes on to describe in detail the numerical symbolism that I have already examined in chapter 3.[31]

Other details of the same building attracted the imagination of the people. There is a story about the one hundred white marble dragon water spouts on the top tier of the platform supporting the temple, a folk version of the great ritual controversy of the Jiajing period, and at least three versions of a legend about the phoenix stone in the floor of the building.[32] The stone set in the floor is very much like the center paving stone on the altar of heaven. Directly above it in the ceiling of the temple is the dragon-pearl motif (yang, male, heavenly). Popular understanding called for the yang-dragon above to be paired with the phoenix (yin, female, earthly) below. The round stone in question is of dark green-black marble, and with the help of a little imagination, one can see in the white markings of the stone the form of a phoenix. At the very least, the stone is strikingly different from the stones that surround it.

There are legends, stories, and explanations for almost all the unique details of the altar of heaven complex: the seven stones of the Big Dipper (found just south of the seventy-two pillar arcade), the echo stone of the altar itself, the whispering wall, which embraces the Hall of the Imperial Firmament, the Cinnabar Platform Bridge. Some of them follow the format we have already examined above. When Qianlong ordered the altar of heaven platform remodeled, for example, he demanded that it express in every detail the yang symbolic numbers, expecially 9 and its multiples (once again, this much is perfectly historical), with the usual threat of punishment if the builders cannot produce a plan in three days.

This time the famous mathematician Tai Jiushao sends a spirit to the desperate workmen. He takes the form of a disgustingly dirty young boy who eats like a pig and keeps wiping his greasy mouth on his sleeve. (Many of the legends have the divine beings or their emissaries appear in the most unlikely forms. As in the case of Milofo, the fat Buddha, humans must look beyond mere externals, a point that Monkey also makes in the *Xiyouji*.) He later disappears and the workmen find a scrap of his sleeve on which is the plan for the altar with all elements in multiples of nine. A similar legend tells of the construction of the Cinnabar Platform Bridge under Yongle.[33]

Besides showing a surprisingly accurate knowledge of the symbolism of the altar of heaven, the legends also incorporate many of the figures of popular religion and tradition: Liu Bowen, Lu Ban, the Queen Mother of Heaven, the Jade Emperor, and Taishang Laojun. The large and impressive grounds of the altar of heaven complex, the marvelous buildings and monumental architecture there must have seemed truly supernatural, a sacred place set apart. Even the vegetation that grew there had a special virtue, unique powers that surpassed ordinary vegetation growing outside the walls. There is for example a medicinal plant that grew there called "motherwort" (*Yimucao*). Besides its pharmaceutical use, it could also be eaten as a tender young plant, and in that case it was called "dragonbeard, a favorite dish in Beijing."[34] The herb was sold (and still is) in pharmacies in Beijing and its efficacy was thought to be far greater than the motherwort grown elsewhere. There is a legend to explain why this is so.

Once, long, long ago, a young maiden named Lotus lived with her parents in a small village near the place that would later become the altar of heaven. They scratched out a meager livelihood farming their land. The young Lotus brought great happiness to her parents because she was both beautiful and devoted to them. Then one spring day tragedy struck. The old man became sick and died. So saddened was the mother that she too became weaker by the day and after six months seemed close to death. Lotus frantically summoned doctors and tried all sorts of medicines, but to no avail. Then an old woman of the village told her there was a miraculous herb growing in the northern mountains that could cure women's illnesses, and Lotus determined to set forth on a quest to find it. (Here the legend uses the term *chujia* ["leaving home," the same expression used when a person joins a Buddhist monastery or nunnery] to suggest the religious nature of the quest.)

Lotus endured terrible hardships on her journey to the north. Completely exhausted one night, she fell asleep and an old man appeared to her in her dream. He told her of the location of the magical herb, and that she must traverse "seven steep slopes and follow eight tortuous roads." She awakened and with great determination continued on her way. Finally she found herself on the top of a great mountain where she met two beautiful young women who gave her the plant she was seeking. They also gave her seeds and instructed her to plant them when she returned home to help other ailing women. She thanked them and began her return home, but before she had gone far she turned around saw that the charming women had changed forms, one had now become a white deer and the other a beautiful bird. They were truly immortals. Unlike the slow and difficult trip to find the herb, her trip home was quick and easy. She arrived in time to save her mother and, following the instructions of the two immortals, planted the seeds to help others. Since that time, long ago, the motherwort has grown at the site of the altar of heaven.

But the legend ends with a postscript. Much later, it says, a certain emperor wanted to build an altar of heaven on the spot and when he saw the unkempt condition of the area angrily ordered workers to have all the wild grasses removed. One minister, whose mother had been cured by the motherwort, said to the emperor that the grass was called "dragonbeard" and if it were torn out that he (the emperor) would not be able to grow a beard! The emperor quickly rescinded his order.

The myths and legends of the altar of heaven are both accurate in their knowledge of the builder-emperors Yongle, Jiajing, and Qianlong, and detailed in their knowledge of the architectural elements of the grounds and their symbolism. And although there was a strict prohibition against ordinary people entering the altar of heaven complex, I believe it was not nearly as carefully enforced as that which prevented their entrance into the Forbidden City. The prohibition on the one hand probably piqued curiosity, interest, and a sense of awe in the people, and on the other hand stimulated the human desire to find a way around the regulation.

One legend gives us a hint of this.[35] It tells of a young orphan boy named Miao who was called the "bamboo flute immortal" because he could play the flute with such amazing skill. In his adolescence he found a home in the Taoist Liturgical Music Academy, located in the southwest sector of the altar of heaven complex. The directors were pleased to add him to the corps of liturgical musicians and found him very trustworthy, so they often put him to work tending the grounds.

In the neighborhood nearby where Miao had previously lived there were a number of sick people, and since they knew he had access to the altar grounds, they came and asked him to help them procure some motherwort. Miao knew of the strict prohibition against entry, but pitied the sick people, so he often slipped into the interior of the altar grounds to get the herb, which he made into a salve and gave to the people. Many were cured, and word of this spread like wildfire. With Bodhisattvalike compassion, the young boy spent his entire day making the medicine, which he continued to give away to the people. Soon the director of the academy heard about it. Although angry at the Bamboo Flute Immortal, he knew a good thing when he saw it and immediately conceived the idea of starting a business, a pharmacy that would sell the salve.

The legend explains the origin of the *Jisheng* (saving life) pharmacy operated by the Liturgical Music Academy. The legend indicates that many workers were required to run the business, to work in the fields, and make the salve. But the presence of the academy also brought numerous people from all walks of life to the altar of heaven for other reasons. During the Ming dynasty, the academy housed over six hundred students learning music and dancing to be performed for the imperial rites. The teachers were mostly Taoist priests, some monastic, some married and living in wealthy private homes, and some poor, living on the grounds of the institution.

Many hundreds of people came and went every day. The southwest section of the altar of heaven became a favorite place for outings and parties, drinking and poetry making. Markets, stores, restaurants, taverns, and pharmacies sprang up. The academy continued to function in this fashion through the Ming and into the Qing dynasty. Qianlong tried to control excesses there by removing the Taoist priests and putting court officials in charge, but it was only in 1803, because of an assassination plot against Jiaqing, that the academy was closed to ordinary people and by and large disbanded.[36]

Besides the academy personnel and visitors, many other ordinary people must have had access to the grounds of the altar of heaven: the guards and soldiers who were regularly stationed there and the added numbers sent there at the time of imperial sacrifice, the hundreds of workers who took care of the grounds, the cooks, butchers, and others who prepared the animals at the time of sacrifice. Just south of the Liturgical Music Academy there used to be the stable for raising the hundreds of animals used for the imperial sacrifices. On its grounds were dormitories for herdsmen and caretakers, a milking barn, farm workers to grow the grains and grasses for fodder, a mill, and graneries. Clearly, although the altar of heaven was forbidden to common people, this prohibition was often breached, and surely thousands were able to see various parts of the grounds. The myths and legend were thus often based on personal knowledge, not just hearsay.

A DIFFERENT SACRAL STRUCTURE

Having looked at a number of myths and legends from a variety of sources, we can see that most share certain similarities. In fact the motifs of Beijing's legends are found in many cities of China. Most of the motifs can be found among Wolfram Eberhard's *Types:* the supernatural conception (#51), the age of men (#71), the body from the lotus (#95), the construction sacrifice (#99), the trick of the handworkers (#100), pilgrimage of the maid (#127), and the miraculous building of a temple (#186), just to name a few.[37] All show a concern with specific places, chiefly the walls, towers, gates, wells, bridges, and temples important in everyday lives. But also, as we have seen, the legends show an awareness of the important sites of imperial religion, especially the altar of heaven. The hills to the northwest of Beijing, with their many temples and shrines, and the imperial park—the Yuanmingyuan (formerly) and the Yiheyuan Summer Palaces—were the most important places just outside the capital.[38] An identifying characteristic of these legends is a love and respect for place, a curiosity about the power and prestige of certain places in and around the city. All this is best explained by the concept of sacred space, that certain places are set apart because of a qualitative difference from the areas surrounding them. They are places of power and the legends acknowledge them as such.

A second characteristic of the legends is the awareness of another world or worlds close by, not too different from the everyday world of common experience, except for its greater power. It is the abode of the gods, immortals, ancestors, and ghosts, and these more powerful figures can cross over into this world quite easily. The beings from that world can cause problems in this one, but many of the beings are benevolent and compassionate, and are able to help humans in their difficulties. They manifest themselves in specific places to help specific persons in their various difficulties. The places where they have appeared and the monuments that reveal their miraculous help mark a "sacred geography" of Beijing.

Finally, the legends clearly reveal a belief that the city of Beijing itself, its location, its form, and its greatest monuments, are given from above, by these powerful and wise beings from the other world. Somehow all the important features of the city are too wonderful, too miraculous, to have been simply the production of human endeavor. The divine source of the city and its monuments is the guarantee of its "rightness," its security, and its ability to endure through the centuries, despite rebellions, wars, and natural calamities. As the old Beijing man says in Lao She's novel, *Sishi tongtang*, on the eve of the Japanese occupation, no disturbance can last more than three months in Beijing, because "in all the world there is no city you can depend on more surely. . . . this city is a city that cannot die."

NOTES

1. It is difficult to place historically most of these legends, dealing as they do with events and persons from the time of Yongle, the builder of Beijing as it stands today, to the early twentieth century. Most of them are probably Qing dynasty, though a few perhaps come from the Ming period. Wang Canchi, *Beijing shidi*, p. 204, lists about thirty books or collections of legendary material from Beijing.

2. For the classical formulation of the relationship of terrestrial and celestial geography, see Edouard Chavannes, *Mémoires Historiques*, introduction and the section called "Celestial Governors."

3. Biot, *Le Tcheou-Li*, 2:532.

4. Needham, *Science*, 3:229–30, suggests that the reason that Chinese astronomy was polar and equatorial, rather than ecliptic or zodiacal like the Greek, was the background of microcosmic-macrocosmic thinking. "The celestial pole corresponded to the position of the emperor on earth, around whom the vast system of the bureaucratic agrarian state naturally and spontaneously revolved."

5. *Rixia jiuwen kao*, I (1), 3–6.

6. These correspondences may be seen at a glance in Schlegel, *Uranographie*, 1:76ff.

7. *Rixia jiuwen kao*, I (1), 13.

8. Chavannes, *Mémoires Historiques*, 1:27, has two brief versions of this battle myth. A good study of the significance of the Huangdi myths is given in Charles Le Blanc, "A Re-Examination of the Myth of Huang-ti," *Journal of Chinese Religions*, nos. 13 and 14 (Fall 1985 and 1986), 45–63. See also Jan Yun-hua, "The Change of Images: The Yellow Emperor in Ancient Chinese Literature," *Journal of Oriental Studies*, 19, no. 2 (1981), 33–34, where Huangdi is called "an ancestor, a warrior, a ruler, a god and the God on High."

9. *Rixia jiuwen kao* II (2), 1.

10. Le Blanc "Re-Examination," says, p. 52, that "as teacher of civilized institutions . . . the following categories should be attributed to Huang Ti [the list does not intend to be exhaustive]: the proper naming of things, astronomy, the calendar, measures, music, writing, historical records, Taoism as an esoteric doctrine, the distinction of sexes, marriage, tailored clothes, sacrificial rites, funeral rites, medicine, the chariot, and so on." I have found that the story of the yellow emperor is still recounted in the textbooks of primary school, both in Taiwan and the Peoples Republic, as part of China's legendary history.

11. Le Blanc, "Re-examination," p. 62.

12. *Rixia jiuwen kao*, II (4), 1.

13. E. T. C. Werner, *Myths and Legends of China* (London: George Harrap, 1922), pp. 328–29. Liu Bowen, or Liu Ji, was an important minister under Hongwu, and died in 1375, long

before Zhu Di left Nanjing to become prince of Yan. Hok-lam Chan says that "his exceptional qualities as a politician and scholar have been attributed to his possession of occult powers, while the stories thus created have transformed him into a legendary Taoist mystic and efficacious prognosticator." In September 1366 Hongwu entrusted him with designing a plan for enlarging Nanjing to ready it as the dynastic capital. We can see traces of both these historic facts interwoven in the story of Beijing as Nezha city. Liu's biography is in *DMB*, pp. 932–38.

14. E. T. C. Werner, *A Dictionary of Chinese Mythology* (New York: 1969), pp. 247–49.

15. The problem of securing good water for the city has always plagued Beijing. Hwang Ming-chorng, "Study," p. 128, discusses the problems of the city's water supply, listing the bitter (polluted) and sweet wells in the Qing dynasty. It is no wonder than wells and water sources were the subject of so many Beijing legends.

16. Yao Guangxiao was in fact an advisor to Zhu Di. He was a Buddhist monk who was both an important religious and political figure, having skills in divination, physiognomy, persuasion, and a conviction of Zhu Di's imperial destiny. After the prince regent became Yongle he made Yao the junior preceptor to the heir apparent, and Yao remained an important figure in court for the next decade. He died in 1418, just after Yongle ordered Beijing rebuilt as the national capital. See his biography in *DMB*, pp. 1561–65.

17. Recounted in Jin Shoushen, *Beijing ti chuanshuo* (Beijing legends) (Beijing: Tongsu wenhua chubanshe, 1957), pp. 23–26. This book has been translated into English by Gladys Yang and published in 1982 by Panda Books.

18. Arlington and Lewisohn, *Old Peking*, Appendix B, p. 338. See the geomantic chart of the city in the form of a human body on pp. 336–37. Unfortunately, the chart cannot be easily understood, since Qian Gate is the only actual element of the city indicated.

19. Juliet Bredon, *Peking*, p. 36.

20. *Shuntianfu zhi*, I, pp. 186–87.

21. Ibid. The appearance and interpretation of this sort of auspicious sign is common in dynastic annals. During the Jiajing reign, the emperor transferred a building of worship for imperial ancestors and gave it a new name. After the ancestral tablets were installed, it auspiciously "rained money." Another source repeats the incident, adding the information that most of the money fell on a military bureau! See Qu Xuanying, *Beiping shibiao*, p. 137.

22. Jonathan Spence, *Emperor of China*, p. 150.

23. Werner, *Myths and Legends*, pp. 232ff.

24. Jin Shoushen, *Beijingdi*, p. 17.

25. Ibid., pp. 17–22.

26. Werner, *Dictionary*, p. 81.

27. Jin Shoushen, *Beijingdi*, pp. 3–16. The legends are those of "the Cricket Vendor's Basket," "the Mender of Large Objects," "Moving a Bell," "the *Fa* Pagoda," and "Pouring out the Honey and Increasing the Salt."

28. We have already seen these symbolic numbers of 9, 18, and 72 as they figured in the construction of the altar of heaven and other important sites. While it may seem surprising that the popular legend has preserved the cosmic numbers so accurately, it is rather common, as we shall see again. Hwang Ming-chorng says that the corner towers are "probably the most complex structures in Chinese ancient architecture" ("Study," p. 53). Lu Ban was the acknowledged patron of carpenters, called upon for building projects great and small. One Western observer, while having a house built, noticed that the workers offered sacrifice to Lu Ban. At the crucial moment of raising the ridgepole, they sang: "the posts must be placed truly when a fortunate day arrives, the ridgepole must be raised when Fate decrees we meet the Star of the Purple Enclosure" (Florence Ayschough, *A Chinese Mirror* [Boston: Houghton Mifflin, 1925], p. 40).

29. Jin Shoushen, *Beijingdi*, pp. 38–40.

30. Jia Qunnuo and Wang Chengyong, *Tiantan jingwu chuanshuo* (Beijing: Zhongguo minjian wenyi chubanshe, 1987), pp. 1–3.

31. Ibid., pp. 7–8.

32. Ibid., pp. 9–10, 14–16, 17–19.

33. Ibid., pp. 23–25, 35–38.

34. Checking this herb in a Chinese botanical dictionary, I found that *Yimucao, Leonurus heterophyllus*, is an herb that grows all over China, and can survive at elevations up to 3400 m. "The whole plant is used to make a medicine which is beneficial to treating various gynecological problems."

35. Wang Chenyong, *Tiantan*, pp. 56–59.

36. Ibid., pp. 39–42.

37. Wolfram Eberhard, *Typen chinesischen Volksmärchen*, Helsinki, 1937.

38. See Zhang Yuchang and Peng Zheyu, eds., *Beijing qingdai chuanshuo* (Beijing: Chunfeng Wenyi chubanshe, 1984), a collection of 75 legends of Qing dynasty Beijing, the great majority of which are set in the northwestern hills.

Chapter 5

Beijing in
Comparative Perspective

> Outside the walls of Peking in 1601 Ricci kept always with him
> some grains of soil from the Holy Land and a tiny cross made,
> he believed, from fragments of the true cross on which Christ
> had died.

—Jonathan Spence, *The Memory Palace of Matteo Ricci*

The purpose of this chapter is to establish the validity of the distinction betwen the two structures of the sacred that have been implicit in this book, the cosmocized sacred city and the city of local sacrality. These are meant as heuristic devices, not exclusive or comprehensive categories. Other categories are possible, such as the "city of the saints," a description that focuses on morality as the defining quality of a certain city, like Geneva of John Calvin's time, or Anabaptist Münster, or Mormon Salt Lake City.

There are other ways to sacralize a city than the two I have dealt with. As he writes about the transfer of the Sri Lankan capital from Anuradhapura to Polonnaruva in the ninth century, Bardwell Smith uncovers a number of ways that rulers attempted to legitimate this move, to "manifest the transcendent within the ephemeral, to generate symbols of unity within the plural."[1] Besides the use of cosmic symbols like Mt. Kailasa, the four world protectors, and building on a large scale, there was, for example, a conscious linking up with the past capital and religious traditions (which is unlike the Chinese situation) by having the kings crowned in Anuradhapura and obtaining the tooth relic and alms bowl as legitimizing insignia in the new city.

When I began research on Beijing, I felt that it was important to establish that it was either a cosmic sacred city or a city of local sacrality. That question now seems beside the point, since Beijing obviously shares characteristics of both types. From the point of view of the emperor and his advisors, the cosmic elements are more important, while from the perspective of ordinary people, manifestations of local sacrality are more significant. In every religiously important city that I have studied, I have found evidence of both patterns embedded in the lore and history of the city. However, I still believe that these types are heuristically useful ways of analyzing the religious meaning of a city. The purpose of this chapter is to test this view in a comparative context.

It is a truism that every culture is different and in a strict sense incomparable. Superficial comparisons can be very harmful to accurate understanding and damaging to the uniqueness of the phenomenon studied. Therefore I undertake this chapter with hesitation and some misgivings. Still, much comparative work has already been done in urban studies, and if done carefully, both similarities and differences can be enlightening. Such similarities as there are have often been explained by diffusionism, which is possible and likely in some cases, but in other cases cultural diffusion is an impossible hypothesis. The similarities rather seem to reveal something about human nature. City as symbol can engender similar patterns of response and understanding, even in cultures cut off from one another in time and space.

Besides developing the typology of the sacred city, the object of this final chapter is to examine how various cultures have sacralized certain of their cities, or better, how people of diverse cultures have perceived the city as a sacred form. Having done this, I will be able to put Beijing in a comparative context, learning not only something about the Chinese, but perhaps something about human nature itself.

Though various cities of the world have been called "sacred" or "holy," it is not always clear what writers mean when they use those terms. And although many such cities have been the object of scholarly research, I am not aware of any study that has looked at the whole range of possibilities in a systematic way. In fact, the assumption often seems to be that "sacred city" always means approximately the same thing. One of the widest ranging and most amply documented studies is by the German scholar Müller.[2] Yet one can immediately perceive gaps in the study, noting that renowned sacred cities like Mecca and Banaras are not considered. And Jerusalem is not studied as a *real* city, but only in terms of the cosmic symbolism that coalesced around it in medieval times. More fundamentally, Mircea Eliade's thought has provided a basic framework for the study of the city as a carrier of sacred meanings. Paul Wheatley's studies of the origins of Asian cities have probably given greater impetus to the study of urban cosmology and symbolism than the works of any other author writing today.[3] Let me add immediately that I do not presume that this chapter can make up for the comprehensive study that is lacking. This book is mainly about Beijing, and I use in it categories that are useful in analyzing it. But I believe that these categories can also be helpful in the study of other sacred cities.

Since these two types I am dealing with have been roughly outlined for the Chinese context in earlier chapters, I will not repeat the distinctions here. In the interests of simplicity I will hereafter call the cosmic sacred city the "sacred city" and the city of local sacrality the "holy city." In the comparative material that follows, my objective is obviously not to attempt an adequate study of any particular city. I am using other scholars' research to aid in my own search for a basis for the religious interpretation of Beijing.

THE SACRED CITY

The first striking element in the sacred city is its orientation in space, its alignment with the geometry of the universe. Tradition has it that Rome, *Roma sacra*, was founded with augury and rites similar to those we have seen used in China.[4] Heaven was thought to be divided into four sections by two axes, *cardo* and *decumanus*. The earthly site for the capital was accordingly oriented by the intersection of the same two axes, *decumanus* running east-west to follow the path of the sun, *cardo* traced north to south from the pole star, and giving the city the name *Roma quadrata*. The outer limits of the city were fixed, according to the ancient Etruscan ritual, by the founder plowing a furrow in a circuit that described the borders of the future city. This was called the *pomerium*, and the clods of earth turned up by the plow were then dutifully thrown within the sacred orbit. When the locations for the future gates were reached, the plow was carefully lifted to avoid scoring the earth. Within this circumscribed area, the space was sacred and called the *templum*.

By the fact that the cosmic axes crossed in the center of the city, Rome was considered to be the center of the world. This intersection was marked by a pit called the *mundus*, a passage to the netherworld by which the *manes*, or ancestors, rose to the surface three times yearly to receive the sacrifices of the living. Thus the stone that covered the pit was called the *lapis manalis*. The orientation and centering symbolism, together with the preliminary augury and geomantic precautions for Rome and Chinese capitals, are strikingly similar.[5]

The sources referring to the foundation are early and fragmentary, and most of these features have been obliterated in the subsequent development of Rome. Archaeological evidence for the ideal Roman city can be found only at Marzabotto, fifteen miles south of Bologna, which was founded about 500 B.C. It had an acropolis with temple and other sacred buildings, and was laid out on a gridiron plan. It had an outer defensive wall, and the inside *pomerium* was oriented to the four cardinal points, with *cardo* and *decumanus*.[6]

Later rapid growth in Rome's population spilled over the *pomerium* and the old religious boundary has completely disappeared. But conceptions of a cosmic sacred capital in the center of the world were never completely lost. In imperial times, these ancient Roman ideals were re-awakened and stimulated by contacts with the Near East. Nero had a revolving rotunda in the *Domus Aurea* (his palace), suggesting that his throne commanded all directions from the center of the world, and he was represented in a number of images as the god Apollo Helios. The poet Lucan exhorted Nero to have his throne in the middle of the universe, or the cosmos might lose its equilibrium. "If you rest on a single side of the immeasurable ether, the axis of the world will not stand the weight. Maintain the equilibrium of the firmament in the circle of the universe."[7]

Orientation and strong centralizing symbolism were also important features of Near Eastern cities up through Sassanian times. In Mesopotamia and the ancient Near East often only small areas of the ancient urban sites have actually been excavated. Yet a careful look at plans and aerial photographs leaves little room for doubt that the principles of orientation, axiality, and centralizing symbolism were key factors in the planning of these cities.

One of the best excavated cities of the Near East is Ur, which occupied an irregularly shaped mound, but had its monumental ritual complex oriented with its corners to the cardinal points. Within the complex were ziggurat and temples to the moon god Nannar, to the divine couple Nannar and Nin-gal, and a sacred way that led through a double gateway into a large paved courtyard, belonging to the temple of Dublamakh.[8] It is commonly said that sacral kingship in the Near East found its expression in cosmic cities, but a precise chronology of kingship and city building is lacking. According to literary sources, both had their origins "in the heavens." The Sumerian king list says that "when kingship was lowered from heaven, the kingship was in Eridu." The city itself seemed so wondrous a thing that only a god could have created it, in Egypt Ptah or Re, in Babylon, Marduk.[9] In the earliest Mesopotamian cities there was apparently no king, but a kind of theocracy through the rule of priests, while the god was said to be "owner" of the city. Whether royal or sacerdotal figures were at the top of the hierarchy, we may see in the orientation, axiality, and centrality of these cities an expression of the desire, already documented in regard to Beijing, to conform to the pattern of the cosmos:

> Analogy was inverted to produce a basic axiom that the topography of the heavens was established first and the world was made in its image. Man, in order to assure security for the world and thus for himself, should in his constructions remain true to the pattern of heaven. Architecture, man's most conspicuous modification of natu-

ral environment, was as a matter of prudence . . . controlled by cosmic imitation.[10]

Besides the basic layout of the city, placement of individual temples, ziggurats, and royal dwellings followed the same principles. Another constant feature was the presence of the sacred processional or arterial way that links the principal components of the nuclear city, often vividly demonstrating the relationship between gods, priests, and ruler. Their remains have been excavated in Babylon, Assur, and Hattusa, and literary sources tell of one in Uruk.[11]

Babylon, oriented with its corners to the cardinal points, is particularly interesting as an example of a cosmocized city. It has been convincingly reconstructed and there exists a contemporary description of the city by Herodotus:

> The following is a description of the place. The city stands on a broad plain, and is an exact square, fifteen miles in length each way, so the entire circuit is sixty miles. . . . It is surrounded, in the first place, by a broad and deep moat, full of water, behind which rises a wall fifty royal cubits in width, and 200 in height. . . . The city is divided into two portions by the river which runs through the midst of it. . . . The streets all run in straight lines, not only those parallel to the river, but also the cross streets which lead down to the waterside. . . . The outer wall is the main defense of the city. There is, however, a second inner wall, of less thickness than the first, but very little inferior to it in strength. The centre of each division of the town was occupied by a fortress. In the one stood the palace of the kings, surrounded by a wall of great strength and size: in the other was the sacred precinct of Zeus Belus, an enclosure a quarter of a mile square, with gates of solid brass; which was also remaining in my time. In the middle of the precinct there was a tower of solid masonry, a furlong in length and breadth, upon which was raised a second tower, and on that a third, and so on up to eight. . . . On the topmost tower there is a spacious temple, and inside the temple stands a couch of unusual size. . . . They also declare (but I do not believe it) that the god comes down in person into this chamber, and sleeps on the couch.[12]

The mention of the ziggurat brings up a problem of interpretation. Earlier authors saw it as a "ladder to heaven," while more recently it has been interpreted as a kind of cosmic mountain and source of fertility.[13] Whatever the interpretation, the ziggurat remains the special point of contact with the gods, the place of worship. In this sense it is comparable to the altar of heaven in Beijing. Both are monumental architectural forms, articulated into the overall plan of the city by their position in relation to the axial-processional way. Both are tiered structures, but the architectural expression is different. The ziggurat reaches up to the heavens, a vertical assertion of human ability to reach toward the gods. The altar of heaven is "open" to the celestial influence, horizontal, and therefore more expressive of human receptivity toward the will of heaven. These contrasting forms, similar in basic significance, are obviously rooted in unique features of each of the two cultures. Furthermore, the two structures were a particularization of the symbolism of the cosmic city, the sacred place where the ruler (priest), mediator between heavenly and earthly realms, contacts the gods. As the myth of Nannar states: "Behold the bond of Heaven and Earth, the city. . . . Behold Nippur, the city."[14]

Besides the pre-Aryan sites of Harrapa, India is not usually considered a home of the cosmic sacred city. However, there are ideals of a cosmic city that can be found in classical Indian sources. They favor a square or rectangular form for the royal city, with twelve gates, and three roads running east-west, three north-south. The royal residence was to be just to the north of the center of the city, while the actual center was given over to the apartments of the gods. An attempt was also made to reflect the framework of human society in the layout of the royal city. Ideally, Kshatriyas (warrior class) were to live in the eastern quarter, Vaisyas (merchant class) to the south, Sudras (servant class) to the west, and Brahmins (priestly class) to the north. Supporting this social segregation was a whole range of correspondences meant to differentiate further the separate areas: a correlation of colors (Brahmins white, Kshatriyas red, Vaisyas yellow, Sudras black), odors, tastes, kinds of trees, and so forth, which reminds one of the endless categories of the five-phase school in China.[15] Furthermore, the royal city also reflected the Indian pantheon. The scheme of the systematizers assigned various parts of the city to many of the important gods of the Vedic pantheon. The central sections were identified with Brahma and the greater gods, the outlying quarters with lesser divinities. Like the Roman *pomerium*, the limits of the Indian royal cities were to be marked by the drawing of the plough, but unlike Rome the Indian city's border was thought to be purified by the droppings of grazing cows.[16] Whether any ancient Indian city approximated these ideal arrangements is a moot question, since there is no archaeological evidence available. Certain cities in Sri Lanka, however, have been reported to show some features of the classical plans.[17]

The manner in which cosmic cities expressed centralizing symbolism varied according to the indigenous concepts of divinity and the role of the sacred king. In the Indian classical ideal, not only was the city understood to be located at the conjunction of the four quadrants, but there was an apartment or temple of Brahma at the exact center of the city. The cities of southeast Asia—Burma, Thailand, and Indo-China—are completely consonant with the cosmic pattern we have been examining. They have orientation, axiality, sacred kingship, and show in addition concrete centralizing symbols at the center of the city, principally the cosmic mountain and the linga.[18] In other cases, as we have seen in China, the urban architectural center is muted or diffused, while the ruler himself is the "living" center.

Although there are no archeological remains of the classic Indian city, today's temple cities, particularly in South India, probably give us a good idea of what they were supposed to be, cities like Kanchipuram and Madurai. Madurai was built according to the pattern of a sacred cosmic diagram or mandala, oriented to the four cardinal directions, with a series of concentric streets delimiting a square and focusing on a temple at the city's center. Before the medieval period, Mandurai was also a "palace city," with the Pandyan king residing in his royal palace at the center.[19]

In the cities of the later Near East, up through the Persian period, as in China, the royal ruler's throne was considered to be the center of the universe and the city. These cities were also oriented to the four directions, but the favored form was round, not square or rectangular. Herodotus again tells us of the great round city of Ecbatana, built by Deioces, legendary first king of the Medes:

> Rising in circles, one within the other. . . . The number of the circles is seven, the royal palace and treasuries standing within the last. . . . Of this wall the battlements are white, of the next black, of the third scarlet, of the fourth blue, of the fifth orange; all these are coated with paint. The two last have their battlements coated respectively with silver and gold.[20]

Since some of the ziggurats had layers of different colors, it is not impossible that Ecbatana was modeled on them, the city itself conceived as a sacred mountain.

The same round plan was employed in the building of Parthian Drabjird and Sassanian Firuzabad, serving to emphasize the exalted status of the sacred king, whose kingdom mirrored the rule of the sun in the heavens. The king, among his vassals and satraps, was a reflection of the heavenly hierarchy, as can be seen in the titles given to Near Eastern rulers from Babylonian through Sassanian times: "Sun of Babylon," "King of the Universe," "King of the Four Quadrants of the World," "Brother of the Sun and Moon":

> Is there not a striking correspondence between the cosmic titles of the king and his place in the cosmic city? Wall and fosse are traced

mathematically with the compass, as an image of the heavens, a projection of the upper hemisphere on earth. Two axis streets, one running north-south and the other east-west, divide the city into four quadrants which reflected the four quarters of the world. At the very point of intersection . . . sits the king, "the axis and pole of the world."[21]

The Persian King Khusrau is said to have had a revolving throne or throne room, serving to emphasize further the central position of his royal throne in the universe. The fixed stars, the twelve signs of the zodiac, the seven planets, and the moon were in some fashion made to move through their phases and revolve around the throne. The source of this idea was the astral religion of the neo-Babylonians, passed on to the Persians from the Chaldeans. Heaven and earth were imagined as interdependent, things occuring in this world being a reflection of the upper universe. The terrestrial order governed by the king mirrored the heavenly order under the Sun God Marduk.[22] Needless to say, this conception finds its exact parallel in the Chinese imperial ideology we have examined.

Even after the Persian period had ended, one can see traces of the same concepts in an unlikely place: Baghdad, built by the second Abbasid caliph Mansur. Evidently the plan of the city was as much influenced by Mansur's desire to follow in the glories of the Sassanian kings as by the religious ideals of Islam. The construction began at a propitious moment in 762 C.E., chosen by Naubakht, the caliph's official astrologer. The foundations were laid with Sagittarius in the ascendency and the caliph set the first brick himself, an act recalling the ancient Sumerian belief that the royal builder should work with his own hands on the building. The city was perfectly round, with four gates on the intermediate points of the compass. Mansur declared that the sovereign should live in the center of all and be equidistant from all.[23]

Since the excavation of the Aztec city of Tenochtitlan in the late 1970s, especially its monumental Templo Mayor, we have learned more about this example of a cosmic sacred city.[24] It provides many parallels to the Chinese tradition. A divine omen, an eagle alighting on a nopal cactus, led the Aztecs to the exact spot for building their city. Successively enlarged as Aztec power grew, the city had four causeways emerging from a ceremonial center and was considered the navel of the earth, the place where the superterrestrial cosmos (with its thirteen layers) was joined to the subterranean realm (of nine layers) below.

There was a fivefold division of space (four quarters and a center), and a great deal of symbols and symbolic ritual dealing with center and periphery. Similar to the rituals at the Chinese altar of land and grain, vassal states brought precious stones to cast into the base of Templo Mayor, a symbol of the integration of the empire. There was also a fundamental dualism in Aztec thought embodied in the twin towers of the temple architecture, one representing the god Tlaloc (rain, night, earth), the other Huitzilapochtli (dry, day, sky).

In an interesting contrast with the Chinese capital, the rituals carried out at Templo Mayor were highly dramatic and meant to be seen by the populace. The temple provided an "impressive visual perspective," and the rites performed, with their "lavish use of gold, splendid feathers, and beautifully woven materials, combined with the dramatic power of the ceremonies, must have had an overwhelming effect upon the spectator—an effect that cannot be grasped in modern secular terms."[25] Obviously an ideal polity very different from the Chinese was at work there.

It would be possible to consider further examples of the same phenomenon, but I hope we have examined enough already to establish the existence of a fairly consistent conceptual pattern.[26] The search for an ideal "type" is always selective, shaving away the edges of variety to achieve an interpretative clarity that does not exist in reality. Yet such ideal types can still be helpful tools of analysis. The cities in the cultural areas we have discussed, while differing in many respects, do share a fundamental conception of the universe and their relation to it. In the celestial vault, source of light and heat, dryness and rain, wind and storms, they perceive an impressive order. They see it in the stars, in the regular movement of sun, moon, and planets. These cultures see in the heavens awesome manifestations of power, given patterns, reference points, predictability, omens and signs, all of which have meaning for the world below. We could say that they saw in *both* the predictable and the unpredictable manifestations of a sacred power (which they admittedly conceive of in differing ways) a reality (or the "supra-real" as Malraux has put it) to which they respond in remarkably similar ways. The result is what we have called a cosmic religion, sacred kings, and the royal cities, which are all attempts to find security in the universe they inhabit.

Let me conclude by summarizing some of the most general features of these cities. (1) Orientation, which is the attempt to lay out a city in accord with the geometry of the cosmos. We have seen this accomplished with both round and square plans. Sometimes the cities are bisected by axial streets leading toward the four directions, sometimes the corners of the city point toward them. The processional way, which graphically articulates the relationship between god, priest, and ruler, is most frequently one of these axial ways.

(2) Symbolism of centrality. In some cases the city itself is called the center of the world, in others there is a further monumental emphasis on centrality achieved by the use of a well to the underworld, a cosmic

mountain, a linga, the temple of the god(s), or a royal palace. The particular expression of centrality seems to be a function of the culture's view of the sacred ruler and his relationship to the gods. In any case, contact with the cosmic power is strongest at the center and flows outward, becoming ever-more diluted as it reaches the boundaries of the known world.

(3) Throne of the sacred king. Though earlier stages, as in the ancient Near East, point to a possible theocracy through the medium of priests, the city inevitably later becomes the throne of the sacred king, whether in China, southeast Asia, classical India, the Near East, Mesoamerica, or Rome. The sacred king is the channel of divine power, the conduit through whom the blessings and warnings of the divine beings are brought to earth. Thus the responsibility for the good or ill fortune of the whole national family ultimately rests upon the ruler.[27]

(4) Stratified social order. The societies that live in the sacred cities we have been considering seem to be inevitably highly structured, hierarchical, with clear differentiation of social functions. The cities are "an expression of hierarchy in concrete form." The social order and urban structure seem to mirror the same underlying reality: the organizational conception that made possible the creation of both city and society. For these cities are clear geometrical forms, not just the result of spontaneous organ growth, an urban agglomeration. They were, in a word, planned, with all that that implies.

(5) The plan of the earthly city somehow takes its model from the heavens, in structure and also in function, for the earthly hierarchy imitates the divine pattern of government. The cosmic city is not just one city among others, but *the* city, node of upper and lower worlds, center and pivot of the four quarters of the terrestrial plane. In certain cases, there is direct reference to a celestial city in the stars, such as the purple protected enclosure of Chinese tradition. Babylonian cities also have their archetypes in the constellations: Sippara in Cancer, Niveveh in Ursa Major, Assur in Arcturus.[28] Rome, too, as we have seen, had its model in the heavens, its *templum* or sacred area reflecting Jove's *templum* in the sky.[29] The same may be said for India.[30] In other cases we have to be content to say that the orientation and planning of the earthly city reflects or harmonizes with the order of the cosmos.

THE CITY OF LOCAL SACRALITY

There is another type of religiously symbolic city that differs in nearly every respect from the type I have just delineated, which I will call the "holy city." It is clearly represented by such religious centers as Mecca, Banaras, and Jerusalem, although the case of the latter is made extremely complex by its long and checkered history, as well as by its connection with three major contemporary faiths. In these cities there is no recognizable geometry of form, no evidence of overall planning, no relationship to a sacred king, no orientation or axial way. To say in a word what characterizes these cities, it is sacrality of place: the man-made and natural objects it contains are sacred, the very ground of the city is holy ground. Therefore, another way of contrasting these two ideal types is by the terms "space" and "place." The sacred city has religious meaning because it is space organized according to a sacred model. The holy city has religious meaning because it simply *is* at a certain locus in the environment. Let us look at some examples.

On the way to Mecca, custom has marked out "stations" called *miqat*, on all the roads that lead to the city. At these places, pilgrims to the holy city must perform a complete ablution, and begin to observe numerous clothing, cleansing, and sexual restrictions in preparation for entering the *haram*, the sacred territory of the city of Mecca.[31] Similarly, there is the *Panchkoshi* or "sacred boundary" forming the circuit of Banaras. Along the length of the road are posted gods to watch over the boundary and it is said that while "even a foot or an inch beyond its precincts is devoid of any special virtue, every inch of soil within the boundary is, in the Hindu's imagination, hallowed."[32]

The condition of local sacrality may be recognized by the desire of persons to die within the sacred precincts or be buried there. It is considered blessed to die on pilgrimage in Mecca. Many thousands lie buried where they fell at Arafa, a testimony to their piety in fulfilling the grueling requirement that even aged pilgrims stand in the hot sun from noon to sunset listening to the *Khatib*'s sermon.[33] Many persons of the Jewish, Christian, and Islamic faiths have been buried on the Mount of Olives in Jerusalem in hopes of rising first on the last day, for it is said that the Judgment will be held in Jerusalem. Earth from Jerusalem was placed in the coffins of Christians around the world in the belief that it would speed the corpse's decomposition as well as its eventual resurrection. Muslims believe that whoever dies in Jerusalem is assured of ascending into heaven and whoever fasts there will escape hell.[34] "Happy the Hindu who dies in Banaras," quotes Havell, "for he is transported to Shiva's Himalayan paradise," whereas if he should die in the unhallowed ground across the Ganges, he would fear being reborn as an ass. Most of the palaces that line the Ganges at Banaras were at one time occupied by old retainers of the princes and nobles, who were given the privilege of spending their last days in Shiva's city, so that when they die they may be transported at once into *Shivaloksa*, the abode of bliss. Anyone at all who dies in Banaras gains liberation from the earthly cycles of samsara.[35]

When we inquire into the source of local sacrality, we are confronted with the same sorts of phenomena already described in regard to Beijing: sacred objects, sacred persons, places hallowed by miraculous events. The story of Jerusalem is too well known by Westerners to require any extended discussion here. The city was founded by the first Jewish monarch, David, on the site of the old Jebusite capital, and its subsequent history provided the scene where the great Hebrew prophets worked and the successors of David ruled. It contained the rock on which the Solomonic temple was built and today has the famous Wailing Wall. It was also, according to the rabbis, the site of the foundational event, for God began to create the entire world from Zion. It was the place where the climactic events of the Christian faith occurred, the crucifixion and resurrection of Christ. Less well known to Christians are many traditions connected with Islam. Muhammad is believed to have experienced the night journey here, when he was carried up to heaven to behold celestial glories.[36]

As I mentioned, the status of Jerusalem is complex. Jonathan Z. Smith interprets the city as originally a sacred city, becoming a holy city (as I am using these terms) only later in its history. Jerusalem is what it is because of the temple, and the temple could have been built anywhere. There were in fact other rival shrines like Bethel, which might have been chosen. Jerusalem was built by royal prerogative at a place of royal choosing:

> Later Jewish traditions will develop a complex mythology of the temple site and its "stone of foundation" stretching from creation to final redemption, but this is only developed in the absence of temple, king, and priest. Under such conditions, the temple needs legitimation, needs to be perceived as not arbitrary, precisely because it no longer plays an ordering role.[37]

To use my own terms, Jerusalem was transformed from a sacred city to a holy city, in both Jewish and Christian traditions.

Mecca is more important to Muslims than Jerusalem, and more ancient. It was first built by the angels *before* creation, then successively rebuilt by Adam, his sons, Abraham, and finally by the Curaysh, the family of Muhammad.[38] Of its sacred objects, by far the most conspicuous was the ancient "temple" at the center of Mecca called the Ka'ba (cube). It partakes of the antiquity of Mecca, having been erected by Abraham from stones quarried in three separate mountains, one overlooking Mecca itself, the others Mt. Hermon and the Mt. of Olives. When the walls reached the proper height, Abraham stepped on a stone that still shows the imprint of his feet. The black stone embedded in the wall of the Ka'ba, which the pilgrims kiss, was sent down from heaven by the angel Gabriel. It was originally white, but acquired its present color through contact with the sin and impurity of the pagan period. There is also a depression along the northeast side of the Ka'ba called a kneeding trough, where Abraham and Ishmael mixed mortar to build the holy place. Nearby is another stone marking the spot where Muhammad and the angel Gabriel prayed together, and on the northwest side a semicircular structure of stone built above the tombs of Hagar and Ishmael.[39]

The religious geography of Banaras is similar to that of Mecca and Jerusalem. The lords of cyclic creation and destruction, Vishnu and Shiva, have left their mark all over the landscape. There is, for example, the Manikarnika ghat, one of the most important, which boasts a well dug by Vishnu and filled with perspiration from his body. Another important object of devotion is the marble slab with Vishnu's footprints, where the god is said to have alighted before beginning to worship Shiva (recall that Banaras is Shiva's city). There is also a huge black stone, six feet high and twelve in circumference, where Shiva issued forth when the gods assembled to offer sacrifice. Among Banaras's many sacred wells, there is another said to be dug by Shiva. But the most significant religious fact about the city is not the many individual places of hierophany, but that Shiva actually *lives* there.[40]

Buddhist sacred sites at the Deer Park at Sarnath, just northeast of Banaras, together with the Hindu sites of the city proper, make the area holy to two traditions. Stupas mark the place where Gautama first turned the wheel of the law, where he predicted the coming of Maitreya, where the latter, then a bodhisattva, accepted his vocation, a reservoir where the Tathagata bathed, another where one can see in the stone the marks of the Buddha's garments, and so forth.[41]

Nearly every temple, shrine, and ghat in the city has a legend connecting a god or divine event with its founding. As one pilgrimage book puts it: "Making a pilgrimage there in Banaras every day for a whole year, still she did not reach all the sacred places. For in Banaras there is a sacred place at every step."[42] But the most important "thing" in Banaras is really not an object, but the River Ganges itself. Sent down from heaven by the goddess Ganga, falling over Shiva's brow, its waters are powerful enough to cleanse both spiritual and physical ailments. Along the banks of the river are crowded the famous ghats where devout pilgrims and worshipers from all over the subcontinent come to bathe and where the funeral pyres are lit on which to cremate the bodies of the dead. So sacred is the water considered that it is carried away by homeward-bound pilgrims for use in domestic ritual and healing.[43]

Using the information that we have examined so far, we can now begin to isolate the characteristics of the city of local sacrality, the holy city. The dominant quality is the city's utter specificity, its uniqueness, while that of the cosmic city is universality gained through imitation of a model or archetype. The city of local sacrality is a clearly defined topos, a portion of land whose very soil is holy. There is an almost physical quality to this holiness because it is connected with things, places, objects. The holy city is also typically a destination for pilgrimage where priests or cult leaders minister to the needs of pilgrims.

The cosmic sacred city, on the other hand, is the product and expression of a highly structured and hierarchical society. Perhaps originally founded by a priestly elite, it later usually comes to be ruled by a sacred king who is also high priest of the rites performed there. The locally sacred city may conceivably have a royal figure and a hierarchical society, but it is not essentially related to the nature of the city and sometimes in fact exists in tension with it. Eck says that Banaras "has rarely been an important political center, and the rise and fall of kings through its long history have had no role in the tale of the city's sanctity told by its own people. . . . It is not the events of its long history that make it significant to Hindus; rather it has such a long history . . . *because* it is significant to Hindus."[44]

In contrast we may recall the cosmic city of the Vedic-Hindu tradition where the center is assigned to the ruler and the four quarters to the four classes of society—priests, warriors, merchants, and serfs—while outcasts are banned. Banaras, on the other hand, has an egalitarian character. It is said to be "without the world," that is, outside the normal boundaries of dharma, which govern society. It is accessible to every caste and even outcastes, for the River Ganges is believed to efface caste distinctions.[45] Similarly, when pilgrims, noble or common, rich or poor, go to Mecca, all don the *muharram* or white robe, and for the time of pilgrimage all normal distinctions are equalized in the one community of Islam. Before God, all are equal.

The quality of "nontransferability" or "nonrepeatability" should also be considered as a possible distinguishing factor between the two types of cities. Certainly individual objects that contribute the aura of local sacrality in a city may be transferred elsewhere, such as relics in the Buddhist, Christian, or Islamic traditions. The Buddha tooth and alms bowl can be taken from Anuradhapura to Polonnaruva. A slip from the Bodhitree can be brought from India to Sri Lanka. It is recorded that the four main gates for Baghdad and the gate of Mansur's palace were taken from a city in Mesopotamia called Zandaward; both the gates and the city were said to have been built in ancient times by King Solomon.[46]

How far the process of transferring local sacrality might go is hard to say. But there is an astonishing story in the Chinese tradition, which ranks as the most extreme case I am aware of. According to the account, the incident occurred when Mongol power had just begun to rise and the Nuchen Jin ruled north China. The latter had heard of a certain "elegant and splendid mountain" in the territory of the Mongols, and connected their rising fortunes with the possession of this mountain. Jin augurs and geomantic experts visited the mountain and pronounced that it had *wang qi* (literally "royal breath," but suggesting that its possession would cause or create a true sovereignty). Believing that it would enhance their own power and authority, the Jin sent an immense force of laborers into Mongol territory to dismantle the mountain and rebuild it in their capital at Dadu.[47] Thus what is said in some religious traditions to be accomplished by faith was effected in China by tens of thousands of laborers!

This story, if true, is surely rather unusual. While objects or parts of objects can be removed from a holy city, it is inconceivable that the entire city should be moved. Matteo Ricci may bring soil from the Holy Land to Beijing, but neither he nor anyone else can bring Jerusalem.

There are two problems that tend to blur the distinction between the sacred city and the holy city. The first stems from the fact that certain cities have both patterns of sanctity in their histories. Jerusalem, as we have seen, may have begun as a cosmic sacred city. We know that it was originally a Jebusite royal city, then was made the capital of the united Israelite monarchy under David and his successors. Solomon was particularly responsible for introducing aspects of cosmic symbolism, borrowed from "the nations," into the temple, sanctuary, and royal precincts. Later centuries saw its development as a locally sacred city through mythic developments deriving from its centrality in all three prophetic religions: Jewish, Christian, and Muslim. Understandably, the city's symbolic values reflect both kinds of sacrality.

But the process of mythic development does not go just in one direction. Later on Judaic and Christian sources began to "re-cosmocize" the city, applying to it all sorts of cosmic metaphors. Pope Urban II, preaching the crusades at Vezelay, referred to it as "the navel of the earth, the royal city in the middle of the world," according to the report of the monk Robert of Rheims. The currency of this concept in the Middle Ages may be seen in the many maps of Jerusalem drawn in that period. They not only place the holy city in the middle of the world, but contrary to the reality of the irregular shape of the city, show it as a perfectly round, walled city in the style of Parthian, Sassanian, and Abbassid cities of the Near East. Furthermore, the maps show a perfect orientation to the four directions, with two axial avenues crossing in the center.[48]

Rabbis called Jerusalem the "citadel and central point of the universe," below which God placed the source of all the earth's sweet water, the fount from which the four rivers of paradise flow. The rock of Jerusalem was situated exactly above the subterranean waters and penetrated down to them, according to the Mishnah. These were the waters of chaos, which existed before creation, called *tehom* (the equivalent of the Babylonian *apsu*), so the rock was said to contain the "mouth of tehom." The Mount of Golgatha in Jerusalem was known in Christian symbolism as the center of the world, the place where Adam was created and buried, and thus redeemed by Christ's blood falling into the ground.[49] In the last example particularly one can see the mixture of both kinds of symbolism.

Roma sacra also shares a long history that spans the founding, republican, and imperial periods of pre-Christian history, and fifteen hundred years of the Christian faith. We have already examined some of the cosmic traditions connected with the founding of the city. Within the Christian perspective, Rome is a city of local sacrality because it was the see of St. Peter, visited by St. Paul, the place of the martyrdom and burial of so many of the early saints. But there was also the Caesaro-papist tradition, which produced much universal and cosmic symbolism. This tradition reached its peak in the thirteenth century under the rule of Innocent III, but still has echoes in certain architectural features of the Vatican, such as the world-embracing Bernini colonade, the rhetoric of the pope's yearly *urbi et orbi* sermon, and generally in the papal claim to universal spiritual authority. So it is evident that the two orientations we are considering are not be identified by different religious traditions. Both orientations exist in India (Banaras vis-à-vis the classical ideal capital), in Isalm (Mecca and Baghdad), in the Jewish and Christian traditions.

There is, however, a second problem involved in postulating a distinction between the sacred city and the holy city. That is the fact that certain kinds of symbolism seem to be "natural" to both types of city, principally images of centrality and creation/foundational myths. We have already seen this phenomenon in regard to Jerusalem. It may also be documented for Mecca, which at first sight appears to be a "pure" example of local sacrality. Using language now very familiar to us, some Muslim traditions call Mecca the "center of the world," "navel of the whole earth, the place of communication with the upper and nether worlds," and the like.[50] Banaras was believed to be the center of space where all directions originate, the place where Shiva's *linga*, the *axis mundi*, first appeared, and it alone does not sink in the waters of destruction at the end of time's cycle.[51] Furthermore, Hindu religious cartographers cosmocized the irregular city into a geometric plan, as illustration 23 shows.

On the other hand, it is just as natural for a planned cosmic city to begin to acquire the mythology of local sacrality, as we have seen in Beijing. The caliph's palace in Baghdad was covered by a large green

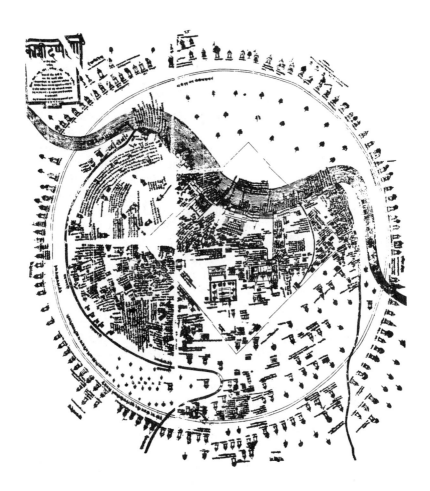

Illus. 23. An old pilgrimage map of Kashi (Banaras).

dome, on top of which was the figure of a horseman. In later times this figure was credited with having the power of pointing its lance in the direction from which the enemies of the city were about to appear. This is a legend not unlike many we have recounted about towers, gates, bridges, and other structures in Beijing. There was also a shrine to the great muslim Saint Ma'rul southeast of the city, which enhanced the local sanctity of the area, for it was said that his intercession with Allah would prevent the approach of evil to Baghdad.[52]

What these shared factors point to is not utter confusion in the types we have proposed, but something about the nature of human symbol making. If Eliade's *Patterns in Comparative Religions* has any validity at all, it documents a kind of logic in myth and symbolism that can be verified in culture after culture. Naturally there are exceptions, but in my opinion they prove rather than discount the rule. Why these cross-cultural similarities should exist is another question, which we cannot go into here. But there is a sense in which the myths and symbols seem to be quite objective, suggesting the same or very similar realities to people of widely divergent cultures. A city, however its genesis be explained, is both a reality and a symbol, and as such has a rather objective capacity to represent or manifest something to human beings. That natural symbols such as trees, rock, water, and astral bodies can suggest the sacred is somehow less surprising than the hierophantic power of things made by human hands such as temples, cities, and houses. But all such symbols strain, as it were, to the full limit of their capacity to represent, and in the study of cities one can see many examples of this process of extension. The form of the city is a kind of container whose contents have stimulated the mythic imagination in many cultures to surprisingly similar results.

Of course it is a vast oversimplification to reduce religious meaning of cities to these two types. Using different methods of analysis, one could derive different categories. Nevertheless the two types we have suggested do seem to correspond to two very common yet contrasting methods of organizing space. Urban geographers have demonstrated the existence of two radically different kinds of cities in traditional cultures, distinct both in their genesis and morphology:

> Throughout history there persist two distinct trends—the one toward the rational and the geometrical, the other toward the irrational and organic: two different ways of dealing with or of mastering the environment. . . . Since the beginning of civilization there have been cities planned according to regular schemes and cities which have grown up organically like trees.[53]

The principle stated here may be verified in many of the cultures we have examined. Needham, discussing the planned city as opposed to the organic city, notes:

> In China there was a rather marked difference between the spontaneously growing village or rural settlement and the town planned from above. . . . Towns and cities in China were planned as rational fortified patterns imposed from above upon carefully chosen portions of the earth's surface.[54]

In India there is also a clear difference between the two types: the unplanned urban settlement that grows up around a holy place, and the planned royal city:

> A healthy place and sacred surroundings are the first considerations for the location of a house. . . . Indians are, by their traditions and scriptural precepts, desirous to erect their humble dwellings by the side of a temple which in times of importance and renown, becomes an object of pilgrimage.[55]

Among Chinese capitals that ideally were planned and cosmoscized, some such as Kaifeng, Hangchou, and Nanjing were originally the product of organic growth and partially intractable to the hands of planners. But just as there are no "pure" types of sacred and holy cities, there are also complications to the distinction between planned and organic cities, even at the level of smaller settlements. After a city in China had grown organically to a certain point, it would have been "absorbed" into the hierarchy of the administrative network by which the imperial system functioned, thereby acquiring at least the basic features of the cosmic city: the *shejitan*, the ancestral temple and local yamen, which gave it an official position in the administrative structure of the empire.

THE PLACE OF BEIJING

> Of all great cities under heaven, there is none more reliable than Beiping. . . . This is a precious place; even the greatest troubles cannot last here more than three months.

> He looked upon China, this millennia-old nation, as the most sacred family.

> —Lao She, *Sishi tongtang*

We may look at Beijing from a number of points of view. From the perspective of political administration, it was the center of a network of power. As in the classical world of Europe "all roads led to Rome," in Ming and Qing China the circuit of authority began and terminated in Beijing. In this context, two aspects of the role of the capital should be kept in mind as particularly significant: Beijing was the vertex of the hierarchy of political authority, and at the same time it was a model for all subordinate centers of the power it shared. Under the national government were the traditional thirteen provinces during the Ming period, and below them the executive centers for local administration: *fu* (prefecture), *zhou* (subprefecture), and *xian* (county), in descending order of importance. Roughly speaking, each prefecture included about three *zhou* and seven *xian*.[56]

Each nexus of authority was threefold. At the national level in Beijing there were sectors dealing with civil administration (*wen* officials), military matters (*wu* officials), and the unique Chinese governmental creation, the censorial ministers. This threefold structure was represented at the provincial and lower levels, so that each unit of local administration was a mirror of the governmental structure at the capital.

Fu, zhou, and *xian* headquarters were naturally located in cities, but these "cities" should not be conceived as independent political units. As Eberhard points out, "there was no concept of the city as a municipality with its own self-government. No concerted action or organization of citizens occurred."[57]

Throughout the Ming and Qing periods, the capital, through its corps of representatives at the lower levels, completely dominated the Chinese state. However, the overbearing nature of this arrangement was offset, at least theoretically, by the familial-religious understanding of the total hierarchy. Not simply a secular political structure, the state was conceived as a macrocosmic family. As the emperor performed his imperial rituals, his representatives at the local level fulfilled comparable obligations for the welfare and the people, sacrificing at the local *she ji* (spirits of land and grain) altar, to local tutelary and ancestral spirits, praying for rain or the recession of floods. As good fathers, they doled out rewards and punishments to maintain order and harmony in the territories for which they were responsible. In the capital, the emperor was called "father and mother of the people," and in the centers of local administration those delegated his power and sacral functions were sometimes called "father and mother officials."[58] The capital was exemplary in both its secular and sacral functions.

STRUCTURES OF DOMINANCE AND SUBMISSION

Many of the studies of sacred cities and sacred kingship stress the role of religion in legitimating the authority and enhancing the power of the ruler. The ideology embodied in the city of Beijing certainly does that, elevating the status of the emperor almost to the level of the divine. He is the son of heaven. But his title as "father and mother of the people" reminds us of another aspect of his role, which is also incorporated in the structure of the capital. There were factors within the imperial ideology that mitigated and limited the exercise of monolithic power.

The greatest practical expression of this was the tradition of the upright minister who was courageous enough to criticize the emperor when he erred. Many such conscientious officials lost their jobs, their wealth, and even their lives when they exercised their moral duty of criticism. That was why it was considered so important for the emperor to hold court regularly, so that he could hear the words of such honest ministers. The major criticism of the late Ming emperors like Jiajing and Wanli was that they isolated themselves in the inner court, failed to have regular audiences with their ministers to conduct the business of government. The great reform in the early Qing was that the emperors were conscientious in hearing their loyal officials at regular audiences. Qianlong wrote:

> I have examined the sacred admonition which says "Reverence heaven (*Jingtian*), take the ancestors as models (*Fazu*), be diligent in governing (*Qinzheng*), stay in communication with virtuous ministers (*Qinxian*)." Though your works go not beyond these four principles, the meaning should extend ten thousand miles. From ancient times those who followed these principles had good government, those who ignored them had disasters.[59]

So important was this notion that the emperor had the last four characters, *Qinzheng Qinxian*, written on a plaque that hung in the *Yangxindian* hall (which, after the time of Yongzheng, had become the main residential palace of the emperors).

There were a number of other factors limiting imperial power, but I am particularly interested in those that were incorporated into the architecture of Beijing. I call these factors "structures of submission," as opposed to "structures of domination," which are the more obvious. An example of the latter would be the axial way, the grand processional road that is the line of dominion reaching from Shangdi in his polar capital and continued on earth in the plan of the capital. I have already considered these structures of domination extensively.

The altar of heaven embodied both factors. On the one hand it displayed the exalted role of emperor as high priest, but on the other, his liturgical station was on the second, not the first tier of the altar, and he had to face north, the position of submission, while kowtowing many times during the ritual. That is to say, his power was limited by Shangdi, who had given him his commission to rule (the mandate of heaven) and could take it away if he ruled badly.

The *taimiao* was another structure of submission. As at the altar of heaven, in the ancestral temple the emperor had to take the position facing north and kowtow during the ritual. Like the head of any family, the emperor had to submit to his ancestors, who as spirits of the dead were more powerful than he. They in fact were the true heads of the family rather than the currently living representative. If he succeeded and ruled successfully, he brought glory to his ancestors; if he ruled badly, he would be ashamed to face them for he had disgraced their name. How important ancestral worship was is clear from the anguish of the great ritual controversy, as emperor and officials argued for years over who should be honored as his father.

Another less obvious structure of submission was the garden. This suggestion may seen farfetched, but a glance at the map of Beijing will show that the only areas free of the absolute geometry of the city plan are the irregular and organic shapes of the imperial gardens to the west of the Forbidden City. The underlying conception and planning of a garden reveals an entirely different spirit from that which created the urban structure. If the capital, with its rigid gridwork plan and walled enclosures, was an image of the Confucian ideal of a hierarchical society, then the imperial gardens were an image of Taoist freedom, spontaneity, and humility before "great nature."

In the Chinese garden tradition, the observer gives up orientation, centrality, axiality, symmetry, and all the predictability of straight line and geometrical space. There is no sense of "progression," no measured progress along a path or road planned to emphasize social and political concepts. There is order, but it is the order of great nature (the *Dao*), which is subtle and difficult to describe in words. Sir William Chambers, though not impressed by Chinese building architecture, was fascinated by their gardens. He commented:

> The art of laying out grounds, after the Chinese manner, is exceedingly difficult, and not to be attained by persons of narrow intellects. . . . this method being fixed to no certain rule, but liable to as many variations as there are different arrangements in the works of creation.[60]

This early (eighteenth-century) perception of Chinese landscape was accurate in realising that its model was nature itself. Or as Denis Attiret put it, writing in the same Qianlong period, "they chuse a beautiful Disorder."[61] Yet present in the disorderly order were the same principles of yin and yang that we have seen so often in urban symbolism. The two major features of Chinese gardens are, as in landscape paintings, mountains (yang) and waters (yin). These are what make up cosmic order, whether expressed the form of the city or the irregularities of the garden.

In the garden, the human being, from emperor to private person, must submit to a different order of being. There is no grand vista, no processional way, no overall pattern to comprehend with the eye. There is only the twisting path, sudden changes, unexpected views, pocked and pitted rocks, twisting watercourses, oddly formed trees, overhanging ledges, and dark grottoes. There is no center, no periphery. In the finest gardens, the visitor is not going anywhere, but simply *is*, one of the elements of nature. As Wing-Tsit Chan observes, ruler or private citizen was called to be humble, for each was just a small part of great nature.[62]

The major imperial gardens in Beijing were those in the west section of the Imperial City, including the three lakes called the northern, central, and southern seas, the Yuanmingyuan (and later Yiheyuan) gardens just to the northwest of the city. These were extensive and elegant areas, yet the remarks made above apply to them as well as to the smaller gardens belonging to private individuals.

In fact, the spirit revealed in the imperial gardens and the gardens of wealthy individuals such as those restored today in Suzhou is the same spirit revealed in the two-dimensional landscape painting of Chinese tradition, and even in the miniature landscapes of the "scenery in a dish" (*penjing*; Japanese: *bonzai*).[63] The overall meaning of this symbolism was therefore one shared at many levels of Chinese society.

Perhaps the best way to understand gardens as structures of submission is to contrast them with royal gardens elsewhere, such as the classical gardens of France and England. The European royal park continues the geometry of the palace and city into the world of nature. Nature at Versailles is nature tamed, trained, and molded to human perspective. Louis XIV wanted uninterrupted vistas from his palace windows, radial roads that stretched to the horizon clearly symbolizing the vast extent of his dominion. The story is told of a certain English gentleman who wished to curry favor with the duke of Beaufort at Badminton. Beaufort had built an impressive estate with radial avenues stretching from his manor house to the borders of his land, so his neighbor had trees planted in rows on his own estate to *continue* the lines of the duke's radial avenues on his own property.[64] It was only in the eighteenth century, when Romanticism began to see a divine spirit in nature, that the Romantic landscape garden began to replace the classical garden in Europe. The Chinese, always perceiving a sort of divine spirit in nature (the *Dao*), were never willing to cut and trim nature to the stature of the merely human. I think it is important to remember these structures of submission as we try to make an assessment of Beijing's comparative status.

BEIJING, HOLY AND SACRED

We have completed an outline of the main features of the cosmic sacred city and the city of local sacrality. The first type demands the existence of a hierarchy of control (usually headed by a sacred king) and a highly stratified society reflected in the very layout of the city's plan. It is modeled on a pattern derived from the stars or cosmic order. It is oriented to the four cardinal directions, usually has an axial ceremonial road, is considered the center of the country and whole terrestrial world. It has monumental architecture, which expresses this symbolism. The second type, the holy city, is a sacred place whose very ground has an aura of sanctity. It is usually the object of pilgrimage and an important cult center, having sites made holy by the occurrence of sacred events, the visitations of divine-heroic persons, and the presence of sacred objects connected with them. Its form is irregular, giving evidence of its unplanned character and organic growth.

Beijing can obviously be analyzed from both points of view and found to have both structures of sacrality. It is certainly a preeminent example of the cosmic sacred city, a point that should require no further discussion. However, there are two features of the holy city pattern that merit consideration. We have looked at the myths and legends that make it not just cosmocized *space*, but a holy *place*. It has its share of divine beings and heroes who have performed wonders and left their mark on the urban landscape in the form of a shrine, temple, tower, well, and the like. Most important is the myth of the Yellow Emperor, founder of Chinese civilization, who built his capital on the site of Beijing. Even today in Taiwan and the Peoples Republic of China the story of the Yellow Emperor is preserved in elementary school textbooks (with cautions that this is myth, not history). Yet outside the legends of the Yellow Emperor and Nezha, the other myths and legends are of local, not national, currency.

There are some other features that set Beijing apart from such cities as Mecca, Banaras, and Jerusalem. One of them is the apparent lack of that intense feeling for the sacrality of its very physical elements. Pilgrims carry soil away from Jerusalem, some wishing to have it placed in their coffins. They carry water home from the well of Zamzam and the Ganges River to heal physical and spiritual problems. There is an almost *physical* dimension to the sacrality, which reminds one of the descriptions of *mana*, *baraka*, *orenda*, *wakanda* given by Marrett and others. Rutter tells of an experience in Mecca that highlights this point. Because it costs money at every step of the way as pilgrims tried to approach the holy Ka'ba, the poorer Muslims were unable to get inside the black cube. When Rutter emerged from inside, a mob of poor people surrounded him, rubbing their hands all over his body, then all over their own bodies, "obliged to content themselves with a little of the Kaaba's virtue borrowed at second-hand from more fortunate pilgrims."[65] I have found no evidence that this *physical* sacrality was reflected in the feelings of the Chinese for the soil of Beijing or any objects within it.

The second point that merits further discussion is the question of pilgrimage to a cult center, which was included in our typology. Pilgrimage was extremely popular in China, but its destination was usually Buddhist and Taoist temples in the mountains and countryside rather than sites within cities. Furthermore, though there were important temples and shrines in Beijing where people gathered on certain days of the year, they were chiefly of local interest, and certainly not national pilgrimage destinations.

Pilgrimage to the sacred center must be seen in a different context in China than in other cultures. As the imperial religion interpenetrated socio-political reality, pilgrimage may also be seen within the framework of that reality. One could develop the intriguing idea that the rulers of border states, the *fan-wang*, or their emissaries *(fanshi)*, bringing goods from their own regions to offer to the son of heaven, were on a kind of pilgrimage in the context of imperial religion. The *Collected Rituals of the Ming Dynasty* cites the custom of tribute missions as a long-standing tradition, going back to the Shang period, when tribes from the area of Tibet came to offer gifts and were granted an audience by king Tang (traditionally dated 1766–1754 B.C.E.).[66] The authors then trace the development of the practice up through the Yuan dynasty, noting the best-known missions that made their way to the Chinese capital in each dynastic period.

While the tributary system is made up of economic, diplomatic, and political elements, its theoretical foundation is unquestionably religious, insofar as it is the expression of the submission of the whole world to the reign of the son of heaven. When the tributary missions arrived in the capital, they were under the care of the Office of the Barbarians of the Four Quarters (the *Siyiguan*). The very title of this bureau presents us with the ancient image of China as the center of the world surrounded by barbarians of the four cardinal directions.

In the Ming period, the emissaries were carefully warned and instructed in the parts they were expected to play in the audience ritual, rites calculated to enhance the status of the son of heaven. On the day of the audience, they were led, in what must have been an awesome progression, through the series of gates and courtyards to the sacred presence of the emperor, enthroned in *Fengtiandian* (which was the *Taihedian* of Qing times).

The chief ceremony the emissaries ("pilgrims") were asked to perform was the kowtow, the three prostrations and nine knockings of the head upon the ground. Lord MacCartney and the other eighteenth-century European envoys were right when they sensed in the extravagance of this gesture something more than mere oriental etiquette, a practice that would drastically reduce their status and that of the rulers they represented. It was indicative of sacral status. There were various types of kowtow required between certain persons on specified occasions, which served to express the relationships involved. But the ninefold kowtow was restricted to the most solemn occasions and reflected the sacred status of heaven and the son of heaven. When the *fanwang* or *fanhi* prostrated themselves before the emperor at the center of the world, the object of their "pilgrimage" was attained. Through the son of heaven they made contact with the power of heaven and could obtain blessings for the four quarters of the world.[67]

Even supposing the validity of this interpretation of the tribute system as a kind of pilgrimage, there are still two main differences between this sort of analogous "pilgrimage" and the normal sort. In the tribute system there is an occasional sending out of Chinese emissaries to outlying kingdoms, an element that seems to have no counterpart in pilgrimage. Furthermore, the tributary system applied particularly to foreigners, so that we would have a case of the Chinese themselves not going on pilgrimage.

At this point in the discussion, it may almost seem that there are two Beijings, one a cosmic sacred city and the other a city of local sacrality. I would rather say that there are many ways of viewing Beijing, depending on whether the person looking is emperor, minister, or of the ordinary class, and to give an adequate interpretation of the city, one would have to try to represent the total fabric.

The remarkable thing is how all these elements worked together in Beijing and how the city represented a body of shared conceptions toward the world, which was the common property of all levels of society. The cosmic conceptions of yin yang, the five-phases worldview, the symbolic numbers, the lore of the *Yijing* were not just an upper-class philosophy, but were shared ways of thinking at many levels of society.

I recall the first time I visited the altar of earth. *Ditan* Park is not particularly popular with tourists, so when I entered the walled area I found myself almost alone. I saw five Chinese persons on the lower tier of the altar, all practicing a form of *qigong*. I walked to the top tier of the altar to count the paving stones, beginning at the center. When I had reached the outer circle and passed near the people, a woman who appeared to be their leader, looked at me and said "588." I must have looked startled, because she said again, "588. That is how many stones there are, but I think that number is wrong. There should be 600." I asked her how she knew the exact number and she said "because I counted them myself." I asked her why she thought there should be 600 and she said because of the *Yijing*, and then launched into a discussion of numerical symbolism. In explaining her views to me, she used a stone to write characters on one of the paving stones, frequently asking her companions for help in making the characters because "she had only graduated from the sixth grade."

This woman reaffirmed for me the existence of a body of symbolic thought shared by all levels of society in Beijing. Though she had very little formal education, she had a great interest in the meaning of the *Yijing*. She is not an isolated case. Even in the limited number of legends I have mentioned there is much evidence that ordinary people were quite aware of the emperors who played a major role in the shaping of the city and in the symbolic numbers incorporated into its architecture, as we saw in the legends of the four corner towers of the Forbidden City and in the Hall for Yearly Prayer at the altar of heaven. The odd appellation of the emperor, "son of heaven of the repetition of nine," *jiuchong tianzi*, is another popular reference to an important symbolic number.

One could give numerous examples of this Chinese knowledge of and fascination with numerical symbolism. The Ming novel *Xiyouji* (abridged and translated as *Monkey* by Arthur Waley) begins with a chapter about the origins of Sun Wukong, the monkey king. The great stone that will give birth to him is described as "thirty-six feet and five inches, which corresponded to the three hundred sixty-five cyclical degrees, while the circumference of twenty-four feet corresponded to the twenty-four solar terms of the calendar. On the stone were also nine perforations and eight holes, which corresponded to the Palaces of the Nine Constellations and the Eight Trigrams."[68] Or at an even more mundane level, a recent newspaper article in the *Renmin ribao* discussed the significance of the numbers 72, 36, 8, 9, and 108, tracing their appearance in early classics and mentioning their use in subsequent literature and belief.

Popular imagination, using the same numerical values, often transformed the real into the ideal, because that was the way it "should" be. There was a commonly held conviction that there were nine gates along the axial way from *Yongding* Gate in the south to the emperor's throne, though in actuality there were only eight. There were many practices and beliefs that reveal the importance of nine, or its multiples. There was a saying among the people that the Forbidden City had thirty-six urns and seventy-two wells. These are a reference to the thirty-six auspicious star spirits and the seventy-two noxious earthly spirits we have already seen at the Hall of Yearly Prayer.[69]

The dragon is probably the best single example of a symbol that was enthusiastically shared by all classes of Chinese society. There is no need to list all the ways dragon imagery figured in imperial cult—it was *the* motif of imperial ceremonial robes, or palace decor, and architctural design. The phrase "dragon throne" referred to the emperor's sovereignty. The dragon symbolized China as a whole. The myths of Beijing mention a body of water called Black Dragon Lake (*Heilongtan*). Official chronicles mention three places in Beijing that have that name, all of them sites of prayer for rain in times of drought. They also describe a place called Dragon King Pavilion, west of the *shejitan*, which was used for the same purpose.[70]

The *Dijing jingwu lue*, a short descriptive piece about Beijing from the late Ming dynasty, states that at the beginning of the Wanli period the emperor visited the imperial tombs to the west of the city and on his return stayed overnight at a Black Dragon Lake. After a severe drought, Wanli sent an official to the lake to offer prayers. When the rains came, the emperor gratefully gave the dragon spirit a title and set up a stone memorial tablet there.[71] I have already mentioned in the previous chapter how many of the popular Beijing legends are about dragons. The references could be multiplied, but those given are enough to show that the dragon as a legendary figure was a unifying symbol in Chinese society and had the same basic meaning for the upper classes and ordinary people.

Another remarkable unifying factor in Beijing was in the uniform architectural style employed. Unlike the royal cities in other cultures we have considered, there was no sharp cleavage between imperial monumental buildings and domestic architecture. Elsewhere, there are ziggurats, pyramids, temples, and palaces that are totally different in style and size from ordinary homes. In China, the temples and palaces were based on the same model as the typical private home, differing only in size. From the small houses of the alleyways (called *hutong*) in Beijing to those of the wealthiest mandarins, all followed the same basic plan. Even the emperor lived in smallish rooms laid out according to exactly the same principles as the houses of the *hutong*.[72]

Needham explains the most important features of this commonly shared domestic architectural model as follows:

> The fundamental conception of Chinese architecture arranges one or more courtyards (*thing yuan*) to compose, sometimes in a very complex way, a general walled "compound" (*ssu ho yuan*). . . . The main longitudinal axis is always (or ideally) north-south, but the chief buildings (*cheng thing, chengfang*) or halls (*tien*) are always placed transversely to it. They thus come one behind another, with the

main entrance of each always in the centre of the long south-facing side. . . .

The long rear wall is almost always unbroken by doors and windows, and forms, as it were, the ultimate statement of the plan, though not its climax, since the largest hall will be placed somewhere north of the central point, and there will be a diminuendo of constructions behind (i.e., north of) it.[73]

Reading this passage with Beijing in mind, one immediately becomes aware of its perfect consonance with the plan of the Forbidden City. The public areas will be to the front, the private areas to the rear. The long rear wall finds its parallel in the always closed northern gate, or the northern wall of the whole city, which had no central gate.

The continuity between imperial and domestic architecture was not simply one of form, however, but also of the principles behind them. The basic elements of the *fengshui* system for the placement and protection of palace, house, and grave, were the same: the directions, the elements, the trigrams, the time periods, the heavenly bodies. Although the application of these factors was probably erratic or unique in specific cases, there were many features of the system known to everyone. For example, the geomantic analysis of Beijing, which I used in a previous chapter, could be also used to determine the *fengshui* of an individual home, which the author does.[74]

But even beyond the question of the form and arrangement of the private home, the dynamic relationships of the family within were also determined by principles derived from the yin yang, five-phase worldviews, the admonitions of the *Yijing*, and most generally from images of congruence with the cosmic forces, the great heavenly bodies and the powers of the earth. Kangxi, in the sixty-first year of his reign, put it succinctly: "There are no two suns in the heavens, nor are there two rulers on earth."[75] The *Liji*, which translated these principles of nature into norms for daily living, teaches: "the *Dao* of Heaven provides the most perfect teachings. . . . The ruler appeared at the [top of the] steps on the east, his wife was in the corresponding place in the west—these positions of husband and wife are in accord with the distinctions of yin and yang."[76]

It can be seen that the models that guide the behavior of husband and wife here are the same as those that were applied to the emperor and empress. The relationships, the hierarchy, the positions of all within the family unit were played out on the stage of the family home, while the order of relationships ritually performed in the architectural setting of the Forbidden City were carried out by the emperor, who had for his total home "all within the four seas."[77] Wright has made the point that when people build cities they do more than satisfy their practical needs, "they dramatize for us their social order—both actual and ideal—their view of the cosmos and their place in it, their hierarchy of values."[78] Perhaps we can add that the genius of Chinese urban planning was its ability to embody a worldview shared by all levels of society.

This worldview was an attempt to bring cosmos and society into a perfect harmony, and the means used was ritual, a ritual whose rubrics were enshrined in both imperial and domestic architecture. But the harmony between architectural form and social structure was unself-consciously manifested. There is only one major architectural manual that has come down to us, a handbook written about a thousand years ago, to give technical guidance to Chinese builders. It contains almost nothing about architectural theory or principles. But it has been recently pointed out that architecture in the Chinese tradition was under the Board of Rites of the imperial government. Strange as it sounds, palaces, halls, and other buildings were viewed as ritual objects.[79] This is true whether the architecture was imperial or domestic.

Let us look at one final passage from the classics, one among many that express the liturgical character of domestic architecture. The following is a ritual of greeting of guests at a noble house:

> When the arrival of the guests is announced by the usher to the host, the host meets the guests in person outside the main gate. . . . The host with a salute precedes them in. The principal guest, with a wave of the hand to the second guest, enters to the left of the door, and the second guest in similar fashion invites the others. All the guests then enter together by the left of the door, and range themselves facing east and graded from the north. Then the host salutes the principal guest thrice in their progress up the court, and on arrival at the steps, after three yieldings of precedence, the host ascends by the eastern steps. The guest then goes up the western steps, and the host, at the top of the east steps, and advanced as far as the rafter under the eaves, faces north and bows twice. The guest, at the top of the western steps, and advanced as far as is the host, faces north and bows in return.[80]

The language of direction, hierarchy, symmetry, balance, and harmony, so long Chinese ideals, is expressed clearly here. The imperial rituals were much more amplified, the customs of ordinary people much more simple, but both incorporated the same principles.

Today we are very conscious of the human impact on the environment, and we think of home building as a manipulation of the environment to suit our own needs. But in traditional China it was rather the reverse. The form of domestic environment was a "given," and was expected to shape humans into the proper mold, indicating their place within the small society of the extended family at one end of the social spectrum, or at the other end of the spectrum, to shape the emperor, his ministers, and family into the proper mold.

Finally, I would say that the remarkable factor about Beijing is not the contrast or conflict of two symbol systems, cosmic and local, but how these two systems were harmonized into a congruence and unity. Our task is not to decide whether Beijing was a sacred city or a holy city, but simply to look at it from as many perspectives as possible. One could probably construct either of the two systems, as I have tried to do, or deconstruct them by viewing Beijing through different eyes. But in the end, when the analytic work is over, it is more satisfying to turn over the fabric and see the tapestry from the right side.

As Lao She's old man tells us, it must have been at times a stirring and reassuring thing to live in Beijing. Even though ordinary people were excluded from the imperial rites, we have seen that they knew a great deal about them and about the symbolism they expressed. Even though the streets were cleared and the windows hung with blue cloth to keep common eyes off the grand processions to the suburban altars, the effects of living in the "capital of the world" must have affected lives and formed attitudes. William James in his *Principles of Psychology* described the way a person's house and possessions, though their effect was unconscious, became as much a part of one's personality as one's knowledge and sentiments, opinions and acts:

> If that is true of the individual, it is even more massively true of the community: for it was by means of new esthetic structures that the city defined a new collective personality that had emerged, and looked with a fresh pride at its own face. If the king or the governor were too high and mighty to be approached except in extremity, the meanest inhabitant could nevertheless identify himself with the personality of the city, in all its power and radiance.[81]

In a very concrete way, the structure of the city of Beijing made clear to all levels of society their place in the cosmic/social hierarchy. And if it did not bring freedom as urbanism did in the mercantile cities of medieval Europe, it at least provided a kind of security and a measure of peace in the acceptance of that assigned role. One had a place in a large family.

At the summit of the hierarchy, the city of Beijing may be looked upon as the house, the possessions, and the "furniture" of the emperor. It was, as we have seen, an embodiment of the ancient concept of the sacred king, an expression of the classical concept of the role and function of the son of heaven. Beijing was the stage (or altar) upon which the Ming and Qing emperors came and went, performed their duties more or less well according to the role assigned to them from the distant past.

One may say that the emperors had little opportunity to choose their "furniture" or dictate their environment, and that therefore the city was not an *active* expression of any one emperor's personality, at least not to the extent that Versailles was the expression of the personality of the Sun King. Yet Beijing was a *passive* expression, not so much of an individual but of the imperial persona, a definition of character handed down for at least two thousand years. If a particular emperor did not fit the pattern, he would still find it hard to escape from the weight of inherited ideals and general expectations. Few emperors had the opportunity to shape Beijing, but the city shaped many of them. In this sense it was a schoolmaster of the emperors, a *paedagogus imperatorum*, and as in any school, some were good students and some were not.

NOTES

1. See "The Pursuit of Equilibrium: Polonnaruva as a Ceremonial Center," in Bardwell Smith and Holly Baker Reynolds, *The City as a Sacred Center* (Leiden: E. J. Brill, 1987), p. 77.

2. Werner Muller, *Die heilige Stadt* (Stuttgart: Kohlhammer, 1961). The purpose of this study, however, is not to examine the sacred city as a phenomenon, but to propose a theory that the cosmic-type city, which the author documents in Eurasian and African cultures, has its origin in pre-Aryan megalithic cultures.

3. Besides references to Wheatley's works already given, I should also mention *City as Symbol* (London: H. K. Lewis & Co., 1969); *Nagara and Commandery: Origins of the Southeast Asian Urban Tradition* (Chicago: University of Chicago, Department of Geography Research Papers, nos. 207–8, 1983).

4. See Muller, *Stadt*, pp. 21ff.; Gutkind, *Urban Development*, pp. 17ff.; and Jerome Carcopino, *Daily Life in Ancient Rome: The People and the City at the Height of the Empire*, trans. by E. O. Lorimer (New Haven: Yale University Press, 1966; first published, 1940), p. 12.

5. Wright, "Symbolism," pp. 669–71. If we could accept Granet's description of the tree supposedly at the center of the ancient Chinese capital, which united upper and lower worlds, there would even be a parallel with the *mundus*.

6. Gutkind, *Urban Development*, p. 27.

7. H. P. L'Orange, *Studies on the Iconography of Cosmic Kingship in the Ancient World* (Oslo: H. Aschehoug, 1953), p. 22.

8. Lampl, *Cities*, p. 14 and figure 20; C. Leonard Wooley, *The Sumerians* (New York: W. W. Norton, 1965), pp. 140ff. The type of orientation found in Near Eastern cities was generally with the four corners to the cardinal directions, as can be seen in the cases of Ur, Nippur, Uruk, Khorsabad, Babylon, Dur-Untash, and Persepolis. See maps and plans in Lampl, *Cities*, illustrations 20–23, 32–35, 40–43, 153–55, 162–65.

9. W. F. Saggs, *The Greatness That Was Babylon* (London: Sidgwick & Jackson, 1966), p. 35; Lampl, *Cities*, p. 7.

10. Phyllis Ackerman, "The Symbolic Sources of Some Architectural Elements," *Journal of the Society of Architectural Historians*, 12, no. 4 (December 1953), p. 4.

11. A. Leo Oppenheim, *Ancient Mesopotamia* (Chicago: University of Chicago Press, 1964), p. 139.

12. Herodotus, *The Persian Wars*, trans. by George Rawlinson (New York: Modern Library, 1942), pp. 97–98. The Zeus Belus precinct was the temple of Marduk and the zigurrat was the famous tower of Babel. Marduk, having been elevated to the position of supreme god in the *Enuma Elish*, is rightly called *Bel* (Lord) by Herodotus and identified with Zeus. For more detailed accounts of the city, see Lampl, *Cities*, pp. 18–19; Saggs, *Babylon*, pp. 354ff., and Oppenheim, *Mesopotamia*, pp. 109–42.

13. The latter interpretation is that of Henri Frankfort. See his *The Birth of Civilization in the Near East* (Garden City, N.Y.: Doubleday Anchor Books, 1956), pp. 56–57. A summary of the various theories on the ziggurats may be found in André Parrot, *Ziggurats et Tour de Babel* (Paris: Michel, 1949).

14. Lampl, *Cities*, p. 9.

15. Kautilya, *The Arthasastra*, trans. R. Samasastry (Mysore: Mysore Printing and Publishing House, 1960; first edition, 1915), pp. 3–4. Binode Behari Dutt, *Town Planning in Ancient India* (Calcutta and Simla: Thacker, Spink & Co., 1925), pp. 55–57. Bredon, *Peking*, p. 20, notes that in Qing times the Manchu bannermen groups were assigned to different sections of Beijing and the colors identified with the bannermen and their quarters reflected five-phase thinking.

16. Dutt, *Town Planning*, pp. 60–61. The areas plowed were later planted and cows brought in to graze upon and "purify" them.

17. See the reports of A. M. Hocart in "Archaeological Summary," *Ceylon Journal of Science*, 1 (July 1924–February 1928), 150–56; (December 1928–August 1933), 86–87. Wickremeratne, "Shifting Metaphors of Sacrality: The Mythic Dimensions of Anuradhapura," in Smith and Reynolds, *City*, pp. 45–59, says that the Sri Lankan capital followed a cosmography that reflected the universe, with Buddhist dharma replacing Brahma and the bodhi tree serving as the *axis mundi*. For diagrams of the various classical Indian town plans, see Muller, *Stadt*, p. 121, and Dutt, *Town Planning*, pp. 145–46.

18. Muller, *Stadt*, pp. 135ff.; Wheatley, *Pivot*, pp. 248–57.

19. Holly Baker Reynolds, "Madurai: Koyil Nakar," in Smith and Reynolds, *City*, pp. 12–13.

20. Herodotus, *Wars*, p. 57. The round unexcavated mound of Echatana may be seen still today. See Lampl, *Cities*, illustration 157.

21. L'Orange, *Studies*, p. 13.

22. Ibid., p. 22.

23. G. LeStrange, *Baghdad During the Abbasid Caliphate* (Oxford: Clarendon Press, 1900), pp. 17–19. There are no remains of Mansur's Baghdad. The author's information is taken from Muslim historians Yakubi and Tabari. See also Richard Coke, *Baghdad: The City of Peace* (London: Butterworth, 1927), p. 36. The reference to the Sumerian practice of royal building may be found in Sigfried Giedion, *The Eternal Present: The Beginnings of Architecture* (Washington, D.C.: Bollingen Pantheon Books, 1964), p. 240.

24. See Johanna Broda, David Carrasco, Eduardo Matos Moctezuma, *The Great Temple of Tenochtitlan: Center and Periphery in the Aztec World* (Berkeley: University of California Press, 1987), especially the Carrasco article, "Myth, Cosmic Terror, and the Templo Mayor," pp. 124–62.

25. Ibid., Johanna Broda, "Templo Mayor as Ritual Space," pp. 67, 69–70.

26. Southeast Asia provides particularly clear examples of the cosmic sacred city because of the availability of literary testimony to the intent of the builders. See Wheatley, *Pivot*, p. 248. Besides Tenochtitlan, other cities of Mesoamerica show orientation, axiality, centrality, and sacred processional ways. The earliest known city in the Americas using the two perpendicular axes was Teotihuacan, built in the third or fourth century c.e. Its principal

features were the Great Compound and Citadel (including Temple of Quetzacoatl) at the southern end of the processional way (on west and east sides, respectively). The immense Pyramid of the Sun was east of the axial way and at the northern termination of the axis was the Temple of the Moon. Similar features may be seen at the Mayan city of Tikal. Jorge Hardoy, *Urban Planning in Pre-Columbian America* (New York: George Braziller, 1968), pp. 23–29, 34–37; figures 5–13, 32. See particularly the conception of figure 33, from a letter of Cortez; summary in Wheatley, *Pivot*, pp. 234–35.

27. Recently, discussions of the genesis of the city have been placing more emphasis on the role of religion, particularly through the coalescing of power in the person of the sacred king and his ritual center. The work of Paul Wheatley has been especially influential in this regard. In a more popular vein, Mumford's writings have developed similar conclusions: "The most important agent in effecting the change from a decentralized village economy to highly organized urban economy was the king, or rather, the institution of kingship" [*The City in History* (New York: Harcourt, Brace and World, 1961, p. 35]. Or in another formulation, Mumford speaks of a "sudden fusion of sacred and secular power which produced the nucleus of the city" ["The University City," in Carl H. Kraeling and Robert M. Adams, eds., *The City Invincible: A Symposium on Urbanization and Cultural Development in the Ancient Near East* (Chicago: University of Chicago Press, 1960), p. 7]. I do not think "fusion of sacred and secular power" a happy phrase, because it suggests the prior existence of a secular power for which there is no evidence. Emphasis on the religious source of city development was made over one hundred years ago by Fustel de Coulanges in *The Ancient City*, so the idea is not new, but in more recent years it had been submerged in theories stressing economic, social, political, and demographic factors, as V. Gordon Childe, "The Urban Revolution," *Town Planning Review*, 21 (1950), 3–17. For other approaches emphasizing the importance of the religious factor, the ceremonial center as urban nucleus, see Wheatley, *Pivot*, esp. pp. 318ff., and A. M. Hocart, *Kings and Councillors: An Essay in the Comparative Anatomy of Human Society* (Cairo: Printing Office Paul Barbey, 1936), p. 245. Despite obvious deficiencies, Hocart has a contribution to make to the study of cities.

28. Eliade, *Cosmos*, pp. 7–8.

29. Varro, *On the Latin Language*, VII, 8ff., quoted in Frederick C. Grant, *Ancient Roman Religion* (New York: Liberal Arts Press, 1957), pp. 13–14.

30. Eliade, *Cosmos*, p. 9; Muller, *Stadt*, p. 117.

31. Gustave E. von Grunebaum, *Muhammadan Festivals* (New York: Henry Schuman, 1951), pp. 28–29. In his article "The Sacred Character of Islamic Cities," in *Mélanges Taha Husain: offerts par ses amis et ses disciples à l'occasion de son 70ieme anniversaire* (Cairo: Abdur-rahman Badawi, 1962), pp. 25–37, von Grunebaum suggests three categories for interpreting the sanctity of Muslim cities, which appears different from the twofold sanctity I have suggested. First, there is the type of sanctity stemming from *baraka*, a purely local sanctity connected with a prophet's tomb, the sanctuary of a saint, or the presence of numbers of Muhammad's descendants (e.g., Hebron). Second, a soteriological sanctity resulting from the role the city has played or will play in *Heilsgeschichte* (e.g., Damascus, Kerbela, or Medina). Finally, a cosmological holiness when the city is considered the center of the world. This is the most holy type applicable only to Jerusalem and Mecca. In this schema, the first two types are included within my "city of local sacrality." Von Grunebaum's definition of a cosmic sacred city is very restricted, including basically the ideas of (1) exaltation above the territories surrounding it, (2) cosmogonic site, (3) center of the world, (4) place of communication with upper and lower worlds. As I see it, this category still lacks more features of the cosmic city, such as geometric planning, orientation, monumental architecture, etc. As will become clear later in this chapter, I would interpret Mecca as a city that acquired certain features of cosmic symbolism as a result of its preeminent local sacrality.

32. Rev. M. A. Sherring, *The Sacred City of the Hindus: An Account of Banares in Ancient and Modern Times* (London: Trubner & Co., 1868), pp. 47–48, 175. The sacral territory here described may appear to be the same as that we have seen in the cosmic city, such as the *templum* of Rome, marked by *pomerium*. The Roman case is, I believe, the strongest case of an

apparent exception. The *kidinnutu* status of Babylonian citizens was divinely sanctioned and indicated by the placement of a *kidinnu*, an object erected at the city gate as a symbol of divine approval and protection. But the *kidinnu* refers more to the status of citizens than the sanctity of the city's ground. See Oppenheim, *Mesopotamia*, pp. 121ff. In any case, one must look at the source of the *templum* sacrality, which derives from the repetition of a pattern. That of Mecca and Banaras has another derivation, as we shall see.

33. Eldon Rutter, *The Holy Cities of Arabia* (London: G. P. Putnam's Sons, 1928), 1:162; von Grunebaum, *Muhammadan Festivals*, p. 32. The plain of Arafa is east of Mecca, an important station in the pilgrimage cycle. The maps of Mecca and Medina in Rutter are quite helpful in giving an overview of the form of the two cities, details of the Ka'ba, central mosques, outlying pilgrimage sites, etc.

34. Normal Kotker, *The Earthly Jerusalem* (New York: Scribners, 1969), pp. 4–6.

35. E. B. Havell, *Benares the Sacred City* (London: Blackie and Son, 1905), pp. 75, 100; Diana Eck, *Banaras, City of Light* (New York: Alfred A. Knopf, 1982), p. 24. Eck's book is the most comprehensive analysis of the religious meaning of Banaras available.

36. Kotker, *Jerusalem*, pp. 4, 6.

37. Jonathan Z. Smith, *Map*, p. 35.

38. Rutter, *Cities*, 1:117ff.

39. Von Grunebaum, *Muhammadan Festivals*, pp. 19–24. There are many other sacred places and objects within the *haram* of Mecca, e.g., the well of Zamzam, Mas'a (where the strange rite of running takes place), Mina (where the devil is stoned) and other places on the way to Arafa.

40. Eck, *Banaras*, pp. 94, 126; Havell, *Benares*, p. 137; Sherring, *City*, pp. 67–68, 71, 117.

41. Sherring, *City*, pp. 368–70.

42. Quoted in Eck, *Banaras*, p. xvi.

43. Havell, *Benares*, p. 100.

44. Eck, *Banaras*, p. 5.

45. Dutt, *Town Planning*, p. 307; Havell, *Benares*, p. 100.

46. LeStrange, *Baghdad*, p. 21.

47. *Jiudu wenwu lue*, IV, 10. When the Mongols captured Beijing, they renamed the mountain *Wansui shan* (Mountain of Ten Thousand Years). Today it forms the island in the northernmost of the three lakes or "seas" in the west of Beijing's imperial city. Kates discusses this incident, calling it a "holy mountain," and translating *wang ch'i* "king-making vital force" ("New Data," p. 180).

48. Muller, *Stadt*, pp. 53ff. For a number of examples of medieval maps, see tables 6a, 6b, 7a, 7b, 8a, 8b.

49. Eliade, *Cosmos*, p. 15; Kotker, *Jerusalem*, pp. 4–5.

50. Von Grunebaum, *Mélanges*, pp. 32–34.

51. Eck, *Banaras*, pp. 294, 296.

52. LeStrange, *Baghdad*, pp. 31, 99.

53. Sigfried Giedion, *Space, Time and Architecture* (Cambridge: Harvard University Press, 5th revised edition, 1967), p. 414.

54. Needham, *Science*, 4:71.

55. Dutt, *Town Planning*, pp. 30–32, 41ff. Henri Frankfort makes the same distinction for the Near East, using Sargon's Khorsabad for the classical example of the planned type. See "Town Planning in Ancient Mesopotamia," *Town Planning Review*, 21 (1950), 106.

56. See discussion in James B. Parsons, "The Ming Dynasty Bureaucracy: Aspects of

Background Forces," in Charles O. Hucker, ed., *Chinese Government in Ming Times* (New York: Columbia University Press, 1969), pp. 175–231.

57. Wolfram Eberhard, "Data on the Structure of the Chinese City in the Pre-Industrial Period," *Economic Development and Cultural Change*, 4, no. 3 (1956), p. 267.

58. Hucker, *Traditional Chinese State*, pp. 66–67.

59. (*Qing*) E Ertai, Zhang Tingyu et al., Guochao gongshi (Beijing: Beijing guji chubanshe, 1987), 1:240.

60. Sir William Chambers, *Designs of Chinese Buildings, Furniture, Dresses, Machines and Utensils* (1757; reprinted, New York: Benjamin Blom, 1968), p. 19.

61. Jean Denis Attiret, *A Particular Account of the Emperor of China's Gardens Near Pekin*, quoted in John Dixon Hunt, *The English Landscape Garden* (New York: Garland, 1982), p. 38.

62. "Man and Nature in the Chinese Garden," in Henry Inn, *Chinese Houses and Gardens* (New York: Hastings House, 1950), pp. 30ff.

63. See Rolf Stein, "Jardins en miniature d'Extrême-Orient," BEFEO (1943), 2:1–104; and Lothar Ledderose, "The Earthly Paradise: Religious Elements in Chinese Landscape Art," in Bush/Murck, *Theories of the Arts in China* (Princeton: Princeton University Press, 1983), pp. 165–83. And Maggie Keswick, *The Chinese Garden* (New York: Rizzoli, 1978).

64. Yi-fu Tuan, *Topophilia: A Study of Environmental Perception, Attitudes and Values* (Englewood Cliffs, N.J.: Prentice Hall, 1974), p. 140.

65. Rutter, *Holy Cities*, 1:216. The author also mentions that the *Ka'ba* is washed down twice a year and Muslims consider it blessed to drink this water.

66. Quoted in John K. Fairbank and Teng Ssu-yu, *Ch'ing Administration*, Harvard Yen-ching Series 19 (Cambridge: Harvard University Press, 1961), pp. 141–42. The authors present a good summary of the tribute system, pp. 136ff.

67. Another religious element connected with the tribute system may be seen in the interpretations of the exotic gifts of the tributaries as auspicious signs. During the Yongle reign, the first giraffe was brought to Beijing from Bengal. The officials announced that this was the marvelous mythic beast called the *qilin* (an auspicious omen said to appear only in the reign of a perfect sovereign as a sign of heaven's approval). A memorial of congratulations was prepared. At first the emperor declined, with a tart response: "Even without the *qilin* there is nothing hindering good government!" But he did go out in great state to meet a second giraffe, which came the next year (J. J. L. Duyvendak, "The True Dates of the Chinese Maritime Expeditions in the Early Fifteenth Century," *T'oung Pao*, 34 [1939], 341–412).

68. Anthonly Yu, trans., *The Journey to the West* (Chicago: University of Chicago Press, 1977), 1:67.

69. Qi Rushan, *Beiping*, pp. 62, 68–69. Derk Bodde's translation of *Yenjing suishiji* (annual customs and festivals in Peking) (Peiping: Henri Vetch, 1936), pp. 88ff., has a number of examples of beliefs and customs concerning the number nine. According to De Saussure, the son of heaven is sometimes called *jiuwu zhi cun*, "the preeminence of nine and five" (p. 226). Another collection which reveals the same numerical symbolism is the ever popular Chinese Almanac, still published each year in Taiwan and Hong Kong.

70. *Rixia jiuwen kao*, XVII (61), 3.

71. Ibid., XXVI (106), 12.

72. Cameron and Brake, *Peking*, p. 116. See the comparative charts and analysis of the basic domestic plan vis-à-vis the Forbidden City's courtyards and palaces on the same page. *Hutong* is a special Beijing word that refers to the tiny streets that make up the gridwork crisscrossing the city. Wu also says that "the house is the basic cell in the organism of Chinese architecture" (*Chinese*, p. 31). "The entire city was made of groups of *fang* in which houses of all sizes were organized. In the case of the capital city, the emperor occupied the central and largest houseyard complex, thereby dominating the walled-in town, and symbolically, the nation" (p. 34).

73. Needham, *Science*, vol. 4, part 3, pp. 62–63. The author has illustrations applying the typical module (p. 62) to a Confucian temple complex (p. 64) and to a traditional home in Beijing (p. 66). Wright, "Symbolism," p. 673, discusses the same module and its applications.

74. P'eng Tso-chih, "Stadtbau," p. 13. In the case he examines, the house does not lie on the ideal north-south axis but is oriented with its corners to the four directions and its main door facing the southeast. Applying the king Wen (*luoshu*) trigrams to this situation, one finds that the axis of the house runs from the *qian* trigram in the northwest to the *sun* trigram in the southeast. The house thus has a *qian* position, and the lucky directions for such a situation are *qian*, *dui*, and *kan*, the unlucky ones are *sun* and *gen*. These are the basic factors that will be used in determining the proper place for the gates, the hall of the ancestors, pavilion, etc.

75. E Ertai, *Guochao*, p. 17.

76. My translation. This passage is found in Legge, *Li Chi*, 1:410–11.

77. Soper, *Art*, p. 217. The words are those of one of the generals of Han Gaozu praising the dynastic founder in 200 B.C.E.

78. Wright, "Symbolism," p. 667.

79. Brian E. McKnight, "Patterns of Law and Patterns of Thought: Notes on the Specifications (*shih*) of Sung China," *Journal of the American Oriental Society*, 102, no. 2 (April–June 1982), pp. 329–30. The name of the architectural manual is *Yingcao fashi*.

80. John Steele, trans., *The I-Li or Book of Etiquette and Ceremonial* (1917; reprinted, Taipei: Ch'eng Wen, 1966), pp. 52–53.

81. Mumford, *City in History*, p. 68. William James's insight is expressed by his brother Henry with equal clarity in *Portrait of a Lady:* "There's no such thing as an isolated man or woman; we're each of us made up of some cluster of appurtenances. . . . One's self—for other people—is the expression of one's self; and one's house, one's furniture, one's garments, the books one reads, the company one keeps—these things are all expressive."

Epilogue

A Tale of Two Emperors

One summer night in Beijing, I stood inside the circular enclosure that surrounds the altar of the sun. It was filled with people enjoying the cooler air of the evening. The thump of badminton rackets and swish of shuttlecocks could be heard all around. On the top of the western steps of the altar sat a young man, playing a guitar, his friends singing along quietly. To the south of the altar a younger and noisier group were playing soccer. Below the guitar player, two little girls took turns sliding down the smooth marble ramp at the side of the steps. They encouraged a timid friend, who was afraid to try.

The thought of sacrilege crossed my mind, but I immediately dismissed it. Like all the sacrificial sites of the imperial religion, the altar of the sun was now merely a public park. Apart from the government of the Dragon throne, these altars had no sacred meaning. When Emperor's rule ended in 1911, so did the religion which supported it. The religion died quickly and few mourned its passing.

But the same fate did not befall *Tiananmen*, which came to be incorporated into the symbolism of the People's Republic of China. In April 1989, as I finished revising this book, the students had begun their protests in *Tiananmen* Square. I wrote at that time: "While it is impossible to know what will come of the marches, they are a reminder that *Tiananmen* is still the center of the city, the place where the interests and expectations of ruler and people intersect. The old north-south axial way has lost its significance. The planners of New China have substituted for it the broad east-west thoroughfare called Changan Boulevard, a significant symbolic restructuring of the city. But the old axial way and Changan Boulevard intersect at *Tiananmen*, which is center still. As always, what happens here will determine the future of China."

As the place where the relationship of ruler and people was focused, *Tiananmen* is a reminder that even in an autocratic state like imperial China, the "the consent of the governed" was a factor of the political reality. The Chinese had never completely forgotten the dictum of Mencius that the people are the state's most valued possessions, and "he who has the confidence of the people may become the Son of Heaven."[1] For over five hundred years *Tiananmen* was the place where the imperial decrees were promulgated, solemnly lowered in the mouth of a golden pheasant. Four decades ago, in 1949, it was the place where Mao Zedong and the revolutionary leaders proclaimed the People's Republic of China. It is still the symbol of Beijing and of China.

Beijing was the emperor's home. Without his presence, Beijing sank to the level of just another historic Chinese city, as had Changan (now Xian), Loyang, Nanjing, and other previous capitals. In the prologue I suggested that the walls were the essence of the Chinese city. Here I want to reemphasize that the sacral meaning of the Chinese capital was only possible in relationship to the person of the emperor, who was the point of connection between heaven above and the people below.

How did the people view their emperor and what did they expect of him? As we have already seen, the popular imagination as expressed in myth and legend is a surprisingly accurate reflection of both historic and symbolic realities. The people's legends and myths know which emperors were most important in the building of the city, which buildings and structures have the most profound architectural and symbolic significance. Their legends and myths show a good understanding of the symbolism behind the ideals of the politico-religious ideology that for so long dominated China. This is all the more remarkable for the exclusion of ordinary people from the Forbidden City and from the sacred altars and temples where the imperial rituals were carried out.

The political-religious ideology examined in this study endured as the official form of government until the revolution of 1911. The great Chinese capitals, of which Beijing was the last, functioned as both throne and altar, the stage on which the rituals of imperial government were performed. Yet this "civic religion," as Robert Bellah would call it, lacked certain dimensions that many persons found necessary in their personal lives, and so they looked elsewhere to satisfy these needs. Even as an imperial ideology, it was not without its competitors. At various times in Chinese history, had circumstances been different, it is conceivable that either Taoism or Buddhism could have assumed a central role as the ideology of Chinese statecraft. But they did not, and therefore their temples, organizations, and leaders have not figured in the writing of this book.

It may seem that this is a glaring omission. Because Taoist, Buddhist, and community temples had much more impact on the everyday lives of ordinary people than any of the structures of imperial worship, a comprehensive study of Beijing's religious history would have to give them extensive consideration. And besides the religious function, the popular temples were centers of community activity, adding color and interest to the yearly round of urban activity in their neighborhoods. Some of them, such as the Taoist White Cloud Temple, the Buddhist Great Charity Temple, the Lamaist Harmonious Peace Temple, are even today national centers of these religions. The famous temple festivals and markets held throughout Beijing were great events in the lives of ordinary people, colorful celebrations that were at once religious, social, economic, and recreational opportunities.[2]

Although imperial civil religion had a transcendent aspect in that it was the point of official contact with Shangdi and the other spirits of heaven and earth, it was not concerned with *personal* transcendence, not even that of the emperor. For those individuals who sought to become immortals or to cross "the sea of bitterness" to the farther shore, Taoism and Buddhism provided aid and succor. The civil imperial religion was public, formal, official, so both emperor and people sought individual salvation and personal transcendence elsewhere. The legends of Beijing reveal this also. At the White Cloud Temple, for example, on the nineteenth day of the first month of the lunar year, there was a commemoration of the death of the most famous Taoist priest of the Jin and Yuan dynasties, Qiu Changchun. People from all walks of life attended, wealthy and noble, poor and ordinary, some to hear the music and stories, some to pray to the immortals. According to legend, the Taoist immortal Lu Dongbin, as well as Qiu Changchun himself, would pass through the crowds. If a person were to see Lu or Qiu, they could become an immortal and rise to heaven. Many of the Taoist monks sat at the foot of the tall pine trees in the temple courtyard awaiting the appearance of the immortals, and the ordinary people also crowded in with the same dream of seeing them. But it is said that Lu and Qiu do not appear in their original forms, but change into the form of a visiting man or woman, a beggar pleading for food, or even a rich merchant or gentleman. Therefore, adds the legend laconically, the immortals are rarely seen.[3]

Buddhism and Taoism dealt with areas ignored by the civic religion of the rulers, but of great concern to ordinary people: everyday morality, work, marriage, wealth, the span of life, fate, causes and cures for sickness, death, and the possibility of continued existence in another world. At their highest levels of imagination, they opened up a vision of transcendence that appealed to persons from all walks of life, even emperors. Jiajing was a Taoist; Hongwu, Yongle, and most of the Qing emperors were Buddhists. Down through the dynastic histories we see many examples of the tension between the religions of personal transcendence and the more thisworldly and collective concerns of the civic religion of the imperial court.

This tension is also recorded in the popular legends of Beijing. It is said that the first emperor after the Qing had "entered the passes," Shunzhi, was not the natural son of the former Manchu ruler, but the product of a miraculous conception and birth.[4] According to the legend, his mother was a poor maiden who lived with her father and mother on a riverboat and made a precarious living by catching fish. One day the eighteen-year-old maiden was washing clothes at the prow of the boat when she saw a large and beautiful apple float toward her. She picked it up and noticing that it was the biggest and most delicious looking apple she had ever seen, took a bite and quickly ate it all. After five months, it began to be obvious that she was pregnant, and her irate father thought about pushing her into the river to eliminate this blot on the family reputation. Her mother, however, pointed out that their daughter had not left the boat nor had they had any male visitors in all this time, so how could she have done wrong? Calmed by these words, the old man decided to wait for the child's birth to see what would happen.

The day of birth finally came, marked by wonders, a strangely red sky, a fragrant smell, and from the womb of the maiden came a large apple. The beautiful fruit then opened and a plump child emerged. The old couple was delighted to have a grandchild, which they told others was "adopted." But during the chaos of the end of the dynasty, as Ming and Qing armies fought, the old couple, the maiden and her child, were forced to flee their houseboat. They were spotted by the Manchu ruler along the roadside as he rode by on horseback. Totally captivated by the beautiful child and himself without male heir, the emperor asked if he could adopt the child (his mother could hardly refuse!). Soon the old Manchu ruler died and at age six, the child assumed the throne as Shunzhi, the first emperor of the new Qing dynasty.[5]

Despite this auspicious beginning, a continuation of the Shunzhi legend brings out the tensions between immanent and transcendent aspirations in the Chinese tradition. Thirteen years later, the regent stepped down and Shunzhi himself took up the cares of government. It was not long before the responsibilities and anxieties of office became a terrible burden to him. He began to understand the misery of the "red dust" (the cares and worries of this world). In his heart he felt the desire to abandon his position as emperor, leave the imperial city, and "enter the void gate" (begin life as a Buddhist monk).

Shunzhi first went to the Red Lotus Temple in the hills west of Beijing. There, with all his heart, he began a life of strict discipline and self-cultivation. If hungry, he ate wild berries; if thirsty, he drank spring water; and if tired, he napped on the ground with a stone as his pillow. Although life was hard, he had no thoughts of returning to the imperial palace.

But one day a pregnant woman passed by the temple gate, lost her footing, and had a miscarriage. Shunzhi, the legend tells us, feared that the Buddha nature he had acquired had been responsible for the woman's misfortune and left Red Lotus Temple, fleeing even farther away to the west.[6] Reaching the White Lotus Temple, he undertook still greater austerities. Early each day, just as the birds began to sing, he would carry a stone from the summit to the foot of the mountain and back to the top again. "How many times he went back and forth, how many summers and winters passed by, is hard to say, but Shunzhi's feet were tired and swollen, his hands rubbed raw, and the drops of his blood reddened the slopes of the mountain." Finally the stone was rubbed smooth to the shape of a round ball the size of a bowl, and at the same time the discipline of his Buddha nature was brought to final perfection.

But not quite. Shunzhi, the legend concludes, became a true Buddha living in the flesh. He sat in meditation like a statue in the temple, called the "terrible old man" (*mowang laoye*), and the hill where his blood had fallen was called the "slope of the terrible old man." But it is said that the head of this "Buddha in the flesh" was ever turned toward the southeast because ever since he first took up his "eternal sitting," he had not yet completely cut out his worldly heart, and at that time still gazed back toward the Purple Forbidden City. The dragons of Tiananmen no doubt looked at him with reproach too, for he had not just abandoned his duties as son of heaven, he had failed to excise the final flaw of longing for his former exalted role.

There is no evidence, of course, that any of the events of this legend actually happened, yet it is precious for the vivid way it portrays the tension between two high callings: to be a good emperor or to achieve otherworldly salvation. The legend shows that when the second path is carried to an extreme, the popular imagination sees it as potentially frightening and repellent, finally incompatible with the expectations of the people. It was well and good for some to enter "the void gate," but that was not what the people wished of their ruler. Historically emperors like Jiajing have always been blamed for carrying their religious pursuits to extremes.

These legends contain fine touches: the fresh hope placed in the young emperor born miraculously from an apple, the poignant description of the bleeding emperor carrying his stone up and down the slope of White Lotus Mountain. It is very significant that the tone of the legend changes at the end, as though extreme austerities become abhorrent and pointless to the popular imagination. Shunzhi is called *mowang laoye*, which I have translated the "terrible old man," but is literally "the old diabolic king." The legend leaves us with the final vivid image of Shunzhi's face arrested in a perverse gaze toward his old throne, like Lot's wife petrified in the act of her weakness.

The legend of the succeeding Qing emperor provides a counterpoint to the repellent image of Shunzhi. Kangxi also leaves his blood mark on the earth, and in doing so acts out the role of the ideal emperor of the people's imagination, because he gives himself to save his people. To the people, the true emperor is not so much a high priest of the civic religion, but a great figure of compassion who cares to learn about the condition of his people and relieve them of their suffering. Perhaps there is some influence of the bodhisattva ideal here, but even within the imperial tradition he is "father and mother of the people." And although far too many failed to live up to this hope, a few did and their memory is honored in many legends.

As is true with most of Beijing's folklore, this legend is connected with a particular place, in this case a ruin in the western hills, which used to be called the Temple of the Stone Buddha. One of the purposes of the story is to explain what at first seems a very commonplace but misleading name. Inside the former temple there never was a stone Buddha, but rather a lump of coal called the "imperial blood stone." The story of this stone begins in the Ming dynasty, with an evil (but unnamed) emperor who feared a popular rebellion might arise, encircle, and entrap him in Beijing. Thinking of the hardships of Beijing winters and how a blockade might leave him without a source of heat, the emperor allowed entrepreneurs to open coal mines in the hills west of the city, but with the stipulation that all coal be sold to the government, and stored at Prospect Hill just north of the Forbidden City. (This, by the way, is why Prospect Hill is also called Coal Hill.)

The work in the mine shafts was extremely dangerous. There were frequent explosions and many men lost legs and arms, becoming disabled for life. But these maimed creatures were the lucky ones! Many others died, and a popular saying went: "For every one thousand who go in, only five hundred come out!" So eventually all the workers fled the mines, and the only way the imperial court could keep the work going was by sending prisoners destined for capital punishment to be indentured forever in the mines. None ever came out alive. The coal mines came to be called the "mines of no return."

This inhumane system of criminal slavery continued into the Qing dynasty until word of it came to the attention of Kangxi, who decided to dress up like an ordinary person and see for himself what conditions in the mines were like. Taking a small stone lantern, the emperor found in the subterranean prison the skeletons of many fallen workers. The stench of the rotting flesh of unburied corpses assailed his nostrils. He thought to himself: "These dead are my people, the people of the great Qing nation. This situation is a disgrace to my rule. The first thing I must do on returning to the Purple Forbidden City is to close these terrible prison pits!" But he had forgotten that now he himself, like the other wretched prisoners, was trapped forever, with no way to prove that he was the emperor. As he tried to make his way to the mine entrance, he was booted back by an overseer. What to do? How could he get a message to the court to come and save him? Finally he thought of a method, and biting his middle finger he wrote the following verse in blood on a large lump of coal:

A true dragon is imprisoned in this mine
Below Guojie Pagoda a good heart in torment,
This writ in blood is by imperial hand.
Quickly return me to the great Qing court.

Sometime later this lump of coal was found on Coal Hill by an alert official, and troops were sent immediately to the mine below Guojie Pagoda to free the emperor. On his return, Kangxi closed the mine prison, punished the overseers, and sent his own men to run the operation. People then built a small temple near the place and on the main altar placed the lump of coal with the emperor's bloody message, a witness to the "good emperor" of Beijing legend. And today if you visit this place, ends the legend, although the little temple is gone, you can still see the place where incense was once burned.

Embedded in the legends of these two emperors are the attitudes of ordinary persons toward the powerful figures who ruled them down through the ages. Most of the "good" emperors gave themselves to cares of the "red dust." Although they may have personally favored Taoism or Buddhism, although the Manchus continued to carry out their ethnic rites in special temples in the Forbidden City, their central duty lay in fulfilling the expectations of an accepted role. In this respect, official and popular expectations coincided. The people, though personally inclined to Buddhism or Taoism, believed that the emperor's chief task was thisworldly: to have compassion on the people, to share their misery, to bring harmony, peace, and prosperity to the Central Kingdom. And so while their legends transmuted Shunzhi into a repellant idol, Kangxi became a savior-emperor in the flesh. The dragons of Tiananmen must have looked with approval as they saw Kangxi being brought back to the Forbidden City.

If we do look upon traditional Beijing as the home of the emperor, then what is the modern city? The dynastic house is gone and its precincts are a museum. The house of Beijing now has new landlords, and the rulers of the Peoples Republic have taken over a home they did not build. Though they are busy with restoration, they must find themselves in a strange and ambiguous position, preserving the elegance and grandeur of the decadent imperial past. They are proud of New China, yet know that of the millions of foreign tourists who came to the city, most are here to see the Forbidden City, the Great Wall, North Sea Park, the altar of heaven, not the memorials to the revolution.

As the trains filled with Chinese tourists and foreign visitors roll into Beijing Central Station, loudspeakers in each car remind them that they are about to enter their grand and historic capital, rich with history and filled with the magnificent monuments of China's past. Though many still visit Mao's tomb, most have come to see the imperial monuments, the altars, the halls, the temples, the parks where emperors lived, played, ruled, and worshiped. I sense an ambiguity in the minds of Chinese who come to their capital. They do not want him back, but the emperor still lives in their imaginations, a reminder of the grandeur and glory of the old "Central Kingdom."

NOTES

1. W.A.C.H. Dobson, trans., *Mencius* (Toronto: University of Toronto Press, 1963), p. 182. In another place Mencius quotes the *Book of Documents:* "Heaven sees as the people see, Heaven hears as the people hear" (ibid., p. 66).

2. Hwang Ming-chorng gives a list of the most important Qing temple markets and festivals in Beijing, "Study," pp. 105ff.

3. This account may be found in Yuan Qixu, *Yanjiu zhuzhi si* (1693), Preface in the collection *Qingdai Beijing zhuzhi si* (Beijing: Guji chubanshe, 1982), pp. 3ff.

4. Le Blanc, "Re-examination," p. 53, mentions the widespread traditions of the miraculous births of dynastic founders, particularly the Yellow Emperor, and the first emperors of the Shang, Zhou, and Han dynasties.

5. Zhang Baozhang, pp. 6ff for this and the following legends.

6. This is obviously a folkloristic understanding of Buddha nature (*foxing*), which is the unborn and undying element in the human being.

Bibliography

CHINESE SOURCES

Beijing difang wenxue lianhe mulu 北京地方文学联合目录 (a union catalog of thirteen major libraries in China on source material relating to Beijing). Beijing: 1959. With classified list of 2,200 titles and articles indexed by number of strokes.

Beipingshi zhengfu, 北平市政府. *Jiudu wenwu lue*, 旧都文物略 (an outline of the culture and artifacts of the capital). Taibei: Guoli gugong bowuyuan, 1971. First published, 1935.

Chen Hongnian, 陈鸿年. *Gudu fengwu*, 古都风物 (customs and sites of the ancient capital). Taibei: Zhengzhong shuju, 1970.

Chen Zongfan, 陈宗蕃. *Yandu congkao*, 燕都丛考 (general examination of Beijing). 1930.

E Ertai, Zhang Tingyu et al., 鄂尔泰　张廷玉等 *Guochao gongshi*, 国朝宫史 (a history of the palaces of the imperial court). 2 vols. Beijing: Beijing guji chubanshe, 1987. First published, 1742.

Gang Tianyu, 冈田玉. *Tangtu mingsheng tuhui*, 唐土名胜图会 (an illustrated collection of famous scenes of the land of Tang [China]). 2 vols. Beijing: Beijing guji chubanshe, 1985. First published, 1802.

Guangyeshushe, 广业书社. *Beiping lishi fengtu congshu*, 北京历史风土综述 (a general study of the local customs and yearly events of Beijing), vol. 3 of *Beijing difang yanjiu congkan*, 北京地方研究丛刊 (general collection of research works on the Beijing locale). 8 vols. Taibei: Guting shushe, 1969. Hereafter cited as BDYC.

Guoli Beiping yanjiu yuan, 国立北平研究院. *Beiping shiji congshu*, 北平史记丛书 (a general study of the history of Beijing). BDYC, vol. 3.

Hou Renzhi, ed., 侯仁之　编. *Beijing lishi dituji*, 北京历史地图集 (a collection of historical maps of Beijing). Beijing: Beijing chubanshe, 1988.

Jia Qunnuo, Wang Chengyong, 贾群娜　王永用. *Tiantan jingwu chuanshuo*, 天坛景物传说 (legends of sights and artifacts of the altar of heaven). Beijing: Zhongguo minjian wenyi chubanshe, 1987.

Jin Shoushen, 金受申. *Beijingdi chuanshuo*, 北京的传说 (legends of Beijing). Beijing: Tongsu wenhua chubanshe, 1957.

Kungang, 崑冈. *Daqing huidian*, 大清会典 (collected statutes of the Qing dynasty). 1899.

Lan Mengbo, 蓝孟博 . *Xian*, 西安 (a history of Xian). Taibei: Zhengzhong shuju, 1970. First published, 1957.

Li Hongzhang, 李鸿章. (Guangxu) *Shuntianfu zhi*, 顺天府志 (the history of the Shuntian prefecture compiled in the Guangxu reign). 16 vols. Taibei: Wenhai chubanshe, 1965. First published, 1885.

Ling Shunsheng, 凌纯聲 . "Zhongguo gudai she zhi yuanliu," 中国古代社之源流 ("the Origin of the She in ancient China"). *Bulletin of the Institute of Ethnology of Academia Sinica*, no. 17 (1964), 1–44. With English summary.

———. "Beiping di fengshan wenhua," 北平的封禅文化 ("sacred enclosures and stepped pyramidal platforms of Peiping"). *Bulletin of the Institute of Ethnology of Academia Sinica*, no. 16 (1963), pp. 1–100. With English summary.

Liu Tong, 刘侗. *Dijing jingwu lue*, 帝京景物略 (a summary of the sights and artifacts of Beijing). 1635.

Liu Zijian, 刘子健 . "Fengshan wenhua yu Songdai mingtang jitian," 封禅文化与宋代明堂祭天 ("two forms of worshiping heaven in Sung China"). *Bulletin of the Institute of Ethnology of Academia Sinica*, no. 18 (1964), 45–57.

Ming Shilu, 明实录. (veritable records of the Ming dynasty). Nangang: Academia Sinica, 1962–1966.

Na Zhiliang, 那志良 . *Gugong bowuyuan sanshinian zhi jingguo*, 故宫博物院三十年之经过 (the experience of thirty years of the National Palace Museum's History). Taibei: Zhonghua congshu weiyuanhui, 1957.

Nilu Guoke, 逆旅过客 (pseud.). *Dushi congtan*, 都市丛谈 (a general discussion of the capital city). 1940. Vol. 2 of BDYC.

Qi Rushan, 齐如山. *Beiping*, 北平 . Taibei: Zhengzhong shuju, 1971. First published, 1957.

Qu Xuanying, 瞿宣颖. *Beiping shibiao changpian*, 北平史表长编 (a history of Beijing arranged in chronological order). Vol. 1 of BDYC.

Shao Yuechong, Lu Jieching, 邵越崇 陆深清. *Xiuzhen Beiping fenchu xiangtu* 袖珍北平分区详图 (a pocket edition of detailed fold-out maps of the districts of Beijing). Shanghai: Fuxing yudi xueshe, 1947.

Shen Shixing, 申时行 *Daming huidian*, 大明会典 (collected statutes of the Ming dynasty). Taibei: Huawen shuju, 1964.

Sun Chengce, 孙承泽. *Chunmingmeng yulu*, 春明梦馀录 (a history and description of Beijing, its palaces, temples, and gardens, and a description of government ministries and bureaus). Hongkong: Longmen shuju, 1965. A reprint of the 1881 edition. First published, circa 1670.

———. *Tianfu guangji,* 天府广记 (an extensive record of Shuntian [Prefecture]). Beijing: Beijing guji chubanshe, 1984. A reprint of the 1962 edition. First published, 1672.

Wang Canchi, ed., 王灿炽编. *Beijing shidi fengwu shulu,* 北京史地风物书录 (a bibliography of the history, geographical places, and customs of Beijing). Beijing chubanshe, 1985.

Wang Chenyong, ed., 王成用编. *Tiantan,* 天坛 (the altar of heaven). Beijing: Beijing luyou chubanshe, 1987.

Wang Ji, 王圻. *Sancai tuhui,* 三才图会 (an illustrated encyclopedia organized on the principles of the three powers: heaven, earth, and man). Taibei: Chengwen chubanshe, 1970. First published, 1607.

Wu Changyuan, 吴长元. *Chenyuan shi lue,* 宸垣识略 (a description of the Forbidden city, Imperial city, inner and outer cities of Beijing). 1876. First published, 1770.

Xu Yigui, 徐一夔. *Daming jili,* 大明集礼 (collected rites of the Ming dynasty). 1530.

Xu Daoling, 许道龄. *Beiping miaoyu tongjian,* 北平庙宇通检 (an index to the temples and shrines of Peking). 2 vols. Beiping: Guoli Beiping yanjiuyuan, 1936.

Yan Chongnian, 阎崇年. *Gudu Beijing,* 古都北京 (Beijing, the ancient capital). Beijing: Chaohua chubanshe, 1987.

Yu Qichang, 余棨昌. *Gudu bianqian jilue,* 古都变迁记略 (a summary of the historical evolution of the ancient capital). Vol. 4 of BDYC.

Zang Lihe, 臧励龢. *Zhongguo renming da zedian,* 中国人名大字典 (dictionary of Chinese names). Shanghai: Commercial Press, 1934.

Zhang Baozhang, Peng Zheyu, eds., 张宝章 彭哲愚. *Beijing Qingdai chuanshuo* 北京清代传说 (Beijing legends of the Qing dynasty). Beijing: Chunfeng wenyi chubanshe, 1984.

Zhang Tingyu, et al., 张廷玉. *Ming Shi,* 明史 (the official history of the Ming dynasty). Vols. 46–50 of Ershiwu shi, 二十五史 (the twenty-five histories). Taibei: Yiwen yinshuguan, 1956.

Zhang Cixi, 张次溪. *Tianqiao yilan,* 天桥一览 (a tour of the Tianqiao district of Beijing). Beijing: Zhonghua yinshuju, 1936. Vol. 2 of BDYC.

———. *Zhongguo shiji fengtu congshu,* 中国史蹟风土丛书 (a general account of the history of Chinese customs). Beijing: Zhongguo fengtu xuehui, 1934.

Zhen Jun, 震钧. *Tianchi ewen,* 天咫偶闻 (history and description of Beijing). 1907.

Zhi Chaozi, 枝巢子. *Jiujing xiaoji,* 旧京琐记 (jottings on the old Capital). Vol. 2 of BDYC.

Zhu Yicun et al., 朱彝尊等. [Qin ding] *Jixia jiuwen kao,* 日下旧闻考 (a description of the history and antiquities of Beijing published by imperial decree). 1688. Revised and enlarged by Ying Lien and others in 1774. Taibei: Guangwen shuju, 1968.

Zhu Xie, 朱偰. *Mingqing liangdai gongyuan jianzhi yange tukao*, 明清兩代宮苑建置沿革圖考 (an illustrated study of the evolution of Ming and Qing building techniques in palaces and parks). Shanghai: Shangwu yinshuguan, 1947.

———. *Beijing gongque tushuo*, 北京宮闕圖說 (illustrations and discussions of Peking's palaces and courtyards). Shanghai: Shangwu yinshuguan, 1938.

———. *Yuan dadu gongdian tukao*, 元大都宮殿圖考 (an illustrated study of the palaces and halls of the Yuan capital of Dadu). Shanghai: Shangwu yinshuguan, 1936.

WESTERN SOURCES

Ackerman, Phyllis. "The Symbolic Sources of Some Architectural Elements." *Journal of the Society of Architectural Historians*, 12, no. 4 (December 1953), 3–7.

Arlington, L. C., and Lewisohn, W. *In Search of Old Peking*. Peking: Henry Vetch, 1935.

Ayscough, Florence. "Notes on the Symbolism of the Purple Forbidden City." *Journal of the North China Branch of the Royal Asiatic Society*, 52 (1921), 51–78.

———. *A Chinese Mirror*. Boston: Houghton Mifflin, 1925.

Balazs, E. "Les villes chinoises." *Recueils de la Société Jean Bodin*, 6 (1954), 225–40.

Barthes, Roland. *Empire of Signs*. Trans. Richard Howard. New York: Hill and Wang, 1982.

Bauer, Wolfgang. *China and the Search for Happiness*. Trans. Michael Shaw. New York: Seabury, 1976.

Biot, Edouard. *Le Tcheou-Li où Rites des Tcheou*. 3 vols. Taipei: Ch'eng Wen Publishing Co., 1969. First published, Paris: A L'imprimerie nationale, 1851.

Le Blanc, Charles. "A Re-examination of the Myth of Huang-ti." *Journal of Chinese Religions*, 13–14 (Fall 1985–86), 45–63.

Bodde, Derk. *Annual Customs and Festivals in Peking*. Translation of Tun Li-ch'en, *Yen-ching sui-shih chi*. Peiping: Henri Vetch, 1936.

Boerschmann, Ernst. *Chinesische Architecture*. 2 vols. Berlin: E. Wasmuth, 1925.

———. "Chinese Architecture and Its Relation to Chinese Culture." *Annual Report of the Smithsonian Institution*, 1 (1929), 39–60.

Boorstein, Daniel. *The Discoverers*. New York: Random House, 1983.

196   Bibliography

Borges, Jorge Luis. *Other Inquisitions 1937–1952*. Trans. Ruth L. C. Simms. New York: Simon and Schuster, 1968.

Bouillard, G. "Note succinte sur l'histoire du territoire de Beijing." *Bulletin of the Museum of Far Eastern Antiquities*, 1 (1929), 39–60.

Boyd, Andrew. *Chinese Architecture and Town Planning: 1500 B.C.–A.D. 1911*. Chicago: University of Chicago Press, 1962.

Bredon, Juliet. *Peking*. Shanghai: Kelly and Walsh, 1919.

Bredon, Juliet, and Mitrophanov, Igor. *The Moon Year*. Shanghai: Kelly and Walsh, 1927.

Bretschneider, Emil. *Recherches Archéologiques et Historiques sur Péking et ses Environs*. Publications de l'Ecole des langues orientales vivantes. Paris: Ernest Leroux, 1879.

Broda, Johanna, Carrasco, David, and Moctezuma, Eduardo Matos. *The Great Temple of Tenochtitlan: Center and Periphery in the Aztec World*. Berkeley: University of California Press, 1987.

Bush, Susan, and Murck, Christian. *Theories of the Arts in China*. Princeton: Princeton University Press, 1983.

Cameron, Nigel, and Brake, Brian. *Peking: A Tale of Three Cities*. New York: Harper and Row, 1965.

Cammann, Schuyler. "The 'TLV' Pattern on Cosmic Mirrors of the Han Dynasty." *Journal of the American Oriental Society*, 68 (1948), 159–67.

———. "Chinese Mirrors and Chinese Civilization." *Archaeology*, 2, no. 3 (Autumn 1949), 114–20.

———. "The Magic Square of Three in Old Chinese Philosophy and Religion." *History of Religions*, 1, no. 1 (Summer 1961), 37–80.

Carcopino, Jerome. *Daily Life in Ancient Rome: The People and the City at the Height of the Empire*. Trans. E. O. Lorimer. Edited with bibliographical notes by Henry T. Rowell. New Haven: Yale University Paperback, 1966. First published, 1940.

Chambers, Sir William. *Designs of Chinese Buildings, Furniture, Dresses, Machines and Utensils*. New York: Benjamin Bloom, 1968. First printed, 1757.

Chan, Albert. "Peking at the Time of the Wan Li Emperor (1572–1619)." *International Association of Historians of Asia Proceedings*, Second Biennial Conference (1962), 119–49.

———. *The Glory and Fall of the Ming Dynasty*. Norman: University of Oklahoma Press, 1982.

Chang, Kwang-chih. *The Archaeology of Ancient China*. New Haven: Yale University Press, 1963.

———. *Shang Civilization*. New Haven: Yale University Press, 1980.

———. *Studies of Shang Archaeology*. New Haven: Yale University Press, 1986.

Chavannes, Eduoard. *Les Mémoires Historiques de Se-ma Ts'ien*. Paris: Ernest Leroux, 1875.

―――. *Le T'ai Chan*. Paris: Ernest Leroux, 1910.

Cheng, Te-k'un. *Archaeology in China*. 4 vols. Cambridge: W. Heffer and Sons, 1959.

―――. *Studies in Chinese Archaeology*. Hong Kong: Chinese University Press, 1982.

Childe, V. Gordon. "The Urban Revolution." *Town Planning Review*, 12 (1950), 3–17.

Chu, Chi-chien, and Yeh, G. T. "Architecture: A Brief Historical Account Based on the Evolution of the City of Peking." In *Symposium on Chinese Culture* (1932). Edited by Sophia H. Chen. New York: Paragon, 1969, 112–37.

Coke, Richard. *Baghdad: The City of Peace*. London: Thornton Butterworth, 1927.

Le Corbusier. *Towards a New Architecture*. Trans. Frederich Etchells. New York: Praeger, 1963.

Couvreur, S., S. J. *Chou King*. Taipei: Ch'eng Wen, 1971. First published, Ho Kien Fou: Imprimerie de la Mission Catholique, 1897.

DeBary, Wm. Theodore, ed. *Sources of Chinese Tradition*. 2 vols. New York: Columbia University Press, 1964.

Deffontaine, Pierre. *Géographie et Religions*. Paris: Gallimard, 1948.

―――. "The Place of Believing." *Landscape*, 2, no. 3 (Spring 1953), 22–28.

Dorn, Frank. *The Forbidden City: The Biography of a Palace*. New York: Scribners, 1970.

Dutt, Binode Behari. *Town Planning in Ancient India*. Calcutta and Simla: Thacker, Spink, 1925.

Duyvendak, J. J. L. "The True Dates of the Chinese Maritime Expeditions in the Early Fifteenth Century." *T'oung Pao*, 34 (1939), 341–412.

Eberhard, Wolfram. *Typen chinesischen Volksmärchen*. Folklore Fellows Communications No. 120, Helsinki, 1937.

―――. "Data on the Structure of the Chinese City in the Pre-Industrial Period." *Economic Development and Cultural Change*, 4, no. 3 (1956), 253–68.

Eck, Diana. *Banaras, City of Light*. New York: Knopf, 1982.

Edkins, Joseph. *Chinese Architecture*. Shanghai: Kelly and Walsh, 1890.

Edsman, Carl-M. "Zum sakralen Königtum in der Forschung der letzten hundert Jahre." *Studies in the History of Religions*, 4 (1959), 3–17.

Eichhorn, Werner. "Die Wiedereinrichtung der Staatsreligion im Anfang der Sung-Zeit." *Monumenta Serica*, 23 (1964), 205–63.

Eliade, Mircea. *Cosmos and History: The Myth of the Eternal Return*. New York: Harper Torchbooks, 1959.

Elvin, Mark, and Skinner, G. William. *The Chinese City Between Two Worlds*. Stanford: Stanford University Press, 1974.

Fairbank, John K., and Teng, Ssu-yu. *Ch'ing Administration: Three Studies*. Harvard Yenching Series 19. Cambridge: Harvard University Press, 1961.

Farmer, Edward Lewis. "The Dual Capital System of the Early Ming Dynasty." Ph.D. dissertation, Harvard University, 1968.

————. *Early Ming Government: The Evolution of Dual Capitals*. Cambridge: Harvard University East Asian Research Center, 1976.

Feuchtwang, Stephan D. R. *An Anthropological Analysis of Chinese Geomancy*. Vientiane: Vithagna Press, 1974.

Fisher, Carney T. "The Great Ritual Controversy in the Age of Ming Shih-tsung." *Society for the Study of Chinese Religions Bulletin*, no. 7 (Fall 1979), 71–87.

Franke, Wolfgang. *An Introduction to the Sources of Ming History*. Singapore: University of Malaya Press, 1968.

Frankfort, Henri. *Kingship and the Gods*. Chicago: University of Chicago Press, 1948.

————. "Town Planning in Ancient Mesopotamia." *Town Planning Review*, 21 (1950), 99–115.

————. *The Art and Architecture of the Ancient Orient*. Harmondsworth: Penguin Books, 1954.

————. *The Birth of Civilization in the Near East*. New York: Doubleday Anchor Books, 1956.

Freedman, Maurice. "Geomancy." *Proceedings of the Royal Anthropological Institute of Great Britain and Ireland 1968*. Presidential Address, 5–15.

Fung, Yu-lan. *A History of Chinese Philosophy*. Trans. Derk Bodde. 2 vols. London: Allen and Unwin, 1952, 1953.

Fustel de Coulanges, Numa Denis. *The Ancient City*. 7th ed. Boston: Lothrop, Lee, and Shepard, 1889.

Gernet, Jacques. *Daily Life in China on the Eve of the Mongol Invasion, 1250–1276*. Trans. H. M. Wright. New York: Macmillan, 1962.

Giedion, Sigfried. *The Eternal Present: The Beginnings of Art*. New York: Pantheon Books, 1962.

————. *The Eternal Present: The Beginnings of Architecture*. Washington, D.C.: Bollingen Pantheon Books, 1964.

————. *Space, Time, and Architecture*. 5th rev. ed. Cambridge: Harvard University Press, 1967.

Giles, Herbert A. *A Chinese Biographical Dictionary*. Shanghai: Kelly and Walsh, 1898.

Goodrich, Anne Swann. *The Peking Temple of the Eastern Peak*. Nagoya: Monumenta Serica, 1964.

Goodrich, L. Carrington, and Fang Chaoying, eds. *Dictionary of Ming Biography.* New York: Columbia University Press, 1976.

Gothein, Marie Luise. "Die Stadtanlage von Peking, ihre historisch-philosophische Entwicklung." *Wiener Jahrbuch fur Kunstgeschichte*, n.s., 7 (1930), 7–33.

Granet, Marcel. *La Pensée Chinoise.* Paris: Albin Michel, 1968. First published, 1934.

De Groot, J. J. M. *The Religious System of China.* 6 vols. Leiden: E. J. Brill, 1895.

Gutkind, E. A. *Urban Development in Southern Europe: Italy and Greece.* In *International History of City Development.* Vol. 4. New York: Free Press, 1967.

Hardoy, Jorge. *Urban Planning in Pre-Columbian America.* New York: Braziller, 1968.

Harlez, Charles Joseph. *La Religion et les Cérémonies de la Chine Moderne.* Brussels: F. Hayez, 1894.

Havell, E. B. *Benares the Sacred City.* London: Blackie and Son, 1905.

Hawkins, Peter S., ed. *Civitas: Religious Interpretations of the City.* Atlanta: Scholars Press, 1986.

Henderson, John B. *The Development and Decline of Chinese Cosmology.* New York: Columbia University Press, 1984.

Henricks, Robert G., trans. *Lao-tzu: Te-Tao Ching.* New York: Ballentine Books, 1989.

Herodotus. *The Persian Wars.* Trans. George Rawlinson. New York: Modern Library, 1942.

Ho P'ing-ti. "Loyang, A. D. 495–534: A Study of the Physical and Socio-Economic Planning of a Metropolitan Area." *Harvard Journal of Asian Studies*, 26 (1966), 52–101.

Ho Yun-yi. "Ritual Aspects of the Founding of the Ming Dynasty 1368–1398." *Society for the Study of Chinese Religions Bulletin*, no. 7 (Fall 1979), 58–67.

Hocart, A. M. "Archaeological Summary." *Ceylon Journal of Science*, 1 (1924–1928), 150–56; 2 (1928–1933), 86–87.

———. *Kings and Councillors: An Essay in the Comparative Anatomy of Human Society.* Cairo: Printing Office Paul Barbey, 1936.

Huang, Ray. *1587, A Year of No Significance.* New Haven: Yale University Press, 1978.

Hucker, Charles O., ed. *The Traditional Chinese State in Ming Times, 1368–1644.* Tucson: University of Arizona Press, 1961.

———. *Chinese Government in Ming Times.* New York: Columbia University Press, 1969.

Hunt, John Dixon. *The English Landscape Garden*. New York: Garland, 1982.

Hwang, Ming-chorng. "A Study of Urban Form in 18th Century Beijing." Master's diss., MIT, 1986.

Inn, Henry. *Chinese Houses and Gardens*. New York: Hastings House, 1950.

Jan, Yun-hua. "The Change of Images: the Yellow Emperor in Ancient Chinese Literature." *Journal of Oriental Studies*, 19, no. 2 (1981), pp. 117–37.

Jochim, Christian. "The Imperial Audience Ceremonies of the Ch'ing Dynasty." *Journal of Chinese Religions Bulletin*, no. 7 (Fall 1979), 88–103.

Kates, G. N. "A New Date for the Origins of the Forbidden City." *Harvard Journal of Asian Studies*, 7 (1942–1943), 180–202.

Kautilya. *The Arthasastra*. Trans. Samasastry. Mysore: Mysore Printing and Publishing House, 1960.

Keightley, David. *The Origins of Chinese Civilization*. Berkeley: University of California Press, 1983.

———. "Shang Divination and Metaphysics." *Philosophy East and West*, 38, no. 4 (October 1988), 367–97.

Keswick, Maggie. *The Chinese Garden*. New York: Rizzoli, 1978.

Koster, Hermann. *Symbolik des chinesischen Universismus*. Stuttgart: Anton Hiersmann, 1958.

Kotker, Norman. *The Earthly Jerusalem*. New York: Scribners, 1969.

Kraeling, Carl H., and Adams, Robert M. *The City Invincible: A Symposium on Urbanization and Cultural Development in the Ancient Near East*. Chicago: University of Chicago Press, 1960.

Kramer, Samuel Noah. *History Begins at Sumer*. New York: Doubleday Anchor Books, 1959.

———, ed. *Mythologies of the Ancient World*. New York: Doubleday Anchor Books, 1961.

Lampl, Paul. *Cities and Planning in the Ancient Near East*. New York: Braziller, 1968.

Lancaster, Clay. "The Origin and Formation of Chinese Architecture." *Journal of the Society of Architectural Historians*, 9, nos. 1–2 (1950), 3–10.

Legge, James, trans. *Li Chi*. 2 vols. Vol. 28 of Sacred Books of the East. Edited by F. Max Müller. Oxford: Clarendon Press, 1885.

———. *The Shu King, The Religious Portions of the Shih King, The Hsiao King*. Vol. 3 of Sacred Books of the East. Edited by F. Max Müller. Oxford: Clarendon Press, 1879.

———. *Yi-King: The Book of Changes*. New York: Dover, 1963. First published, Oxford: Clarendon Press, 1879.

Li Xueqin. *Eastern Zhou and Qin Civilizations*. Trans. K. C. Chang. New Haven: Yale University Press, 1985.

Livy. *The Early History of Rome*. Trans. Aubrey de Selincourt. Harmondsworth: Penguin Books, 1960.

Lynch, Kevin. *The Image of the City*. Cambridge: Harvard University Press, 1960.

McKnight, Brian. "Patterns of Law and Patterns of Thought: Notes on the Specification (Shih) of Sung China." *Journal of the American Oriental Society*, 102, no. 2 (April–June 1982), pp. 323–31.

March, Andrew L. "An Appreciation of Chinese Geomancy." *Journal of Asian Studies*, 27 (February 1968), 253–67.

Maspero, Henri. "Le Ming-T'ang et la crise religieuse chinoise avant les Han." *Mélanges chinois et bouddhiques, 1948–1951*, pp. 1–71.

Meyer, Jeffrey F. "Fengshui of the Chinese City." *History of Religions*, vol. 18, no. 2 (November 1978), 138–55.

Mote, Frederick W., and Twitchett, Denis. *The Ming Dynasty, 1368–1644*. Vol. 7 of the Cambridge History of China. Cambridge: Cambridge University Press, 1988.

Muller, Werner. *Die heilige Stadt*. Stuttgart: Kohlhammer, 1961.

Mumford, Lewis. *The City in History: Its Origins, Its Transformations, and Its Prospects*. New York: Harcourt, Brace and World, 1961.

Needham, Joseph *Science and Civilization in China*. Vols. 1–6. Cambridge: Cambridge University Press, 1954–1984.

Oppenheim, A. Leo. *Ancient Mesopotamia*. Chicago: University of Chicago Press, 1964.

L'Orange, H. P. *Studies on the Iconography of Cosmic Kingship in the Ancient World*. Oslo: H. Aschehoug, 1953.

———. "Expressions of Cosmic Kingship in the Ancient World." Numen supplement, *La Regalità Sacra*, 1959, pp. 481–92.

Pelliot, Paul. "Review of Osvald Siren's *The Walls and Gates of Peking*." In *T'oung Pao*, 24 (1926), 78–79.

P'eng Tso-chih. "Chinesischer Stadtbau unter besonderer Berüchsichtigung der Stadt Peking." *Gesellschaft für Natur und Volkerkunde Ostasiens, Nachrichten*, 89–90 (1961), 5–80.

Pope, Arthur Upham. "Persepolis as a Ritual City." *Archaeology*, 10, no. 2 (1957), 123–30.

Rosemont, Henry, Jr. *Explorations in Chinese Cosmology*. Chico, Calif.: Scholars Press, 1984.

Rutter, Eldon. *The Holy Cities of Arabia*. 2 vols. London: G. P. Putnam's Sons, 1928.

Saggs, H. W. F. *The Greatness That Was Babylon*. New York: Hawthorne, 1962.

Saso, Michael R. *Taoism and the Rite of Cosmic Renewal*. Pullman: Washington State University Press, 1972.

de Saussure, Leopold. *Les Origines de l'Astronomie Chinoise*. Taipei: Ch'eng Wen, 1967. First published, Paris: Maisonneuve Frères, 1930.

Schlegel, Gustave. *Uranographie Chinoise*. 2 vols. Taipei: Ch'eng Wen, 1967. First published, Leiden: E. J. Brill, 1875.

Sherring, Rev. M. A. *The Sacred City of the Hindus: An Account of Benares in Ancient and Modern Times*. London: Trubner, 1868.

Siren, Osvald. *The Walls and Gates of Peking*. New York: Orientalia, 1924.

———. *The Imperial Palaces of Peking*. 3 vols. Paris: G. Van Oest, 1926.

Sjoberg, Gideon. *The Pre-Industrial City: Past and Present*. Glencoe, Ill.: Free Press, 1960.

Skinner, G. William. *The City in Late Imperial China*. Stanford: Stanford University Press, 1977.

Smith, Bardwell, and Reynolds, Holly Baker. *The City as a Sacred Center*. Leiden: E. J. Brill, 1987.

Smith, D. Howard. "Divine Kingship in China." *Numen*, 4 (1957), 171–203.

Smith, Jonathan Z. *Map is not Territory: Studies in the History of Religions*. Leiden: E. J. Brill, 1978.

Soothill, William Edward. *The Hall of Light: A Study of Early Chinese Kingship*. London: Butterworth, 1951.

Soper, Alexander. In Sickman, Laurence, and Soper, Alexander, *The Art and Architecture of China*. 3rd ed. Harmondsworth: Penguin Books, 1968.

Speiser, Werner. *Oriental Architecture in Color*. New York: Viking, 1965.

Spence, Jonathan. *Emperor of China: Self-Portrait of K'anghsi*. New York: Knopf, 1974.

Steel, John, M. A. *The I-Li*. Taipei: Ch'eng Wen, 1966. First published, London: Probsthain, 1917.

Stein, R. A. "L'habitat, le monde et le corps humain en extrême-orient et en haute Asie." *Journal Asiatique*, 245 (1927), 37–74.

———. "Jardins en miniature d'Extrême-Orient." *Bulletin of the Museum of Far Eastern Antiquities*, 2 (1943), 1–104.

———. "Architecture et Pensée religieuse en Extrême-Orient." *Arts Asiatiques*, 4, fasc. 3 (1957), 163–86.

Steinhardt, Nancy Shatzman. *Chinese Imperial City Planning*. Honolulu: University of Hawaii Press, 1990.

LeStrange, G. *Baghdad During the Abbasid Caliphate*. Oxford: Clarenden Press, 1900.

Tacitus. *Complete Works*. Edited by Moses Hadas. New York: Modern Library, 1942.

Thompson, Lawrence G. *Chinese Religion: An Introduction*. Belmont, Calif.: Dickenson, 1969.

Trewartha, G. E. "Chinese Cities: Numbers and Distribution." *Annals of the Association of American Geographers*, 41 (1951), 331–47.

———. "Chinese Cities: Origins and Functions." *Annals of the Association of American Geographers*, 42 (1952), 69–93.

Tuan, Yi-fu. *Topophilia: A Study of Environmental Perception, Attitudes and Values*. Englewood Cliffs, N.J.: Prentice Hall, 1974.

Valery, Paul. *"The Yalu" in History and Politics*, vol. 10 of The Collected Works of Paul Valery. New York: Bollingen Pantheon Books, 1962.

Turner, Victor. *The Ritual Process*. Chicago: Aldine, 1969.

de Visser, M. W. *The Dragon in China and Japan*. Amsterdam: Johannes Muller, 1913.

Von Grunebaum, Gustave. *Muhammadan Festivals*. New York: Henry Schuman, 1951.

———. *Medieval Islam*. 2d ed. Chicago: University of Chicago Press, 1953.

———. "The Muslim Town." *Landscape*, 7, no. 3 (1958), 1–4.

———. "The Sacred Character of Islamic Cities." In *Mélanges Taha Husain: offerts par ses amis et ses disciples à l'occasion de son 70ieme anniversaire*. Cairo: Abdurrahman Badawi, 1962.

Von Heine-Geldern, R. "Weltbild und Bauform in Südostasiens." *Wiener Beiträge zur Kunst und Kultur Asiens*, 1932, pp. 34–35.

Waley, Arthur, trans. *The Analects of Confucius*. New York: Random Vintage Books, 1968. First published, New York: Hillary, 1964.

Wang Kuo-wei. "Ming-t'ang-miao-ch'in-t'ung-k'ao, Aufschluss über die Halle der lichten Kraft, ming t'ang, über de Ahnentempel miao, sowie über die Wohnpalaste ch'in." German translation by Jonny Hefter. *Ostasiatische Zeitschrift*, neue folge (1931), pp. 17–35, 70–86.

Welch, Holmes, and Seidel, Anna. *Facets of Taoism: Essays in Chinese Religion*. New Haven: Yale University Press, 1979.

Werner, E. T. C. *A Dictionary of Chinese Mythology*. New York: Julian Press, 1969. First published, Shanghai: Kelly & Walsh, 1932.

———. *Myths and Legends of China*. London: George Harrap, 1922.

Wheatley, Paul. *The City as Symbol*. London: K. K. Lewis & Co., 1969.

———. *The Pivot of the Four Quarters*. Chicago: Aldine, 1971.

———. *Nagara and Commandery: Origins of the Southeast Asian Urban Tradition*. Chicago: University of Chicago Department of Geography Research Papers, nos. 207–8, 1983.

Willetts, William. *Chinese Art*. 2 vols. New York: Braziller, 1958.

———. *Foundations of Chinese Art*. New York: W. W. Norton, 1965.

Wright, Arthur F. "Symbolism and Function: Reflections on Changan and Other Great Cities." *Journal of Asian Studies*, 24 (1964–1965), 667–79.

————. "Viewpoints on a City: Changan (583–904); Chinese Capital and Asian Cosmopolis." *Ventures*, 5 (1965), 15–28.

————. "Changan." In Arnold Toynbee, ed., *Cities of Destiny*. London: Thames and Hudson, 1967.

Wu, Nelson I. *Chinese and Indian Architecture*. London: Studio Vista, 1968. First published, New York: Braziller, 1963.

Yang, C. K. *Religion in Chinese Society*. Berkeley and Los Angeles: University of California Press, 1967.

Yu, Anthony, trans. *The Journey to the West*. Chicago: University of Chicago Press, 1977–. 4 vols.

Yutang, Lin. *Imperial Peking: Seven Centuries of China*. New York: Crown Publishers, 1961.

Index

Praise for

Hooked

An ALA-YALSA Quick Pick

A TeenVogue.com 25 Must-Read Summer Books Selection

"What keeps this strong debut on course is its accumulation of myriad, closely observed details." —*Kirkus Reviews*

"New beginnings are informed by lessons learned in a happy, if not happily-ever-after, ending." —*Booklist*

"*Hooked* is a lovely and timely romance and a moving tale of family lost and found. As poignant as it is pertinent, it's a wonderful read for young and old."

—Galt Niederhoffer, author of *The Romantics*

"It's impossible not to get hooked into this tender and moving story—it totally won my heart."

—Rachel Cohn, coauthor of the *New York Times* bestseller *Nick & Norah's Infinite Playlist*

"Catherine Greenman has an innate knowledge of her characters. She lets you into their hearts and then asks you to stay—until the very last page."

—Cecilia Galante, author of *The Patron Saint of Butterflies*

Hooked

catherine greenman

EMBER

Text copyright © 2011 by Catherine Greenman
Cover photograph copyright © 2011 by Brandy Anderson/Flickr/Getty Images

All rights reserved. Published in the United States by Ember, an imprint of Random House Children's Books, a division of Random House, Inc., New York. Originally published in hardcover in the United States by Delacorte Press, an imprint of Random House Children's Books, New York, in 2011.

Ember and the E colophon are registered trademarks of Random House, Inc.

Visit us on the Web! randomhouse.com/teens

Educators and librarians, for a variety of teaching tools,
visit us at randomhouse.com/teachers

The Library of Congress has cataloged the hardcover edition of this work as follows:
Greenman, Catherine.
Hooked / by Catherine Greenman. — 1st ed.
p. cm.
ISBN 978-0-385-74008-1 (hardcover) — ISBN 978-0-385-90822-1 (lib. bdg.) —
ISBN 978-0-375-89888-4 (ebook) [1. Teenagers—Fiction. 2. Teenage pregnancy—Fiction.
3. New York (N.Y.)—Fiction. 4. Domestic fiction.] I. Title.
PS3607.R464H66 2011
813'.6—dc22
2010023542

ISBN 978-0-385-74009-8 (tr. pbk.)

RL: 6.0

Printed in the United States of America

10 9 8 7 6 5 4 3 2 1

First Ember Edition 2012

Random House Children's Books supports the First Amendment
and celebrates the right to read.

For my parents

acknowledgments

There were hundreds of moments when I wanted to bury this book deep inside folders within folders on my computer, like a little Russian doll. I would like to thank Jonathan Rabb, Ellen Horan, Martha Chang, Brendan Kiely, Esther Noe and Rob Weisberg for keeping me going. I'm also deeply grateful to Jennifer Rudolph Walsh, Erin Malone and Alexia Paul for their early insights and support, and to Polly McCall for her bottomless well of encouragement. My heartfelt thanks go to my agent, Alice Tasman, and to my editor, Stephanie Lane Elliott, for their willingness to ride the bumps with my characters and to ask the prickly questions I might otherwise have avoided. Thanks also to Krista Vitola and Jen Strada for their watchful eyes and to Hilary Weekes for her kind help. I'm forever indebted to Julie Moore, who set me free to write this by looking after my kids with amazing dedication and love. And finally, thank you to Richard d'Albert, my husband. When I give it my best shot it's always with you in mind.

part one

1.

I met Will Weston during a fire drill on a gray, freezing February Monday, a few days after I turned seventeen. I was in metal shop when the bells went off, and had to go outside in my smock. Why didn't they have fire drills during homeroom, when we still had our coats? I hid behind a tree to block the wind, and as I studied the gloomy, red-bricked façade of the school for any signs of real fire, I spotted him. Will was leaning against the stone wall, hugging himself in a thin, black sweater. He was tall and he had large, square, hulking shoulders that reminded me of Frankenstein—an aberration in a sea of boys with shoulders so narrow you could lift them off the ground by grabbing their knapsack straps together in one hand. This guy looked too old for high school. His chin was ducked toward his chest and he stared at me forever, and it was clear that he didn't care that I noticed. I remember looking around, wishing there was someone to talk to, but I was surrounded by the dicks from metal shop. Metal shop was the great dick-alizer—we all behaved like we were in preschool, cutting each other in the soldering lines, hogging the drying shelves, all for the easy As Mr. Blake was famous for doling out. It was not lost on me that an A from Blake would finally kick my average up to an A-minus, a longtime hurdle. Anyway, one minute Will was undressing me from afar, and then he just appeared, as if in a blink.

"Blake or Dolan?" he asked, peering into my face.

"Uh . . . Blake," I said, cursing my telltale gingham smock.

"I had him. A girl in my class lost her eye."

"You were in Lisa Kwan's class?" I asked, marveling.

3

"I was." He nodded modestly.

"What happened? He told us she poked it out."

"Her vise was loose," he said. We both tried not to smile. "You don't use them anymore, vises. Right?"

"No, everything's on the table," I explained. "He helps you when you need to make a cut. He's sick of me. I'm always recutting." I realized then that there was something weird about *his* eyes: the left eye was looking at me, but the right eye drifted off toward the Hudson River. It was both off-putting and death-defyingly hot. It also somehow made him seem too smart for me. I wondered if he was a brainiac, like everyone else at Stuyvesant High School, where I'd somehow landed like an alien on the wrong planet. In math and science, at least, which Stuy held sacred above all else, I was the opposite of a brainiac. Not quite a dumbass, but close. I felt like I was working twice as hard to do half as well as anyone else.

"You'll get an A," he said, rubbing his forearms for warmth. "Don't worry. Has he shown you his oliver?"

"His what?" I asked, thinking, He has the most beautiful hair: brown, wavy, and longer than I initially thought.

"His oliver."

"Oh God. Don't tell me. Another pervy—"

"Go on, ask him to see the oliver," he said. "He'll love you if you ask him."

"What is it?"

"You don't want to be surprised?" he teased.

Part of me did, but I shook my head.

"It's his silver tin of green olives," he whispered, so that the metal-shop dicks couldn't hear. "He keeps it in his pocket for martinis. 'Always keep your oliver on your person.' That's what he used to say. You're a junior?"

4

I nodded.

"I had him freshman year. He's toned it down since then. I think he's a less-happy drunk these days."

"Aren't we all," I said.

"Settle down there, Dorothy Parker." He held out his hand. "I'm Will Weston."

"Thea Galehouse," I said.

"I know." He smiled proudly.

"How do you know?"

"That yearbook picture of you, sleeping on the desk. Your name was in the caption. 'Thea takes a breather' or something stupid like that. Was that during a class? Or homeroom?"

"Homeroom, I think. I was tired."

"No shit. I could never sleep like that. In the middle of everyone. I wish I could. You have the same hair still. Like wet grass stuck to your face." He pushed a clump of loose hair into my cheek with his thumb as people started to stream back into the building. "Anyway, don't stress about Blake." Will took the steps two at a time, so I did too. "He skews it to the pretty ones."

We got inside the double doors and I faced him. "Do I look stressed out?"

"Little bit."

I hate offhand comments about my moods. My mother still makes them constantly. But the way he said it made me think, Maybe I *am* stressing out about stupid freaking metal shop.

"You know," Will said, "ever since I saw that picture of you, all schlumped out all over that desk, I've wanted to meet you. Do you like burgers?"

"Love 'em," I said.

"Have a burger with me, then."

5

He said it in the nicest way. It was one of the shining moments of my life. A total shock and yet right as rain.

The huge oil painting of peg-legged Peter Stuyvesant, our school's namesake, loomed over Will by the staircase. School, the place where we spent so much of our time, was so deathly dreary at that moment. It was like Will put it all—the gray walls pockmarked with painted-over thumbtack holes, the gummy stair railings that made your hands smell like spit—into relief. He glanced at a short girl in clogs walking by. She almost stopped to talk, then didn't. He looked back at me and I got the first jolt. The first java jolt. The first whiff of desire for his big, scary, manly-man body. And the desperation to be included in his thoughts. Me, Thea.

We made a plan to meet Friday.

I tried to think of some cool exit, but I ended up smiling and doing my weird secret-wave thing that my best friend, Vanessa, always makes fun of me for.

"Ask to see the oliver!" he called. I looked back at him. He stood there smiling at me, the sea of people jostling past him.

When I pointed Will out to Vanessa during lunch, he was standing outside between two parked cars, talking to an Asian guy in a ski jacket.

"I see what you mean, kind of," she said, twirling her long brown curls behind her shoulder.

"What do you mean, *kind of*?" I asked, annoyed at her.

"I like his little slump," she said, appeasing me, "like he can't hold up all that tall, like it's a real burden. Poor thing. He has a nice smile."

I stared down at the ripped, stepped-on backs of Vanessa's long jeans, afraid to look. "What's his deal?" I asked her.

"I don't know, he is so not a hipster, but I've seen him hang out with them. He almost has an anti-look, it's so nondescript. Midcentury Gap. White T-shirt–ville." She looked at me. "It's fine, though. Completely inoffensive."

"Do you think he looks like he's just met someone?"

"Someone meaning you?" Vanessa continued staring blatantly. "I think he went out with Judd Lieberman's sister."

"When?" I asked, the squeak of sneakers on the marble floor grating on my nerves.

"Last year," she said, putting her hand absently on my shoulder. "She graduated. Calm down."

I went to the library and found Amanda Lieberman in the yearbook. She was pretty in a neat, preppy way I wasn't: clean, shiny brown hair and wide, bony cheeks sort of like his. I was more blobby—cherubic, not chiseled. I kept my highlighted blond hair dirty because washing it made it limp. When it got too greasy, I sprinkled it with powder, like I read George Washington used to.

At home after school I fell asleep on our gray sectional and had a dream that Will and I were lying together on a car hood in the blazing sun in our underwear. It's funny how love is like the flu, how one minute you're fine and the next it digs in and takes over.

"Have you finished your homework?" Mom asked, rousing me out of my coma.

"Haven't started yet," I said. "I don't start till after five."

"Since when?" she asked, glancing at her Canal Street Chanel watch.

"Since always." I pried myself out of the split in the sectional.

"You'll never guess what just happened," she said, jamming the sleeves of her blazer up her arms.

"What?" I was sitting up now, braced.

"I think I just sold my first flat. The two-bedroom on Astor. Can you believe it? The client made an offer and the seller accepted. I just got the call." She waved her cell phone around, then combed her fingers into the front of my scalp, "lifting" my hair. "Would it kill you to wear your gorgeous hair down one day? It looks so grotty when it's in that godforsaken mess at the back of your head."

"Anyway, congratulations," I said, falling back onto the couch, taking in the whole picture of what she was wearing: a short black skirt that was possibly shorts, black tights and high-heeled boots that went up to her knees. It was her signature look: a Barneys version of Madonna's Danceteria phase.

"You wore that to the showing?" I asked.

"Got a problem with it, honey chile?" she asked, her working-class-and-proud-of-it English brogue morphing into a pathetic attempt at ghetto. She strutted into the kitchen, her wavy blond hair hitting her cheeks as she uncorked an open bottle of pinot grigio. "'Cause yo momma is some hot shit now, yo momma is yo real estate ho."

I rolled over onto my stomach. I needed sugar.

"They finally gave me my business cards today," she called. "Come see."

I stumbled into the kitchen and she handed one to me. Her fire-engine-red grin ate up the postage stamp–sized photo in the upper left, and in the middle, in royal-blue italics, were the words "*Fiona Galehouse, Sales Associate.*"

"*Galehouse?*" I asked, flabbergasted.

"It sounds nicer than Addison," she sniffed, dropping an ice cube into her glass. I slumped at the kitchen table. Only my mother would take her husband's surname once they'd finally *divorced*. "It has a better ring for sales." She avoided my eyes and I realized the real reason for the switch: she wanted to distance herself from the whole tax-evasion thing. My mother had gotten into some kind of trouble when I was twelve and Fiona's, her nightclub, was winding down from its heyday. It had to do with taxes, and all I know is that Mom secretly blamed Dad for it, for not being "aggressive enough," even though it was never really clear to me that he'd had anything to do with it. He worked at an investment bank and never spent time at Fiona's, or with us, for that matter. It didn't help that the tax thing coincided with the summer Dad stopped drinking. Everyone was weirdly on edge that summer—Mom screaming on the phone all day, Dad coming home from work with five bottles of Clamato—but then after making such a huge deal about getting Dad to quit drinking, Mom went and divorced him anyway.

After they did the intervention on him and Dad went away to rehab, Mom realized that she was pissed as hell that it took Dad's *boss* to get him to stop, when she'd been pleading with him for years. She'd tried leaving—I remember trekking out in the middle of the night many times with my hamster and staying at her friend Maryanne's—but we always ended up coming back to the same routine: Mom in the bedroom with her plate of cheese and crackers, her phone and the TV, Dad in his leather swivel chair in the living room, ignoring us, with his headphones and piles of paper. They had an uncanny habit of never being in the same room together. But when the almighty Bill Mindorff told Dad he'd get the ax if he didn't sober up, only *then* did he take it seriously. Bill Mindorff. I'd never met him, but the picture of him in my head was crystal clear: red tie with little blue polka dots, white shirt, feet up on his desk, wielding his untold powers over Dad.

"Apparently we don't factor in nearly as importantly as the

possibility of not becoming a bloody managing director," Mom had said one night while Dad was away "drying out." I'd dabbed my pinky into the tub of her cold cream and swirled it around on my forehead, wondering how Dad could love his job more than us. But the fact that he was gone for all but maybe five hours on the weekends meant it must be true.

"I've got some beautiful asparagus for dinner," Mom said, wiping her hands on the blue-flowered dish towel. "It's after five. Start your homework."

"I met a guy," I said, fishing a rice cake out of its plastic pack.

"Ooh," she said, downing a sip of wine.

"He's a senior. His name's Will Weston."

"Is he cute?"

"Beyond."

"Well, well, well, I'm really pleased, Thea," she said unconvincingly, wiping her lipstick off the rim of her glass. "I'm not surprised. You're a knockout." She smiled at me and I studied the crescents of her red-rimmed brown eyes, eyes that looked like she could be crying even when she smiled, as if even though she was smiling, she was never, for a second, forgetting how screwed up the world was. I wondered if anyone thought she was an addict. My mother was a vegetarian who drank wheatgrass shots and herb tinctures and did yoga every day, but she still had red-rimmed druggie eyes. She banged her glass loudly on the slate countertop. "You could have anyone you want. Just take your hair out of that hive."

2.

The week crawled by until Will and I went for burgers that Friday, four days after the fire drill. The restaurant was in the basement of a garment industry building with fake wood paneling and head shots of soap actors. There were a few suits at the bar and that was it.

"She's beautiful, my friend." A guy with a bow tie cupped my elbow as I caught a glimpse in the mirror of my too-yellow, flat hair, which Mom had made me wear down. "Where do you want to sit? You have the place to yourselves."

"He doesn't say that about just anyone," Will said as we headed to the back of the room. I looked at the empty booths, awash in red-webbed candlelight. The last thing I wanted to do was eat. I was dying for a drink but didn't want to get carded, so I ordered a Diet Coke. Will got a beer. He clinked my glass, still on the table.

"Glad you agreed to dine with me." He swallowed with a quick jerk of his head, like he was swallowing an aspirin. He leaned forward, his wide, square shoulders pointing at me through his wrinkled button-down. "So tell me about you," he said. "Where do you live?"

"I live in Chelsea with my mom," I answered. I was having trouble figuring out which eye to look into. Looking into the left one, the one that worked, felt too focused, too intense. It made me feel like I was ignoring the right one, but looking into the right seemed wrong, since I didn't think he could see out of it. I pushed the paper off my straw, deciding to just get it over with. "So can I ask you . . ."

"The left one." He smiled assuredly. "You're good. Most

people skirt around it for years. Just ignore the right one. Pretend it's not there."

"Okay." I sipped, catching some lemon pulp, trying not to make lemon lips. "Were you born with your eyes that way?"

He shook his head, sucking in his cheeks to quickly down the beer he'd just swigged. "I looked up into a tree when I was three and an acorn popped me in the eye."

"Did it hurt?"

He shrugged, smiled, didn't answer.

"So where are you going next year?" I asked, focusing on the left side of his face.

"Columbia," he said. "Got in early. I hope it's less of a waste of time than this place."

"Well, you get to stay in New York. That's a plus."

"That's right," he said. "Close to home. I'm a city boy. A New York boy."

He explained that his dad was a financial analyst who did consulting with big banks. "He works two days a year," Will said. "The rest of the time he walks up and down Broadway. He's a big walker. He goes to the movies a lot. He's seen everything." I told him that my own father worked endlessly, was consumed by his job, and had very little personality to show for it. Will had two brothers. He got along with Johnny, the younger one, but not Roy, the older.

"What about your mom?" I asked.

"Mom's got a degree in public health management, whatever that is." He sighed. "Yet she spends all of her time baking desserts no one eats and puttering. How many times can you leaf through a twenty-year-old *National Geographic*, I ask you?" He shook his head in wonderment. "You got any siblings?"

"No," I responded, worrying about my hair.

He snatched a French fry off my plate. "That was a test," he said. "Good sharing. You passed with flying colors. How are you with attention? Do you need someone's undivided attention all the time or are you more of an independent-spirit only-child type?"

"Independent-spirit only child. Type."

"Good. Actually, now that you tell me that, I see it. You have a lonely way about you."

"I'm not lonely," I protested. "My mom's home all the time."

"That doesn't count," he said dismissively. "All the time?"

"Yep."

"Is she okay?" He leaned back. "I know what you're going to say. Depends what you mean by okay, right? Does she work?"

"She used to. She used to own a club."

"What kind of club?"

"A club club." I shrugged. "Fiona's."

"No way," he said, his left eye widening. "Did you ever go?"

"Only when it was closed. It scared me when I was little. The guys dancing in cages, you know, half-naked, dog collars . . . she sold it when I was twelve."

He bit off giant bites of his burger, dipping what he had left in a pile of mustard. He said he didn't like ketchup. Only mustard. My mom drowns everything in ketchup, including Chinese food.

"Didn't she . . ." He paused, examined his bun. "This is awkward. Didn't she get, like, busted for tax evasion or extortion or something like that?"

"She took a plea," I answered quickly.

"A plea?"

"Some kind of plea-bargain thing that let her off," I said, dousing my fries with more salt. "You can tell I so enjoy talking about this, right?"

"Sorry." He grinned, his good eye lasering into me. "What's she doing now?"

"Watching *Days of Our Lives*," I said. "Moisturizing."

"What about Dad?"

"They're divorced," I said.

He looked at me pensively. "Did you take it hard? How old were you?"

"I was thirteen. Of course I took it hard, although I never saw him." I slid my empty, wet glass around on the table. "Doesn't everybody?"

"Don't deflect. Some people are waiting for it, or expecting it."

"I wasn't expecting it," I said.

"So your mom sold Fiona's and then right after, went about getting a divorce?"

"Sort of makes your head spin, doesn't it?" I chirped.

He peeled at his beer label. "Does it make you not want to get married?"

The room blurred behind him into chunks of brown and red light. "I do want to get married," I said.

"Awwww." He pretended to swoon.

"Walked right into that one, didn't I?"

He reached for my hand and patted it.

"Boys," I sneered. "Anyway, now that they're finally divorced, she's decided she wants Dad's name. How weird is that? She was always Fiona Addison, now she's Fiona Galehouse."

"Okayyy." He smiled.

14

"Hopefully it's just on her business card."

"So she *is* working."

"Yeah, sort of," I said. "She's started selling real estate. Apartments. She's always made a big deal about working. 'You never want to be financially dependent on anyone,' she tells me that all the time. 'It's the most important thing. Financial independence. If you don't make your own way, you'll have no choices in life.' When I was little, I had no idea what she was talking about. Whenever she said 'choices,' I always pictured parting my hair on the left, then shaking it out and parting it on the right. To this day, when I hear the word *choices*, I think of parting my hair."

He sat very still as he listened, which made me worry that I'd been rambling. After a moment he cleared his throat dramatically. "So Thea," he said, looking at me sideways. "You seeing anyone?"

"Who, me?" I asked, my tongue feeling as though it had quadrupled in size.

He looked down at his plate, then up again, waiting.

"I'm not seeing anyone at the moment," I said. "What is that, anyway? Seeing someone?" I made a peekaboo gesture. "I see you!"

He waved for the bill. The bow-tie guy threw the billfold across the room like a Frisbee, and Will caught it and folded in money.

"Thank you," I said. I wondered if his family watched the Oscars together. And if he'd ever seen his parents naked.

We navigated the dark stairs up and out into the empty street. The sidewalks were streaked with black ice, and the howling February wind shot up and down the street. Will put my arm through his and we walked hunched into the cold like

15

old people. He told me about his favorite building, which we were nowhere near.

"Did you know that if you work in the Seagram Building, you can only have your shades all the way up, all the way down or exactly in the middle?" he asked.

"That's assuming you have a window office."

"I'm going to assume that," he said emphatically. "I'm an optimist. You have to be an optimist in life. No one told me that, by the way." The wind screamed at his face, making his eyes water. "Shiver me timbers."

"I feel like I've seen shades in that building that were five-eighths of the way down," I said as we both stopped to find our gloves.

"That would be hard to believe, Thea."

"Well, I think I have," I said. "Actually, I'm sure of it now. I have."

"Well, why don't we go verify that?"

"We're twenty blocks away."

"It'll be worth the trip. Let's make it interesting. If there is one shade not in its rightful place—high, medium or low—it's five dollars. For you."

"Okay, deal."

"All right, then," he said, straightening up with purpose. "We'll be there in no time."

It felt like we were crossing Antarctica. I had no hat and my ears burned. We barely said a word, it was so cold, and I didn't want to complain. When we got to the Seagram Building, we went up the steps and stood in the middle of the plaza.

"There, I see one," I said. "The shades are three-quarters down. Six floors up, four from the left. We have to stand back a little."

"Jeez, you're right," he said, surprised. "How did this happen?"

"It must be busted." I held out my hand as he fished for the five.

"I appreciate that deep respect for order, I must say," he said, slapping it into my hand. "Philip Johnson, he liked things in their place."

We stood there for a long time, freezing our asses off. It was so beautiful—the ceilings on every floor were illuminated, rich, deep blocks of orange. All those squares, hovering over all the private conversations about God knows what that I would never know about, all I would never know. Will was looking up at the top of the building, pensive and still, a smile frozen on his face. Finally he turned to me and I knew what he was going to do, so I stood still and waited, letting the fantastic terror of those tiny milliseconds crawl through me as his cold face came to mine. Everything that had been moving around us—the revolving door pouring out late-night stragglers, the Poland Spring truck plowing its way through the avenue traffic—everything seemed to come to a halt, as if we were all in a weird game of freeze dance. I felt incredibly grown up and hoisted out of my life, kissing him in his black coat, a shock of black in the orange haze. He stood back, slowly stamping his feet as I cupped my ears and blew into my gloves.

"It was Mies van der Rohe," I said. "He was the guy who designed it."

"Really?" he asked, not minding being corrected. "Well, maybe Johnson helped."

We got a cab back to my house and he walked me to my door.

"Want to meet my mom?" I asked nervously, hoping she was wearing something other than that dumb yoga tank with the stick figure of the guy doing a sun salutation.

"Not tonight." He winked, taking my hands.

More kisses in our dim, carpeted hallway, quiet except for the echoing wind in the elevator shaft. Who were his friends? I wondered. Why me? Did he like tall, thin girls? Because I was tall but not exactly thin, and I wasn't sure he'd realized that yet. We kissed and kissed, that new kissing you could do forever. I wondered how long my turn with him would last.

3.

"I want to make this," I said as I sat on Vanessa's bed in her large, powder-blue bedroom. I handed her an old photo I'd found of me standing on the beach on Charter Island in a red, white and blue bikini.

"Look at you!" Vanessa said, examining it. "What a cutie. How old were you?"

"Sixish," I said, peering at it next to her.

"You look like you have a big boat sponge or, like, a gigantic maxi-pad under your crotch," she said, and she was right. The bikini bottom sagged in the crotch because the suit was made of crocheted wool. When it was wet, it would stay cold on my skin and never, ever dry. I remembered it being incredibly itchy, but there was something about it I absolutely loved, and looking at the picture reminded me of how much I loved it.

"My grandmother made it for me," I said. "She made blankets mostly, in hideous mustard tones, but she made the bikini, too. I wish she'd made more." I grabbed the photo out of Vanessa's hands. "I remember her taking that picture so clearly. We were on the beach on Charter and it was really early in the morning. We were hiding from my parents after some giant brawl in the middle of the night, after Dad got bombed and called Mom a shit-hair."

Vanessa burst out laughing. "What the hell is a shit-hair?" she asked, reaching over me to a yellow apple on her desk. "Are they dumber than shit-heads? Meaner? Ted, man, he's got a way with words. Thank God he quit the hooch. Now we just need to find him a together young lady." She bit into the apple, spinning it around between her thumb and index finger. "I'm officially off Snickers. I think I'm turning diabetic."

"Do you think I could find a pattern for the bikini?" I asked, tapping the photo.

"I can't imagine who would publish a pattern for something like that," she said, pulling an old canvas tote out of her closet.

"Well, I can," I said. "People are weird."

"Why don't you start with a scarf and see how it goes?"

"I don't want to do a scarf."

"I don't wanna," Vanessa whined. Her black bra strap burrowed into her shoulder and she shoved it to the side. Vanessa had big, beautiful boobs. No points, just circles. "Now, if I'm going to show you, you cannot get frustrated." I sat up against the wall and she moved next to me, pressing a gray, metal crochet hook into my hand. It was thin and cold and I liked the way it felt.

"I won't, I promise," I said.

She fished around in the bag and pulled out a large, messy pile of dark purple yarn. Then she yanked a line off it and took the hook from me. "The first thing you've got to do is cast on, which is basically a series of little knots, also known as chains. Repeat after me . . . *chains.*" She did the first two, then moved my fingers around the hook until I got it.

"Do about thirty for a scarf. You want it long and skinny, right?" Her head knocked against mine while she watched, and I could feel her breath on my hands. "Tell me about last night. What's he like? Is he all Arthur Miller–tortured or is he normal?" She lifted my index finger and bent it, like it was a piece of Play-Doh, farther down the hook.

"Vanessa, I like him so much it's freaking me out," I said, clutching the loop that hung precariously from the hook.

"Be specific," Vanessa implored. "What was the place like?"

"Dark and steak-housey, and sort of desolate and empty."

"Sounds *awful,*" she said, holding my elbow out as I tried another chain.

"He's a little weird," I admitted.

"How?"

"Well, his family sounds pretty out there. His dad works two days a year and spends the rest of the time going to movies, and his mother's got a degree in public health management, whatever that is, but he says she spends all of her time baking and leafing through old magazines."

"Weird!" Vanessa exclaimed, intrigued.

I remembered to bring the yarn around from the back of the hook, thinking of Will's face, his body, his stillness. "I feel sick," I said. "Is he going to call me?"

"Don't go rexy on me," she said, turning the hook toward my chest.

"I won't."

"Or bulimic. You better not." She took another bite of her apple and chewed loudly. "He'll call. Then you'll 'bandon me for the boy. Perfect, you're getting it. Do a few more and then we'll start the first row." She dropped her apple on the bed, where it made a wet stain on her quilt, and fished in the bag for another hook, this one with a square of flecked beige hanging off it.

"Ooh, what's that?" I asked enviously.

"I just started it." She spread the chains across the hook proudly. "It's going to be a sweater."

"How come you get to do a sweater and all's I get to do is this crap scarf?"

"God, Thea, you're *so* impatient." She rolled her eyes dramatically.

"Do you think when I'm done with this boring eighties scarf, I'll be able to do the bikini?" I asked.

"Let's jump off that bridge when we get to it," she said with a sigh.

4.

By the end of March of my junior year, I had a life-ruining B average. I'd finished the first semester in December with a B-plus, not great compared to everyone else but good enough for me and, more importantly, good enough for Dad.

Dad was forever dreaming up ways in which I could be improved. That was the secret to our relationship. It's what kept him interested.

I went to a "specialized high school" for math and science geeks, but I hated math and was terrible at it. If Dad hadn't quizzed me for a year with those little flash cards held up to his chin, I never would have gotten in. Even though I always majorly screwed up in math, I was usually able to offset it with As or A-pluses in English and history and dumb, extraneous classes like metal shop. But by the end of March of my junior year, I had a B-plus in biochemistry, a C-plus in geometry, a measly B in English and a B-plus in history. I was screwed.

The problem was, I'd stopped doing homework. Will was a second-semester senior and had none, so it became too hard to face mine. I didn't want to do homework. I wanted to be with him. We took long walks after school to the East Village for French fries, or to a café between our place and Dad's, where we drank hot chocolate and lounged for hours on the black velvet couch in the back. The homework was always there, the obscure stress of not doing it getting louder and louder as the afternoons wore on.

When the March grades came in, Mom called Dad and he cornered me at one of our Wednesday-night dinners.

"Look, Thea, you need to try harder," he said, yanking his tie loose. "You're a junior. This is your most important year, for Christ's sake. The grades at the end of this semester are crucial. This is it, kiddo, you know that. You've got to get it back up to at least a B-plus. At *least*! I don't know what's going on—Mom says you've got some new boyfriend. Maybe you're going through something, but you've got to try harder."

"I *am* trying," I squealed, pissed that Mom had told him about Will.

"What's the situation with the tutors?" he asked, curling his hands into problem-solving fists.

"I'm going to Binder for biochem and geometry."

"He does both?"

"Mmm-hmmm."

"How often do you go?"

"Once a week. We do an hour on each."

"That's it?" he demanded, shoving his glasses up the bridge of his thin, narrow nose.

"That's *enough*." I thought of Mr. Binder sitting at his dining room table in his boiling hot apartment, waiting for me in his yellow undershirt. How my elbows would get sore from leaning on his lace tablecloth. If Will, science-fair-finalist Will, found out I had a tutor, I thought, he would realize what a dumbass I truly was and that would be it. Game over. I had a fantasy of going to some progressive private school where my homework would be to read *Madame Bovary* and to create and perform an interpretive dance based on it. But Dad believed in public education. "If you don't go, who will?" he said. He actually believed that if he sent his daughter to public school, other investment bankers would follow.

"Well, I'll say it once again, this semester is crucial, Thea," he said, pausing with his hands in the air.

"I know, I know," I said, watching him chew. He always looked like he was grinding his teeth rather than eating.

"So what's your first choice these days?" Dad asked, taking a roll from the basket in front of us.

"I don't know," I said, relieved he'd changed the subject but annoyed at his lame, forced switch to the aspirational, his fallback. "I'm thinking it might be good to stay in New York."

"What about Wesleyan?" Dad had gone to Wesleyan. We both knew it was rapidly becoming a pipe dream, given my plummeting grades, but he liked to dream.

"I'm a New Yorker. A city girl. I think I'd get bored."

"Hardly," he said.

"NYU's still within my reach if I do well on the SATs. And I'd be close to home."

He threw salt from the shaker onto his roll in jerky bursts, as though the salt weren't coming out.

"What's wrong with that?" I asked.

"Nothing," he said. "Let's get cracking on the grades so we have some options, shall we?"

"'Let's'? I believe it's 'You get cracking, Thea.' Last I checked, you've been out of school for, like, decades?"

He took a deep breath, as though trying to suppress some deep, white-collar rage he felt toward me and my lack of ambition. "You know, Mommy never finished school," he said.

"Yeah, but who cares? She ran her own business."

"I think she suffered for it," he said. "She's savvy but undisciplined. That, in my mind, is a result of not having a good, solid education. I don't want you traveling down that route."

"None of her friends in Gloucester went to college. If you're smart and creative, it's a waste of time."

"Not exactly," he said, his left eye twitching slightly, as if he were imparting some secret knowledge he wasn't supposed to. During moments like those, hearing his tight, confined sentences and comparing them to Mom's loud rush of words, I wondered how they ever got together in the first place.

I sat back, tossing my napkin onto my plate, knowing how much Dad hated seeing dirty napkins on plates. "I should get home," I said. "I have tons of homework."

"Let's get you home, then," Dad said, wincing at the napkin or me, I couldn't tell.

5.

Mom went to a real estate conference over a long weekend in May. I was supposed to stay at Dad's, but I'd neglected to mention to her that Dad was going to be at a banking conference in Bermuda, and they didn't bother checking with each other anymore.

"Who is it?" I asked, even though the doorman had already told me on the intercom.

"It's the plumber," Will answered in a low monotone. "I've come to fix the sink." He jumped just a little when I opened the door, and it occurred to me that he was nervous too.

It was weird having a boy in our white, fluffy-kitten apartment. Mom rarely had any men over. Alex, her married, veiny-templed boyfriend, occasionally. But Alex was so wimpy, slithering into her room like it was a hole in the wall, like a mouse fleeing danger. Will was different. A foreign mass our house had to reconcile itself with. We sat down on the living room couch and he picked up Mom's long strand of wooden beads, spinning them around on his finger.

"This place is cool." He smiled, looking around. "It's exactly how I pictured it. Took you long enough to invite me."

"I've invited you before," I protested, mashing my knees together to make my legs look thinner.

"Just that one time," Will said. "When I walked you upstairs, the first night we went out. After that, nothing. What I can't figure out is whether you're scared to have *me* meet her or to have *her* meet me." He leaned toward me and batted his eyes.

"Need I remind you that I've yet to meet your parents?"

"You will, sometime soon," he said. "Not that that's anything to look forward to. Anyway, your mom has nice taste. Minimal, for lack of a more imaginative word. My parents are stuck in Shakerville. When people come over, they're like, 'Dude, you Amish?'"

"Maybe they like to keep it simple," I said.

"Nah, they're just too depressed to figure anything else out. To change anything. They're big wallowers."

"But you," I said perkily, "you're not depressed. You're an optimist."

"That's right," he said, sticking his thumbs under his armpits, mock-proudly. "I said that on our first date, didn't I?"

I nodded, pulling my hair out of its messy knot, subconsciously channeling my mother and trying to "lift" the front.

Will stretched, reaching his hands behind his head. "So what do you and Mom eat for dinner?"

"Salad in summer, stir-fry in winter," I said, pulling my T-shirt down over the lower bit of my stomach as I leaned back next to him. "That's pretty much the way it works around here. She's a vegetarian."

He took my hand and slowly waved it around with his. "Rembrandt's was closed this week because of a flood," he said, referring to the restaurant his parents went to every night for dinner. "They almost couldn't cope. Dad made us breakfast last night. Ham and cheese omelets and a head of iceberg with salsa. Real lettuce scares him. He came home at five last night. I couldn't believe it. Usually he's home after seven. He likes us to think he's coming home from a long day at the office, but everyone knows he's actually been at the Israeli market buying cashews."

"He really works only two days a year?" I asked, looking

26

at the brown, braided belt around his impossibly narrow waist, which only reminded me of my never-ending, visceral need for underbaked chocolate cookies.

"Yes, and he wouldn't have it any other way. He's not exactly a people person."

"He must be very smart," I said.

His left eye darted around my face quizzically. "I don't think you have to be that smart to get a job like that."

I didn't say anything. Even after three months of being together, there was something so intimidating about him.

"Anyway, this is too friendly, what we're doing," he said, his gaze fixed on the black and white photos of me and Mom across the room. "I don't want to be friends right now."

"You don't?" I asked, feeling my stomach flip.

"I do want to be your friend—who wouldn't want to be your friend." He said it fast as a statement, not a question, putting his hand, which was hot and shaking just a little, on my knee. "But right now I want to jump on you. And if we keep talking, I'm worried it will be too late."

We looked at each other for this crazy, scary moment that seemed to stretch on and on as the white living room grew gray and hazy behind him. He pushed me backward on the couch and got on top of me, kissing my face, then my mouth, our bodies matching up in a straight line, all the way down. He was heavy, almost too heavy, but I felt safe and enclosed as he undid my jeans with his confident, searching hand. He did whatever it was that he did to me and I felt the couch somehow drop away, and it was like for a few seconds I entered some alternate universe where everything was humming and buzzing and not really real.

It's not like I was a novice. I had two boyfriends before

Will. First was Bo Brown, the summer after seventh grade. We fooled around a lot. Never anything past second, but he basically had his hands and his mouth all over my boobs all summer. I never got tired of it. We swam out to the rocks that led into the Charter Island harbor once and Bo did his thing, his spit, metallic-tasting from his braces, washing over me with the salt water. It must have been the weekend, because Dad was there. I remember seeing his big, bald head from the water, shining in the sun. He was up on a ladder, painting something on the side of the house.

"Thea Galehouse, for Christ's sake, are you aware that there's a riptide?" he yelled at the house, not at me, which made him look deranged. "It could have swept you right out. Jesus!" I hoped he'd seen us.

Michael Cunningham was the second. I was fifteen and he said he was nineteen, but it turned out he was actually twenty-four. I met him hitting tennis balls against the backboard in the park across the street from our apartment. But he was a stoner, and after a while it started to freak me out. There's smoking pot and there's smoking pot. Mom got it way before I did, after meeting him for a split second in our lobby.

"Tell me it's just marijuana," she said.

"Huh?" I asked.

"What's he on?"

I shook my head. Too dumb to play dumb.

"I'd rather you didn't spend time with him. Irrelevant, I realize, but don't do drugs with him. Come to me if you want to get high."

But the stuff with Bo and Michael had been nothing like *this*. I get it now, I kept thinking as I lay underneath Will, I get it. After a while I felt a wet spot by my hip.

"I told you, I'm a class act," he said, embarrassed. "Sorry."

I nudged him to my side and we lay like that forever, in a little astrodome of lips and rough, salty skin amid the fading Friday-afternoon light.

"Galehouse Rock," he said, running his finger along my hairline. "G-Rock. Your eyes are always open. Every time I open my eyes, your eyes are open."

"Like bug-eyed?" I asked. "Like I'm a meth addict?"

"No, you freak." He laughed, prying my eye wider with his thumb and index finger. "You're just taking it all in. You don't look like you have a lot of judgment going on in there. I like it."

"I judge," I said.

"I know you judge yourself. I'm going to bet you give yourself the business. Anyone who has Fiona Galehouse for a mother can't help but be a little cracked."

"Thanks," I said.

"I mean it as a compliment," he said, bumping his nose against mine. "You're welcome."

We ate hummus and carrots, drank Mom's white wine and talked, finally falling asleep on the rug under the coffee table. We woke up Saturday and fooled around all day, did everything but, then did it for the first time Sunday. We were going to do it, then we weren't, and then we finally did, right before he was about to leave.

"You don't want to wait a little longer?" he asked, sliding a condom on dexterously with one hand. It was clear to me he'd done it before.

"Nope," I answered.

"Big of me to ask, though, right?"

It was a big deal, but not in the way I expected. I was

expecting to be transformed into someone I felt like I was supposed to know, but hadn't met yet—the ten-years-older version of me. I'd imagined her hiding behind a midnight-blue velvet curtain, and I thought that when I finally had sex, the curtain would go up and there she would be—the new me, and the *old* me, that little girl digging her short fingernails into an orange on a January night, she would disappear forever. But she was still there, with her goofy secret wave and all.

After we did it, I took a picture of Will lying in between two of my bears. They lay in the same position, the three of them naked with my pink flannel sheet covering their chests, each with their left arms sticking out stiffly at their sides. I lined up their heads in the frame and got on top of Will.

"You know," I said, framing the shot, "when I was little and I went to work with Mom and saw that guy in the cage at Fiona's, his giant penis scared the crap out of me. It was covered by his green leotard, but it was, like, you could see the outline of it, which was almost scarier than the real thing. But yours is different. It's friendly looking. Pretend you're sleeping."

Will closed his eyes, trying not to smile. "Do you think the bears have feelings?"

"Of course," I said. "I know they love *you,* for one thing. They just have a hard time showing it."

I heard heels clonking down the hall and froze. "I'm home." Mom peered into the room. The clock on my desk said six-thirty. The last time I'd looked it was two o'clock. I was straddling Will on top of the covers and thanked God I'd thrown on a tank top and my underwear. "I see you're having a cozy time of it."

Will stared up at the ceiling, frozen like the bears.

"How was the conference?" I asked, not looking at her.

She moved farther down the hall to her room without answering. We got a grip, threw on some clothes and crept toward the kitchen. Will was right on some level: I hadn't had him over because I wasn't sure Mom would like him. You had to prove yourself first, have a story of intense personal suffering to be worthwhile in her eyes.

"Why is everyone so stupid today?" she said, crashing into the kitchen counter with some plastic shopping bags. "That damned Rolf." To an outsider she would definitely look slightly mad, with her red eyes and smudged fire-engine-red lipstick.

"What'd he do?" I asked, relieved that the focus was off us and our sexual misadventures.

"He's just a tosser," she said simply. "That thing I needed to go out Friday morning before I left is still there. Such an attitude. I wish they'd fire him." She looked pointedly at Will. "Hi."

"Mom, this is Will," I said.

"Hello, Will." She held out her hand.

"How do you do," he said, shaking it.

"Very well, thank you," she said, an amused smirk sneaking across her face at his formality. She turned away and pulled toilet paper and toothpaste out of the bags.

"What's going on?" I asked as nonchalantly as possible.

"Sort of a rubbish weekend," she muttered, twisting the plastic bag into a knot and throwing it into the cabinet under the sink. "Had an unpleasant meeting with Don Trainer. I've known this man for twenty-five years. But he's a bridge burner, which you should never be in that business." She peeled waxy paper away from a hunk of dark yellow cheese. "Will, would you like to try some Old Amsterdam?"

"I'd love some, thanks."

She scraped a thin slice. "I shouldn't share this, it's too good," she fake whispered.

"I appreciate it, Fiona," he said. I looked at Mom. She didn't seem to mind the first name.

"I thought you said you didn't want to work with that guy," I said.

"I didn't but he called again, and you know."

"Mom."

"What?"

"Lose the losers in your life."

"Don't I know it." She winked at Will, chewing.

"You're right, this is very good," he said. He got up and went to the fridge and pulled out a can of Diet Coke, which he cracked open and drank. Again, Mom didn't bat an eye.

"You keep saying you want to pursue the real estate thing, so why don't you partner up with someone you actually like?" I asked.

"I don't know, Thee." She sighed, leaning toward the kitchen counter. "I don't know."

Will stayed for dinner; he helped Mom by chopping up broccoli and dumping it into the pot when she said, "Okay, now."

"I like him," she said when we were on her bed later that night. "He's gorgeous, Thea, you didn't tell me."

"Yes, I did," I said. I was sitting next to her on the bed with the purple mess of yarn Vanessa had given me to crochet the scarf. It had been sitting in a sad pile on my radiator for months, but for some reason that night I was determined to untangle it and roll it up into a neat ball, even though I had many, many unread pages of biochemistry sitting on my desk.

"What's that?" she asked, as though I had a dead mouse on my lap.

"Just some yarn Vanessa gave me," I said.

"Anyway, he's gorgeous in that truly American way," she said, fishing for the TV remote, which was buried under a pile of magazines and notes to herself. "Like someone is pointing a blower at him, keeping him awake and bushy-tailed. He's got no pretension. He's an old soul."

I rolled my eyes, leading the end strand of the yarn through a series of snarls and pulling.

"What?" she asked. "I'm not saying it lightly. He has a maturity about him."

"When you say 'old soul,' it cheapens it."

"Oh, well." She scowled. "Terribly sorry to cheapen it. What's wrong with his eye?"

"You mean, how it wanders?" I asked, rolling what I'd untangled into a small, kitten-sized ball. "He looked up at an acorn tree when he was little. Isn't that cute?"

"He can get it fixed," she said, muting the TV. "He's quite funny, actually. He'll seem sort of serious, but then he breaks into that lovely grin, quite at the drop. Which is nice. You don't want anyone too heavy, Thea. That's for sure. I was always going for the darkish ones. Like Daddy. But dark is actually boring, lo and behold. Anyway, Will is welcome anytime. You can tell him I said that."

"You're not mad at me?" I asked.

"I'm not mad," she said. "A little jealous, maybe—"

"Mother!" I said, dreading what was coming next. I don't like talking about sex. I don't bond over it. My mother has always provided me with far too many details. About how Bruce, her orange-tanned, social-worker ex-boyfriend, nibbled

33

his way up her thighs until he found her spot and brought her off, or how one of the backers of Fiona's who she ended up screwing had a penis that curved like a scimitar. Mom was purposefully graphic because, she said, she didn't want me to be a victim.

"I'm kidding," she said, laughing. "That was tacky. Sorry. Just don't do anything stupid. Should we put you on the pill?"

"I don't know," I said. The pill was for older, more mature people who were serious about sex. "Yeah, maybe. Please don't tell Dad."

"Oh God, why would I do that?" she said, starting to read the program guide on the screen. "He'd just blame me. You're seventeen, for God's sake. It's none of his business."

By the time I untangled the last bunch of knots, I had a nice ball of yarn the size of a tennis ball. I squeezed it, letting little images from the amazing, perfect weekend with Will drift by. The way he slept in a fetal position with his leg curled up around my waist reminded me of the framed *Rolling Stone* cover on the wall in Mom's bathroom where John Lennon is lying curled up around Yoko Ono. I took the crochet hook and stabbed it into the ball. It looked like a piece of sculpture or artwork, full of weight and purpose. When I pulled the hook out, it brought a couple of strands of yarn with it and I thought, That's my heart right now—stabbed by a blunt object, with little bits of heart mush oozing out. That's my heart. My heart is hooked.

6.

All spring, I expected Will to graduate and that would be that. He would realize how silly this thing with me was, given the sea of women about to become available to him in September. So June took on a Lifetime-television-for-women quality, like soon Will would . . . die tragically of leukemia.

But we didn't break up. When school ended, we got summer jobs, me at Mom's friend Ella's shop on Lexington Avenue, he at a law firm, and we'd meet every day for hot dogs in Central Park, sweaty and irritable.

We drove to Charter Island one weekend in July and made it to the station by 8:05 to pick up Dad, who'd caught a train at Grand Central after work. I saw the train pull up and there he was, his head in the window, looking down at some "important documents." I thought of Mom and her fits of rage as they were splitting up. "Tosser marches off to rehab the second Bill Mindorff raises a red flag, but we don't count for rubbish."

Was it true? If it was true, why didn't he try to change? To shift his priorities around a little bit? It seemed stubborn and selfish of him not to try, and look where it got him: facing backward on a train on a Friday night, his shoes stuck to old newspapers, another summer closing in on him.

"I can't understand why anyone would want to endure I-95 when there's that perfectly nice Metro-North," Dad said as he got into the car, carrying stale train air with him. "You must be Will." They shook hands and I saw it right away in his eyes: this was the reason his daughter wouldn't be going to Wesleyan.

"Nice to meet you, Ted," said Will. Dad glared at Will.

I knew he was put out by the first name. I wished he would relax and not sit so straight in his seat, his wide head like a cement block in front of me.

"We had decent luck on the way up, not much traffic, thank God," Will said as we pulled out of the parking lot.

"I have a car, but it sits in the garage by my apartment most of the time," Dad responded.

"What kind of car do you drive?" Will asked in an overly chummy way.

"An eighty-four Aston Martin."

"Oh man, I would love to see that."

"A fellow at work sold it to me when he took a job in capital markets in London," Dad said placidly.

"So I hear you're a banker," Will said, stopping a little too short at a red light. "What area are you in?"

"It has to do with risk," Dad said vaguely, as if Will couldn't handle a complete definition.

"Is that why you're in it?" Will asked.

I squirmed in the backseat. The question was sassy and Dad ignored it.

"Did you two have dinner?" Dad asked.

"We did," I said. We'd stopped at McDonald's on the way up, and the car still smelled like heat-blasted strawberry milk shakes. "We were starving. Sorry."

There were whitecaps on the water that glowed under the moon as we drove toward the house. We parked on the gravel and I led Will to the guest room, where he dropped his bag and swung old tennis racquets and picked up books from the stacks on the table. I was glad Dad was still upstairs when Will went to the kitchen and opened cabinets. The snack cabinet was packed with family-sized bags of chips and Goldfish

36

that Dad kept around in case people came over for a sandwich or drinks. I wondered if Will thought it was weird that a grown man who lived in a house by himself had giant bags of junk food in his closet. I was always wondering what Will thought. He took an old metal pinwheel off a shelf in the library and went out to the porch to watch it spin. I sat down next to him on the damp wicker couch and before long, Dad came out in jeans and a brand-new Harvard Business School sweatshirt.

"So, nice to have you up here." He nodded and raised his Coke to us ceremoniously before he placed it deliberately onto a coaster, then pulled the legs of his jeans up and lowered himself to his chair.

Will leaned forward on the couch next to me. "This is a beautiful spot, Ted. It must have been wonderful to grow up here." I looked around. It was what you would call a casual house. Sailing trophies were strewn around on shelves, and a rack of croquet mallets jutted out into the living room. But that was my grandmother. Not Dad. Dad was so uptight, so stiff and ill at ease, I wondered how he could have any friends. I could tell that Dad thought Will was out of line, calling him Ted again. I could almost see him squirming and seething in his chair. He sat with his knees together, as though he were holding in pee, gripping his glass on the table next to him.

"Thea doesn't come up as much as she used to," he said. "This is a treat."

"What are you talking about?" I said. "I was here last weekend."

"We've got to get you up on skis," he said, turning to Will. "We took her out last weekend and it's the damnedest thing. She just can't stand up."

"You rev the engine too much," I said, making a fist and turning it. "You've got to go lighter. You jerk me around. Literally."

"She's never gotten up," he said to Will, ignoring me. "I can't figure it out. Her feet are exactly where they should be, her legs—"

"Dad, hello? What did I just say? It's too much of a jolt."

"No one else . . . the Hendricksons didn't seem to have any problem with it. I think it has more to do with your stance. You lean over too far."

"Well, how about I lean back next time and you pull the throttle to half where you were pulling it." I remembered floating sickly in the water, hanging on and wanting to let go, anticipating the smack down. Everyone on the boat turned to the water, watching me, except Dad, his head turned away, hand gripping the throttle.

"We'll get you up one of these days," he said. "By golly, we're going to make it happen!"

Why had he brought this up out of nowhere? I heard Jim, the caretaker, come in through the kitchen door and start to get Dad's dinner ready. Jim had looked after the house for my grandmother, and after she died, Dad kept him on and the job somehow evolved into shopping and cooking for him on the weekends. The house looked more formal, fancier, than it actually was. Dad sighed and closed his eyes in forced relaxation, then glanced at Will.

"How'd you like to go fishing tomorrow morning?"

"I'd love it," Will answered, overly enthused. "What time?"

Dad got up and walked over to the tide chart hanging on a pillar.

"The optimum is three hours or so before dead high," he said. "So, five or six."

"Ouch," said Will.

Dad looked at Will like he'd said a word he didn't understand.

"What the hell." Will slapped his legs. "I'm game. Morning air. Good for the brain." He broke into a wide, jovial grin. He looked slightly ignited, a little too hungry, next to me in the dim light.

"All right, then," Dad said. "We have a taker."

Dad had never once asked me to go fishing. Sailing, yes, but fishing was a man's thing. This infuriated me—how he could complain that I didn't spend enough time with him, then spend the day devising new ways to get away from me when I was actually there.

"Let's go for a walk," I said to Will.

"Sure," he said.

Dad stood up. "I'll tap on your door at around quarter of tomorrow," he said.

"Would that be quarter of five or quarter of six?" Will asked.

"Six," Dad said. "Let's sleep in a little." He winked as if he'd just said something very sly. I cringed. What a nerd. "You two have a nice walk," he said, and started for the dining room. Will and I went out and found his sandals on the front porch. We headed down the street, and through a crack in the hedges I could see Jim lighting two tall, white candles and pouring water into a crystal glass. Dad tucked his napkin into his sweatshirt collar, lord of the manor, commencing his meal.

My bare heels banged against the pavement, and our shadows grew taller and thinner under a lone streetlamp.

39

"How glad are you that you're not a fifty-year-old divorced investment banker with no life?" I said.

"*So* glad," Will said, looking back toward the dining room window. "Who's that guy waiting on him?"

"It's just Jim," I said. "He's been around forever. He helps Dad out on the weekends."

"Nice," Will said, his expression hard to read underneath the dim yellow streetlamp.

7.

They went fishing the next morning for three hours while I sat on the porch eating Grape Nuts, worrying Will would catch something and show Dad up, or not catch anything at all and feel like a failure. He ended up catching one lonely snapper, which he threw back.

I watched Jim go into the kitchen that night with moving brown-paper bags, remembering how Mom would run screaming from the kitchen when she saw those bags. Eventually she would boycott lobster night altogether.

I pulled out some old green-glass salad plates shaped like crescents.

"I'd wash them," Jim said sheepishly. He filled the big black pot with water.

When the water was boiling, Jim squeezed the tops of the lobsters' heads, which he said deadened the pain, then threw them in. Will came downstairs and smiled, his back to the pot, when he heard the lobsters hissing.

The wind had died down, so we ate outside on the porch while Jim cleaned up the kitchen. Dad focused on his food, and we would have eaten in complete silence if Will hadn't started talking.

"Did you spend a lot of time here when you were a kid, Thea?" Will asked me, his lips glistening with butter and salad dressing.

"We would come up for a week or two in the summer," I said, "but most of the time I went to day camp in the Bronx. Mom didn't like it here."

"Fiona was not one for island life," Dad said as the claw he was cracking fell into the butter. "This island, anyway."

"That's hard to imagine," Will said. "It's beautiful here. It's one of the most beautiful spots I've ever seen."

Dad stared at his plate, chewing, avoiding Will's eyes. I begged him in my head to at least acknowledge the compliment.

"When Thea was little, she used to think lobsters were monsters," he said. "She'd see the bags and run outside, all the way out to the end of the bluff. Remember, you wouldn't come in until they turned red?"

"Well, it was hard to watch Mom freak out and not think something terrible was happening."

"Thea was also afraid of rain." Dad rose suddenly, scraping his chair, and went to the pillar in the corner. "See what I did here? I haven't shown you, have I? I moved them."

"Moved what?" I asked.

"Your height measurements."

I got up and went over, followed by Will.

He turned on a lamp. "I marked it all up on a tape, so I think it's still pretty accurate." I looked at the markings, immediately remembering the sensation of a pencil being leveled on top of my head: the first when I was around a year old, then every few months after that, the gaps ranging from incremental to gaping, depending how much time passed in between. The original markings had been done in different-colored pens, and Mom had done some of the early ones, so the handwriting looked different from year to year, depending on which one of them wrote it. But now the markings were uniformly etched in black graphite, Dad's script as neat and tight as a calligrapher's.

"Why did you move them over here?" I asked.

"The chairs kept smacking against the pillar by the table, so when the porch was finally painted last fall, I transferred them over here, out of harm's way," Dad said. "It's a wonder you ever grew at all, given how much you hated vegetables. Do you remember how crazy we used to get?"

I nodded, remembering the nauseating stench of corn-on-the-cob steam escaping from a jiggling lid. Nana, of course, blamed my mother and her lack of discipline in raising me.

"But now look at you," he said. "A broccoli fanatic. And salad. Salad was the first thing you started to come around on, if I remember correctly. Salad with little cherry tomatoes."

He looked me up and down, arms stiffly at his sides, and it was like I could read his mind: she needs to lose a few pounds. After the divorce I'd become Mom's property and therefore vaguely distasteful to him.

"Let's eat," he said, steering us back to the table.

"So where do you get the lobsters?" Will asked. "Do you guys have a trap out there?" He elbowed toward the water.

"No, it's illegal now, you need a license. Thea, why are we eating salad off ashtrays?"

"What?" I asked. "I thought they were salad plates."

"These were Nana's and they're actually ashtrays," Dad said, picking up his plate and holding it at his chest. "This gives you an indication of how much they used to smoke. They would lay these out all over the house during cocktail parties."

"They really do look like plates," Will mused. "Were you ever a smoker, Ted?"

Dad nodded, mashing his napkin across his mouth. "Two packs a day at one point. I'd somehow resisted temptation all through college. I raced crew and played lacrosse, so I took that very seriously. But when I met Thea's mother, actually, that's when I took it up."

"Right, all her fault," I chimed in.

"I'm not saying that, Thea," he said, looking at me pointedly. "No one to blame but myself on that front." He pushed his bowl of empty lobster shells away from him, toward the glass-enclosed candle in the middle of the table. "I think I got caught up in all the headiness of it, you know, the parties, the scene, all that. They all smoked."

"What brand?" I asked. I pictured him slouched in his chair in the living room, drunk.

"Camel Lights, whatever was around. Anyway, needless to say, I hope you don't fall down that little rabbit hole," he said, rattling his glass of ice and draining it of water. "Nicotine addiction is no prize. It's been, what . . . almost a decade? And still, I'd kill for a cigarette."

"Really?" I laughed.

"Oh, absolutely," he said, smiling and shaking his head. "Absolutely. It never really went away for me. And sometimes at work . . ." His voice trailed off.

"What about a drink?" I blurted, surprising myself. His drinking was more of a taboo subject for me than sex. To bring it up was not just embarrassing but dangerous. I still had pervasive, floating fears that he'd start again. And somewhere in my head I believed that if he started again, it would do him in. Whether it was true or not, that's what I believed.

"That too," he said, his face stiffening, closing up. He watched Will's reaction, gauging how much I'd told him.

"I could see how they'd go hand in hand," Will said.

Dad nodded, chuckled skittishly. "Not too clearly, I hope."

"How did you stop?" Will asked.

"The same way I stopped drinking," he said quickly. "I put my mind to it." He leaned back in his chair and crossed his leg.

"Was it hard?" Will asked, wide-eyed, encouraging. I could hear it in his voice. He was digging for color, but I knew he wouldn't get any. "Did you have, like, withdrawal symptoms?"

"With the drinking I did, sure," he said. "The smokes were more of a habit. But like any smoker, I guess, a beloved one."

"What do you miss most?" Will asked.

"What, about smoking?"

"Or the drinking, or both."

Dad arched his eyebrows skeptically. "You're extremely interested. . . ."

"I just mean a successful guy like you, you know, you had these . . . demons that you conquered, so to speak." Will sat back and crossed his legs, jiggling his foot on his thigh. "The partying, you know, you and Fiona, boozing it up, getting high, it seems very glamorous from where I'm sitting."

Dad looked at Will carefully. It was definitely crossing the line into too-personal territory and we all knew it, but for some reason Dad talked. "I wouldn't say I miss anything about it. It's more that I miss my youth, and the requisite reckless-ness. I'm in my late forties. I'm human. I feel old."

"You're not old," Will said.

"I'm not young." He let out a forced, theatrical sigh. "You know what's funny? I miss being married. It's funny how I associate smoking with marriage."

"You miss being married?" I asked.

"Of course I do. Does that surprise you?"

"Uh, yeah," I answered in my best teenager voice. Mom once told me men were like dumb little pups, sitting in a window waiting for a home, any home.

"Well, it shouldn't." He smiled. "Enough about me and my checkered past. Who wants dessert? I think Jim picked up a Fruits of the Farm pie."

Jim appeared silently in the kitchen doorway. I wondered what he'd heard.

"Jim, were you able to get your hands on anything at Chelmsfords?" Dad asked conspiratorially.

"I got lucky," Jim answered.

"Music to my ears," Dad said, rubbing his hands together as Jim brought out the pie and set it in front of him. "Who wants a slice? Food. Pie. That's my downfall now. Who?"

8.

Mom stood by my door with a pair of jeans under her arm and her white sunglasses on top of her head. "What in God's name are you doing?" she asked.

"Crocheting," I said, gathering the ball of purple yarn farther up my lap. "Vanessa taught me."

"God, you're giving me chills," she said. "You are single-handedly conjuring the horror of Evelyn Galehouse," she murmured, meaning Dad's mother, my grandmother. "The way her fingers twitched when she made those awful blankets! She would always *appear* to be so engrossed, but every time I looked, I caught her glaring at me, like the evil little witch she was. Anyway, how can you even look at heavy yarn like that in this heat?"

"It's August, Mom," I said. "It's hot outside. Deal with it."

"What's wrong with you?" she asked, rolling the jeans into a little bun.

"Nothing." I gripped the loop I'd just done tightly with my finger. "Will's moving his stuff up to Columbia today."

"Well, we knew the day would come," she said matter-of-factly. "Honestly, Thee, do not get so wrapped up in this. You have the rest of your life to need a man to be happy."

"I'm not wrapped up."

"Good. Do you have anything for Josephine?" she said, referring to the tailor who worked at the dry cleaners downstairs.

I shook my head. My phone buzzed and Mom jumped. She hated loud, sudden noises and looked at me like the phone ringing was somehow my fault.

"G-Rock, money-love," Will whispered as Mom waved and left. "Wanna come up here and check it out? Help me unpack all my bongs?"

"Okay," I said, squeezing the ball of yarn and smiling from ear to ear. I thought it would be weeks or months until an invitation came. "Do you need anything?"

When I got out of the subway at 116th Street, there were plantains at the vegetable stand on the corner instead of bananas, and the plantains spoke to me. They said: We dare you to succeed in our strange new world. We dare you to try to hold on to him.

The street outside the main building was a sea of cars with lampshades, stuffed animals and stereo speakers on their roofs. A girl ran by in a tennis skirt with a purple boa around her neck.

"Mom, wait!" she shrieked. "I have the keys!"

I walked through two stone pillars into a grand, imposing courtyard and had a flash that I was in some other part of the world—one of those piazzas in Florence, where I'd sucked face with some now-almost-faceless boy—and that I'd be leaving soon, getting on a plane or something. I went into the building, up the stairs and around a corner with a bulletin board displaying ads for used couches and rides. There was a note card tacked to it: "To whoever made a grilled cheese in the lounge toaster 4/23 . . . clean it out, asshole!" I wanted to stare at that board for every clue of what life would be like for him, but I continued down the carpeted hallway, which smelled of cigarettes and Doritos. I passed a huge, plastic black cat with a skinny neck and a pointy snout. It was almost as tall as me, its creepy, imperious eyes following me as I stopped at room 208.

Will's door was ajar and a tall man gazed at me with a sandwich perched at his mouth. I smiled at him and then registered the woman sitting on the bed reading. She didn't look up. A wave of something close to panic overtook me. Will had neglected to mention his parents would be there.

"G-House Rock!" Will yelped, stepping down from a grimy wooden desk chair. He hugged me with a mix of enthusiasm and awkwardness, turning me around by the shoulders to face his parents. "Thea, this is my mom and dad, Phil and Lynne Weston. Guys! This is Thea!"

"Pleasure to meet you," Mr. Weston said, crumbs dangling from his lips. His handshake was surprisingly limp. Mrs. Weston crossed her arms and didn't stand up. Her dark hair was pulled back in a messy ponytail, with little bullets of unruly strands sticking out at the sides. She looked at me with her spooky gray eyes and heavy, arched eyebrows, which somehow had the ability to angle down at me even though I towered over her as she sat on the bed. She and that creepy plastic cat in the hallway automatically morphed into the same person in my head.

"Hello, Thea," she finally said. She had a switch on–switch off smile that zipped across her face, almost like a tic, then disappeared.

"This is my special fwend you've heard so much about," Will said in an off-putting baby voice. On the desk there was a fish tank with two coral reefs and a fake Campbell's soup can propped in the corner of it. A green fish with rainbow-colored gills swam around in a plastic bag inside the tank.

"I didn't know you had fish," I said.

"Not fish," Will said, holding up the plastic bag. "A fish. Ricky, meet G-Rock."

He turned to his father. "Did you remember to throw in the extension cords?"

Mr. Weston nodded blankly at Will. "I should go check the car," he said. He turned to me and I noticed little lakes of long-ago stains on the navy-blue polo shirt that stretched across his belly. "Will is under the impression that double parking is now allowed under some new citywide ordinance," he said, winking at me. "Do you find his laissez-faire attitude toward life as refreshing as we do, Thea?"

I shrugged like a dumb teenager, cursing my cutoffs and

wishing I'd been somehow better equipped for meeting them. I felt blond and fat and didn't know where to stand.

Mrs. Weston picked up a framed poster of a big tree with violins hanging off it like Christmas ornaments. It was for a music festival in the Berkshires in 1969.

"Where do you want this, sweetheart?" she asked, standing to face the dingy, cinder-blocked wall as Mr. Weston almost tripped over a laundry basket stuffed with hangers on his way out.

"I'll do it later, Mom." Will looked at the digital clock that had been plugged in but was still sitting on top of an opened box. "We should go to this reception thing . . . it's already started. Dad, just meet us there, it's down the hall." I saw Mrs. Weston look away as Will put his arm around me, and I had a moment to take in what she was wearing: a white tank top under a too-big, untucked denim shirt.

"Will you be my l'il date, G-Rock?" Will asked, batting his eyes at me.

A large tray of white and orange cheese cubes was the only splash of color in the drab, olive-hued lounge. About thirty kids stood around, some forming triangles with their parents. A guy with short, black hair and a sweater tied around his neck stepped toward us.

"Excuse me, I saw you across the hall from my room," he said. "You're the other lucky one." Mrs. Weston, Will and I stared at him blankly.

"Oh," Will said, "the singles, you mean?" He rubbed his hand through his hair. "Yeah, that was a break, I guess. I tend to be lucky in things that involve sweepstakes."

"My name's Olivier, nice to meet you." He shook Will's hand.

"I'm Will, and this is my mom, and my girlfriend, Thea Galehouse."

Olivier nodded, assessing me with his French eyes. "Listen," he said to Will, "I've asked some people from the hall over for a little thing tonight. I hope you can swing by." He looked and sounded like he couldn't care less if Will came. I dubbed him "Sweaterboy" in my head. So far college seemed like an endless series of "little things" where people stood around avoiding each other. After some more small talk Olivier cleared his throat. "I'm just off the plane from Paris this morning, so I'm starting to fade. Time for a catnap." He nodded again and sort of bowed to Mrs. Weston, whose smile switched on and off as he walked away.

"So, Thea, you're a senior now, is that right?" Mrs. Weston nibbled on a cube of cheese and bored into me with her gray eyes, which looked somehow icier now that she was standing by a window. "What are your plans? How is Thea Galehouse going to set the world on fire?"

"Good question," I said, belching out a stiff, truncated laugh. "Haven't quite tackled that one." I looked around the room at all the tall, tanned kids oozing summer relaxation in their new olive-hued lounge, and felt suddenly overwhelmed. How was I going to face senior year without Will? Take the SATs? Apply to colleges? Write essays? How was I going to do any of it? Dad's face flashed in front of me. His intense, steely scrutiny, demanding results and performance. How was I supposed to be a normal high school student when I had this rope pulling me here? It wasn't fair that Will had gotten away to this place, to his own room with the plastic cat in the hall and Sweaterboy across the way, while I still had this mountain to climb.

Mrs. Weston must have read something on my face

because she paused, orange cheese cube in midair, and said gravely and urgently, "Be positive, Thea."

I nodded, seething at her new age–claptrap comment. Be positive. Could two words in the English language be more meaningless?

"Frankly, I think your generation has it made," she said, folding her arms. "Mine was still scatterbrained. Too many mixed messages from our mothers." She tapped her bony temple with her fingertip. "Anyway, Thea, I wish you every success. We need strong women like you out there, forging ahead with great things." Will looked at me, wide-eyed, as if to say, Don't mind her, she's crazy.

Mr. Weston appeared next to Mrs. Weston and cleared his throat. "There's an officer circling the cars downstairs. Lynne, I think we should make ourselves scarce." He seemed to always have the same smiling expression on his face, as though he were cracking deeply ironic personal jokes to himself all the time. He pulled his glasses off and rubbed them with his shirt as he turned to Will. "You all set?"

"Yep," Will answered, giving his father a hug with half his body and patting his back.

Mrs. Weston turned to me and held her hand out formally. "Goodbye, Thea," she said pointedly, and I understood the gesture right away: she believed she was saying goodbye to me forever.

They ambled side by side through the swinging doors as Will started to reach for a toothpick to pick up a cube of cheese. He glanced at me and retracted.

"You could have told me they'd be here," I said.

"I didn't tell you?" he asked. He reached again and this time popped a cube into his mouth. "Sorry."

"Your mother hates me."

51

"What are you talking about?" Will rolled his eyes and stuck the toothpick in the side of his mouth. "She wouldn't know how to hate you. What was all that about setting the world on fire, or whatever she said? She's a repressed bra burner, stuck in the seventies."

"Did you hear her tell me to be positive?" I asked, realizing that other people in the room were tentatively striking up conversations with their hall mates. I felt like I was holding Will back. He looked around quickly at everyone, then leaned toward me.

"I must have you. Now. Let's blow." He chucked his toothpick into a grimy, black wastepaper bin and we pushed through the swinging doors.

Back in his room, Will lifted the vinyl-upholstered bolster running along the side of his bed and gestured to the shelves underneath. "You can put your exfoliators and night creams and whatnot in there," he said, grabbing my ass. He pushed me down on the bed, angling my body away from a bag of opened fish-tank gravel as a warm rush accosted my stomach. It never ceased to amaze me how quickly sex worked.

"Nice intro to your bad boy," I said. Usually he played around with me down there before the main attraction. "Don't mind me, I'll just lie here."

"Sorry, I'm feeling very . . . focused," he said, thrusting.

"You like fucking me in your new room?" I whispered.

"God, yes," he said. There was the sound of footsteps running down the hall and I felt that letting-go, almost sick feeling, our backs growing sweaty on his bare, unmade mattress.

We lingered in what felt like timelessness afterward as the room got darker, listening to the constant stream of noise out in the hall. The bad thoughts started crowding back in. *Be positive*. Schmee schmositive.

"Have I mentioned that your mother hates me?" I asked.

"She doesn't hate you," Will said, running his fingers along my boobs. "She's just an odd bird. They're in their own little rabbit world." When the room was pitch-black, I got up and felt around for my sneakers.

"Do you really have to go?" he asked, pulling my hand.

I nodded and kissed him, turning on a light. I wanted to stay, but my heart was already aching at the thought of leaving and I wanted to get it over with.

"Good night, G-Rock, Rocker-G, Special Sauce." He stood up, naked, his distracted, disgruntled expression reminding me of Dad's whenever I left at the end of a weekend. Like he didn't want me to go, but at the same time his head was already somewhere else.

part two

9.

As a special parting gift from Stuyvesant—a final act of cruelty—
I was awarded zero-period gym my senior year, which meant
I had to be in the girls' locker room by quarter of eight each
ever-darkening morning. After school Vanessa and I had SAT
prep on Twenty-Third Street, and then we'd go for coffee and
anxiously bark vocabulary words at each other while doing
our other homework.

I got home late one night in October and heard Mom's TV.
I was in a phase where I'd decided to stop worrying about her.
She'd passed the real estate test and she had two new listings,
so she had stuff to keep her busy. I was glad she was awake, in
bed with a hunk of white, runny cheese, her latest obsession.

"How was the class?" She held a cracker out at me, still
looking at the TV.

"I'm totally fried," I said. "It's too much. I can't wait till it's
over."

Mom said nothing and went back to her cheese. Her bed
was overgrown with mail and dry cleaning hangers. I made my
way to it, using the flashing TV light to navigate.

She was watching a movie where two kids were getting
married, and they didn't want a big wedding but their parents
did. It was a movie from the fifties. I could tell because the girl
character started every sentence with "Why," as in "Why, I
wouldn't dream of going to the picnic without you."

The guy on TV was yelling. "Maybe we should forget the
whole darn thing!" he said. I turned and leaned my head
against her leg. Her duvet smelled like nail polish remover.

"Why can't you be more like them?" Mom asked, her head
gesturing up at the screen.

"What are you talking about?" I asked.

"They're just so polite and . . . obedient. They respect their parents."

"I respect my parents," I said, although I could hear my own mocking tone of voice.

"Right," she said. She'd cast the cheese onto the pillow next to her and was patting Pond's onto her face. My mother had a penchant for cheap drugstore beauty products. "That rental car company is still breathing down my back. Honestly, Thea, I got another bill from them today. It's been months since that little episode."

"Really?" I asked sheepishly.

"Yes, still," she said. "We gave you our hard-earned money to go and be on your own and study in another country, and what did you do?" she asked. "You took that money and paraded around the continent doing God knows what." She set the Pond's jar down on her chest and yanked the tie on her robe.

"God, we've been through that so many times already," I said. "Can't we laugh about it yet? Can't it be a story that we have now that we like to pull out of our hats from time to time at parties?"

"Don't be flip, Thea," Mom snapped. "There is absolutely nothing amusing about that episode and there never will be, to me or to Daddy. You could have been in a much more serious accident, or gotten raped or murdered, and we might never have found you."

They'd given me three thousand dollars for a work-study program in London, where I was supposed to take some "new math" course at UCL (Dad's thing) and a design class at Central St. Martins (my thing). I stayed at Mom's older sister's in

Fulham and got a job at a café. But by the beginning of August I was getting really bored. Vanessa was doing an exchange student thing, living with a family outside of Venice, so two weeks before the classes ended, I quit my job, told my aunt, who was clueless, that I was going to visit a friend, and I met up with Vanessa in Italy. I had a thousand euros from the café job and from what Dad had given me, and Vanessa had more, so we took off. I'm not sure why, but I felt like I deserved to do what I wanted, and what I wanted was to go with Vanessa to Portofino and then up to the top of the Matterhorn in Switzerland, to watch the sun rise, and then to Ireland or Scotland, if we had money left, to check out all the beautiful yarn. I love yarn, especially raw, prickly yarn straight off a lamb, in rich, dark colors. It was the best two weeks. We were the dirty Americans. We got drunk and found cute guys everywhere, made out with them in cafés, behind crowded market stalls, in smelly bathrooms. We slept in hostels or in two-star hotels, or sometimes in the train station, on our bags. We'd wake up sweaty and hungover and change our minds about where to go next and find some cheese and bread and stay another day. I'd called Mom and lied, lied, lied, saying I was still in London. I knew she'd never check in with her sister because they didn't get along—Dad had actually been the one to call her and arrange my visit. We would have gotten away with it if I hadn't sideswiped someone in our rented car in Galway, on our way back to Dublin, right at the end. It was the first time I'd used a credit card the whole trip, and I thought I'd be home in time to intercept the bill. But when I returned the car, the rental company called my mother, the primary cardholder, to get her insurance information. After that it was a shit show.

"Such callous disregard, Thea," Dad had said, the pain of

deception knitted into his thin, gray brows. "I'm deeply, deeply, disappointed." Well, so am I, I remember thinking. I'm disappointed that you couldn't figure out a way to stick it out together so I wouldn't have to pack my stupid rolling Swiss Army suitcase every weekend like a traveling monkey and waste my allowance on cab fare to your stupid house by the river—far, far away from any subway, when I'd rather just stay put at Mom's.

"I would think twice before you ever pull a stunt like that again," Mom said, slapping the lid on the Pond's jar.

"Actually, there's this arts program at Edinburgh next summer that I wanted to talk to you about," I said.

She muted the TV and glared at me.

"I'm kidding," I said. The phone rang in my room and I rolled off her bed.

"Don't stay on long," she called. "I can hear you, you know."

"College is so boring," Will said when I answered. "They're all next door. I can hear them."

"Are they eating pineapple pizza?"

"Yeah, that's right, and friggin' taco sandwiches. Hell, I just want to go to sleep. With you. I wish we could be together all the time. I wish you could live in my drawer. I wish I could uncork you from a bottle whenever I wanted. God, I just miss you, Thee."

I breathed in his voice, little pinpricks moving across my chest, as though my heart were waking up from falling asleep.

"Imagine we're really old and you die and everyone sees me trudging up and down First Avenue with my boots undone," he said. "They'd say, 'Poor Vic.'"

"You changed your name?"

"Yeah, I changed my name to Vic, thinking it would make me feel better."

"But it doesn't," I said.

"No, it does not," he said indignantly. "But they all say, 'Poor old Vic, lost the love of his life,' and the other widowers bring me Ovaltine and doughnuts, which I can't eat because I'm so bereft. And they ask me out."

"The widowers? You've gone gay?" I watched puffs of cottony smoke billow from a tower outside my window, thinking, White looks so strange in the dark.

"No, I mean widows," Will said. "The ladies. I take one out a few times, but soon enough, wouldn't you know it, she starts to bug the shit out of me."

"Let me guess, she gets on you about exercising."

"Right. 'Fitness first,' she cackles over and over, like a parrot, so I break up with her because she just reminds me that I don't care about fitness anymore because you're not there. At night I'd lie in my little single bed, remembering G-Rock, my flower girl. Your green eyes that catch fire when you're in the sun and the way your face automatically points to the sky when you laugh. I'd look out my window, at the little sliver of moon and I'd say, 'Damn you, moon, give me back my girl.' I'd curse, then I'd beg, then I'd curse, then I'd beg, all night, every night, till I finally died too."

"Wow," I said.

"Sad, right?"

"So sad."

"Well, maybe it'll end happier than that," he said. "Maybe you won't die and I won't die and we'll live happily ever after forever. We'd be the first people to live forever."

"That'd be nice," I said. I stretched my legs to a cool part

61

of the mattress and pictured us living in a tiny, gold-wallpapered apartment in Paris on the Seine, next to that famous bookstore. How great and weird would it be if we stayed together forever, I thought. High school sweethearts. How great and weird.

10.

"I can't take it," my friend Jill said as she squeezed a slimy lemon onto a wedge of washed-out-looking honeydew. We were cutting fourth period at a coffee shop near school on a brisk morning just before Thanksgiving break. Jill's mother raised Pomeranians and sold them at cut rates. I used to see the handwritten ad at a deli near my house. A sketch of a pug-nosed dog inside a lopsided heart. There were something like twelve Pomeranians living in Jill's apartment, and Jill's mother made her walk the bigger ones every night before she went to bed.

"She makes me carry these tiny wads of tinfoil, which aren't big enough to pick up the poo," she continued. "Then, when they get their periods, they walk around in public in little doggie diapers. People stare at me on the street. I hate her." As I pictured twelve diapered Pomeranians dancing at Jill's feet, a cold, sinking feeling rushed through me. Where was *my* period? I quickly calculated the dates in my head and realized I was a few days—maybe even a week—late. How could it be? I was a sophisticated, sexually active teenager on the pill. But then I remembered the Friday night a few weeks earlier, when

I'd told Mom I was staying at Vanessa's and instead I'd stayed at Will's. I hadn't brought my stuff with me. I'd told myself not to worry and to just forget it and had done a good job of it, until then.

I obsessed over whether or not to test when I got to Dad's apartment that afternoon. Mom was away at a spa in France, and I didn't think I could handle all those days in a row with Dad if the results were positive, so I decided to wait, wishing the weekend were already over. Will was leaving with his family to spend Thanksgiving at his aunt's in New Jersey, and Vanessa was going upstate somewhere. Dad and I were having Thanksgiving dinner at home. A trader who worked for him was coming with his wife.

I went into my bedroom, found my crochet hook and yarn and curled up on Dad's stiff canvas couch, grateful for a tactile distraction. I'd kept the project by my bed at home and I picked it up sometimes when I was on the phone late at night with Will, but after a while it hurt to crochet and hold the phone in my neck, and the phone always won, which meant I never got very far. But I liked having it by my bed, marking time, waiting to be finished.

Dad's apartment was silent except for the noise from my grandmother's antique clock on his desk. I looked up at the slats of dark wood, the old warehouse ceiling that was Dad's favorite thing about the apartment. Sitting there reminded me of all the nights I used to stay up late, reading his old photography books, waiting for him to come home so I could say goodnight and go to bed. He'd been in that apartment on West Twelfth Street a while, two years maybe, and it was so much better than the dump on Twenty-Third Street he went to right after he moved out. Nothing was more depressing than that.

The elevator buttons were the really old kind that lit up when you touched them, but they were so dirty and disgusting I'd only touch them with my elbow, which was hard when I had a coat on. A never-ending hallway with grassy, dentist-office wallpaper led to his scuffed-up metal door. He'd open it on Friday nights, his living room a murky brown hole behind him, and hug me and my knapsack with some strange kind of desperation, like he was drowning.

He came home that night at around seven, his phone jammed to his ear. "A Maserati's a fine car, as long as you drive it in a straight line." He chuckled. "That's right. Well, enjoy. Don't do anything I wouldn't do." He took off his coat and smiled at me, slipping his shoes under the chair in the foyer. "How was school? Any homework?" He kissed me on the forehead and headed toward his bedroom. He did that all the time—asked a question and walked away or asked a question and looked down and read something. It drove Mom crazy. I try to look at it as some form of adult attention disorder. It could hurt your feelings if you let it.

"It's Wednesday night," I called after him.

He came out of his room, still in his suit pants and a brand-new white undershirt. His undershirts and socks and towels always looked brand-spanking-new. It was a complete mystery to me. He either bought new ones all the time or it was some secret of Rula's, our longtime housekeeper who Mom and Dad shared after they split. It was his one fashion statement. "Why not get it over with, that way you'll have the whole weekend free in front of you."

"Uh-huh," I said, unwinding some more yarn from the ball.

"What are you doing?"

"Crocheting," I said.

"Crocheting what?" He went toward the cluster of plants in the corner, arranged as precisely as a landscaped garden, and stood over each with his brass watering can.

"A scarf, it's just practice. I just learned."

"No kidding," he said, looking up at the sculpted bust of the headless, armless woman in the corner. He'd bought it at an antique show, and whenever I looked at it, I wondered if Dad secretly hated women. "I'm all for hobbies where you're actually making something. People don't make things anymore. But start your homework soon, okay? How's it going? Any tests this week?"

I told him I got a B-plus on a geometry quiz I'd taken that Monday.

"Where does that leave you?" he asked, setting the watering can down and balling his hands into fists at his sides. "Where does that leave your average?"

"I'm in good shape, don't worry."

"You're sticking with that idiotic plan of yours?" he blurted, his metal eyeglass frames catching the light as he flinched in disgust. I'd applied early decision to NYU, which had effectively snuffed out his dreams of my attending Wesleyan for good.

"My idiotic plan?" I asked, stopping what I was doing to glare at him. He was completely incapable of editing himself. It was like thoughts came into his head and he would vomit them out without thinking about how the other person might react. Mom said he had Asperger's syndrome, that it just hadn't been diagnosed.

"I'm sorry," he said flatly, plucking a dead leaf off the rubber tree plant he'd had forever. "I'm just really, really disappointed."

"NYU is a great school and it's the perfect fit for me," I said, borrowing lingo from Ms. Weiss, my college counselor at school. "If they ding me, then I'll apply everywhere else. It's a waste of time, pursuing other schools right now."

"Well, I couldn't disagree more," he said, tossing the dead leaf angrily into the wastebasket by his leather chair. "You did yourself a huge disservice, not leaving your options open." He sat down in his leather swivel chair and started opening mail, the sharp sound of ripping envelopes cutting through the thick silence. I focused intently on my hook, torn between explaining to him, calmly and coolly, how carefully I'd thought about applying to NYU, and telling him to go screw himself for being his usual jackass self.

I looked at the photograph of *Mixed Nuts,* his beloved sonar racing boat, on the bookshelf. Ever since I was a tiny thing, Dad had found countless ways to demean me via sailing. When I was four, he took me out on his boat and tried to teach me how to read the wind. "It's there, Thea, you have to pay attention," he said again and again, flailing his arms in frustration. "Pay attention." But the wind was completely lost to me. I couldn't see it, only the menacing August jellyfish dotting the water and our big, brown shingled house gone all Shrinky-Dink from afar. When I started sailing lessons, he bet me I couldn't get to the nun in the harbor a half a mile from our house, so of course I had to try. I got to the nun easily, but getting back took hours. Every so often, Dad would emerge on the lawn and watch with binoculars, as passively as if he were watching TV. I sailed the boat to the end of the bluff, my hands blistering from gripping the lines, then diagonally back toward the house, over and over, telling myself I was making progress.

"Why couldn't you get in the dinghy and help me?" I asked when I finally made it in, freezing from my still-wet suit yet burning with rage.

He lowered the paper he was reading and looked up at me, as if he'd just realized where I'd been. "You're going to have to get in a whole lot quicker than that, kiddo, if you ever want to race with me."

That's how life was with him, I thought, seething as he crumpled up paper and tossed it into his basket. My potential was the only interesting thing about me. If there was something to be achieved—winning a sailing race, getting into Stuyvesant, getting a high grade—count on Dad to swoop in, demanding dedication and results. Otherwise, I wasn't worth his time.

I went to the kitchen and looked in the fridge for something for dinner. There was Old Amsterdam Gouda wrapped in wax paper in the drawer, just like at Mom's. I made grilled cheese sandwiches with an overripe tomato and we had them on our laps in the living room. He ate his while I squeezed mine and tore it apart, feeling sick from imagined pregnancy symptoms. Part of me was afraid he'd be able to discern my potential problem just by looking at me, and I got a shiver down my spine at the thought of him finding out.

"So when is the turkey coming?" I asked.

"Tomorrow morning, between nine and eleven," he answered, not looking up from his paper.

"Do you think they'll drown it in rosemary bushels again?" I asked. Thanksgiving always came from some herb-crazy caterer uptown, which we joked about every year.

"I don't know, Thea," he said lifelessly. He could go

forever without talking. When I was younger, I'd sit in the living room with him, and the silence compared to Mom's chatting actually confused me. But that night I could tell he wasn't talking because he was still pissed off about college. I picked up the empty plate from his lap and went to my room for the rest of the night.

11.

"I wish the weekend weren't over," Will said on the phone Sunday night. "Four days without you. Sucky."

"I know," I said, telling myself I wouldn't mention the potential problem until I knew for sure what the deal was. "I'm so sick of Dad, I can't wait to get out of here."

"Uh-oh, what happened?"

"Nothing specific," I said. "Wait, that's not true. Let's see, I spent Thanksgiving morning making these hors d'oeuvre–y things he likes, or at least I thought he liked."

"What did you make?"

"Devils on horseback," I said. "Mom made them for parties all the time when I was little and he would devour them." I remembered hearing her heels clomping restlessly around the kitchen as she filled the hors d'oeuvre tray with olives and toothpicks. Mom was always really animated when she threw parties. When it was just me and Dad, she was bored. "But when Dad's guests came on Thanksgiving, I put the hors d'oeuvres out and he wouldn't touch them. The pudgy trader guy and his wife ate all of them. When I mentioned that Dad used to eat entire plates of them when Mom made them, he glared at me as though I'd insulted him. 'Well, that was then, Thea.' I swear I can't win with him. You're lucky your parents are still together."

"My dad says divorce is overrated," Will said.

"He's right!" I said.

"Yeah, but it sort of sounds like he's considered it as an option." He laughed. "Parents."

"Parents," I said.

"What else?" he asked. "Did I mention I wish you were here?"

I threw the blankets off and sat up. "Will, I'm scared," I said, immediately wishing I'd waited. "I think I might be pregnant."

"What? We've been on the phone this whole time and you don't say anything until now?"

"I wasn't going to say anything until I took a test."

"You're on the pill!"

"I know, but it can still happen. Remember when I stayed up there a few weeks ago? I skipped it that day," I said.

"That was one pill!" he said.

"Well, I'm probably just late," I said, remembering that Vanessa's cousin had done the same thing—skipped one pill—and gotten pregnant. There was a long silence. A door slammed on his end.

"I almost wish you hadn't told me. How am I going to sleep?"

"Sorry," I snapped. "Don't worry. You don't have anything to worry about."

"What's that supposed to mean?"

"I mean, I'll take care of it. It's not your problem."

"It's not my problem? Of course it is."

"Well, it's not even a problem yet. I'm just a little worried."

"In a way it'd be cool," he said.

"What would?"

"Having it," he said.

I heard Dad walk by my door on the way to his bedroom and turn out the light. "What do you mean?" I whispered.

"I don't know. I know we can't. It's just nice to think about. A little green-eyed G-Rock baby, rockin' the bridge."

"It's late," I said, lying down and pulling the covers back up. I looked at the ceiling and found the streaks of light shining in from the building across the street. They formed a distorted face across the beams—eyes, nose and straight, mean mouth. She looked like a mean queen.

"Call me tomorrow," he said. "It's going to be okay, okay?"

12.

I waited until Monday morning to take the test at school, a weird place to do it, but I thought taking it there would make it less likely to come out positive. I was wrong.

Debbie Marshall was on the phone with her mother outside the stall as I was waiting to look at the stick. The volume was so high I could hear both sides of the conversation. She was telling her mother how all the seniors liked her, and how she was the only freshman invited to the holiday dance. I saw the lines the same moment Debbie's mom cackled that the only reason they liked Debbie was because of her "big booty butt."

I stepped out of the stall and breathed the cold air coming through the crack in the window. All I could think was, Where would it sleep? My room at Mom's was tiny. Dad had carved it out of the living room when I was two and they'd decided I should have my own room. It was hard getting me to sleep in there at first. "Daddy had to come in a hundred and fifty times the first few nights to put you back in bed," Mom had said. "It was our fault for keeping you in our room for so long. We were hippies about that one particular thing." My room didn't have real windows, just a couple of glass blocks along the curved side of the wall to let in light from the living room. Babies needed windows. Air.

It would be easier in Vanessa's room, I thought. She had a deep closet you could fit a crib into, if you took off the sliding doors. I had a closet at Dad's but not in my room at home. Just an armoire. Mom had made this stripy pattern all over it with a comb when the paint was wet. There was the armoire and my bed, which took up the whole wall on one side. My desk stuck out along the wall across from it. I had to walk sideways in between my desk and my bed because the pile of clothes on my chair would fall off if I walked straight. I thought, We could build a loft bed, where I'm on top, and the baby's in a little crib underneath. That's the only way it could fit. Or we could not build a loft bed and I could get an abortion.

I left the bathroom to find Vanessa. She was in homeroom and I wasn't supposed to go in there. Mr. Scarpinato eyed me like I was going to start an insurrection.

"It's an emergency," I whispered, and for some reason he let me pull her into the corner.

"What?" she asked.

"I'm pregnant."

"No!" she said, her smile catching me off guard. It made me smile too.

"Yes."

"Have you told him?"

"Not yet."

"Okay, well, do that, and we'll figure out the rest." She looked out the window, thinking. "We can find out who Jamie's doctor was." Jamie was her cousin in New Jersey who'd had an abortion a year earlier. "I'll call her."

I ran my finger along the radiator dust, picturing Jamie, her red hair falling off the sides of a doctor's table, her freckly, pointy knees sticking up in the air. I looked at Vanessa, who was watching me with her arms folded. "What the hell?" I said, shaking my head at her.

"Don't worry," she said, grasping my shoulders. People were staring at us. "We'll figure it out."

Mr. Scarpinato cleared his throat, pulled a piece of chalk out of his brown polyester pants and started writing on the blackboard for his next class.

I went back to the bathroom to call Will.

"So, yeah," I said.

"No way," he said. "What do we do?" Any trace of wistfulness in his voice from the night before had vanished.

"We're finding a doctor."

"Well, I'll go with you."

"No," I blurted. "It's okay. Vanessa's going to come." I knew right away I had to keep him out of it. In the back of my head I worried that any shared downer experience would be dangerous for us, and I couldn't have that. I hung up, stuck my phone in my jeans pocket and stared at myself in the bathroom mirror, the new me.

13.

I sped out of Dad's house that night like it was any other night and I'd just spent the weekend there instead of ten days. I'd told Will, and now I had to tell Mom.

"See you Wednesday?" I called from the door.

"See you Wednesday," Dad answered from his leather chair in the living room, where he was surrounded by piles of paper he'd dragged home. Mom used to pick up his briefcase and call him "the brick salesman." I could tell he was hoping for a little more departure fanfare—a hug, for example—but I wasn't up to it.

Mom was unpacking when I got home.

"So how was it?" I sat on the love seat next to her bed.

"We had a great time," she said. "It's a beautiful area. We'll go when you're old enough to drink."

She threw me a couple of blouses, catching my eyes for the first time. "Can you throw those in the dry cleaning? How are you? How was Daddy's?"

"Okay."

"I love Beryl," she said. "She's a bit over the top and socially ambitious, the complete opposite of me. But she's good on trips."

"You met people."

"We met people, no one earth-shattering, other single type-As, mostly from New York."

She circled the bed, arranging piles, pouring shoes out of bags, not yet ready to stop moving. I knew I was about to catapult her back here, home, where she didn't really want to be.

"I don't know why I brought these." She licked her thumb and wiped a smudge off a strappy grape sandal.

"Mom, something's happened."

"Oh no," she said, putting the sandal to her chest.

"Don't worry. No one died. I'm not sick."

"Then what?"

"I'm pregnant."

"What?" She walked around the bed, dragging a scarf that had attached itself to her leg. She stood over me, inspecting.

My silence must have confirmed it. "Jesus!" she said. "Since when?"

"Mom, wait," I said, not sure what I was asking her to wait for. "I took the test this morning."

"It's Will?"

"Yes, it's Will. Who do you think?" I started crying.

"How could he—you're on the pill, for Christ's sake. Do you bother taking it?"

"Stop yelling."

"I'm not yelling." She grabbed the scarf that was stuck on her leg and hurled it across the bed, and it fell on the floor. "I don't understand, Thea. Why do I bother? Why did I bother getting you that gynecologist's appointment?"

"Look, it happened," I said, picking up the scarf. "Now I have to deal with it. It's no one's fault."

"Did you take your pills?"

"Yes!"

"All the time?" she asked, her eyes ablaze.

"Yes!" I lied. Why couldn't it be Will who had to remember to take it? I was so *bad* at it.

"Vanessa knows a doctor," I said. She pushed the overflowing suitcase aside and sat down, facing me, fists in her lap. "She says he's very good."

"Have you called him?" The crease in between her eyebrows was deep, deep, deep.

"Not yet," I said. "I wanted to tell you first."

"I'll ask around and find you someone tomorrow," she said, rubbing her temples. "The timing is really unfortunate, with all you have coming up. Honestly, Thea."

"It'll be okay." I rolled the numbered dials of her suitcase lock until they all hit zero. "I'm sorry," I said, because it seemed like the right thing to say.

14.

"The thing I figured out when I was doing it is that they're stupid the way video games are stupid," Will said, pushing the floppy SAT book up toward the edge of his bed. "The more you do them, the better you get. That's really the only trick. You just have to take, like, a million practice tests." Our elbows fell together on his flimsy mattress. 2320, I thought, over and over, as I watched Will's quick, confident face scanning the pages. He'd gotten a 2320 on his SATs. I imagined I felt a little flutter as I lay on my stomach. Mom had called to schedule "the procedure" with someone named Dr. Moore, but the appointment wasn't until later in December, when I was further along. In the meantime, I had the SATs to keep me distracted.

We went over a question about a motorcycle stuntman riding over the walls of a circular well.

"So if the radius of the well is five kilometers, the distance he travels is . . . ," Will said, his voice rising expectantly, like a preschool teacher's, trying to engage me. I wondered if stress could make you miscarry.

"I don't know, three and a half kilometers," I guessed. All I could think of was the economics homework still on my desk at home. It had taken me two hours that morning to do the supply schedule and to make the stupid line go straight up, and I hadn't even gotten to the supply curve. We were only a couple of months into the semester, only a couple of months of watching Mr. Goff's skinny, Levi'ed ass tottering on the edge of his desk while he took that same bag of pretzels out of his desk drawer every day to demonstrate the endless stream of economic principles, principles that slipped from my grasp almost as quickly as they piled up. I shut the SAT book suddenly, folding some of the thin pages over. "I'm tired."

"Let's take a nap, then." Will slid his finger through the folded pages, laying them flat, then dumped the book on the floor. He smiled with his face inches from mine and closed his eyes.

"I'm sorry you have to, you know, go through this with the other stuff going on," he said, rubbing my temple. "Not exactly great timing, is it?"

I shook my head, my eyes welling up.

"Not exactly looking forward to it, are we?"

"What, the SATs or the abortion?" I asked.

"Both, I guess." He sighed. "I'm sorry."

"It's okay."

"You can totally do this, Thee," he said urgently. "You're much smarter than you think you are."

"This is you trying to cheer me up," I said, sulking.

"I mean it. You're weird."

"I'm not weird."

"Oh, let's see," he said, drumming his chin with his fingers. "You memorized your eye doctor's vision chart. That's weird. You like saggy, dead trees, that's weird, and your peach-pit collection? That row of fossilized little pits on your windowsill?" He reached for my hand. "That's really weird, G-Rock, I hate to tell you. But weird equals smart, at least in my book." He curled his leg over me. "You just have to test your ass off over the next couple of weeks."

I stared at the wall. He'd finally hung the Tanglewood poster up, and slats of bent light from the trashed Venetian blind zigzagged across the floating, fuchsia violins. 2320. Stick with it. I fell asleep with my head burrowed in Will's neck and woke up to him kissing me twenty minutes later. Screw econ, I thought. Screw everything. Still half-asleep, I got his jeans down to his knees, pinning his legs together, and started going down on him as he splayed his arms out across the bed, like he was making an angel in the snow.

"You didn't have to do that, you know," he said as he walked me to the subway. "But it was nice that you did."

"I don't *have* to do anything," I said, squeezing his waist. We were going down Broadway, and a transvestite with neon-blue hair glanced at us as we went by. Her eyes dismissed us, as though we were dull white-bread kids, which was completely opposed to how I actually felt. I felt like I was roiling. In love to the point of roiling. I thought of the crochet hook plunged into the ball of yarn on my radiator at home. I was still hooked.

Will stopped in the middle of the street we were crossing and kissed me. We stood there on a wide, white crosswalk strip until cars honked. He pressed his forehead against mine, a straightforward, matter-of-fact lust on his face, piercing through the dusk, and still didn't move. "I love you."

"I love you too," I said.

"I said it first." He smiled. "I win."

We walked the rest of the way to the subway without a word. A guy outside a pizza parlor was whistling and shouting at a brown van moving down the street. Everything moved, bendy buses, skinny dogs on leashes, bike messengers in army jackets whipping around corners. The city had an evening glow, an anticipation, which would normally depress me a little, make me feel like I was missing something, but I didn't feel that way then.

"Sayonara, milady." He grabbed my hands and rubbed his lips across my knuckles. "Take a test tonight. For me, okay?" I didn't want to go but I also did. I wanted to pore over this weird new feeling, trust. I trusted him.

"Uh-huh," I mumbled.

"Uh-huh," he repeated. "You've still got a week before the big day, so test your brains out. I'll call you later to see how you did."

15.

I took the SATs on a Saturday morning at a dank-smelling vocational school near my house. The test room had rows of puke-yellow chairs with holes in the back that made them look like lifesavers. A week later, on the morning of "the procedure," Mom sat on my bed, pulling a feather out of my comforter. "Do you want me to come? Because I will if you want me to," she said. It sounded almost like a threat.

"It's okay, Vanessa's meeting me," I lied. For some reason I'd gotten it in my head that it would be easier to go alone, to just go alone without anyone feeling sorry for me or worrying about me. I'd have to fudge the exit—someone was supposed to take me home—but I'd figure some way out of it.

"Okay," she said. She seemed both hurt and relieved. She pressed her red fingernails up against her eyebrow, fanning it out. "Call me if you need anything, okay? I know this probably feels hard, but you're doing the right thing." She patted my leg and stood up.

I put on sweats, thinking, If it really hurts, they'll be easy to get back on when it's time to go home. I tasted rotten orange peels in the back of my mouth on the subway. Was that a pregnancy symptom? I looked at a woman in front of me wearing a thick, bulky cardigan that disguised her shape and thought of something my friend David told me: that there were hundreds of people in New York City walking around with guns, you just couldn't see them. It might be the same with newly pregnant women like me who aren't showing yet, I thought. Little secret pocket dolls, hiding from you.

The office was packed with rows of women sandwiched

between fake birds-of-paradise. I took a seat and pulled out my yarn, thinking my scarf-in-progress could stand in as a security blanket. My hands were shaky and I pulled at the yarn like a skittish kitten. A door swung open and I spotted three empty cots in a row. They reminded me of giving blood with Vanessa in the basement of school freshman year. I remembered sitting next to her, both of us squeezing the red balls, racing to fill up our bags. Then we ate four-packs of Fig Newtons and drank apple juice while the nurse had us recline for twenty minutes. Vanessa said the apple juice looked like urine.

A redhead in a flowered pajama top and a name tag that said *Annie Kay* walked by. The young-looking woman across from me in a khaki pantsuit burped. I focused on my yarn, embarrassed for her. I looked up again and she was staring at the wall, clearly worried. I thought of Mom's sister, Pat, who'd had a hysterectomy when she was thirty, and I began to wonder why the fuck I'd come alone. Annie Kay stepped into the doorway and called my name into the room, like we were all there for an audition and it was my turn to read.

"Do you have someone here with you to take you home?" she asked me, scanning the seats around me.

"Yes," I lied. "She's downstairs getting a magazine." I wondered if I was making a big mistake but thought I could always call Vanessa and have her come get me if I was dying from the pain or out of it. Annie Kay made a motion to follow her down the hall and I hoped that was the end of it.

Dr. Moore was the kind of person you'd want to get an abortion from. Blond hair cut very straight above her shoulders, and skin that clearly got frequent, maybe compulsively so, peels. She stepped quietly into the room, followed by a nurse, and everything immediately grew very serious.

"Thea Galehouse," she said, looking at her chart. "So, you think you're about eight weeks along, correct?"

"Something like that."

"We'll just take a quick look." She asked me to scooch down the table and picked up the phallic-looking magic wand. It was dark in the room and the screen illuminated her face, making it bright blue. She stared at the screen for a long time, then took the mouse and moved it around, clicking and clicking.

"Okay," she said, letting out her breath. Something was printing out. "Eight, nine weeks looks about right. I'll be back in a minute and we'll start."

She and the nurse left. I sat up on my elbows and pulled the screen toward me without thinking. A circle inside a larger gray circle, frozen on the screen. The littler circle was shaped like a comma that you could color in, or a cartoon bubble for voices.

I looked away from the screen and looked back again, and when I looked back, I got scared. For some reason I thought of Sam Negroponte, the artist guy who died across the hall in our building. I bugged Mom until she fessed up that he'd hanged himself. He was dead in his apartment for almost a week. I was in fourth grade, and when I got off the elevator one day, the smell crept into some part of my brain that registered exactly what it was without needing words. You're not ready for this, my brain said. Not ready to know this smell and what it is or what it means.

The same thing happened when I looked back at the screen. Not ready. I'd just take a little more time. I got off the table and threw on my clothes like you'd imagine putting your clothes on in the middle of the night if your building's on fire.

As fast as you can, thinking and not thinking at the same time. I sped down the narrow, empty hallway and ducked past the receptionist, who was deep in discussion with a woman at the counter about her insurance co-payment. No one noticed me leaving, and it struck me how easy it was to become invisible when you needed to.

I walked outside, gathering my down vest around me to fend off the December wind. Someone had discarded a perfectly healthy-looking pine tree on the corner. Christmas was still a couple of weeks away. I imagined some perfectionist Upper East Side housewife throwing it out because it was too short or something and immediately connected the unwanted tree, with its wide, wet stump, to whatever was growing inside me. I got a smoothie on Seventy-Second Street and sat on a hard stool in front of the window for an hour. Then I went home. Mom was at the dining room table paying bills when I walked through the door. She asked how it was. I told her Dr. Moore was very competent and professional, that it hardly hurt, that Vanessa was a huge help, that I was glad it was done.

"Anything for insurance?" she asked.

"They're mailing."

"You don't feel crampy?"

"No," I said, making a mental note to complain later. "Not yet."

"I bought a big thing of Advil," she said. "You can take more than the bottle says. Take some the second you feel anything." I started for the kitchen, but she was swinging an envelope between her second and third fingers like a little white flag. "Something came for you this morning." She smiled.

"No way," I said. "You opened it?"

"I'm sorry, I couldn't stand it, and I wanted to prepare for

82

bad news in case there was some. But you're in. Early decision."

I grabbed the envelope. "New York University" in purple letters in the top left corner. My SAT scores had been online for a couple of weeks, but I'd been too afraid to look. I rubbed my thumb along the mangled edge where Mom had opened it and felt an almost dizzying surge of relief and pride: I'd done it. I thought about all the nights with that freaking SAT phone book on my lap, the desperate hope that I could somehow absorb the contents via osmosis. All the Saturdays I'd spent that fall staring at the backs of plastic red chairs at the Princeton Review, missing Will and desperate to be with him instead of there. I'd done it. Maybe all the stressing over econ and calc had somehow been enough to maintain a B-plus average. Maybe stressing was as effective as working, because I definitely did more stressing than working. But it had all somehow come together.

"Well done, you clever girl, as my mum used to say to me once in a blue moon," Mom said, standing up and coming toward me. "You pulled it off and now my baby is flying the coop at last. But you'll be a stone's throw away. I'm getting the best of both worlds. I can hardly believe it." She stood up and walked over to me with her arms extended, and I saw myself in our flecked mirror above the stereo console as she hugged me: a smiling, rooty blond girl with a thorny secret.

16.

I kept my laptop screen tilted away from my bedroom door. It was January—a month since my un-abortion—and I jumped every time the radiator in my room clanked, thinking it was Mom coming home from dinner. No, I did not want to become a member of Babylove.com, I just wanted to quickly see what it looked like. I signed in as a guest, and the Web page asked for the conception date. I didn't know for sure but guessed it must have been sometime in late September, after Will moved up to Columbia, since he'd been away with his family before that. It took me to a page that said my twelve-week-old baby was two inches long and developing reflexes. The page said, "Click here to see what your baby looks like."

I'd called Dr. Moore's office the afternoon I got home from the un-abortion in December, afraid they'd call me and Mom would answer. They'd asked me if I wanted to reschedule, and I'd made another appointment for the following Friday. I gave them my cell phone number and asked them to call that, not my house, to remind me. When Friday came, I'd left school early, without saying anything to Vanessa. I'd gotten a 6 train to Moore's office on the Upper East Side, but as the train flew past Eighth Street, then Fourteenth, I started to feel sick, the collar of my down jacket choking me. I focused on the lawyer advertisements plastered up and down the train, but I felt dizzy, like if I took my eyes off the subway ads, the rest of the world would go black. So I got off at Forty-Second Street and grabbed a shuttle to the West Side. I thought if I could just tell Will how sick and scared I felt, he'd understand and know what to do. I got on a 1 train uptown and when I got to Will's hall, I spotted him in the lounge, sitting at a card table doing a million-piece puzzle with a red-haired girl. I paused to spy for a moment but didn't get the sense that there was anything going on with her. As I moved toward them, I realized the puzzle was all white. Every single tiny piece.

"G-Rock!" He looked surprised but happy to see me. "It's the Beatles' *White Album*," he said, maneuvering me onto his lap. "Melanie and I have committed to finishing it by Sunday. Right, Melanie?"

Melanie nodded and we smiled at each other. The air around her smelled like cigarettes.

"You're going to help us, right?" he said, nuzzling my neck, sending a delicious chill through me that for a lovely moment overpowered everything else. "We neeeeed you."

So I ended up staying and doing the puzzle, thinking we'd go off to his room and I would tell him everything, that I hadn't had the abortion yet and that I didn't know what to do. But we didn't go to his room. He seemed so happy that night—so unlike the lovelorn soul he was on the phone with me, complaining about how it was too loud in his dorm and how there were too many people around and how maybe this place wasn't for him. It sounds lame considering what was going on, but I didn't want to spoil it. Or maybe I just wanted to escape it too. Someone turned on the TV and then a stereo blared out of a room near the lounge, and someone brought in some beer, and Will smoked pot with a guy in a purple rugby shirt, and we did the puzzle and talked with whoever came through, until it got late and I told him I had to get home, and he walked me downstairs and got me a cab.

I clicked on the tab to see what my baby looked like. Someone had done a line drawing of an enormous head on top of a small tadpole-like body. Big, wide-set black eyes and holes for ears. So, this was my baby, I thought. How had someone drawn it? Had they studied a printout of an ultrasound or was it something else, where the baby wasn't alive anymore? Not ready, I said to myself. Not yet. I pushed away the thought that I was almost three months pregnant, that the tiny person inside me was now larger than a quarter, and as I heard Mom's keys in the door, I felt a strange, visceral urge to defy the hopelessness of it all.

17.

I had to ask Ms. Jedel for a recommendation to get into an English seminar at NYU. I'd sent the application in, but the recommendation was way late. When would I ask her? At the end of the day or the beginning? Which day was the best day to ask for something like this? Friday? Inside the classroom or outside? What would I say? *"Ms. Jedel, I know I haven't been doing so terrifically, but I wondered if you would consider . . ."*

Ms. Jedel had a very formal demeanor, and she wore tailored pencil skirts and navy patent-leather pumps, which made her stand out even more next to the bedraggled male teachers in jeans and sneakers. When I had her freshman year, she stood at the blackboard, holding the chalk in her fingers like a cigarette. "If you cannot spell *separate*, you are not up to par," she would say. I'd imagine her going home at night to her apartment with a single paper grocery bag nestled in her arms—

dinner for one—and I imagined her pushing her glasses daintily up her nose as she undressed next to the closet door. I always pictured her wearing a beautiful cream silk slip under her skirt and blouse, and imagined her getting undressed down to that, then padding off to the kitchen to ladle her take-out risotto onto a white plate and eating it sitting down with a tall glass of water. In some weird way, she gave me hope that my adulthood would be elegant.

"Ms. Jedel, I have a big favor to ask you. . . ."

Then senior year something happened. I took her film class and she discussed *Dog Day Afternoon* and *Raging Bull,* in her same skirts and pumps, and she was too far removed from real life. She was a nerd. And a spinster. I ended up getting a B-plus for the fall semester.

"Ms. Jedel, believe it or not, after my less-than-stellar performance so far in the film class, I'm actually thinking of majoring in film. I know, I know, but this year has been hard for me. I'm deeply in love, and now I'm with child, actually. Could you cut me a break, Ms. Jedel? Could you?"

I endlessly put off asking her, until I finally got up the nerve on February twelfth, my eighteenth birthday. I thought that asking her on my birthday, even though she didn't know it was my birthday, would somehow mean she'd say yes. I was wrong.

Vanessa was waiting outside in the hall.

"What'd she say?"

"I can't believe it," I said. "She turned me down."

"No!" she said, her eyes widening. "So obnoxious. I'm sorry, Thee. I can't believe it. Come with me later and we'll do birthday ice cream, and you can help me buy tennis sneakers. I'll cheer you up."

"Okay," I said, thinking, This birthday is turning out to be complete rubbish, as Mom would say. Mom had asked me if I wanted a party, but my last big birthday, my sweet sixteen, took place at Dad's squash club with too many kids I didn't know smoking pot on the dark empty courts. I just wanted this one to come and go.

I went with Vanessa after school to buy tennis sneakers on Thirty-Fourth Street. She'd picked the last semester of our senior year to join the tennis team. I was jealous because I knew she'd be good at it and probably get really skinny, whereas I was a depressed slob, getting fatter by the second, coming home from school every day and crashing onto the couch like a plane.

A mop-topped boy brought out a stack of boxes and popped the lid off the first one.

He bent down and took the heel of her foot.

"How's Fiona?" Vanessa asked. "Still howling at the moon?"

"She's okay," I said. "She just sold her second apartment, so she's all excited. Maybe the real estate thing will be her . . . thing."

"That's so great. She's found her calling, I know it." She looked at the white leather lace-ups that made her already narrow foot look even narrower. "What do you think?" She twisted her ankle around. "You're coming to my first match, right?" She grinned and gathered her long brown curls into two ponytails on either side of her head. "Promise margarine?"

I nodded, trying to conjure up watching a game on the shiny new aluminum bleachers in Battery Park. My favorite sunglasses had split in two at the nose when I had sat on them the summer before. They were still on my dresser, sitting, sitting, sitting, as if one day I'd magically take them into the kitchen and Scotch tape them perfectly together. Why couldn't I just throw shit *out*?

"Ness, I'm really fucked up," I said, a shelf of misery forming in my throat.

"What is it, babe?" she asked, taking the sneaker off and gripping it. "You still thinking about the you-know-what?"

"I would be," I said, staring at the stack of boxes. "If I'd *had* the you-know-what."

She froze. "What do you mean?"

"At the appointment, I don't know, I freaked out," I said. "I hopped off the table."

"Thea, that was way over a month ago—why didn't you tell me?"

"I don't know," I said. I honestly didn't. "I'm going back. I just had a little moment that day. I'm going back."

"Aren't you running out of time?"

"There's still time," I said. "It's not too late." The boy returned and paused in front of us with another box, which he set on the floor by Vanessa's feet.

"I'm going to take these, thanks," she said, pointing to the sneakers and quickly getting her boots back on. We went to the counter and Vanessa pulled out a crumpled wad of twenties. I didn't know what she was thinking; she'd gone mute. I'd been sort of coasting with this fuzzy problem in the back of my mind for weeks, but the look on her face—she looked like she'd seen a ghost—brought it raging to the front.

We got outside and the tide of people on Thirty-Fourth Street coaxed us toward Seventh Avenue.

"Will doesn't know, does he?" she finally asked. "You have to tell him."

"I'm going to tell him. It's so hard to find the right time."

"There won't be a right time, Thea, it doesn't exist. Just get it over with."

"I know." We got to the corner and waited at the light.

"Thea, do you really think you and Will are going to go off and, like, just blow off college and get sucky jobs and live on love in some prairie town, with a baby?" she asked. "What's going on? What's going on in your head?"

"I—I don't know," I stammered. "Maybe part of me thinks that. I can't help it. What's wrong with me?"

"If you decide to go ahead and have it, I'll shut my mouth, but right now it seems like a bad idea." She held her knapsack, with its prickly pink rubber key chain dangling off it, in front of my face, as if to prove a point. "We're really young, in case you haven't noticed."

"How different would it be if we were, like, twenty-four?" I asked.

"That's still young!" she exclaimed. "But at least you'd have a college degree. You'd have a shot."

"Is college really necessary anymore?"

She shook her head. "What are you talking about?"

"I don't know, is it?" I shrugged.

"I don't know what to say, Thee," she said, brushing her hand across my stomach. "Jesus, babe, what a moosh you are. You can't let go of anything, can you?"

18.

I got it into my stupid head to tell Will at Dad's Pave the Way benefit a few days later. I didn't know what I'd say or how I'd say it, but I thought a gorgeous candlelit ballroom would help romanticize the whole thing and make him see things my way, even though I wasn't sure what my way was. I'd found an old forest-green suede tunic of Mom's and dressed it up with long beads and a black chain belt that hid my stomach and showed off my arms.

"That is so Fiona," Vanessa said when I tried it on for her that afternoon. "I'm so having a visual of Fiona with her bangs and her huge black leather bag, walking around in that a few years ago. God, she has the best clothes."

"It's okay, right?" I asked, tugging at the sides and cinching the chain belt around the narrowest part of my waist, which at that point was up around my rib cage. I looked up and caught Vanessa staring up at my bulging stomach.

"What?" I asked.

"Nothing," she said, still staring. "You haven't told him yet, have you?"

"No," I said. "Check out my scarf." I gestured to the balled-up crochet project still on my bedside table. "It's coming out lopsided. What am I doing wrong?"

She looked at me long and hard and I braced myself for a lecture. She'd been silent on the subject and I, of course, never brought it up, so it was hard to know what she was thinking. She just rolled over and grabbed the scarf while I quickly pulled the dress over my shoulders.

I was the first one to arrive at the hotel that night. I was watching a guy in the lobby jewelry shop take coral necklaces out of the window boxes when Will slid through the revolving door, eyes darting around. He spotted me and walked across the lobby.

"Hey." He gave me a nervous kiss. "You look great."

"So do you," I said. "You okay?"

"I'm fine," he said, looking at me like I was crazy. "Why wouldn't I be?"

"Why are you answering my question with a question?" I said.

"What, does that bother you?"

"Does it bother me?" I asked.

"Does it bother you?" he repeated.

"Shut up."

"No, you shut up," he said.

"No, you."

Dad came up the steps behind us. I was sure he'd heard Will tell me to shut up.

"Hello, kids," Dad said. His tux was blacker than Will's. I'd thought black was black, one shade. "Good to see you again, Will." Will missed a beat before shaking Dad's outstretched hand.

"You too, Ted."

"Where's Elizabeth?" Dad's eyes started darting around the room like Will's, and I thought maybe it was a survival thing men did when they were nervous. Elizabeth Ransom was Dad's friend from growing up on Charter Island. I didn't think they'd ever done it, but I wasn't positive.

I shook my head. "We just got here."

I wished Will would say "Thanks for inviting me," or "What does Pave the Way do, exactly, Mr. Galehouse?" But he

92

just stood there, his tux accentuating the broadness of his shoulders.

"Are you speaking tonight?" I asked Dad, putting my arm through Will's.

"Naw, no," Dad grumbled. He waved to an older couple, lowering his head as they walked by. "Harry's speaking. I don't do it unless there's a gun at my head."

Will smiled appreciatively.

Elizabeth blew in. "Sorry, sorry, sorry," she called from across the lobby. "I've just had the afternoon from hell. Corky chewed up the Pearsons' baby ball. I had to stop at Mary Arnold and have one messengered over, of all things."

"Do us all a favor, Lizzie, lose the yippy little sausage," Dad said, kissing her on both cheeks.

"Nevah," she cackled.

Elizabeth was a decorator and had gotten Dad his living room furniture. Big brown leather stuff with buttons, and a couple of stripy-wood end tables that struck me as very him: unadventurously tasteful, directly linked to the great outdoors. He wouldn't let her do anything else with his apartment. He said she was too expensive.

"How are we all this lovely evening?" she asked, gathering her diaphanous wrap around her, and before anyone could answer, said, "Shall we mingle with the masses?"

Dad put his hand on the small of Elizabeth's back and guided her to the elevators, alerting me to the fact that Elizabeth's ass was half the size of mine. The ballroom upstairs was a patchwork of sumptuous black fabric—chiffon, gabardine, taffeta—all swishing around over the gaudy, Saudi-palace carpet. Will and I were the youngest ones there. I hoped we stuck out in only a cool, sexy way.

"Can I get everyone drinks?" Will asked, his voice fading into the din.

"Champagne?" I asked Dad. "C'mon, one glass."

"One glass," Dad said. "Lizzie?"

"White wine, please. Emma!" she called to a woman a few heads away. "That wasn't your show—Diane's? Where the lights fell down on the stage?"

Emma shook her head solemnly.

"Thank God!" Elizabeth yelled, a little softer but with exaggerated emphasis. "I read that and thought, Oh my God, I hope that wasn't her show."

If she'd said "I hope that wasn't Emma's show," instead of "her show," it would have come out sounding nicer. Elizabeth reminded me of Mom a little, the way you couldn't always tell whether she was on your side or not.

Will stepped over to the bar a few feet away. I heard him say "Can I get a white wine . . ." and saw Dad wince. He was always on me to say "May I please have" instead of "Can I get." "It's vulgar, Thea," he'd say. "The kids who work for me say it all the time too. Their breakfast orders in the morning make my head hurt. 'Can I get an egg and cheese?' You all need to be reprogrammed. It's basic English." At least I did it too, and people at work. Not just Will.

Will came back with Dad's seltzer with lime and Elizabeth's wine, then my champagne and a beer for himself, which he drank out of the bottle. The four of us stood in an awkward huddle.

"Teddy tells me you're at Columbia," Elizabeth said to Will.

"Yeah." Will nodded uncomfortably. I saw Dad look away.

"That's a wonderful school. My nephew just finished up there."

Will swigged his beer.

"So who are we sitting with?" I asked, molding my cocktail napkin around the base of my flute. "Work people?"

"Mostly, yes, and some friends of Harry's," Dad said.

A woman wearing a polka-dot dress and green glasses was talking near me. "Bruno, my youngest, loves the ladies," she said, her tall husband nodding in agreement. "He likes to escort them down the steps of his preschool and bid them good afternoon."

We found our table, close to the stage. Elizabeth put her tiny handbag, shaped like a turtle and covered in rhinestones, next to Dad's chair, and another couple quickly parked themselves on his other side. The other free seats were across the table, so any further Dad-Will bonding wasn't in the cards. We spent the night talking to a pale, pudgy Australian guy who worked for Dad. "I love this city," he kept saying, as though trying to convince himself. "I love the Upper West Side."

Mostly we snuck out into the atrium for drinks, our first trip right after the salads. We ducked behind a big pillar decorated with fake orange lilies, our buzzes escalating at the same time in a whirling rush.

He leaned toward me and winked. "You are the fairest of them all, milady. Ma'am. Your Honor."

"Gee, thanks," I said, fluttering my eyelids. I kissed him, noticing how every angle of his body inspired a crazy-making, lustful lurch inside me. I wanted to step into him. Just get in him and live in there. I leaned against the pillar, cold against my bare back.

"You know, I love you so much," Will whispered, brushing his lips across mine just like he did when we had sex. Even then I knew that chances were, I loved him more. Will was drunk. It reminded me of when I was younger and Dad had scrawled the words *I love you more than you can dream* on the back of a picture of me in our living room one night when he was bombed out of his mind. I'd come home from school and found it, next to an ashtray filled with butts, the table sticky with beer from the previous night's all-nighter. I had crossed it out, making deep, pissed-off Bic-pen indentations into the cardboard. I remember thinking he could only bring himself to love me when he was shit-faced.

Still, I loved hearing Will say he loved me, over and over.

"Will, I have to tell you something," I said.

"What," he said, kissing my neck and pulling the chain around my waist.

"I'm still pregnant. I didn't go through with it, that day I was supposed to. I couldn't."

He looked at me and his body seemed to lurch backward in slow motion.

"I didn't mean to hide it," I said. "It's hard for me to explain."

"Jesus Christ," he said. I tried to find a trace of something I could recognize, in his eyes, in his expression, but his face reflected back only the worst—that I'd done something very wrong by not telling him.

Someone had made an announcement I didn't hear and everyone started to file back into the dining room.

"I'm out of here," Will said. He started for the elevators, then kicked open the fire-exit door and let it slam behind him before I had a chance to call his name.

19.

The tangle of Mom's belts hung off my desk chair when I woke up the next morning. A couple of them were on the floor. Mom loves her clothes and preserves them fastidiously in her closet like museum pieces. My first thought was actually to get up, roll the belts and put them on my desk before she saw them like that. Then I remembered the previous night and wondered if I could just close my eyes again and have everything end right there. I felt like someone had run a bulldozer over my body and wondered how I was ever going to get out of bed, get clothes on, deal with Mom in the kitchen and get out the door to school. I remembered Dad's face when I went back into the dining room and told him that Will had gotten sick and that I was going to take him home. He'd sat back and laid his dessert fork down as if he were trying not to wake someone, even though the room was ringing with the sound of silverware through the drone of voices. "Okay," he'd said flatly, taking a sip from his sweaty water glass, and I could read his thoughts like a news feed running across his face: Here we go again, Thea's up to her old tricks—she's drunk and her boyfriend's drunk and she's let me down once again. I'll let her go before she embarrasses me any further.

I told Mom that the party was fun and that Will loved my dress and that I was late for zero period, slathering some peanut butter on a piece of toast I knew I would throw into the junk-mail can in the lobby.

I somehow made it to school, to my spot on the floor in zero-period gym as Mr. Boone paced and talked about muscle recovery.

"When you work a muscle group to its maximum capacity, they need a period of time to reoxygenate," Mr. Boone said, weaving around us like we were cones on a road.

The reality that I wouldn't ever again lie in Will's bed at Columbia and see that Nerf basketball hoop hanging off his door, that I wouldn't get to touch his hair, flatten it out along the back of his neck, was starting to hit home. I realized I understood what the expression "hot tears" meant. There were so many of them going down my face, I gave up wiping them away. Wiping called attention to them. I didn't feel like dying. I felt dead already. Will hadn't abandoned just me, but also the beautiful, mysterious thing growing inside me that we had made together. I remember watching the track team come panting through the big metal doors from their run and having the feeling that the level of pain I was experiencing was way more than I bargained for. It was pain I didn't know existed. Mr. Boone passed by my spot and looked straight at me for a moment, and it was almost like he knew *why* I was crying, but he did a stand-up job of pretending nothing was wrong. I wondered over and over why I'd done what I'd done and what I was going to do next.

But then later, as I went outside for lunch, there was Will. He stood in the middle of the sidewalk with his arms folded across his chest. It was freezing cold and it reminded me of the first day I met him. He was standing by himself then, too.

"I'm so hungover." Will smiled, shaking his head. "Staying up all night didn't help."

"Do you want to go somewhere?" I asked. I saw Vanessa walking toward us in her maroon down jacket, but she saw my face and turned and went around the corner. I hadn't even told her yet about the night before.

"Tell me what you were thinking, Thea," he said.

"I-it was just . . . avoidance," I stammered. "I was avoiding it. I thought I'd go back when I was ready."

"You were scared," he said.

"I was scared," I repeated. "I *am* scared."

"What are you scared of?"

"I'm scared of doing it, I'm scared of not doing it," I said, looking down at my knapsack slumped at my feet on the curb. "I don't know what to do."

"What are you more scared of?"

"Getting an abortion," I said. "I don't know why."

"Shit, Thea," he said, setting his hands rigidly on his hips. "I wish you'd just told me. You could have told me you were screwed up about it. We could have talked about it. What did you think I'd do?"

"It's lame, I know," I said. "It's like I couldn't do anything. Except let another day pass. In a weird way, I know it's pathetic and awful, but I liked that it was getting bigger."

He looked at me, his good eye boring into mine. "You actually want to go through with this," he said slowly. "You want to bring a baby into the world. A child."

I love the sound of your voice, I thought. Your voice is my drug. All I'll ever need. "It's you, you know, how could I not?" I said, barely getting the words out. "It's you."

More staring. A gust of wind blew our hair up.

"What are you thinking?" I asked.

"I'm thinking, holy shit." Mr. Plumb, a history teacher, walked up to us, eyeing Will in his big, black down parka.

"Well, if it isn't . . . ," Mr. Plumb said, not finishing the sentence.

"Hello, Mr. Plumb." Will mustered a quick smile.

"The girl's reeled you back here, eh?" Mr. Plumb smiled, his crazy eyes bulging out of their sockets. "Where you at now?"

"Columbia," Will answered.

"Very nice, very nice," Mr. Plumb said, slapping Will on the back. "Well, I'm going to get a slice. Be a good boy, now."

"I will," Will muttered.

"All I can think is, Why not," I said. "Do you know what I mean?"

"No." He sighed, running his thumb over my palm. "But I can try, I guess."

"You can't do it just because you love me," I said.

"There's no other reason, Thea, sorry."

We both turned to stare at the big double doors at the top of the steps, watching as kids streamed into the street, chatty and enervated in the gray midday light. I wondered how close Will was to walking away.

"My parents are going to freak out," he said quietly.

"What do you think they'll do?" I asked, not sure what direction he was going in yet.

"Hell if I know." We looked at each other and hugged, and I imagined us in one of those telling soap-opera hugs, with him frowning behind me without me realizing.

20.

I thanked the bartender for the ginger ale, envisioning the straight, sharp lines across Dad's forehead. I wondered how he might come between us. What he could say or do to change Will's mind.

"I *knew* you wouldn't go through with it," Vanessa had

said when I'd told her that morning at breakfast that I'd decided to keep the baby. She stirred the streaky cream in her coffee as the words poured out of her. "I don't know why, but I feel like it's meant to be this way. I didn't want to say anything, I know it'll be tough, but if anyone can do it, you can. You're a *pioneer*. You make the rules. How did Fiona take it?"

"She's not speaking to me," I said, amazed at how Vanessa had so swiftly changed her tune to support mode without blinking an eye.

"Shocker," Vanessa said, squeezing my hand. "Typical Fiona, so constructive. Don't let it get to you. She'll come around."

Now Will came in and sat at the bar without taking off his coat. "So I told them," he said, breathing fast. "They're pissed, but weirdly, I think they get it. Deep down, they're closet hippies. I told you that. This is normal to them on some level. They want to meet with your parents." He flagged the bartender and mouthed the word "Heineken" after he'd gotten his attention.

"Okay," I said. "What else did they say?"

"They said that if it's what I want, they can't really stop me. But I know my dad was this close to having a stroke. My future up in smoke, all that." I tried to read Will's face, unable to tell if he felt that way too. "But I have to hand it to him. They may have some ulterior thing cooking. I have no idea."

"Like what?" I asked, feeling sweaty and sick at the prospect of Dad walking into the restaurant at any moment.

"Like hiring our dry cleaner who's also a hit man to off you?" he said, pulling out his wallet.

"You think?" I asked, folding down my straw.

"I don't know, I don't think so, but we can't be positive."
He smiled tightly and took a big swig of his Heineken. "Just be
extra careful."

"C'mon," I said. "What else did they say, really?"

"That they'd talk to my aunt Florence, try and work something out with us living in her apartment while she's teaching
in Africa. Florence doesn't want to sublet to anyone she
doesn't know, so we may have a leg up in that sense. They actually wondered why they hadn't thought of it earlier, since
it would be cheaper for me to live there than to board at
Columbia, because of the rent control. They want me to stay
in school. They said they'll do *anything* they can to help as
long as I stay in school."

"Do you think they hate me?" I asked, realizing how juve-
nile the question was.

"They didn't say." He rolled his eyes.

Some Italian ballad bellowed out of the jukebox speakers.
The whole normal world went on around us.

"Mom asked about your parents," he said, his eyes scanning the bar nervously up and down.

"What about them?" I asked, tugging on the arm of his
coat to pull it off.

"Like whether they approve and whether they'll contribute."

"Oh," I said.

"Then my father got to how much." He stood up and got
his coat off, looking around for a place to hang it up.

"How much what?" I asked.

"How much 'everyone,' by which he meant your dad, was
going to contribute. I'm not sure if they think he's going to
foot the whole thing, but they might." *Foot the whole thing.* It

came out casually and awkwardly at the same time. I wondered if Will thought that too.

"We'll work it out," I said quickly.

"Well, they should meet." He glanced up at the muted news on the TV. "Does your father have any conception of time?" Will asked, incredulous, pulling his phone out to look at its digital clock. "It's quarter of. How is he not here yet?"

"Sorry, he's completely anal about everything else." I looked at Will's profile against the blue lights from the window. He looked jittery and scared. I was just grateful that he cared about any of it, that he was in the restaurant with me and that he wasn't making me get an abortion or dodging me.

"What the hell is he going to do?" He shook his head. "What do you think?"

"It'll be okay. Just follow my lead. Let me talk."

Dad appeared at the front of the bar, a navy-blue cashmere scarf neatly crossed around his neck.

"Waiting long?" he said, moving toward us. This was how he apologized. Fleshy splats of spring rain disappeared into his trench coat.

"Not too long," I said.

"Good." He kissed me and flagged the host. "I didn't know you'd be joining us, Will," he said, his chin rooting around in the air, which meant his feelings were hurt that I didn't ask him first if Will could come. He kissed me and his cheek was cold, and he smelled like his office. Like black glass and paper.

We sat and Dad hid behind his menu, pulling at his eyebrows, changing lanes in his head. Will and I dove into the bread basket, keeping busy.

"So Dad, we actually have something pretty big that we

want to talk with you about," I said. I poured olive oil onto a plate and put it in the middle of the table for us all to dip the bread into, a loving cup.

Dad took off his coat and hung it around his chair. "What?" he asked, looking at me quizzically. "Did I do something wrong the other night?"

"What? At the benefit?" I asked. "No, why would you think that?"

"You two left sort of abruptly," he said.

"Oh, sorry about that," I said, looking at Will, who was studying the menu. "No, you were in the middle and everything."

"What, then?" he asked, lifting his water glass and sipping. "What's wrong?"

"Nothing's wrong." Will leaned forward, jamming his hands under his bum.

"Don't freak out, okay?" I said, smiling as though I had a terrific surprise.

"Why would I freak out?" Dad asked.

"Because," I said. The waitress drifted over in her black sneakers with red laces, then retreated when I said, "I'm pregnant."

"Wh-who," he stuttered.

"I am," I said, looking at Will. "We are."

He stared at me, glass in hand, frozen.

"We're going to have a baby," I said. "In July."

"Thea, I don't understand." He sat back in a way that made me feel contagious.

"It wasn't intentional," said Will. "But I guess you could say it is now."

I expected anger or disgust, but not death. Dad looked like someone had just died.

"How pregnant are you?" he whispered.

"About four months. Dad, I know it's a lot, but we're figuring it out. We're making plans."

"Please God," he whispered.

"It's not a please-God situation." I laughed. "I know it wasn't exactly in anyone's plan, and I know it's going to be tricky, but it feels like the right thing." I felt like I was talking to an old man. Will and I stared at each other, wide-eyed. I looked over the top of Dad's head, toward the lights above the bar, letting them pin in and blur out.

"I'm sorry, no. That's quite enough." He stood up, pulled some bills out of his wallet, even though we hadn't yet ordered, and grabbed his coat off his chair, then stalked toward the door. We sat there paralyzed, our empty white plates shining at us.

"Quite enough," I said. "Jesus."

"He's clearly not a fan of mine," Will said.

"It's not you," I snapped.

"He couldn't even look at me."

"I was not expecting that," I said. "It was like he didn't even see us."

"Only his broken dreams." Will downed his beer, shaking his head. "What now?"

Outside the window, people were walking home from work with briefcases and bags from the Food Emporium. I thought about a cab ride I had taken with Dad once. An old Jennifer Lopez song had been on the radio, and at the end of the song Dad had said, "There's a place in this world for Jennifer Lopez." He'd said it matter-of-factly, with no derision. That's how I'd imagined him being about the baby. That he'd figure out a place for it. That or better. I'd fantasized that Dad would see it as something unique to me, like parents see

105

certain gifts or talents in their children. That he'd see it as something I was somehow destined for. But that was how *I* saw it, I realized. Not him.

"He's going to call Mom," I said. "I should go home."

I raced home, unlocked the door and went straight to the bathroom, turning the tub water on. I got in and when I turned off the water, I could hear the defensive quality in Mom's voice as she talked to him on the phone. Except now it was more like a schtick. Like Alice and Ralph Cramden, black-and-white and gritty and muted. Firecrackers shooting onto garbage cans and sputtering off.

"She told me last night," Mom said, not caring if I heard. "She said she wants to have it, the same thing she told you. It's a crusade, Ted, she's clearly on a crusade. . . . For Christ's sake, of course I have . . . unequivocally. . . . My daughter's fallen pregnant . . . you think I'm swinging from the rafters? . . . You'd think if she'd learned one thing from me, it's independence. . . . Most of the time she's going to the bloody opposite . . . so this is perfect. . . . Stop it . . . if you act for one second like this is my fault . . . one second, Ted . . . I mean it . . . She's got it all *mapped out,* Ted, for God's sake. . . ."

I heard a pause and then she said, "Fine, so come and talk to her about it. . . . No, tonight . . . tomorrow's no good." She hung up and called from her bed.

"Daddy's coming over."

"Now?" I yelled. "It's almost ten."

"Now. Get out of the tub."

I put on sweats instead of a nightgown and opened the door to my tall father and his runny nose. He glared at me and headed for the living room, pausing by the dining room table. It had been years since he'd been to our apartment. The table was littered with change and receipts and shopping bags with tissue paper hanging out. A chair had a stack with my folded laundry on it from when Rula had been there. I hadn't yet brought it to my room.

"Do you have some water?" he asked. He looked as though his thoughts had hardened into slabs of granite.

I went to get him water as Mom came out of her room in her bathrobe and sat on the ottoman, the Nivea on her calves smelling up the room. Dad sat on the couch, still in his coat. I sat in the white armchair, dragging it a little to face them as a wave of thick, intractable loneliness crawled over me.

"I'm disappointed you didn't feel like you could come to us before this point," he began. "What prevented you from having a conversation with one, or both of us, at the very least?"

"I found her a doctor, Ted," Mom said, throwing her arms up. "As far as I knew, it was taken care of weeks ago!"

"Is that true?" he asked me.

I nodded, feeling guilty for not including him in that chapter.

"I want to just clarify something." He leaned forward on his elbows, his fingertips touching. "And it's delicate, so I'll just ask it. . . . An abortion is . . . no longer an option. Is that correct?"

"I could probably find someone if I tried, but I don't want one."

"Then, Thea, we have to seriously consider adoption."

"No," I said, picking at the seam of the chair.

"You're bringing a human being into the world," Dad said. "That alone is enough for an eighteen-year-old. That would be an accomplishment."

"Not happening," I said, probably too quickly. I looked down and saw that I'd ripped the seam and put my hand over it. Mom didn't notice because she wasn't looking at me. She stared straight ahead, her face expressionless. She'd already given up on me. Dad looked at her for help, and for a minute I thought it had switched to Dad and me against her.

"What is it about adoption you're opposed to?" he asked.

"I don't know," I said. "But I know I couldn't do it."

"You have to do better than that," Dad said.

"I just . . . This baby is already mine, I can't explain it," I said. "I can't imagine giving it to someone else."

"Well, I've clearly lost the plot, Thea," Mom sniffed, pressing her crossed arms to her rib cage. "Exactly how do you plan to keep it? To support it?"

I stared at the glass bowl on the coffee table. Dad had used it as an ashtray when I was younger. It had little bubbles on the bottom, and I remembered I used to picture the bubbles rising to the top of the ashtray and popping.

"I guess I'm hoping you can help us," I said, the room humming with silence as I realized, for the first time, what I was asking. What I was asking of everyone. How I was crowding up their lives with this mysterious, massive thing.

"I know it's a lot to ask," I said. "I know."

Mom turned her head toward the window, her face a tight ball of disgust.

"Maybe whatever we do, we could treat it as some kind of five-year loan or something," I said. "Or ten years. We think we've got a place to live. Will's aunt Florence is teaching in Africa for two years and may sublet her apartment to us."

"Where?" Dad asked sharply.

"It's in the Village, it's a big studio, I haven't seen it, but it's

108

a rent-controlled apartment, so it's like nine hundred dollars a month or something like that."

"So when you say you've got a place to live, you mean you've got a place to live that we have to pay for," Mom practically spat.

"I'll get a job if you want," I said, pulling my knees up to my chest.

"Good luck with that," she said. "No one will hire you if they know you're pregnant."

"You want to keep it." Dad sighed. It was like he'd fallen behind and had to review the basic facts. It was like I was with Mr. Binder, my tutor.

"I want to keep it," I repeated.

"Thea, forgive me if I'm having trouble envisioning you as ready to take on the burden of raising another human being," Dad said. He stood up and paced between the couch and Mom's pink birdcage-as-artwork in the corner. "It was just a couple of summers ago that you were not even capable of handling *yourself* in a responsible manner."

"Not that again," I said. "Look, I know, I was a bad, bad girl. I get it. But this is not the same thing at all."

"Tell me this, then," Mom said, the dark roots on top of her head coming into full view as she looked down at her cuticles. "What, exactly, has changed? You've gone and screwed us over again, have you not?"

Dad sat down and cleared his throat. "Thea, I'm going to say this once. Ever since you were born, I've dreamed of you going to college. You can roll your eyes all you want, but I've dreamed of it."

"Why?" I said. "Why is it so important?"

"Because when it's the right fit, it affords you the rare

opportunity to learn things about yourself. On your own, without anyone . . . interfering."

"It's not like I'll never go."

"You'd have a child," he said, pulling off the scarf around his neck. "You'd be distracted, not to mention burdened. It wouldn't be the same."

"He dragged me to his reunion before you were born," Mom said, suddenly changing the tone of the conversation. "They kept calling him Tinny—why, I'll never know. They went out into the cornfields and tipped cows and left them there like that."

"You start to carve out your life," he said, ignoring her. "It's an exciting time. It's wonderful." His voice cracked.

"And it can all be yours," Mom said, imitating a game show host.

"I can go later," I said, trying to reassure him.

"Thea, this is beyond comprehension to me," he said, thrusting back on the couch, gripping his knees. "How are you going to live? Will's going to take care of you? Will's going to have your health and the health of the baby as his first priorities? Fiona?"

"That's the plan," said Mom.

"Well, I don't think moving in with Will is the solution."

Mom shook her head. "She's going to do what she wants, Ted. You're being a bit thick. If you'd been tuning in for the last year, you'd have realized that she's obsessed with him."

"I'm not obsessed with him, Mom," I said. "Will wants it this way too."

She looked at me for the first time since we sat down. "He wants it because *you* want it and you've managed to convince him it's the right thing to do. Don't think for a second he'd have come to it on his own."

"Okay, calm down, everyone," Dad said. "Fiona, we need to help her."

"She's had a ton of help, Ted. She's had nothing but help."

"Stop making it sound like I've turned on you," I said. "Like I'm turning on you and like I'm just some manipulative . . . slut. I'm just trying to figure out the best thing." I thought of Will and felt a sharp stab of fear—did he secretly hate me for wanting this? I hated Mom for making it sound so bad. I remembered Dad chasing Mom around the house when I was little, Dad yelling, "Come back here, you little minx." I remembered Mom half-naked with a hairbrush in her hand.

"Mom, what's a minx?" I'd asked.

"A minx is a devious little thing," she had yelled into the doorframe of my bedroom. "A vixen. A cunning little trollop." Her eyes had poured out something hard and feminine and she'd run off, but Dad had caught her under the armpit and led her away like a cartoon cop dragging a baddie into custody, Mom screaming and laughing, Dad slamming their bedroom door behind them.

"The best thing would be for you to grow up." Mom stood and headed to the kitchen, clearly sick of being my mother.

"Thea, there are hundreds of very good placement agencies," Dad continued. "Parents who would give anything for a child. You have no idea. I know of people, women at work who can't have children. People who are desperate to have families, who can't have babies by themselves. Thea, please, I'm begging you. Think about it. Take some time and really think about it."

"Give it up, Ted, she's already gone." Mom came back in, chewing a handful of pretzels. She thought this was all his fault.

"I'll think about it," I said.

"Oh, please, don't lie," said Mom.

Dad stood up. "Fiona!"

"What?" she screamed. "You think she's listening to a bloody word you're saying?"

"At least I'm trying," he said.

"Right, and you're really reaching her, Ted."

His eyes seemed to recede beneath his eyebrows. Was it anger or hatred, or both? I'd seen it on his face before, and I understood how there would be no turning back about someone after that. How no amount of talking or making up or whatever could undo it. He paused for a moment, shaking his head at me, then walked out, slamming the door.

"Yeah, that's it." Mom exhaled loudly, her mouth O-shaped, like she'd just finished a sprint and was catching her breath. "Useless coward."

21.

"What if it's a girl?" Vanessa turned to me while we were stopped at a red light on our way to Stash, a knitting store on Charlton Street. "I envy you."

"Yeah, you envy me," I said. "You envy the looks Mr. Kushman gives me throughout the entire forty minutes of calculus, like I'm all woman now."

"Ew!" she yelped.

"I think it's a boy," I said, changing the subject. I pictured a baby in a yellow undershirt that snapped under the crotch. A baby rolling around on the lawn, on the mildewed quilt that hung on a nail in our shed on Charter Island.

"I wonder what it will say to you, the boy," she said. "What will it say?"

"They don't talk right away," I said, holding her back against the curb as a taxi whizzed past us.

"Of course not," she said. "But imagine him saying, 'That skirt looks so nice on you,' or 'Don't wear that lipstick, Mommy,' or 'I'm tired, Mommy,' or 'I love you more than my Thomas trains, Mommy, I love you, I love you, I love you, Mommy.'" Vanessa's head bobbed and swayed like a belly dancer's. "Could you just?"

"Maybe I should turn the scarf into a blanket for it," I said.

"Or you can start something else for it."

"What do you think it would like?" I asked.

"It could use a lot of things—a blankie, some sockies, you name it, it could use it."

"It," we both said, doing our Madonna blinks at each other. A cowbell jangled over our heads when Vanessa opened the door to the yarn store. A pale-faced woman in a tie-dyed thermal shirt looked up from her computer.

"Those bells are loud," she said dryly.

Vanessa strode across the white floor, her rubber biker boots clomping as loudly as rubber could. "Hi, we want to buy some yarn." She popped the gum she was chewing.

The woman got up slowly from her stool and walked around the desk, her faded black cargo skirt trailing threads from the hem.

"Are you starting something or do you need to replenish?" she asked, sticking a pencil behind her ear.

"Replenish," Vanessa said. "I'm making something for her baby. It's a secret." The woman arched her eyebrows at me, more in benign surprise than disapproval, and I felt what it was like to be pregnant, out in the open, for the first time. It still seemed like it was happening to someone else.

"How should we do this?" she asked Vanessa. "Do you want to whisper it to me?"

"It's okay, I'll go over here," I said, walking to the opposite corner and seeing the table of thin, glossy, hardback books. *Leona's Big Book of Caps. The World's Coolest Socks.* There was another woman sitting in an office in back with straight, reddish purple hair and severe bangs. She was knitting something tartan, and Jimi Hendrix was playing on her computer.

"Ella?" the woman in the cargo skirt called to her.

"Yes?" Ella called back, not looking up.

"Do we have any more skeins of Mongoose Forty-Four?"

"Skeins." Vanessa smirked at me from across the room. "I love that word."

Ella glanced at the ceiling in the office. "It's on order. I'd give it another month."

"Shit!" Vanessa pouted.

The woman looked over at me and whispered something to Vanessa.

"I know," Vanessa said. "I could do that." I looked away. The walls were lined with little box-shaped shelves filled with yarn, and by the window there was a big wooden spinning wheel with a crank that looked very old.

"I'm considering just showing you so you can have a part in this decision," Vanessa called, being overly serious. "I'm at a crossroads and may need to change tacks."

"Okay, so show me." I shrugged and walked over.

She pulled it out of her bag and held it up. It was the same beige yarn she had shown me the day she taught me to crochet in her room, only now it was half of a hat.

"I thought you were making a sweater," I said. That day in Vanessa's room seemed like a million, trillion years ago.

"I undid it. I thought it would be a cool baby hat. I'm going to make a tiny brim in front, so it's kind of trucker. Except now I need to do the top in a different color. I don't want to wait a month. What about a light green?" She swiveled the unfinished hat around on her fingers. "You don't like it."

"No," I said. It was hitting me hard at that moment that I would soon have a tiny infant who I would have to feed and change and be responsible for every second of every day for the rest of my life. The room went a little foggy. "It's cute. I love it."

Vanessa turned to the woman.

"So if I go with the green, how do I do it?"

"Just finish the row and switch." The woman blinked. "You pull the new color through the loop. You know how to do that, right?"

Vanessa nodded, but I could tell she was too proud to admit she didn't know how to do it.

"If you have a little yellow left, you could do the very top in a little gather, or you could do a little pom-pom. Up to you."

"Hmmmm, cunning," Vanessa said, stealing a glance at me. "But I don't think the baby will be the pom-pom type. Do you, Thee?"

"Hard to say," I said, watching the woman walk over to the green shelf. She was maybe ten years older than us, and she inhabited the room in the way that a place becomes a part of someone after they're in it for a long time. It was the same way Mom was at Fiona's. Like she owned it and it owned her, too. There was something about this woman, something funny.

That bell is loud. I looked back at the beige nubs of yarn on Vanessa's needle. There was a tiny hole near her hand.

"But we'll go with the green, right, Thee?" Vanessa asked. "I'll take a *skein* of the green, and then I've got to split. Have to get uptown for Miles's thing." She plunked a credit card down on the high Lucite counter. I reached into my jacket pocket for a tear-out from *Vogue* of a woman in a crocheted dress with a blue, yellow and green zigzag pattern. It was the kind of look I wanted for a new version of the crocheted bikini from the photo of me on the beach. I was still obsessed with making it, and I had that photo with me too.

Vanessa stuffed the new green yarn into her straw beach bag. "You coming?"

"I think I'll linger," I said.

"I'll call you later. Byeeee." She waved, clanging the cowbell on her way out.

It felt easier to approach the woman now that Vanessa was gone. I looked at the shelves again. Everything was arranged by color, and when you looked across the shelves, it was like looking at a very detailed rainbow spectrum, blue into teal into green into yellow, each color predictable yet surprising. I thought about zigzaggy sunburst patterns and interwoven squares in primary colors. Thinking about the crocheted bikinis made me feel like the world was opening a window into another world. I went up to the counter, where the woman was staring into her big flat-panel computer screen.

"Paper cutters, my new fixation," she said. She turned the screen to me and pointed to a white paper cutout of a woman with a huge skirt. "There are people out there who spend hours with, like, tiny razor blades, cutting these incredibly meticulous designs. It's just bizarre. But beautiful, right?"

I looked at the screen. The woman's skirt had hundreds of

swirls and what looked like little unicorns all over it. "Wow,"
I said. She was right, it was absolutely beautiful. And a little
heartbreaking. All the painstaking, obsessive effort that went
into it.

"So can I help you out with anything else?" she asked, eyeing the tear-out in my hand.

"Well, I had this idea and I was hoping you could help me
find a pattern, or you know, some instructions."

I pulled out the bikini photo and handed it to her.

"Is that you?" she said, moving it closer and farther from
her face.

"Yes, when I was younger, obviously. I was hoping you
could help me find a pattern that, you know, looks like it."

"Hmmm . . . interesting." She studied the photo, fiddling
with the green stone on the thin, black satin choker around
her neck. "Was there elastic in the waist and leg?"

"Yes," I said, distinctly remembering the feeling of rubber
bands against my skin.

"I guess you could lead some kind of elastic through when
you were all done." She looked at me, considering. "Have you
worked on other projects or will this be your first?"

"I've done a few things," I lied. "Though this seems like it
will be more complicated."

"It will, but no biggie. I don't have a pattern, but it's pretty
straightforward stuff. I could probably figure it out for you."

"Really?" I asked, trying not to sound too excited.

"Sure." She lifted the stone again and dropped it. "It'll take
me a few days. I'll have to look at a pair of undies. What size
are you? This is for you, I take it?"

"Medium," I said. "Normally, that is. Yes, it's for me—I'm
not sure I was actually planning on *wearing* it. In my current
state, and all."

"You just want to re-create it," she said. She continued studying the picture. I could tell she was intrigued by the situation: a practically adolescent pregnant girl clinging to a remnant of her troubled childhood. "Yours looks like it was more of a tube top, right? It might be nicer to do a halter."

"I love halters," I said.

She started sketching on her blotter. "How's this?"

I moved behind the counter. "Is the bottom a little skimpy?" I asked.

"You want it to go higher, toward the belly button?"

"Yeah, I think so." She kept drawing and it became clear to me. "I want it sort of big, like a pair of big, unsexy Carter's briefs."

"Cool." She nodded enthusiastically. "A little weird, but cool. You sound like me. I detest thongs. I find them aggressively disgusting."

"I just think they'd look cool sort of big and, you know, like you're covered up."

"Like Marilyn Monroe. Marilyn wore big undies and big bikinis. Cool!"

"Right, like Marilyn," I said, getting excited. "Everyone wore big cover-up bikinis in the fifties, right? That's what I want."

She drew a little more. "That better? You could even do a cute band across the top."

"No, I want to do zigzags." I fished the *Vogue* zigzag dress out of my wallet. "Like this."

"Ahhh. Sort of a seventies vibe."

"Well, not obviously seventies, right?" I asked.

"No, it'll depend on what colors you use." She flipped a paper clip on the blotter, which was framing a calendar that had Xs marked through the days, and notes written in script with a fuchsia highlighter. She'd doodled the word *Expo* over and over again in the margins. "I think it could look very cool. I'll work out a pattern. Can I hold on to the photo?"

"Sure."

"I won't lose it," she said, pressing it to her chest. "Promise."

"Wow, thanks. I'm so excited."

"My pleasure," she said, moving a bowl of Red Hots toward me. "That's what yarn-store ladies are for."

22.

The parents got together one night in May to discuss our future. I took it as a good sign that the Westons were willing to come downtown.

Will called while they were out. "Notice how they didn't invite us?" he said. "It's like we're little children they need to sort out."

I sat on the living room couch and pulled the purple yarn I'd crocheted into half of a scarf out of its scarf form. The woman at the yarn store had told me to use some scrap yarn to practice new stitches I'd need for the bikini. I was feeling cheap and I wanted to save money for the good stuff once I figured out how to do it. I loved that about crocheting—how yarn could transform into something else just by pulling the hook out and unraveling. When the yarn unraveled, it bent in this cool pattern, like long, crimped purple hair.

I leafed through the crochet magazine I'd bought that showed the new stitches and watched the clock, envisioning the four of them. Dad would spot Mr. Weston and walk over to him with his arms extended, the way he walks across the lawn to greet someone at a summer party, and then he'd grasp Mr. Weston's elbow as he shook his hand. He'd introduce Mom to the Westons, and for a moment, the formal introduction would soften her heavily bleached hair and her fire-engine-red lipstick, smudged around her lips in a way that was okay for a Saturday visit to art galleries but foreign and a little odd to people who had a basketball hoop in their living room.

I imagined them sitting at an outdoor café on lower Fifth Avenue, the May breeze billowing through Mom's pretty blond hair and Mrs. Weston's scraggly ponytail. How they'd order drinks and the Westons would wonder about Dad's choice of plain tonic with lime, but at the same time they'd notice his quiet, distinguished demeanor and understand that whatever battles he'd had were in his past, and they would respect him for overcoming them. Dad would smile at Mr. Weston's twinkly-eyed attempts to lighten the situation. He'd take out a legal pad to figure out our finances and Mr. Weston would make a joke about the pad, and Dad would laugh gruffly and say, "Well, I am a numbers guy." Mrs. Weston would watch Mom in her low V-neck, black jersey wrap sweater and wonder why she didn't try to dress like that every so often instead of in her usual baggy button-downs and jeans. She'd wonder where she could find clothes like that, stuff that was for every day but that also had a little edge. She'd be tempted to ask Mom, but decide to do it when they'd see each other again. Toward the end, they'd give each other knowing looks of resignation and talk about Will's and my endearing, exasperating habits, like how Will comes home from school and records basketball games that he never watches, and wastes Mr. Weston's DVR space, or how he leaves his socks balled up under the dining room table like little cow pies, or how I leave the caps off everything—toothpaste and especially medicine bottles—and how I'm going to have to be careful about that when the baby comes. "They're in for it," I imagined Mom saying as they put on their coats, and I pictured them giving each other knowing looks, behind which would be little flickers of joy and anticipation for their unborn grandchild, as if he or she were already in the restaurant with them, drawing them together into an intimate football huddle.

Mom walked through the door at ten on the dot.

"Hi," I said, rolling up from the couch.

"Were you sleeping?" she asked, undoing the belt of her coat.

"Uh-uh," I said. "How did it go?"

She threw her coat on a chair and went to the kitchen. I heard her unlock the dishwasher and start clattering stuff onto the counter.

I followed her and sat down at the table. "So how did it go?"

"One of these days you could empty the dishwasher."

"Sorry," I said. "What happened?"

"We talked." She tossed some forks into the tray, then picked up the small strainer she used to rinse berries and shook it dry.

"About?"

"Money, basically. We're each going to give you ten thousand dollars. You're going to keep separate bank accounts and be responsible for your own expenses. We'll see how far that goes. I hope they hold up their end."

"Wow, okay," I said, feeling suddenly like a helpless child.

"Like I said, we can treat it as a loan. We'll pay you back over time."

"I won't hold my breath," she said. "You won't exactly be employable, and Will's parents appear to be keen on him staying in school. Daddy is also hell-bent that you keep your spot at NYU until the time is right for you to go back." She shut the silverware drawer and turned around. "Honestly, I don't understand this country's obsession with education. Will should get a job, in my opinion."

"Well, thank you," I said, fingering the Bloomingdale's catalog on top of the stack of mail, too embarrassed to look at her. Money had a way of doing that.

"Other than that, we discussed our disappointment that you couldn't be persuaded," she said. "That took a while."

"Mom, I'm done. I'd always wonder. I know enough to know I couldn't live with not keeping it. Can we move on now?"

"Move on. My only daughter is wrecking her life. Move on."

"What did you think of Mrs. Weston?"

"What did I think?" She reached down to pull the plates out of the dishwasher. "What does it matter?"

"She's sort of bug-eyed, don't you think?" I thought about how so much of what I said came from rotten, anxious places. "She's more with it than she comes across, but she seems a little spacey, right?"

"I didn't notice."

"You were just together for two hours. You didn't notice anything?"

"Thea, don't." She shut the dishwasher with a neat click and dried her hands. "I know she wants more for Will, things that don't involve this crap." The way she drew out the word

122

crap, I felt like a trampy, knocked-up cretin with big buckteeth, wearing dirty, light-blue corduroys. "I sometimes wish you could just be me for a minute so you could understand how much this stinks."

"You know, what about just thinking about what *I* think is right for me?" I asked. "What's meaningful to me? It is my life, after all."

She turned around and faced me, one hand on her hip. "I forget who once said to me, 'Children are thankless,' but they were right. They were absolutely right." She pulled a Toblerone bar out of the butter door of the fridge and went to her room.

"I said thank you!" I yelled after her.

23.

The morning of graduation, the sky was a deep, sharp blue and the wind made the spouts of the Lincoln Center fountain bend in different directions like a frothy liquid compass. My purple polyester gown, striped with creases from the box, slithered against my now giant stomach. Vanessa took my hand and we skipped to the hall underneath the murals of dancers. I wished Will could have been there, but when I had asked Mom if I could invite him, she had given me a "Don't-even-think-about-it" look.

"I have no interest in celebrating your achievements with someone who's essentially destroyed your future," she'd said, and I had taken that as my cue to drop the subject.

The ceremony took two and a half hours, enough time for

four hundred kids to march across the stage and get their diplomas. Afterward, Stephen Bustello, a kid in my class everyone lusted after, stood on the granite ledge of the fountain and threw his cap in, and it floated on top of a spout before falling into the bubbles. The diamond stud in his ear caught the sun and reflected little dots of light onto someone's shoulder. I'll probably never see him again, I thought. I pictured him flying over the city like a superhero, laughing at all of us.

My parents and I went with Vanessa's parents and her brother, Miles, to a dark Greek restaurant with a big stone fireplace that had no fire in it because it was almost summer.

"Why there, why not someplace more fun?" Mom had asked.

"We want to go somewhere close by," I had said. It seemed important to have lunch near the actual event.

"Lincoln Center, yuck," she'd responded.

When Vanessa and I had graduated from junior high together, we'd had lunch at Tavern on the Green. Now when we sat down at the Greek restaurant, Vanessa's mother passed around pictures of twelve-year-old Vanessa and me sitting in tall brocade chairs, holding up glasses with ginger ale and cherries in them. We were the only ones at the table. My hair was too long and lemon yellow, and there was a blue ribbon hanging off the side of my head. I was grinning and looking sideways at Vanessa, and she was looking into the camera, her shoulders neat and narrow, her eyes smart with secrets.

"To the girls," Dad said. He sat across the round white table, next to Mr. March.

"To the girls," we all repeated.

"To the graduates," said Vanessa's dad. "The cream of the crop."

124

"All the best to both of you," Dad said. Mom fidgeted with her gold bangle bracelets and her vodka tonic and studied the people at other tables.

"To bravery," Vanessa's mom said. I knew she'd never wish my situation on Vanessa, but she winked at me.

"To stupidity, more like it," Mom muttered. No one else heard her. I slathered triangles of pita bread with olive oil and taramosalata and crumbled feta cheese, starving. The waiter brought plates of calamari and stuffed olives. Mr. March talked to Dad about how much our high school had changed since his father had gone there, when it was boys only.

"Constant brawls," Mr. March said. "He used to say it was like Rikers, I'm not kidding." Mr. March was skinny with a small potbelly and wore the same glasses Diane Keaton wore in *Annie Hall*. Dad chuckled politely, his index finger stretching his brow toward the ceiling. Dad injected something celebratory into the dim room. But he hardly said a word.

"I just want to lie on Thea's dock this summer," Vanessa said, stroking my cheek. "Kay?"

"Don't torture me, Vanessa, please," said Mrs. March. "We begged and borrowed to get you that thing at Nickelodeon."

"I knowww, but I just need a li'l breaky," she moaned.

"Breaky, I'll show ya breaky," Mr. March interjected, making a fist with his pudgy hand.

"What am I going to do without my Nessy around to rattle my chain?" Mrs. March mused at the menu, shaking her head. "Who's going to give me lousy pedicures?" She looked at my mother. "The first one to go, Fiona. My heart's about to snap."

Mom smiled empathically at Mrs. March and then her face faded behind a cloud. I realized she wanted *me* to go. I straightened my forks and had the weird sensation of being there in my body, sandwiched between Mom and Vanessa, but with the rest of me vaporizing out of the restaurant to a place where I existed completely alone with my thoughts and worried plans.

24.

I celebrated the first Monday of no school by going to Stash. The cowbell clanged and the woman behind the counter looked up as I entered. I was the only one in the store.

"So I think I figured it out," she said cheerfully, recognizing me right away. She pulled open a drawer, fished around and walked toward me with a piece of graph paper that had about twenty numbered instructions and a lot of capital-letter abbreviations. The photo of me in the bikini was paper-clipped to the top.

"What's that?" I asked, pointing to the letters *SC*.

"Single crochet," she said. "Which is mostly what this is, for tightness. Have you ever worked with a pattern before?"

"Actually, no, I've only done a scarf. Is it hard?"

"It's not hard," she said, and from the way she looked at me, I knew it would be. "It's just there are a few things you need to familiarize yourself with. If you have a minute, I could quickly go over it."

"That would be great," I said.

"You're lucky—I got nothing doing at the moment," she said. She went through the pattern abbreviations and got me started, casting on the first side with some practice yarn from a basket by the counter.

"It's basically a series of single crochets, joined together by chains and slip stitches," she said.

"Slip stitch?" I asked, staring at her blankly.

"I'll show you, don't worry."

"I'm glad the original was crocheted and not knitted," I said. "I've tried a few times to knit and I always screw up. I have these big ambitions with knitting and I can never follow through."

She smiled in an understanding way. "You just need someone to help you get started." She took my hook and checked it, then handed it back. "Crochet's a different game, maybe more fun, I sometimes think. More air. I'm a hard-core knitter, but crochet is airy. And it's more forgiving."

"You mean if you mess up," I said.

"If you mess up, and the flow, I don't know." She mimicked winding her fingers and an imaginary needle. "I'm obsessed with it all. Sometimes I think it borders on pathological." She sat back in the chair. "It makes everything better."

"How long have you had Stash?" I asked, spreading out the chains so I could see them better. "I'm Thea, by the way."

"I'm Carmen." She smiled. "Two years. It was my husband's idea. We were trying to get pregnant and I couldn't stop cleaning. I would go through, like, five bottles of 409 a week. So he was like, 'You have to stop cleaning.' He said I should open a shop."

"Well, it's a great place," I said.

"Thank you." She looked around contentedly and checked my hook again. "Okay, you did three of those, right? Now it's time to connect them with a slip stitch." She reached my hook across the three chains and pulled the yarn through. "It's basically just a connector stitch. No biggie. There, you got it. So when is your baby due?"

"In the summer," I said. "I'm moving in with my boyfriend."

"Are you in school?"

"I just graduated from high school."

"Wow," she said. "That's brave."

"What?" I asked.

"I don't know, having a baby barely out of high school."

"Well, we didn't exactly plan it. Our parents are still in freak-out mode."

"Yikes," she said. She looked at me like she wanted to ask a million questions, but instead she turned back to the pattern. "You're doing really well. You'll probably get stuck, make some mistakes, have some questions. Feel free to come back anytime. Come back anyway. I want to see how it turns out."

I stood up and thanked her, a little embarrassed by how much she'd helped me. She walked me to the door and saw me off, standing on the sidewalk with her arms folded, as though she were saying goodbye from her house. I started down the street, stopping at a light to jam the pattern into my bag, not knowing where to put the photo of me in the bikini so that it wouldn't get any more beaten up than it already was. I looked at my face in the photo; I had a sort of Mona Lisa half smile going, but even ten-plus years later, it was immediately raw and decipherable. Me and my grandmother on the beach, after breakfast—toast and milk and orange juice, in side-by-side glasses. She was keeping me out of our house after another four a.m. blow-up.

"Why in the world would I want to go to Alan's with you?"

I remembered hearing Dad shout as I lay in bed. I'd crept to the top of the stairs and peeked. He was standing in the middle of the round woven rug, towering over Mom in a rocking chair. Then Mom stood up, my grandmother's dark green bathrobe draping at her feet. "If you don't like it, don't buy it," she'd said. "I can't imagine why they'd want us in the first place." She'd pretended to shake hands in the air, then turned and looked at her feet. "Uh, hi, uh-uh-uh, Alan, nice tacking out there, uh, today?" I didn't know what she was talking about, just that she was making fun of him. I focused on the big rusty fan in the corner of the upstairs hallway, feeling the silence in every pore, its terrible, inescapable vacuum. I wondered what it would be—one of the sailing trophies on the mantel? The TV? But this time, she struck first. He spat at her and gave her the infamously cryptic title of "Shit-Hair," and that was when she swung the storm lamp in an upward swoop, as though she were swinging a tennis racquet, slamming it at his ear. I remembered not needing to pretend to be asleep by the time the cops came, and after they left, Mom taking me upstairs to sleep in the guest room with the door locked.

"That's it, I promise," I remembered her whispering. I stared at the roses on her nightgown, which grew more and more detailed as light crept into the room. My eyes skipped from one rose to the next, and the white spaces in between them became the spaces between me and Mom and Dad, and I thought about how she wasn't scared of him, and it seemed stark, that fact. Something to be afraid of, maybe, in and of itself.

As I crossed the street, I caught a woman in a trench coat and heels glancing at my belly and then at my face. If she thought I was too young to be a baby mama, she didn't let on. I nudged the bikini photo into the chest pocket of my jean jacket, where it would be safe, as it started to rain.

part three

25.

I packed CDs, no shrieking ballads by women with angry, suffering voices. This was my new life; I was done with those. I took the salad spinner Mom didn't use. She used to pull the string too hard, making the top fly off, then gasp like someone had snuck up on her. I took a rusty peeler instead of the good one with the thick plastic grip, an old nail kit Mom didn't use anymore and washed-out gray bath towels with strings hanging off that she wouldn't miss. I packed and thought about how being with Will might be like chess, how you can play at that first level, a level that's hard but not too hard, and how getting to the next level would require the kind of concentration and willpower that you might not have, but that you wouldn't know whether you had it or not unless you tried.

I jammed my makeup into Dad's old Virgin Airlines travel case made of spongy fake leather. I took five to seven of each thing, underwear, short- and long-sleeved shirts, things I could wear pregnant and not pregnant. I left my turtlenecks—they reminded me too much of school.

Mom was in her room as I dragged my big duffel down the hall.

"So goodbye." She sighed, tossing a catalog to the side of her bed. "This is so utterly bizarre, this situation, I'm honestly at a loss."

"I love you," I said, which sounded weird; we never said I love you to each other. I looked at the white brick wall I'd gazed at from Mom's bed my entire life, and thought, This *is* utterly bizarre: I'm moving out. "I'll call you later."

* * *

Will opened the door to Florence's apartment. "Welcome to the pleasure dome," he said, walking backward with his arms extended. I followed him down the long hallway lined with posters by the cartoonist who hid the *Ninas*, into an airy, white room with high ceilings. There were two tall windows on one wall with multiple lead-pane squares, and a wood-paneled kitchen along the opposite wall. A sagging mohair sofa bed lined the window, and a leather armchair that looked as though a cat had had its way with it for decades sat across from it. A black upright piano with yellowing keys sat in front of the far window, and a narrow, thin-legged coffee table stood in the middle of the room. A very beat-up Oriental carpet covered almost the entire floor, bathing everything in a faded-pink glow. I loved it.

"How was the first night?" I asked, dropping my bag.

"The cars sound angry because of the cobblestone, but you get used to it," he said. "You sleep like the dead anyway."

It was hot. There was an air conditioner hanging out the corner window.

"Does that work?" I asked.

"I've spent the last two hours getting it out of the closet and screwing it into the window," Will said. "She had it wedged into the lower shelf of the bedroom closet. It was a nightmare. We need to go out for some of that insulation tape stuff that goes between the window and the unit."

"Unit?" I asked, smirking at his wonky word choice. I took his waist and pulled him down to the prickly, mohair sofa bed with me, and we had slow, side-by-side afternoon sex, throwing the cushions off to make room for my huge body.

At four o'clock I unzipped my duffel.

"Let's go for a walk," he said. He lay naked on the couch, combing through the wisps of hair under his arm.

"I want to unpack."

"Let's do it later. I have to make room first." He waved at the lone tall maple dresser with brass handles. All the drawers were open, his stuff hanging out.

We went out into the breezy June heat. There was no hiding my stomach anymore. I let it just hang out, feeling the ache in the small of my back. Will took my hand and we walked that way for a couple of blocks, but before long we were too sweaty and dropped hands.

We spotted a hardware store on West Twelfth and went in. The entryway was so narrow we had to turn sideways to get past the line at the register. I almost caught my belly on a rack of plastic key rings as Will chuckled from behind me. "Choo choo," he said. I shot him a dirty look. "What?" he asked, trying not to smile.

Will got into an involved discussion with an older hardware guy about how to properly seal in the air conditioner while I studied the back wall of seed packs, somehow comforted by the fact that there were so many of them, so many different kinds of things people would consider growing. I looked at Will and the guy, facing each other, their arms folded in manly collaboration. I picked up a roll of thick white rope wrapped in an orange sleeve and tried to imagine crocheting with it. The rope reminded me of the bumper ties on Dad's boat. Being in the hardware store felt like a whole new life. Will bought a thing of thick rubber siding and we stepped outside into the heat, which was visibly rising from the street, even at five o'clock. When we crossed the street, there was a guy outside selling ices from a sidewalk freezer. Will got two scoops of chocolate and I got a scoop of rainbow. I looked at the incredibly familiar Gino's sign that I felt like I'd seen in the window of every pizza store since I was born. Will handed me my ice and dropped a bit of cherry onto my stomach. He pushed a napkin into my T-shirt and looked up at me.

"I know everyone in the world was once inside someone else's belly," he said, licking. "I realize that and everything, but it still doesn't take away from the fact that it's just the weirdest concept imaginable."

"I know," I said.

We walked into a mattress store just as we finished sucking the last juicy bits from the soggy paper.

"We could ditch the couch and get a real bed," he said. "Florence wouldn't mind."

"What, you're just going to plop her old one out onto the street?" I asked. He hopped on a bed in the back and did all the stupid things people do on a mattress in public. Then he rolled onto his hip and whispered, "Come," caressing the mattress seductively. I lay down.

"Can my princess feel the pea?" He pushed my head back on the plastic pillow and kissed me as I heard a salesman clear his throat.

We went home and ordered Chinese, eating it on Florence's flowered plastic plates. There was no dishwasher, so we stood next to each other, me washing, him drying and doing the bump with me. After that we opened the sofa bed, throwing the stiff cushions into the crack in the corner.

I took the bikini pattern and the skein of lemon-yellow practice yarn I'd bought at Carmen's out of the paper bag as Will turned on the TV. Everything felt weird and new, but having a project helped. I studied the pattern for a while, then realized that before I started, I had to wind the yarn into a ball.

The skein was basically a big circle of yarn that would get too unraveled and messy if I just pulled from it. It had to be wound into a ball first. Carmen had a contraption clamped to a table in her store that wound skeins of yarn into balls, and she'd asked me if I'd wanted her to wind it for me. As I started to wind the skein around two fingers, I wished I'd taken her up on it. The yarn kept sticking to the rest of the skein whenever I tugged at it. Then I had an idea. I got up and went to the foot of the bed.

"Outta my way." Will craned his neck to see the TV. He was sprawled across the bed, licking the melted remains of a Reese's Peanut Butter Cup off his fingers.

"I need to borrow your feet," I said, looping the circle of yarn around his bare, outstretched feet. "Keep them flexed, okay?" I stood to the side of the TV and started winding. It went much faster with his feet.

"This is a huge help," I said, interrupting his *Law & Order* stupor.

"What are you doing?"

"I'm winding this yarn into a ball so I can crochet a bikini."

"A bikini?" he asked, not looking away from the TV.

"A bikini," I said. "I had a crocheted bikini when I was little that I'm trying to remake, sort of."

"What, so you can run around like G-House Rock, pregnant bikini-monster?"

"No, jerk," I said. "I'm not going to wear it now, don't worry. But thanks a lot."

After a while he let his left foot go slack. I pushed it against my leg to flex it again. A commercial came on and Will watched the yarn as it came up from each end of the loop. "Why are you spending money on stuff that you're not going to wear?" he asked.

"It didn't cost much," I said, guiltily remembering the thirty-buck receipt. "Who made you money cop?"

"I'm not money cop," he said. "But we've got to watch it. You don't even have a job."

"I'm eight months pregnant. We've already talked about this. I'll get a job when the baby's old enough to go to day care." I yanked the yarn, accidentally catching it on his toe.

"Ow!" he said. He pulled his foot out from under the loop. "This is stupid. I'm not doing it. Let's just go to bed. You're tired and I have to get up early."

"Fine," I said. I took the remaining loop off Will's foot and shoved it back into the bag along with the ball I'd started. He turned off the TV and reached over to the floor lamp next to the bed.

"Thanks for your help, by the way." I lay on my side in Florence's old sofa bed, feeling as though my head were lower than the rest of my body. Will didn't answer. Our first night together, I thought miserably. The lights from outside made shapes on the ceiling that, put together, looked a little like the mean queen from Dad's house, the evil, frowning stepmother queen, who followed me wherever I went.

26.

Will left the next morning for his job at the law firm—the same job he'd had the summer before—without speaking to me after the stupid fight. I pulled out the bikini pattern and the ball of yellow yarn and started in, ready to apply myself. "Chain four,

138

join into a ring with a slip stitch." Easy. But then it told me to single crochet three times into the center of the ring and there was a problem: I couldn't find the ring. Carmen said it would be obvious, where the ring was, because it would look like a hole. But I poked at it and separated the stitches and I could not find it. I crocheted three times into the center of what I thought was the ring, only to realize it wasn't. A few rounds of that and I realized I was screwed, unable to start the bikini I was dying to start.

"Damn it!" I yelled. I hurled the yarn, furious at it, wanting it away from me. It landed on the rug by the coffee table as the buzzer rang. Mom and Vanessa were coming over for a makeshift shower-breakfast, which was really just an excuse to see our new place.

They arrived together, not on purpose, throwing their coats on Florence's accordion rack in the hallway. Mom plunked a Babies "R" Us shopping bag onto the coffee table and pulled what looked like a stereo receiver out of a box inside it.

"What's that?" I asked.

"It's a pump," she said. Vanessa and I looked dumbly at her.

"Tell me you know what a breast pump is." The black box was connected by clear thin tubes to a pair of baby bottles with suction cups on top. She plugged it into the wall, but nothing happened.

"I don't think that outlet works," I said.

"Of course it doesn't," she grumbled as I glanced nervously at Vanessa, whose brilliant idea it had been to get together that morning. "Is there one that does?"

"The other side of the couch," I said.

Mom lifted the black box and plopped it onto the far end of the coffee table so that the cord could reach the outlet. A whining whirr came and went in waves. She held up the suction cups with the tubes dangling to the floor.

"Annie had one of these," she said. Annie was one of the managers at Fiona's. She'd had her daughter, Tamsin, when she was forty-six. "You attach these little cups to your nips and it leaves your hands free to drink coffee and open your mail. Come here."

She reached over to the armchair where I was sitting and lifted up my shirt.

"Don't!" Vanessa cried. "You'll make her go into labor! I read that in her book. Nipple stimulation can bring on contractions."

"Why are *you* reading *her* pregnancy book?" Mom glared at Vanessa. "You don't have anything better to do?"

"What, it's fun." Vanessa crossed her legs, embarrassed, and pushed the plate of chocolate croissants she'd brought toward Mom.

"Anyway, after the first month Annie stopped nursing altogether and just pumped." She took a sip from the latte in her paper cup and looked at me pointedly. "She said it saved her booby dolls."

"I'll remember that, Mom," I said. "But I'm not as obsessed with my booby dolls as you are." If my mother weighed 130 pounds or under, she liked to wear her Steven Sprouse polyester button-downs from the seventies that she'd bought at a flea market in London. She said she couldn't wear them if she went over 130 because the fabric would stretch across her chest and stomach in between the buttons and she hated the way that looked. I knew what she meant, but I thought it looked trampy in a good way. When she wore the shirts, her boobs were her booby dolls, her friends, as in, "My booby dolls and I are going to Healthy Bagel." But when she felt fat, she'd lie in bed and watch them fall off to either side, her chin burrowed into her collarbone, scrutinizing. Then they were her "craven globes." "Fie on thee, craven globes," she'd say. When I was little, I thought she'd said, "Pie on thee." I thought it meant Dad had made his chocolate-chip pecan pie, which he did sometimes when he was hungover.

"So it's nice here, right?" I asked Vanessa, afraid to look at Mom. "It's a great deal. We're paying her rent, and she's on rent control. It was perfect for her because she didn't want to sublet to anyone she didn't know and she didn't have any takers in the two months she's been away. We lucked out."

"I love it," Vanessa said quickly. "It has a cool, Village-y artist vibe. Is she an artist? I love the windows."

"She's a sculptor," I said. "And she makes jewelry. And now she's teaching in Africa."

"Where the hell is it going to sleep?" Mom asked, shaking her head in dismay. "The closet?"

"The baby doesn't need anything at first," I said, lifting the wrapped box Vanessa had brought out of the bag. "Anyway, we can't afford anything else."

"Please," said Mom. "No poor-unwed-teenager thing. Please. We're avoiding that like the bubonic plague. Remember."

Vanessa chuckled, which eked a hint of a smile out of Mom. I watched Mom as she cut one of the croissants in half, and I was grateful that she'd at least made an effort to bury her disappointment in me and come over.

"Vanessa, when do you leave for school?" Mom asked.

"End of August." Vanessa sighed. "We're going to Maine for two weeks after Nickelodeon ends, then we're back for, like, a night, and then I go." She made a sad face at me.

My phone flashed. I reached for it on the side table and saw a text from Will. "Sry I wuz a jrk last nite. I luv u."

I shook Vanessa's box, relieved and happy about Will's apology. "Clothes," I said.

She rocked mischievously back and forth on the couch. "Open it."

It was a stuffed dog with calico patches all over it and lop-sided men's ties for ears.

"Isn't he cool?" she asked, hopping in her seat. "I thought it was the cutest thing."

I smiled, thinking about all of the stuff we still needed—a crib, a baby tub, those onesie suits that covered their feet. All of a sudden it seemed totally pathetic, my shower—Mom shifting around on the couch as though it had nits on it, my teenage best friend who didn't know any better than to buy me an ugly stuffed dog.

"It's very sweet," I said. "He or she will love it."

"When are you going to find out the gender, for God's sake?" Mom asked. "It's so creepy–new agey not to find out right away these days."

"We want it to be a surprise," I said.

"It's a surprise no matter when you find out," Mom said impatiently.

"Well, I should go. It's ten-thirty." Vanessa stood up, hiking her wrinkled linen pants over her hips.

"You're skinny," I said.

"Are you kidding?" she said. "Anyone looks skinny to you right now." She patted my belly and kissed my mother on each cheek. "Bye, Fiona."

"Call me later," I said.

She nodded and slung her big fake white-leopard-skin bag over her shoulder. "It's great, Thee, really. I wish I were living here."

The door banged loudly, the metal of the old locks jangling with it. Mom pressed her finger on the plate, retrieving fallen croissant flakes. For the first time in my life with her, there was a heavy and awkward silence.

I looked at my blinking phone again. Another message from Will. I hadn't answered the first one. "Helu? You forgive me, yes?" I quickly texted him back. "Y. I luv u." I tossed the phone where Vanessa had been sitting, feeling grown up and proud of us for maneuvering through our fight so gracefully.

"You know, I've been thinking," Mom said slowly. "About that stuff with Dad. That night, when he came over."

"Oh." I shrugged. I wondered why she was bringing it up out of nowhere.

"It must seem like we've always hated each other, he and I."

"I know you don't hate him," I said.

"That's not what I was going to say." She recrossed her legs and I watched her small, round knees move underneath her black pants and wondered how it was that I had such big knees, such big bones. "He's waiting for this to blow up too," she said. "It's all we can do. It's hard. For both of us, in our different ways, it's hard."

"It might not, you know," I said. "Blow up."

She looked at me as though she were considering something. Music from a car radio drifted in. I had a weird urge to tell her that her life with Dad had not been a waste. That she hadn't wasted her life, that she'd been living a full life then, with its long, loud red nights at Fiona's and its siren voices and

143

everyone's love problems and drama. That her having me and raising me hadn't been a waste of time either.

"Thanks for coming," I said. The visit was sliding away from me, but I felt unready for her to leave. I wondered how sometimes my mother could feel so familiar—the smell of her room, the way she tapped her brush against the sink before she turned on the hair dryer—and yet how I could still have such an unclear picture of her. How I could not know whether she was happy, or what made her happy, what she thought about when she shut her eyes at night. I thought of her unbuttoning her shirt and throwing it onto the silk chair in her room, and the pull of skin across her cheeks after she washed her face, but it was like looking at her through a window from across the street.

"And thank you for the money, and the pump, and everything else," I said. "Have some faith in me, Ma." I tried to say it jokingly, but the words spilled out of me in an awkward rush. "The details might not be all there, but the feelings make sense. It feels real. That's important, you know."

"It feels real," she repeated, looking to me. "What does that mean?"

"It feels like what we're doing is right. Can you just believe me that it does? Even if it doesn't seem right to you? We're going to make it work. I love him. We're going to make it."

"I'd like to believe you." She pulled a tissue out of a pack in her bag and brushed any loose crumbs off her lipsticked mouth. "I would."

27.

The morning I went into labor, I crocheted and watched the Movie Channel, thinking it would teach me something about life. I'd finally found the ring, and as I did more of them, I was able to recognize what the ring looked like (it looked like a hole!) and how it changed shape a little after each stitch. After a few hours I finished a yellow, slightly lopsided version of the bikini bottom that didn't look half bad. It was a far cry from the multicolored zigzags I'd pictured, but it was a step.

I decided to walk downtown and across the Brooklyn Bridge because I was a week past my due date and my doctor had told me to walk. My water broke just as I reached the high, arched midpoint. I stopped short and doubled over, and a guy running behind me crashed into me.

"Jesus, watch out," he said. We were both sprawled on the wooden walkway, bikers and cars whizzing past. He was practically on top of me, his flimsy blue nylon shorts draping my leg. Then he saw my huge belly and my wet, streaked jeans.

"Shit, are you okay?" He stood up and held out his arm. "Can you stand up?"

"I need to get to the hospital," I said, dusting myself off.

"I don't have a phone!" He waved his arms frantically around his skimpy shorts.

"I do," I said. I dialed Will at school.

"It's happening," I said. "My water broke. Meet me at NYU."

"Where are you?"

"On the Brooklyn Bridge. I'm going to try and find a cab." I started walking back to Manhattan, the guy in shorts following me.

"I'm okay," I said, wanting him to go away. Nothing hurt yet. "Thanks."

"You sure?" he asked tentatively, looking relieved.

I nodded and started walking faster. My flats made awful squishy sounds as I got to the end of the bridge and then to Chambers Street. I passed a discount store where a guy in the window was blowing up soccer balls and throwing them into a big bin. There were people moving everywhere, stepping on and off the filthy curb to get past each other. I had a stolen, surreal moment, thinking of my high school just a few blocks west on Chambers as the banners in front of the discount store waved at me in the wind. A cab stopped in front of an ice cream store a few feet away and someone got out.

I stood in front of the driver's window so he could see me, wanting a little drama. "Can you take me to NYU Hospital?" I yelled.

He nodded offhandedly, as though he were just another cabbie carting another pregnant woman to her hospital cot.

"You gonna be okay?" he asked when we got there.

"You bet," I said, hauling myself out.

A rush of people crowded around me at reception, and a nurse got me into a room and helped me into a gown. Will showed up just as some masochist attendant came in to do something called "strip the membranes," which shocked me into submission and started me on a runaway train of screaming pain. I got an epidural, but all it did was numb my left leg. The hours crawled and flew, the door to my room swinging endlessly open and shut, Will holding my hand, sitting, leaning by the window, texting, yawning, looking freaked.

At one point toward the end I started to panic.

"I feel like I could die," I said to him. He was standing next to me, holding my foot in the air.

"I know you do," he said, "but you're not going to."

"You're going to be fine," said the Irish nurse holding my other foot. "You're doing great—just stay with us and push when the doctor says to push."

I wiped my sweaty forehead and the weirdest thought flashed through my head—Mrs. Weston in the Columbia reception lounge with her serious, urgent, expression: *"Be positive."*

As the head came out, I stared at the ceiling and imagined karate-chopping my way through it. I felt like I was on fire, along with the rest of the world. "It's a boy!" the doctor shouted, and I looked down and they flopped the baby onto my bare chest, slippery and bewildered, looking right at me with wide-open, alien eyes.

"Oh my God," I cried. I said it over and over and over again.

28.

They helped me into bed and I rolled gently onto my stomach, which was like sinking into a forgotten, beloved pillow. The nurse left and I remember Will watching me from the chair next to me and shaking his head and smiling.

"Wow," he said.

"Yeah," I said.

"All that blood. It was like a slasher movie." He held my hand and I drifted off to sleep, wondering where he was, the baby, but I was too tired.

Someone turned on a fluorescent light over my head.

"He's over eight pounds, which means you should try and

feed him every three hours," the nurse whispered, wheeling the baby in, his face slightly magnified from inside the plastic rolling cot. His eyes were open and his mouth was shaped like a Cheerio. The nurse lifted him out, a clump of warm, white flannel with pink and turquoise piping, and aimed him at my boob.

"You want his chin to jut out a little," she said. "That's how you know he's properly on." But his chin never jutted out. We tried, but he kept closing his eyes and drifting off and then waking up and squirming around. The nurse manhandled his head, nudging his mouth to where it needed to be.

"How about you leave us for a while and we'll see if we can figure it out?" I finally asked.

"Fine," she said, picking up a blood-smeared towel at the edge of the bed.

After that it was just me and moon-face, high above town, some lit-up bridge outside our window, and Will, asleep in the bed next to us.

"Hello, little man," I said. "Are you hungry?" He gazed into the space between us, his cheek pressed against my chest. There was something incredible about speaking to him for the first time, even though he didn't understand me. It felt almost as though I were speaking to a part of myself who had just been born and who was in the room with us too.

I spent the rest of the night nudging him onto my nipple. He eventually latched on, squeaking a little as he sucked, and at some point I fell asleep with him splayed across my chest. I woke to the sound of heels clomping down the hallway.

Mom arrived with daisies and a bag filled with Pellegrino, pretzels and Milano cookies.

"All the stuff I would want," she said, looking at Will, who was still asleep. They had not been in a room together since she'd found out I was still pregnant. "I'm only staying a few minutes."

"Can you wash your hands?" I asked. She paused to take off her coat and put it behind the chair, then headed for the sink in the corner.

"I couldn't believe it, what she went through," Will said, sitting up as if he'd just dozed off in the middle of a conversation. "I've never seen anything like it in my life. She pushed for, like, three hours. I thought her eyes were going to explode out of their sockets."

"Lovely," said Mom, drying her hands. "When he came out, did he look angry or did he look worried?" she asked.

"Neither, I don't think." I thought of his eyes, blank and searching, when they put him on me.

"He didn't scream bloody murder? You screamed your head off, but then after a while you got it together."

"I think *I* was screaming," I said.

She peered into the cart, where I'd deposited him at some point when the sky was still dark, and looked at me and Will. "So?"

"We like Ian," Will said. "Ian Galehouse Weston."

"Ian," she said, jiggling the cart lightly with her hand. "You don't think it sounds too much like Theeeeeaaaaa?"

"That's part of why I like it," I said. "Can you like it too?"

"Wasn't Ian the name of that daft road manager in *Spiñal Tap*?" She sat down in the chair next to my bed. "How do you feel?"

"Okay," I said. Ian stirred, sticking his hand up out of the blanket he was tightly swaddled in. I reached over to pick him up. "He should eat again."

"He's a furball," Mom said, looking at him and forcing a

smile, folding her hands in her lap. "Where did he get all that fur?"

"He's a baby, Mom," I said, my shoulders stiffening. "Not a monkey."

Will flipped his feet onto the floor, facing us from the other bed. "Did I ever tell you that my name is not short for William?" he asked, looking at both of us. I thought about where I'd seen his name in print: on a list of AP physics tutor volunteers, in the yearbook, on his gray high school sweatshirt, which was suddenly okay to wear now that he'd graduated. The name was always Will.

"It's not?" I asked, pushing Ian's face onto my nipple, which was already sore. He squirmed and butted at me, not latching on.

"My name is actually Willbraham," he said.

"What the hell is that?" I asked. "It's like Baberaham. Baberaham Lincoln. What were your parents thinking?"

"I'm named after a town they rode through on a bike trip," he said, fiddling with the crank at the end of the bed. "They biked through Switzerland on their honeymoon. Can you imagine my mother on a bike?"

Mom crossed her legs and sucked her lips in, which made her lipstick smudge over her lip line.

"Yeah, so . . ." Will stood up and touched Ian's head, looking over his shoulder as someone came in to change the wastebasket. "It was this little town where, they said, everything was very plain, very workhorse, but then the houses all had tulips growing around their doorways and it was really simple and beautiful and . . . crisp. That's the word they used to describe it."

"Like crispy tofu," I said stupidly, looking at Mom. Both of her elbows rested stiffly on the arms of the chair.

"And they spent the night there," Will said. "In some pensione or whatever."

"Some *dieflockerhaus,*" I said, my neck starting to hurt from craning down at Ian.

"Yeah, some *dieflockerhaus,* and they woke up and sat at the café and they saw all these people riding by on their bikes and they all had kids, little babies riding in seats behind them or in sacks or whatever, and they thought it was very cute. And my mom said that's when she decided she wanted to have children."

"That's kind of sweet," I said.

"They were such hippies, in a way," Will said. "What the hell is wrong with William?"

"Why didn't they name you after your dad?" I asked.

"Mom didn't want to," he said, winking at me with his good eye.

As if on cue, Mr. and Mrs. Weston walked into the room in matching Dalai Lama–style jackets with silk cord fasteners. Mr. Weston was carrying a basket from Zabar's. "I figured you could use food more than flowers," he said, placing it on the windowsill. "So I believe congratulations are in order."

Mom stood up. "Lynne, Philip," she said tightly.

They all stood there until Will went over to hug his parents. Ian's face was buried behind my nipple and I desperately wanted to cover up, but my hospital gown was stuck underneath me. All of a sudden the room felt too warm and too crowded.

Mrs. Weston searched out Ian's face, Mr. Weston thankfully hanging back. "He's beautiful," she said matter-of-factly, her switch on–switch off smile in action. I hadn't seen them since that day in Will's dorm. "What's his name?"

"We're going with Ian," Will said.

"Ian," Mrs. Weston repeated. "Lovely. Can I hold him?"

"I think he's finished." I yanked my gown across my chest and handed him up to her. "He's supposedly not getting much now, anyway."

"She didn't wash," Mom said accusingly.

"Oh," Mrs. Weston said. She looked at Mom and handed the baby back to me. "I guess I'll go wash, then."

"Thea, can I get you anything before I head out?" Mom asked, gathering her coat from the chair.

"I'm good," I said. "You're leaving?" She was inches away from me, but it felt like miles. I looked at her, trying to draw her in closer. "When are you coming back?"

"Are you sure?" she asked, not hearing me. "Just call me if you do."

Mrs. Weston lifted Ian out of my arms and Mr. Weston was behind her in an instant. "Look at that," he said, jingling the change in his khaki pockets. They looked like your average, over-the-moon grandparents.

"He's got Will's face, from the nose up," Mrs. Weston murmured. She divided Ian's face in half with her hand.

"Definitely his eyes," I said. They carried on gazing as if no one else were there.

"Well, it's a big day," Mom said on her way out. "Thea, I'll ring you later."

I sat back, shrugging my stiff shoulders. Will moved next to his dad. Both were swaying lightly with Mrs. Weston as she rocked Ian.

"I'm just so happy he's out and safe and healthy," I said.

"You should have seen her," Will said. "I had no idea it was going to be like that."

Mr. Weston looked at me, then inspected his watch. I wondered just how greasy and limp my hair was, whether my face was still puffy and if my nose still had red dots on it. Mrs. Weston moved to sit down with Ian, laying him on his back on top of her legs. "Will used to love to lie like this," she said without looking up.

"Did the money land in your account, Will?" Mr. Weston asked, leaning against the windowsill.

Will nodded. "It did, thank you."

"Thank you, Mr. Weston," I said, feeling unbelievably tired all of a sudden. The adrenaline rush I'd had since I woke up was quickly evaporating, but I felt an odd relief I couldn't pinpoint. I opened my eyes and looked at Mrs. Weston, who was still gazing at Ian's sleeping face. She looked up and smiled at me and it was a completely different expression from the borderline-patronizing looks she shot me that day at Columbia, when she called me forth to face my future as a strong, independent woman. Now she pitied me.

After they left, I called Vanessa. She was with her parents in Maine, and then they were driving her to Vassar toward the end of August. "It's a boy," I said. "I was right. I'm glad I didn't find out, but I had a feeling it was a boy the whole time."

"Oh my God, I'm shocked. I was so vibing girl. Tell me everything. How bad was it?"

"It hurt like hell," I said, pulling at a loose thread on Ian's flannel blanket.

"Really?"

"Really."

"What did you do when you first saw him?"

"I don't think I could ever describe it," I said.

"Listen to you," she said. "How was Will?"

"He was amazing. I'm on a cloud. So crampy. They put me on Percocet."

"La, la," she said.

"I know. I'm flying. He's so beautiful, Ness. Not pruny at all. He's the most beautiful baby."

"I know he is, Thee. I'm so proud of you. Will you *please* email me a pic? Or send me one from your phone."

"You know my phone is messed up and can only send texts, no pics."

"Have Will figure it out. Is it weird yet?"

I looked over and smiled at Will, who was sucking on a chocolate milk shake, watching CNN. "Not yet."

"Maybe it won't be."

"Maybe."

I hung up and dropped my head back on my pillow, watching Ian sleep. I wanted to ask the doctor about Ian's head, which seemed squishy and too big for his body. I wanted to ask her about his neck. How he didn't seem to have one. A few hours later my phone buzzed. It was Dad.

"I'd like to meet him. Are you exhausted?"

"Kind of, yeah."

"Well, it's getting late. When are you leaving?"

"Tomorrow," I said.

"How about I pick you guys up and take you home?"

"Okay, if you want," I said.

"I'll bring the camcorder."

I hung up and drifted off to sleep. Will had gone home for the night with instructions to bring the car seat back in the morning. I woke up after a while, feeling acutely sore and spongy, waiting for Ian to wake up, not knowing what to do with myself until he did. Whenever I looked over at him, I got a feeling of déjà vu, like he'd always been there next to me, my little prince, asleep in his plastic throne.

29.

I was bending Ian's ears when the pediatrician arrived the next morning. She woke him up and pulled at his legs, uncurling him.

"He looks great," she said. "You're nursing?"

"Yes," I said.

"How's it going?"

"I'm a little sore."

"That will pass in a few days, just stick with it," she said, passing him from the rolling cot to me. "I don't need to tell you how good it is for him. Is he latching on?"

I nodded.

"Great," she said, watching as he started his butting, squirming, sucking routine. "Looks like you're both doing just fine." She scribbled on her board. "Things you want to look out for—projectile vomiting. Spitting up, even in large quantities, is normal, but projectile vomiting, or vomit that looks greenish in color, is cause for concern. Are you circumcising?"

"No," I said. I blurted it out without thinking about it, but after I did, I realized I'd blurted out the right answer.

She grinned, her thin, lipsticked lips reminding me of Glenda the good witch. "I have my own opinions about circumcision for nonreligious reasons," she said. "I'm glad we'll both be spared that little chat this morning." She glanced at me and looked around the room, and the bluster left her voice. "Who's picking you up?"

"My boyfriend. He'll be here any minute," I said. I would have liked to stay longer. It was safe and orderly there, the nurses with their thermometers and paper cups of Percocet pills and Jell-O.

"Here's my card," she said, brushing my arm with her smooth cotton coat. "Call me anytime, day or night. No question too dumb, and I'll be happy to do the follow-up with you in two weeks' time."

She and Will passed each other in the doorway without saying anything.

"When can you leave?" He stood over me, patting Ian's sleeping, furry, black-haired head.

"Not sure," I said. "I think she has to give the okay and then we sign out." My phone buzzed.

"I'll go see about signing out," Will said, walking out purposefully.

"I just have to finish up something," Dad said. "I can be there soon."

"Okay, but I think we're leaving," I said.

"Call me if I'm not there when you need to go," he said. "But I'll be there."

I hung up, annoyed that I'd have to manage him again. Will didn't come back for a long time and I thought for sure Dad would get there first. I pictured Will hitching a ride to Montana on a Mr. Softee truck, getting a job on a dude ranch. When he finally showed up, he looked sweaty and I wondered if it was too hot outside for Ian. "There was a shitload of paperwork at the desk," he said, setting his jacket on the swinging bed table. "I've been out there forever. This kid is like a minute old. Unbelievable."

I passed Ian to Will and he tensed up a little, the crook of his arm almost swallowing Ian's head. Will looked up at me and for a moment it was like someone had zapped an unbreakable blue force field around the three of us. I collected stuff at the sink and threw them into my bag.

"You think he's eating enough?" Will asked anxiously. "He's sleeping so much."

"The doc said every three hours," I said. "I don't think they eat much the first few days. They said my milk won't come in for a while anyway. Whatever that means."

"What *does* it mean?" he asked. "What does it mean, 'come in'? Why don't you have it yet?"

"I read in the book that I'll know when it comes in because my boobs will get 'engorged.'"

"Sounds scary," he murmured, his face turned back to Ian.

"I know. Engorged. So sexual," I said, untying my gown in the corner so Will wouldn't see my deflated pooch of a stomach. "But the doc said they sleep eighteen hours a day in the beginning."

"You'd think he'd be a little curious, after being cooped up in there for so long," he said. "Can you imagine how boring it must have been? Just sitting there, endlessly in the dark?"

"Tell me about it," I said.

We pushed out of the revolving doors toward the street, and everything outside—the low roof of the atrium, the blowing trees—felt menacing. I saw Dad at the end of the driveway and my heart sank: How were we all supposed to fit in that tiny car? How were we going to get the car seat in? I realized I'd forgotten to call him, and couldn't believe he was actually there. He was pointing a video camera at us through the driver's-side window.

"Glad I caught you."

We walked to the car and Will tried to hoist the car seat up a little higher so Dad could get a look at Ian. It was a weird scene: us standing frozen in front of the car while Dad filmed Ian asleep in the seat. It was like he couldn't take the camera away from his face and just look at him.

"Hey there, little man," Dad finally said, getting out of the car. He paused the camera and turned to study me. "How do you feel?"

"Fine," I said. "Glad we're going home. How are we going to do this?"

"Well . . ." Dad opened his door again and pushed the tan bucket seat as far forward as it would go. I crouched into the back, snagging a hole in the cellophane of the Westons' Zabar's bag, and waited for someone to hand me the car seat. Will was the first to try, angling the square plastic base away from the top of Dad's headrest, but it was too wide for the car seat to get through.

"Easy!" Dad said, pushing the seat-back down, clearly worried about tearing. As I leaned forward, a jar of Bonne Maman jam somehow rolled out of the car and smashed on the curb. Ian's head was dangling in a way I did not like at all.

"Watch his head!" I said.

"He's okay, Thee," Will said, huffing, kicking the jam glass out of their way. The car seat was now completely stuck between the ceiling and the seat.

"Let me have at it," Dad said. He reached in and now there were men's arms and hands groping and grabbing in front of me. I was surprised at how similarly tanned and hairy they were. Eventually Dad nudged Will aside and extracted the car seat back out into the blazing sun, Ian still sound asleep.

They wound up squeezing the car seat, with Ian still in it, through the space between the two front seats.

"Remind me not to get a ride with you again," I said, pushing the seat belt through the holes in the base like the instructions on the side of the seat said. "I'm sure I'm doing this wrong."

Dad put his foot on the clutch and the car lurched out of the driveway. He drove his car just like he drove his boat, as though it had a single stop-start button. I immediately thought of waterskiing, or *not* waterskiing.

"So this is the famous Aston," Will said, stroking the burled-wood window panel.

"This is it," Dad said. "Where am I taking you to again?"

"Ninth Street, between Fifth and Sixth," I said, watching Will push a panel in front of him that revealed an empty slot.

"Don't tell me, this is where an eight-track player used to live," he marveled.

Dad glanced at him, unsure of what he meant.

"I read that you're supposed to walk them around the house and introduce them to everything," I said.

"I'm sure he'll appreciate that." Will smiled, turning back to me.

"You never know how much they can take in," Dad said, his voice weirdly animated, like he was a game-show host trying to psyche up his contestants. I felt a pang of appreciation that he was being such a good sport. "I always thought you were wise beyond your years when you were a baby."

We got to Florence's apartment and hoisted Ian back out the way we got him in. Dad made a big deal of holding open the doors and carrying my bag, looking for things to do. We climbed the three flights, Will gripping the car seat. The stairs were dark except for a bulb with grubby fingerprints on it dangling from the second landing. Dad would be seeing where we lived, where Ian would be living, for the first time. We all watched Ian in his car seat, levitating up the stairs.

Will put the seat down to open the door and Dad picked

it up and walked in, looking around for a place to set it down. He finally nestled it into the crook of the couch, and set my bag down next to it.

"Do you want a drink or something?" I asked.

"No, I should run along," Dad said, fixing his eyes on Florence's hanging wall-quilt. "How about I run out and get you guys a few things first? Something for dinner? Some fruit? A chicken?"

"That's okay, thanks," said Will. "I'll run out later."

"Are you sure?"

"Yes," we both said.

Dad went over to Ian and bent down to kiss his forehead. The kiss seemed to last forever. I made a face at Will from behind him.

"Okay, you guys," he said, coming up for air. "Call me if you need anything."

"Thanks for taking us home," I said, walking him to the door.

"I'm glad everything went well." He opened the door with one hand and threw his other arm around me in an awkward hug.

I shut the door and turned back down the hallway. "What was with that kiss? It was like he was anointing him or something."

"Give him a break," Will said. "It was nice of him. Do you think he was horrified by this place?"

"Of course not," I said.

"He looked horrified to me," Will said. "Considering where he lives, I'm sure it was not up to par."

"You haven't seen where he lives," I said, sitting down on the couch next to the car seat.

"Yes, I have, and it's slightly grander than this."

"You don't know what you're talking about," I said, trying to undo Ian's straps. "He doesn't care about that stuff."

"Bullshit," he said. "You don't have a job like that, you don't work like that and not care. Anyway, I'm starving."

Will went out and came back with four slices of pizza stacked in a white paper bag. Ian slept on a blanket next to me on the couch while Will figured out how to straighten all four legs of the Pack 'n Play at the same time. Dad had ordered it online and had it mailed to us, along with a stroller that carried the car seat, and another regular stroller. After we'd unpacked everything, a mountain of cardboard, plastic wrap and Styrofoam engulfed the living room. I couldn't help but think how lucky we were to have benefactors on our side who had sent us everything we needed. No matter how hard things might get, I thought, we were lucky. I told myself to remember that.

The Pack 'n Play had a plastic U-shaped bar that hung across the basket and shined lights and played music.

"I bet we never turn this thing on," he said.

"You never know," I said, inhaling my second slice.

"There's something very *Rosemary's Baby* about it." He wound it up and moved his eyes from side to side, imitating a marionette. He glanced at Ian from where he was on the floor.

"I have a son," he murmured.

"You have a son," I said.

The Pack 'n Play clicked down and Will leaned over to turn the dial in the middle of the base, his boxer shorts puffing out of the top of his jeans. Every part of his body still struck me in the same way that a piece of art or the idea of heaven did: enduring and pure and a little bit out of reach.

He stood up, fists on his hips, proudly assessing his

handiwork. I went over to him, feeling all banged up and contorted inside, and put my arms around him. "This is totally freaky," I said, "but kind of fun."

He smiled and pressed his forehead to mine. "Yup."

"I can't help being a little happy."

"Me too," he said.

"Really?"

He nodded slowly, glancing at Ian. "He's so cool. His tiny little everything. Did you smell him? When he first came out? I'll never forget that smell."

I put Ian on Will's chest and they both fell asleep in Florence's armchair. After that, Ian woke up every twenty minutes, sometimes to eat or cry. I thought of what Mom had said when I used to stay up late watching old reruns of *The Dick Van Dyke Show,* fixating on the wool furniture and swinging kitchen doors and married life: "Once you lose sleep, you can never get it back." I remembered my old self, how I used to brush my hair by the radiator and make it stand up. How Vanessa and I would lie in bed and talk in the dark, and it was like our universe hung in the air and we were somehow talking about everything and the night would go on and on. An unbelievably loud motorcycle roared down the street and I waited to hear the sound of someone cursing out their window at it, but it never came and then everything went quiet again, Will on my left side in the creaky, lumpy bed, Ian on my right, where he'd fallen asleep at my boob. It seemed easier to hold him there; he cried when I put him down. I couldn't move an inch, but I didn't care: it was warm and still and us.

30.

"Whoa!" I yelled into Florence's empty apartment. Ian's umbilical cord stump had popped off as I bathed him in the battered porcelain sink. It fell onto the floor and I picked it up and looked at the TV and there was footage of a submarine coasting along the bottom of the ocean, sand puffing out of its way. I dipped a Q-tip in alcohol and rubbed it around Ian's belly button like the doctor said, which made him scream his nuts off. I picked him up, featherlight and sweaty, and walked around the room, wondering what Will was doing at his job. Was he sitting at a desk, holding a pencil? Was he doodling a baby's head with a curly sprig on top? The air conditioner was barely working and we were smack in the middle of a heat wave. Was he relieved to be out of our house?

Ian fell asleep and I spotted the yellow, rolled-up bikini bottom sitting on the second shelf of the side table. It felt like a million years since I'd touched it. The last time I worked on it, I didn't have a baby, I thought. I set Ian down in the crook of the sofa bed and silently picked up the bikini. It was time to start the top, so I cast on fifteen chains, like the instructions said, which would be the bottom right triangle. I told myself the top would be easier compared to the bottom because it was triangles, which meant dropping stitches instead of gathering them into a circle. I sat for hours while Ian slept, the bed creaking underneath when I uncrossed my legs, and thought about all the people in the world who had crocheted who were now dead. I felt a sense of connection with all those dead people, with my dead grandmother sitting on another couch in another house in another time with her large, star-patterned, mustard-colored blanket. I wondered what she'd been thinking about as she'd crocheted my bikini. Did she worry about her son, my dad? Did she worry that his life was out of control? That he drank too much and that his wife was a shrew? My grandmother hated my mother. Why did she hate her so much? As I worked, I noticed that my stitches were becoming more even and less lopsided. I was getting better at it, and it felt like the only thing in the world I was getting better at. The rest of the time, I was in a haze, unable to get out the door.

In the movie on TV there was a blond girl with a ponytail and bangs cut very sharply across her forehead, exactly the way Mom used to wear it when I was younger. It reminded me of Mom sitting in a seafood place on the Charter Island harbor with me and Dad when I was younger, around the time Dad had come back from "drying out" in Arizona. I remembered, out of nowhere, I'd asked them where I was conceived. Dad was sitting across from me, but I looked at Mom when I'd asked. "My friend Sherry was conceived in Mexico," I'd said. "That's why she loves Mexican food. Where was I conceived?"

Mom pretended to choke on her popcorn, shocked.

"Interesting question," she'd said. She was about to launch into something, but Dad interrupted.

"Fiona, not appropriate," he'd said.

"What's not appropriate?" she'd asked. The familiar dynamic: Dad gruff, Mom innocent.

He shook his head and said nothing.

"What's not appropriate?" she asked, louder.

"She's twelve," Dad said, not looking at me.

"Oh Ted, relax," Mom said, dismissing him with as few

words as possible. She picked a single piece of popcorn from the basket, crunched and turned to me.

"I was managing the Kettle, my first job in charge, so I was the big stuff, and I knew it and Daddy knew it. He showed up every night. Didn't you, Daddy?" She looked at him, but his eyes were up at the bar TV.

"He would come when he was done with work, at around eleven or midnight, and he always stayed till the last set. In the beginning I thought it was his abiding, unrequited passion for music, you know, the poor, trapped artist inside the banker thing, but soon I realized it was really just a ploy to catch me as things wound down for the night."

A trace of a smile crossed Dad's face, but he stayed on the TV.

"Anyway, he'd gotten into the habit of waiting for me to close up, very gentlemanly. And then he'd take me home to his place on Warren Street. I was afraid of his lift. It had one of those metal accordion doors, and Daddy would start kissing me and I worried I'd get my hair caught or lose a finger on the way up."

"Fiona, can we leave it?" His chin burrowed into his hand. His other hand rubbed his graying, wiry sideburns. He'd let his hair grow out while he was gone.

"She asked, so I'm telling her," Mom said. "What's the problem with that?"

He leaned hard on the table, the weight of his elbow bringing it toward him.

"I don't think it's necessary for her to hear the gory details at this stage."

"Gory? Lighten up, Ted." She leaned toward him, her hair falling across her eyes. For a second I thought she was going to

165

kiss him. "Please don't let this little rehab stint deplete what's left of your sense of humor. Please. Reformed is one thing. Puritanical, another entirely."

"Humor has very little to do with it," he said. "Can you wait on anything? Can you let anything wait?" He was talking in a way where the corners of his mouth seemed to be trying to seal his lips shut. It was something his mouth did when he drank, which confused me because he'd just stopped.

"You're right, Ted, I should just continue waiting. That's what I should do." She picked up the big menu and closed herself behind a pissed-off tent, where she remained, it seemed, until the end. They split less than a year later.

By the time the movie ended, my neck was killing me from hunching over the yarn. I took Ian out for a walk in the scorching August heat, and Vanessa and everyone else from my old life were like ghosts in my head, conversing and vivid, floating and following my every move. A truck emblazoned with the words *Halal—Schwarma Kabob* emblazoned on it stopped at the corner. I laughed with imaginary Vanessa, who by then was at freshman orientation at Vassar—"What the hell is a schwarma?" I imagined her teasing me: "You've lived in New York City your entire life and you don't know what a schwarma is?"

31.

Will came home that night in a good mood because all the summer associates were getting five-hundred-dollar end-of-summer bonuses. "Maybe we can fix up this dump," he said, ruffling Florence's dusty quilt on the wall. "Let's go celebrate," he said.

I packed Ian in the sack and Will carried the car seat to the coffee shop down the street, where he wedged it into the seat of a booth. The waitress made faces at Ian as she took our order.

Will looked around with a self-satisfied smile. "We could get married and have the party here," he said, balling up his straw wrapper.

"In the back room of Aristotle's?" I asked, confused.

"Sure, it'd be fun. Why not? That guy could host." He nodded at the guy stacking cups by the coffee maker, the guy who'd asked me and Will, "How are you, my friend?" through his mustache. I reached over to stick the pacifier back in Ian's mouth. Will had a strange, forced grin on his face. He looked almost embarrassed, like he'd said something he shouldn't have.

"Seriously," I said. "Do you ever think about it?"

"Yeah," he said a little too casually, lifting his spoon to his mouth. "Every once in a while. Not every second, mind you—I'm a guy."

"Meaning what?"

"I'm a wild and crazy guy," he said, bobbling his head from side to side. I stirred the paper cup of coleslaw on my plate with my fork. I didn't understand where he was coming from and it was making me nuts. He was being offhanded and nervous at the same time.

"If you'd really thought about it, you wouldn't have mentioned it like that."

"Like what?" he asked, wide-eyed.

"Like it was nothing."

"Who said it was nothing?"

"Forget it," I said, wanting to dig our way out of the conversation. The truth was, I thought about getting married—or dreamed about it—more than I cared to admit. And I realized as I watched him, mashing crackers into the bottom of his bowl, that he did not. He looked up at me and I could tell he knew he'd been busted. But busted for what? Did the fact that he didn't think about getting married mean he didn't love me? The thought sent a chill through me as I watched the little tabs of phone numbers on the ads for music teachers and cleaning help flutter in the breeze from the door whenever it opened and closed.

At home Will held Ian and watched TV while I tried to catch a couple of hours' sleep before Ian woke up again. I put the pillow over my head, but I could still hear the sounds of buildings exploding and people yelling at each other. I decided I hated TV.

"Can you turn it down?" I asked, watching as one volume bar went black on the screen. "A little more?" Two more bars. I squeezed the pillow closer to my head, starting to get pissed. He rarely offered to hold Ian during the night; come to think of it, he never did. Granted, I had the boobs, but could he *offer*? And why couldn't he deal with the idea of getting married?

"Will, it's too loud!" I hissed, bolting upright.

"What's your problem?" he asked. "Is that how you ask?"

"I asked, and it's still too loud," I said. "I'm tired. I need to get some sleep."

"Whatever," he said. He turned it off and lay motionless in the dark with Ian asleep on him. "Get some sleep, then."

"Oh, screw you, don't make me out to be the big bad bitch." I waited for him to say something, wondering what had gotten into me. "Look, I'm sorry," I said, my hand grazing his shoulder. "I'm just so tired."

When I woke up the next morning, Will had left to register for his fall semester classes without saying goodbye. I got up, put Ian in the sack on my chest, brought the laundry downstairs, drank coffee, took a walk, went to the drugstore, talked to Mom, watched TV, changed Ian, fell asleep with Ian, went to the supermarket and came home, all the while expecting to see a "We're okay" gesture in the form of a text on my phone from Will—which never came.

32.

Vanessa finally came home from Vassar one weekend in September to meet Ian.

"Paposan!" she bellowed as Will opened the door.

"You're past due," Will said, following her in.

"What am I, a gallon of milk?" she asked.

"Mamosan!" Vanessa kissed me and I pulled her inside to where Ian was lying on the couch.

"Oh my God, he's beautiful," she said as I picked him up.

"Thanks."

"No, I mean it," she said. "He's really beautiful, Thee." She hugged me, sandwiching Ian between us. I hadn't seen her since she'd left with her family in July. She looked older; her curly brown hair was longer and she had more wisps and chunks of it flying around her face. She smelled like cinnamon and trees. "I can't believe it. Can I hold him?"

I put Ian in the crook of her arm.

"I can't believe it," she said again.

"I brought you a belated housewarming present." She pointed to a large floppy rectangle in a plastic bag. "Open it."

Will picked it up, letting the bag drift to the floor. It was a horsehair welcome mat that said GO AWAY in big black letters.

"Perfect," Will said.

"I'm totally behind on Ian's hat," she said. "I need more yarn. Can you believe I ran out again? I need to go back to that store."

I smiled at her, feeling resentful that she'd been too busy hanging out, eating pineapple pizza, to finish it by now. Vanessa sat down, holding Ian in the same position as I did when I fed him, which made him root around, darting his head at her chest.

"Uh! Look at that," said Will, as if proving a point. "He wants to eat again. That's all he ever does." He gestured his head at me. "She's the only thing he wants. How's Vassar? Are you a Vassar girl yet?"

"It's good," she said. "Though there are a lot of wonks and posers from the Midwest. Or worse, *California*. Let's see." Vanessa looked over Ian and examined herself. "Black turtleneck, check. Big ass, check." She pulled up her sleeve. "Uh! No marks! Uh, not a cutter. Guess she's not a Vassar girl yet."

"Ew," I said.

"It's all mock," she said. "Like taking aspirin to kill yourself. Everyone is sooooo intense. Fucking Nick Cave, dude . . . bad seeeeed. You guys are Little Mary Sunshines next to them. And you, little lump o' love." She held Ian up to her face. "Make out with me. I love his little male pattern baldness. Sooooo hot. Does he ever open his eyes?"

"Not so much." Will swiveled in the chair, spinning a CD on his finger.

"He opens them," I said dumbly, bringing a glass to the sink. Will's plate from the previous night was still there, untouched, with dry food all over it.

"Will, this is fucking gross," I snapped, holding it up. "If you're not going to wash it, at least *scrape* it."

Will and Vanessa exchanged a "What's her problem?" glance.

"I'm sorry, but help out," I said. "Did your mother show you how to do dishes? Let me guess the answer to that."

"I can't believe *you're* a mother," Vanessa said, quickly changing the subject.

"I know," I said.

"No, I *really* can't believe it. You're, like, crazy out there now. My crazy mother friend. Are you guys all, like, walking around the Village, going to, like, tea salons? Do you wear berets? All three of you? Matching berets?"

Will and I couldn't help smiling at each other. "Yeah, that's us," he said. "We're part of the movement."

"We're organizing," I said.

Vanessa and I went for a walk while Will stayed with Ian.

"So how's it going?" she said, taking my arm in hers and moving in long strides down the street. "God, I miss New York."

"You do?" I asked.

"Shit, yeah. There's nothing to do up there. So navel-gazey."

"But do you like it?"

"It's a lot of lying around," she said, stopping to roll up her jeans. She was wearing jeans with black flats that looked like ballet slippers. All of a sudden I wanted to roll up my jeans too, but I was wearing clogs. It would have looked dumb. "There's a girl, Helen, on my hall, she's pretty cool. At first I thought she was a huge narcey-marcey. Totally self-absorbed. She sneaks into the room as if anyone in there cared, and her eyes dart around, paranoid, like you've been talking about her all day. But she's funny. And she has beautiful skirts, which she wears every day. She only wears skirts. With black tights."

"Is she your new best friend?" I asked. We'd gotten to the small park near Christopher Street and I steered her to a bench. I was so exhausted from being up all night with Ian that my tongue itched.

"I don't know, Thee. A million times a day I wish you were there."

"Awww," I said.

"I'm serious." She dug into her pocket for a shredded pack of gum and offered me a piece. "What about you? What's going on?"

I watched a little girl in grimy pink leggings waiting by the swings with her mother. "It's scaring me how I can love him so much, and yet every second of the day, I think about how I could lose him," I said, taking the gum. "That's the hardest part."

"Will, you mean?"

I shook my head, surprising myself. "Ian."

"Thea, you're not going to *lose* him," she said.

"You don't understand, Ness," I said. "I *could*. He could get sick, he could suffocate, he could just . . . slip away." She squeezed my hand and shook her head slowly, as though she couldn't believe the things I put myself through. Then she popped her gum and I had a sudden memory of the two of us skateboarding down Seventh Avenue, and her stopping at a traffic light with an exploded bubble all over her face, a long, long time ago.

"Anyway, I'm trying to get him on a schedule," I said, "like the books say. Dinner, bath, bottle, bed."

"Almost the same as mine," said Vanessa. "Dinner, read, vodka, sex, pot, pizza, bed."

"Yours is more fattening," I said. "By the way, I meant to ask you, what the hell is a schwarma?"

33.

On the subway with Ian I overheard a woman in a fitted white shirt and piles of cool, long, gold-chain necklaces talking to someone about a miraculous all-natural sweetener.

"I'm serious, I cut out *all* sugar," she said, fingering her chains. "I don't miss it one bit. Whenever I need sugar for tea, or whatever, I just use this. Now I'm never tired."

When I got up out of the subway, Ian was overdue to eat, but I *had* to get that sweetener. It was the key to quashing my unrelenting, insatiable sweet tooth and therefore the key to losing my baby weight. We trekked against the gusty October wind, a few blocks to a health food store on Twenty-Third Street, and once we were inside, Ian started with his trapped squirm thing, puffing his chest out from his stroller straps like a fat Superman. Then I moved down the aisle and the stroller got wedged in between a stack of boxes. I shoved it through hard, and Ian lost it, big bubble tears bursting out of his eyes, his mouth eating up the rest of his face when he opened it and screamed. I gave the counter lady a bunch of singles for the sweetener and bolted without getting the change.

I was pissed when I got home, the usual thing, how Ian ruled and how I couldn't do something I wanted to for three seconds without him flipping out, how I was stuck with him all the time while in the meantime everyone else on the planet had a life. It was harder when Will went back to school—school felt more threatening to me than his dumb summer job, maybe because his job seemed like real life and school seemed more like a "lifestyle." Everyone shuffling around in their flip-flops, off to class with their Clif Bars. I put Ian in his bouncy seat on the kitchen counter and filled a pot of water to boil some penne. I dumped some butter in a plastic container of leftover peas and nuked it. When the pasta was done, I reached across Ian with the pot in one hand to get the salt, because Dad always throws salt on pasta when he drains it. Then my cell phone rang in my coat, making me stop short. The pasta water spilled all over Ian's leg and seeped through the bouncy seat, a steamy puddle rising on the counter.

Whenever his screams get too loud in my head, and they still do, even now, I try to remind myself that I actually dealt that day and that we didn't just both fall down and die right there. I remembered Dad was a paramedic after college and called him at work. I had to run into the bathroom to hear him. The thought occurred to me that maybe I could just go downstairs, out into the street, away.

"Run the shower and put him under it," he said. "Not too cold, or he'll go into shock. Keep him there for a few minutes if you can. Then get him to the hospital."

I held Ian under the shower by the armpits, almost grateful

he was screaming and crying so much because it meant he wasn't dying. At the same time, I noticed a weird thing happening to me, which was that I wasn't panicking. It couldn't have been more black-and-white to me: he was going to be okay. The driver turned off the radio the second we got in the taxi and got us to the hospital. I had no money. He took us anyway.

They pried Ian out of my arms when we got there and disappeared, which was a huge relief. I stood in the hall, pinching the skin on my neck, saying to myself, Please God, please God, please God, please God. The doors swung open and it was Dad.

We followed purple footprints down the hall and around a corner, over to a woman in green scrubs standing by a cot with metal rails.

"I'm Dr. Lyons," she said. "I'm a resident here. Have you given him anything?"

"I tried to get him to swallow some, you know, liquid aspirin," I said.

"You gave your baby aspirin?"

"Tylenol, I mean."

"Good," she said. "You should never, ever, give your child aspirin. It can really mess with the growth of their brain, not to mention it can cause them to bleed internally. So no aspirin. Acetaminophen only. Tylenol is fine."

Ian wailed and writhed on the cot. I waited for the doctor to stop looking at me.

"Got that?" she asked.

"She gave him Tylenol, did you hear her?" Dad shouted. He pushed his hands together, breathed. "Let's have a look at the leg, shall we?"

"What about the pain?" I asked, pinching my neck. "Is there something stronger you can give him?"

Dr. Lyons straightened Ian's leg. They'd stripped him naked.

"Easy," she murmured. She grabbed some gauze pads off the counter and started dabbing. "It looks like the burns are second degree. That's good news. But I want to have someone else check."

Ian started screaming like he had screamed at home and trying to bend his leg under her grip.

"Is there something you can give him for the pain?" I asked again, frantically.

"We can give him something, yes." She pulled a tube out of a drawer. "This is a topical analgesic. It will numb the area for a while, as well as disinfect it." Ian screamed bloody murder, but as soon as Dr. Lyons was done, he calmed down. She looked up at me again.

"Can you tell me exactly how it happened?"

"Well, I was boiling some . . ."

"On second thought," she said, raising her hands to stop me, "I think I should go find someone who can talk to you . . . privately."

"I spilled water on him," I said. "Boiling pasta water."

"Let's wait, please." She tried to smile, but her smile was urgent and then gone immediately and that's when I realized she thought I did it on purpose.

Dad cleared his throat. "That's fine," he said. "We'll speak to whomever you need us to speak to."

"Are you nursing him?" she asked.

"I am." I picked him up as carefully as I could.

"I'll be back in a flash," she said.

"I'm going to step out there and call Will," I said, reaching into my jeans for my phone.

"Go ahead," he said, pulling out his BlackBerry.

"We had an accident," I said, the hallway doors swinging behind me. "But he's going to be all right."

"What happened?" Will asked.

"I was making dinner and a pot of pasta water banged against something and some of it spilled onto Ian's leg," I said.

"Thea, Jesus Christ," he said. Something in his voice said he was expecting this to happen, as though it were inevitable. "What the hell."

"It was an accident," I said.

Dr. Lyons walked past us with an older guy in a white coat. "Whenever you're ready," she mouthed, pointing to the room I'd just left.

"Where are you?" Will asked. "I should call my parents."

"Just come. You can call them later. Dad's here."

"Your dad?"

"Yeah. I called him first because I thought he'd know what to do. He was a paramedic in college."

"Your dad was a paramedic?" he asked, disbelieving.

"Come soon," I said.

When I hung up, Ian was sleeping in my arms. The gauze pads on his leg were soaked through with a mix of ointment and pus. It hit me how badly I'd screwed him up, but I pushed the thought away. I went back into the room where Dad and Dr. Lyons and the guy in white were talking.

"Thea, this is Dr. Evans," Dad said, as if he were introducing someone who had arrived at his house. "I explained to him what happened."

"Hi there." He winked at me. "Maybe it's a good idea to

have a look while he's asleep." He craned his neck to look at Ian's leg as the rest of his stout body stood erect. Ian flinched but didn't wake.

"Yes, folks, that's a burn," he said cheerfully. "But I'm happy to report we're not going to do anything drastic about it. No scary surgeries. We're just going to hang out and watch it and swab it with cream and let the skin do its magic tricks."

Dad exhaled like he'd been holding his breath. "Okay," he said.

Dr. Lyons moved behind me and must have made a gesture directed at me.

"So tell me what happened," Dr. Evans said. "Some kind of freak accident with a pot of something?"

"I don't know how it happened, I really don't," I said, scared that they were going to haul me off. "It just spilled over while I was bringing it to the sink. I feel so stupid." I shook my head while Dad and the doctor hung their heads to the floor. "You understand that it was an accident, right? That's all it was. An accident. I made a mistake. I'm very careful with him, you know. I am. Dad?"

"I know you are, Thea." He sighed, shaking his head. "You just have to be *more* careful."

I thought of all the hours with Ian, the endlessly repeating, looping thoughts about whether he was eating enough or pooping too much. I saw myself tiptoeing and holding my breath when he slept in the morning. How I walked down the street with him in the stroller, seeing nothing else but his face in front of me. The thanklessness of it all numbed me. I burst into tears.

Will came into the room. "What's the word?" he asked, panting.

"I'm Dr. Evans, and I take it you are the father." The doctor held out his hand. The room we were in was full of computers on carts, and a nurse sat nearby reading CNN and watching us. "He's going to be okay. We're looking at second-degree, superficial burns. Lots of blistering and clear fluids, not pleasant to look at, but he'll be okay."

Will hovered over Ian's leg. "Poor thing," he whispered. "Mama's gonna order in from now on. Don't worry." He smiled and looked up at me and squeezed my arm. It was the last time I remember him being on my side.

34.

Dr. Evans said he wanted to keep Ian in the hospital overnight. There was a single room open in Pediatrics at the end of the hall.

"You should go home," I said to Will when we got to the room. "Get some sleep."

He looked at the single bed, at the sole chair where Dad had already parked himself. "You going to be okay?"

"Just bring him a new onesie when you come tomorrow," I said. "The long-sleeved, blue, striped one. And maybe some socks."

Will kissed my cheek, then Ian's. "Hang in there, little guy," he whispered on his way out.

I held Ian, looked at the soaked bandages and winced. Clear fluid was normal, the doctor had said. Normal. Dad leaned forward in the chair, reading my mind, and it hit me with a rush how glad I was to have that sage, stuffy, older life-form that was my father perched in the corner. "It'll heal," he said. "The feeling Dr. Evans gave was that it looks worse than it is, thank God."

"I know," I said.

He forced a tired smile. "You should call Mom."

"You know how she is with gore."

He nodded, like he was enjoying some personal, fond joke about her. Then he closed his eyes and rested his head against the orange leather seat while I dialed Mom.

"How serious do they think it is?" she asked. Her TV blared in the background.

"Can you turn that down?" I asked, hugging Ian closer. "They said it's second-degree burns."

"So he won't need a skin graft, thank God." I heard the TV go silent, and her voice sounded all of a sudden oversized and echoey. "But he'll probably have scarring. I hope for his sake it's not a real deformity. Are you sure you don't want to switch hospitals? Lenox Hill is really the only one in this city worth its salt."

"No, Mom, we're fine," I said. "They know what they're doing."

"I hope so," she said. "Will's there, right?"

"Yeah," I lied.

"Okay." She hesitated. "Do you want me to come?"

"You don't need to," I said. "We're getting out tomorrow morning."

"Good," she said quickly. "Call me when you get home."

When I looked up, Dad was watching me on the phone, playing with the curtain cord. "Well, I guess I should head out," he said. "Let you guys get some sleep." Change fell out of his pocket as he stood up, and it rolled all over the floor. He looked to see if it had woken Ian up. "Sorry," he whispered, gathering the coins. "Call me if you need anything, okay?"

"Thanks," I said as the door swished closed. I angled the small task lamp on the side table away from us, then turned it off. I carefully lay Ian down into the same plastic box he was wheeled around in when he was born, and I lay flat on the bed. It hit me how recently we were all there and how different things felt now. A nurse peeped through the door, saw me staring at the ceiling and went away. I felt a weird, jumpy urge to see if Ian was okay, and as I stood up, watching his blanket move up and down as he breathed, something happened. I stood over him and thought about how purely, wholly good he was and how I was never going to be able to protect him from or make up for all of my mistakes. I wondered what the hell I'd done, not just with the accident, but the whole thing. Having him. What had I done? Why had I brought someone into this world? I imagined Ian in a calculus class, struggling like me and feeling like shit, and I imagined someone making promises to him, about a job or something else, and him getting his hopes up and the person not making good on it. I imagined Ian loving someone like I loved Will and that person dropping dead on the street. I thought about blood and accidents until a cyclone of grief mashed me up and I wondered how the hell I'd ever thought it was okay to disappear that summer with Vanessa. How could I have done that to them? A trolley rolled down the hall outside my room, one of its wheels catching and banging on every turn. It stopped at my door and a guy peeked in.

"No trays, ma'am?" he asked.

I shook my head and the smell of old food seeped into the room as sobs ripped through me. I thought about Mom and

Dad. Was life nurturing, in some inexplicable way, or was it just a never-ending string of losses in different shapes?

I whispered to Ian, "Remember when you were born and I couldn't stop saying, 'Oh my God?'" He slept on his back with his head turned all the way to his shoulder. At that angle his head looked like it could have spun right around. Did infants have ligaments? Connective tissue? I lay down on the bed and fell asleep in a splinter of light shining from the bathroom door, thinking, This sadness, whatever it is, somehow binds me to Ian, and as a result, to this world, like it or not.

35.

The next morning a nurse griped to someone outside our door over the sound of clattering dishes.

"Without saying anything, she just *took* it from me," she said. I opened my eyes and saw Ian sprawled across my chest on his side; he felt cooler, less clammy, and he had a content pucker on his lips. I couldn't remember the last time he'd eaten. Things felt strangely, wonderfully calm between me and him. A feeling hit me that I'd always somehow known him, or if not him, his spirit; I felt like his spirit had always been with me, climbing the stairwells at school, crossing Fourteenth Street, drinking a soda inside the movie theater on Third Avenue. But I wished I could look down and see his leg healed, the damage I'd done erased.

Will walked into the room with his mother a couple of hours later. He handed me Ian's striped onesie and a pair of white socks, then went straight to the windowsill where my jacket was. "Do you have anything else? Mom's going to drive us home."

I lay Ian in front of me on the mattress to change his diaper and get him dressed. The doctor had said to keep his leg uncovered and I wondered how I was going to keep him warm against the October chill. Loose blankets, I decided. Will was staring at Ian's leg from across the room.

"It's okay," I said. "I know it looks horrible, but there's a topical anesthetic in the cream, so it's not hurting him, right? Otherwise he'd be screaming."

"Do you want to go wash up or anything?" Mrs. Weston stood next to the bed with her hands on her hips, at the ready. Be positive, I laughed to myself. I finished changing Ian and handed him to her, my shirt still open, not caring what she saw. "Ooh, poor baby," she said, taking him gingerly.

"Mom, I'll hold him," Will said, walking quickly over. "Why don't you go get the car and bring it around and we'll meet you downstairs."

"One day," I said, on my way to the bathroom, "I'll stop beating myself up about this, at least I hope I will." I tried to catch Will's eye, but he was looking down at the table, at the instructions that came with the medication.

The elevator stopped at every floor on the way down.

"Hi," I said, leaning toward Will. "Missed you last night. Glad we're going home."

"Me too," he said, staring at the elevator numbers as they lit up and dinged.

I got into the backseat, where Will had already laid Ian's car seat. I wondered how the hell I was going to get the strap over his leg.

"Just do one side," Will said. "You don't have a choice." Then he went around and got in front next to his mother. "Take it easy, Mom," he said. "I don't want him banging around back there. He's been through enough."

"Of course," Mrs. Weston said as she sped down Seventh Avenue.

Ian's leg was smeared with greasy cream and covered with thick, gauzy bandages. He looked like a tiny maimed soldier. Someone honked behind us and Mrs. Weston swerved, trying to get out of the way.

"Forget about him," Will said sharply. "Just focus on taking it slow." I remembered Will saying Mrs. Weston was a shitty driver, that she'd point to something she saw out the window and then steer toward it.

"Did they send you home with anything?" she asked.

"Just more cream," I said. "The doctor said I should call if Ian seemed distressed or feverish but that the pain should be subsiding."

"Yeah, half his leg was almost scalded off," Will said. "But it shouldn't hurt a bit by now."

"It wasn't scalded off," I said. "The doctor's more concerned with potential infection at this point. Making sure the leg stays clean. He said any scars from the burn will heal completely within a year."

"Sure, he's young," Will scoffed, turning the radio on. "He'll get over it."

"I think your cells do multiply more quickly, the younger you are," Mrs. Weston said, catching my eye in the rearview mirror. Was she actually sticking up for me?

"Yeah, well, he'll only need a hundred billion or so." Will sat back and gripped his knees.

"Did I ever tell you about when I spilled coffee on Roy?" Mrs. Weston said.

"Uh-uh." Will stared out the window.

"This whole thing made me think of it," she said. "We'd just gotten a new coffee percolator, I think it was a late wedding present, and I was trying to figure out how to use it and the whole thing exploded."

"Oh no," I said.

"Yup. The whole thing blew, and bits of grinds and hot water sort of showered on top of his head," she said cheerfully. "Bits of coffee grinds on his cheeks, it looked like razor stubble."

"How bad was it?" I asked. "Was he burned badly?"

"I don't think so," she said. "I don't remember. I don't even remember what we did. Can you believe that?" She stopped suddenly at a red light.

"Watch it!" Will said, gritting his teeth. Ian jumped in his sleep as the car heaved to a stop. I loved those flinches. Like he was sending out little smoke signals of alertness and life while he slept.

We got into the house and I sat down to give Ian the boob while Will and his mom took the gauze pads and other stuff from the hospital out of the paper bag. I pointed to the big square pillow on the armchair, the one I used to lay Ian across.

"Can you pass me that?" I asked Will.

Mrs. Weston rushed over to get it. "Here you go."

Will went to the sink and threw water on his face and wiped it with the towel hanging on the refrigerator door.

"Are you all set as far as things from the drugstore?" Mrs. Weston sat down next to me on the couch.

"We're all set," I said. I looked at her face, remembering

again how I'd been afraid of her when I'd first met her. Had she changed or had I? *Be positive.*

"Okay." She looked at Will. "You all right, honey? Can I get you guys some sandwiches?"

"I have to get back to school," Will said. "I've already missed too much."

"They'll understand, I'm sure," said Mrs. Weston. "How could they not?"

"Yeah, it's not every day—"

"Can't you stick around for a little bit?" I said, cutting him off. Ian started to scream. The burned part of his leg was brushing up against the pillow, so I flipped him to the other side.

"I really can't," he said, taking some books out of his backpack and stacking them on the desk. "Is he okay?"

"He's okay, he just has to lie a certain way, off his leg," I said.

Mrs. Weston hunched down and kissed Ian's foot. She patted my leg and gave me a "Hang in there" look. "I'm here and available if you need anything, Thea. Please take me up on it. If you need some time to yourself, to take a nap, to recharge, just call me. Promise?"

"Thank you," I said.

She fished through her big canvas tote bag for her car keys. "Maybe you could bring him around this weekend and we could watch him for a few hours. Give you guys a break."

"Let's see how he's feeling," Will said. He stroked Ian's head for a few seconds and picked his keys up from the table. "I'll walk out with you."

When they left, I ordered chicken with broccoli, an egg roll and a carton of rice and ate it all while Ian slept. He slept on and on that night, barely stirring.

I picked up the yellow yarn, still on the lower shelf of the side table, out of a panicky sense of boredom. It had been a while, but I was relieved to find that my stitches didn't look disastrously different from the last time I'd worked on it. I got all the way up to the top of the triangle—it went faster as the triangle narrowed—and then did the series of chains that made up the tie around the neck, which went faster than I'd remembered. At around midnight, the bikini was done. I held it under Florence's rickety, red metal reading lamp, the night dust circling around it like little fireflies, and thought, This is pretty cool. I marveled at the details Carmen had written into the pattern—how the strap that tied around the back was just a little bit thicker than the strap that tied around the neck. And how the band at the waist had started to roll over just a little since I'd finished it a few weeks earlier. I couldn't wait to show it to her.

When I opened my eyes, Will was standing over me and staring. It was one o'clock and I'd fallen asleep with the bikini top splayed across my chest. He picked it up and the ball of yarn dropped onto the floor. He fished around on the floor in the dark, found the ball and put the top and the yarn back on the second shelf of the side table.

"You're still working on that thing?" he asked.

"I finished it," I said. "Not that you'd care. Where were you?"

"Studying."

"You smell like beer," I said, pulling the blanket up to my shoulders.

"Who the hell are *you*?" he asked, throwing his coat on the chair.

"Nobody, apparently. It doesn't occur to you to call? To see how he's doing, at least?"

"I figured you were taking care of things. Like you've been doing so well."

"Subtle, Will," I said, leaning up on my elbow. "We had an accident. Deal with it. *I* am."

"I didn't say anything." He sat by my legs, his sneakers flopping to the floor.

"You don't have to."

"Let's go to sleep," he said. "You're tired."

I lay there waiting for him to drift off, hating him for the stupid, selfish wall he'd put up, hating him for inserting me so deeply and squarely into the middle of the night, awake and alone. Ian woke up and we sat in the chair by the window. He fell asleep at my boob almost immediately and I wondered for the millionth time what to do. Whether to put him back in the Pack 'n Play or wake him up to keep nursing. I peeled the gauze off his leg, praying he wouldn't scream. I nudged Ian and he startled awake, his jaw starting to move, barely detectable, his arm drifting around my chest, banging it a few times, then drifting up in the air behind him. I wondered if his thoughts were as floaty as his arm. I imagined his thoughts as light phantoms that had no names, just floating and settling, free of synapses or endings. His hand finally settled at my collarbone, and I tried to imagine a future moment when Will wouldn't look at me as though he didn't trust me with Ian, when I wouldn't hate him for looking at me like that. If Will mistrusted me so much, why didn't he step in? If I was really doing such a terrible job, why didn't he just take Ian and run away? Ian breathed in sharply; I tried in the dark to decipher the *New York Times* headlines on the ottoman a few feet away, tried not to think of my own crimes, my honest mistakes.

36.

Will's uncle Dave, Mrs. Weston's younger brother, died of a heart attack in Prospect Park while Ian and I were in the hospital. He was fifty-three. I put Ian in the sack and went with Will to the memorial. We walked around piles of wet leaves and vast, muddy puddles toward hundreds of people huddled on a hill near where he'd been jogging. Dave's wife, Carol, stood by a tree in a navy-blue suit, their three kids next to her. Mrs. Weston was on her other side, her gray eyes sunken and red. She saw us and reached her hand over, where it rooted around aimlessly, touching my cuff, Will's knuckles, Ian's bum in the sack. Amanda cupped Ian's cheeks. "So this is Ian."

"This is Ian," Will said. "And this is Thea."

"He's just beautiful," she said. "I'm sorry we haven't gotten over to see you guys."

You guys, I thought. We were not "you guys." "You guys" were bustling, intertwined; they picked cereal up off the floor and went out to the park, swinging their kid between them. We were not "you guys." I looked at Will, who was shuffling his feet, his eyes fixed on the ground. I missed him in a way that felt like homesickness.

"I'm sorry, Aunt Carol," he said, his hands digging stiffly into his pockets. "I really am."

A guy next to us reached for her. "Hello, Carol," he said. "Don't know if you remember meeting a couple of years ago at Dave's fiftieth. Bob Rosen."

She nodded, looking up at the guy, and smiled in a way that unpacked her grief for anyone to see. "That was such a lovely night, wasn't it?" she said.

The oldest son spoke during the memorial service at a club in Brooklyn Heights. He talked about family camping trips and how his dad loved hideous, cheap light fixtures and was stingy with paper towels and toilet paper to the point of ridiculousness. Black candle smoke drifted up to the ceiling and I wondered for the millionth time, How would I be a good mother? What would it take?

Will went to school after the service, and I went home thinking about how I'd stop snapping at Will when he took his socks off in the middle of the room or threw Ian's dirty diapers directly into the kitchen garbage. It was a Friday night and for some reason, maybe to forget about Dave, Will came home later that night with some people from Columbia and a case of beer.

It was Mark and Maggie and Helena from his hall and Lester and Tina and Jason, all in our small room with Ian nursing and sleeping on me. Maggie and Mark had something going on, but she held on to Will like he was hers; she put her hands around his waist when she spoke to him and they swayed to Neil Young in front of me on the rug. I wasn't supposed to mind. Lester sat next to me on the couch and passed a bong around, taking a hit between each person.

Helena swung her leg over the leather armchair and let her foot float to the music in the thin air. "How often do you have to do that?" she asked me.

"Feed him?" I asked, getting up to open a window. "All the time." She looked away, her puffed lips and her spacey, bored eyes telling me how she believed it was her right to be there, taking up space in our apartment. I looked for her hips, tried to trace them toward the middle of her body, but they were hidden from me. Will sat down at Florence's old upright piano, so dark and unshiny it could have been made out of a blackboard, and played something I recognized by Eric Clapton or a band from the seventies that had a one-word name, and although it was short, it took me around the room in a spiral of aching memories of Will and the way we were together, before Ian, while people talked. It was the opposite of listening to a song over and over until it sinks in and you like it. It was inescapable, lilting love. I didn't know he played piano. What else didn't I know? Will's back was to me, but I could see the side of his face, and he moved around on the bench as though he were in a conversation with someone, as though he were talking, and I thought about being the one he was talking to, how nice that would be, and although I understood all of it for what it was, I still felt as though part of me could step into a cloud of sad love for him and stay there, with Will drifting into the cloud and out, visiting me and then leaving me by myself.

When everyone left, Will threw his clothes in a heap outside the bathroom and flopped onto the bed. I pushed his hip to the side and let my hand wander down, hoping to coax him to life. Usually he took two seconds, but that night he slipped through my fingers. "Will . . ." I whispered, wanting it right between us. Wanting to fuse. Wanting. I rolled on top of him and kissed his forehead.

"What's wrong?" I asked.

"I don't feel good," he said. He let his head fall toward the wall, avoiding me.

"Sick?" I asked.

He shrugged. "Just weird," he said, looking back at me.

"What is it?" I said, rolling off him. "Tell me."

He folded his arm behind his head and stared at the

ceiling. "You could have killed him, Thea," he said, as though he were reciting an age-old, unavoidable fact. "He could have died."

Now it was my turn to stare at the ceiling. I gazed up at the exposed water sprinkler, trying to untangle my defensive thoughts from the truth of what he was saying.

"Do you ever think about how crazy it is?" I finally said. "With Ian, I mean? You must. It's so scary, how could you not. It's like, I know we could lose him at any moment. It's on my mind all the time. Something bad could happen at any minute of any day. But I have to believe it won't. I have to believe we'll keep him safe, that our love will somehow protect him." I found Will's hand under the blanket and held on to it. "The thing is, we can't stop loving him just because we could lose him. I'm trying so hard to just . . . be brave. You can't really be any other way." The sprinkler in the ceiling was starting to resemble a prickly black flower. I thought about Ian's little mouth, how it contracted even smaller when he wanted something, and the familiar aching sadness came right up to me, like a bus getting too close when it rounds a corner. "It's sick, how much I love him," I said. "He is so helpless and I just love him so much." I felt the embarrassing tears popping out of my eyes, rolling down the sides of my face toward my ears.

Will burrowed his arm under me and squeezed, which was such a relief I almost lost it. He squeezed and stroked my rib cage, and relief came to me in soft, warm waves. Finally, a connection, I thought. He didn't say anything, but I felt it: he understands what I mean and he feels the same way I do. It's going to be okay, I thought. We are back in this together.

37.

Ian woke up at six the next morning, and I brought him to the bed and gave him the boob till we both fell back to sleep. When the alarm went off, I heard the shower go on, then later the sound of drawers opening and later still, the sound of shoes shuffling around the apartment. Each time I woke, I remembered Will and me, holding each other the night before, and drifted off into a peaceful, happy sleep.

But a while later I opened my eyes to Will standing in front of the bed with wet hair and a stiff face.

"You shouldn't sleep like that when he's in bed with you," he said. It felt like a kick in the stomach. "You could suffocate him." I picked Ian up and stumbled over to his Pack 'n Play, where he remarkably stayed asleep after I laid him down. Will watched me with his arms folded as I crossed the room. I wondered what had happened, how it had slipped away so easily. I thought he'd been right there with me. I stopped at the kitchen trash bin and tugged the red plastic garbage tie to keep it from spilling over. I didn't know anything anymore.

He sat down on the edge of the bed.

"I don't know if I can do this," he said, his voice sounding thick, underwater.

"What do you mean?" I asked. I sat down next to him on the bed, the first inkling that we might not make it plowing through me, spreading fear over me like seeds. "Will, we're *doing* it. We may not be doing it great, but we're doing okay, which is enough for now." I wanted to keep going, to tell him how full of messy hope I was for us, to tell him we had to keep trying because when the three of us were in bed together, Ian kicking up at the ceiling, the two of us sandwiching him, wasn't it amazing? Didn't he wonder how people could ever let go, after being together like that? The three of us on an island, how could you ever say goodbye to those moments? Just let them go? How did *my parents* ever let them go? How was it possible?

"I want to give him up." He stared straight ahead at the wall. "For adoption."

My eyes skidded over to the Pack 'n Play. For a second I felt like Will was going to get up and take him away. "Don't say that," I said. "That's cruel."

"I'm not trying to be cruel," he said. "I don't know, Thea. When I came to the hospital that morning and saw him in bed with you, lying in front of you on the bed . . . his leg looked like it had been blown off, Thea, I'm not kidding. I can't stop thinking about it. It hit me that morning, so hard. It isn't right, what we're doing. I've been trying to tell myself we'll be okay, but this isn't right. It's not right for him."

I knelt down on the floor in front of him and gripped his knees. We were both crying. "That's not true and you know it," I said. "You're hungover and you feel like crap."

"No," he said, shaking his head. The shades were down and the room was dark, but I could still see his eyes. "I really do believe it, Thea."

Over in his Pack 'n Play, Ian's foot stuck straight up in the air, his toe pointed like a dancer's. I thought of that first night, walking to the Seagram Building with Will in the freezing cold, the fiery orange squares of office lights, how they sort of exploded inside me, little pops of bright, burning sun. I believed they were also exploding inside him. That first night, he told me he was an optimist and I believed him. I looked at that face, into those uneven eyes I didn't know yet, and believed he'd do anything. From the very beginning, I'd thought, This is a guy who'll do anything.

Ian started his coughlike cries. Could Will take him away from me? I stood and went to pick Ian up as Will gathered his stuff for school and left.

38.

"I think he knows the word *poo*," Dad said, dropping the high chair, still in the box, near the sink. I'd spent the day letting the morning's scene with Will play out in my head a thousand times. I would talk him out of it when he got home, I kept telling myself. When Dad buzzed that evening, I panicked for a moment, thinking that Will had called an agency and that they were coming to get Ian. I'd forgotten that Dad was coming to drop off the high chair so that Ian could start eating "real food." I'd told him that it was still a couple of months too early to start with the food, but he'd insisted on bringing it over anyway, "just in case."

"I swear I heard him say 'poo' when we were in the hospital with his leg that night," Dad said, leaning the large box against the coffee table. "Did I tell you that?"

"He's not even three months old," I said.

"Well, he's advanced," he said, ripping through the packing tape with his keys. I rolled my eyes. "Seriously," Dad countered. "The way his eyes dart around when someone enters a room or when that Noah's Ark thing snaps shut. He's very alert. Unusually so."

"Okay, well, take it easy," I said. I was in a black fog, but I couldn't help smiling. "He's got his whole life to buckle under the pressure."

"Of course." He smiled, leaning over Ian, who was on his back on a blanket. "I'm sorry it's taken me so long to get this over here. Better late than never, eh? How is he?"

"He's good," I said, folding up the bed in a hurry. "His leg looks much better."

Dad looked at me, pushed my hair off my forehead. "You all right? You seem . . ."

"I'm okay."

"You don't sound okay."

"Will's still upset about the accident." I stared at Ian on the floor, unable to look anywhere else.

"It was a very rough thing to go through," he said. "But he'll come around."

"I'm not so sure."

"Look, you're giving this everything you've got," he said. "Not everyone is as capable as you are, at your age, you know. If he doesn't realize that . . ."

I escaped to the sink to rinse out glasses and lost it. Horrible, embarrassing, convulsing crying.

"Thea?" Dad walked toward me like he was walking toward a sick animal.

"It's okay," I said.

"Really. What's the matter? What's wrong? What's he doing?"

"Nothing." I was afraid to tell him that Will thought we should give Ian up because I was afraid he'd agree.

"Honestly, this situation . . . ," he muttered, his voice trailing off. He started to lean against the pillar with his hand. Instead he bounced himself off the pillar and then smacked it.

"It's not your fault," he said. "It's not your fault." He leaned his hands up against the counter, just like Will had done that morning, and we both faced the sink.

"I'm fine, Dad," I choked. "It's okay."

"This isn't working here." A quick, embarrassed smile crossed his face as he raised his arms to encapsulate "here." "You look so unhappy. Not just today. How long have you been feeling like this?"

"Since Ian's accident, maybe before."

"Look, just come stay with me for a while, Thea, okay? Take some time apart and figure out what's what."

It made sense, I realized, to be the first one to go. To get out first, like Mom did, before he could take Ian away from me. So I said okay, setting the last dripping glass on the rack.

part four

39.

We got a cab with as much stuff as we could carry, and I sat holding Ian and watching the trees thin out as we made our way west toward Dad's place on the river. Mom called when we were stopped at a light on Tenth Avenue.

"I can't find my black leather belt with the rivets," she said. "Do you have it?"

"No," I said.

"Are you sure?" she asked.

"I'll double-check when I get a chance," I said, moving Ian's fingers away from his mouth. "I'm with Dad, on my way to his place, actually. Will and I had a fight."

"Oh no . . . ," she groaned.

"What do you mean, oh no?" I asked. "You want us to stay together now?"

"I just . . . Wait, how did Daddy end up in the middle of all this?" she asked.

"He brought over a high chair," I said.

"And?"

"And I agreed."

"Agreed to what?"

"We just decided that I should stay with him for a while," I said. "It's not forever, it's just a break."

"You could have called me, you know," she said, sounding strangely forlorn.

"I know, it just happened." I couldn't tell if she really wanted me to go home to her or if she was simply miffed that Dad had "won." "Anyway, we're here now, let me call you later."

"Okay, don't forget," she said.

My room was dark, and as I walked in, I could see the mean queen, elongated by the light from outside, sneering at me from the ceiling. I dumped my bags onto my bed, thinking of all the times I'd dragged Vanessa with me to Dad's to avoid being alone with him. Vanessa always lightened it up. She was so good that way. "Where are we going to find you a good woman, Mr. Galehouse?" she'd say. "What's your type?"

Dad would wince and make a pathetic attempt to play along. "I don't know, uh, Vanessa, your guess is as good as mine."

She set him up once, with Jana, a very blond Czech masseuse. We told Dad she was a *physical therapist,* and that she worked with people with sports injuries.

"Honestly, it made me want a drink," he said when I asked how it went. Vanessa's mom said Jana thought he was cute but that they didn't click and that Jana didn't like that Dad didn't throw his popcorn box into the garbage when they left the movie theater.

"So what? Who cares?" I said, thinking, How cruel. My poor, hopeless, littering father.

When Dad dated Nancy, the violinist, Vanessa and I had made fun of the way her nose twitched like a nervous rabbit's, and the fact that she was twenty years younger than Dad and not even remotely hot.

"He's handsome and rich," Vanessa said. "He could have anyone he wants, and look what he does. Goes for the cellist with stringy hair. King of the midlife-crisis freaks, that one."

I put my mess of underwear in the top drawer, before Dad could see it strewn all over the bed. I stacked Ian's Pampers in a row on top of the dresser, thinking about all the nights sophomore year Vanessa and I did our faces in the bathroom and drank vodka out of Diet Coke cans until I was spinning by the time we went out the door, only to stand in line at some club, get in and walk around, dancing and scream-whispering and drinking more vodka Diet Coke, until we stumbled home. Dad waited up at first, but by the end of sophomore year he was always in bed, Nancy long gone.

And now Vanessa was gone too. I had a flash of her slumped in the corner, drunk and sneering, the tinkling sound of bangles on her wrist as she rolled a joint. Dad tiptoed into my room with Ian's Pack 'n Play. Ian kicked his legs at the ceiling from a blanket on the floor, and for a second I thought Dad wouldn't see him and would step on him.

"He's a happy little guy, isn't he?" he said, hunching over at him. "You done with these?" He straightened up and pointed to the empty duffels.

I nodded and he picked them up and folded them until they were a quarter of their size, then lifted them to a spot in the hallway closet. The room was a large rectangle, one you could easily fit two double beds into, and I wondered what would happen when Ian got older, whether Dad would let Ian take the third bedroom or whether we'd still be in there like siblings. Or whether Will would come to his senses and rescue us. Dad tiptoed into the kitchen and I stayed in the bedroom as long as I could, feeling how slowly the minutes went by when you were stuck in a house with someone who believed you lived your life carelessly.

I called Vanessa and immediately started sobbing.

"I took Ian to Dad's," I said. "I left Florence's."

"Oh no," she said.

"He wants to give him up for adoption," I said.

"He what?" she shrieked.

"Can you believe that?" I said. I put my hand on Ian's stomach as he squirmed and gassed on the floor. "He said that ever since the accident, he hadn't felt right, or whatever. Vanessa, he can't make me give him up, can he?"

"Jesus," Vanessa said. "It's like he has postpartum depression or something. Crazy. No, he cannot make you give him up. No matter what."

"Really?"

Dad appeared in the doorway, looking like a timid puppy. "I was going to make some penne with pesto," he said. "That sound okay?"

I nodded at him, trying to smile.

"Really. You're a *great* mom." Girls laughed and doors slammed in the background.

"What's that noise?" I asked.

"Nothing, some idiotic tea party. Have I mentioned I hate it here?"

"Vanessa, what am I going to do?" I whispered.

"I'm so mad at him." She sighed. "I'm sorry, Thea."

I hung up, wondering if Will had gotten home yet, whether he realized I was gone. I couldn't imagine speaking to him, so I sent him a text. Whenever I thought about what he had said, about giving Ian up, I felt sick to my stomach. "We went to Dad's," I typed. "Don't do anything. Let us go."

Out in the kitchen Dad blasted water into a pot and the showering sound filled the apartment, drowning out my shaky sense of connection to anything.

40.

I woke the next morning at 7:22, stunned that Ian had slept through his 3:00 and 5:30 a.m. snacks. Maybe there was an upside to being at Dad's after all. Maybe my room had secret powers. Maybe the mean queen on the ceiling had cast a spell on Ian. I tiptoed out into the foyer. Dad's shoes were gone from under the chair and there was a note on the table and money: *Home tonight. Pick up some sirloins?* I envisioned another night with him and felt instantly done-in. There were Christmas cards from people who worked for Dad lining the chest by the wall. Young guys, all with short crew-cut hair, all smiling with three kids. I thought of how things had been a year earlier, when Ian was just an about-to-be-aborted grain of rice and Will and I lay on his bed at Columbia, studying for the SATs. I remembered Will's face when I was going down on him after we napped. I missed his body, missed it wrapped around mine. John and Yoko. I looked at the marble bust of a woman on a pedestal in Dad's corner, her arms, legs and head chopped off. I felt like her.

Ian woke up, his wails streaming hollowly down the hallway. I leaned over his Pack 'n Play and picked him up, wondering if it was possible for cheeks to be any chubbier, and held him above me, making him fly. Will's voice blew through me like a cold gust. *"I want to give him up."*

I remembered what Vanessa said and tried not to think about anything else. "Let's go get some yarn today," I said to Ian. I nursed him for a long time, then bundled him up, cramming him into the sack and walking the fifteen blocks to Stash. We clanged the cowbells right after it opened.

Carmen popped up from behind some shelves by the window.

"Thea!" She beamed. Her hair was down and in a jagged, punk-looking part. I wasn't sure, but I thought she'd put streaks in. "It's been ages. How are you?" She crossed the store and peered into the sack. "And look who you've brought!"

"Hi, Carmen." I was so happy to see someone outside of my normal cesspool of a life that I could have kissed her, and did. Ian lifted his head and kicked, also finding it hugely refreshing.

"Oh my God, what a butterball," she said, giggling. "Wow." She made an O face and Ian was transfixed, unblinking.

"So I finished an attempt at the bikini," I said, pulling it out of the bag and laying it on top of a white shelf. "It took me long enough, right?"

"Well, I can imagine your hands are a bit tied." Carmen said, still ogling Ian. I remembered the last time I was there, she said she'd been trying to get pregnant.

"Now I want to do one with teal and royal-blue zigzags," I said. "It's funny how you get these urges, right? I'm, like, possessed now. I have no intention of wearing it, but I *have* to make it."

"I know what you mean," she said, nodding vigorously, studying the bikini. "It's like once the urge takes hold . . . But this one's fantastic."

"Really?" I asked.

"It's fantastic," she repeated. She picked up the yellow top and draped it across her white tank top. "I love how it turned out. It looks homegrown but in this very cool way. It looks like it would sell for five hundred dollars at Barneys."

"You think?"

"Yes! Totally," she said, strutting around with the top. "The Brazilians? Who are always waxing themselves silly? Some rich Brazilian would snap this up in a second."

"They like skimpy stuff more, no? To show off their waxes?"

"Yeah, but I could see them, you know, wearing it a little stretched out, maybe even bunching up a side." She bunched up her own fuchsia underwear, under her skirt. "The thing about crochet is that it drapes so nicely. It's got the whole drape-hug thing going for it."

"Maybe I should try and sell it," I said.

"I'll sell it for you!" she exclaimed. "Believe it or not, I sell a ton of stuff in here." She pointed to the hats with colorful nubs and the baby sweaters hanging from the rafters on hangers attached to fishing wire. "I know it seems like no one's ever in here, but some days I make more money from the clothes than the yarn." She held the top up to the window, seesawing it back and forth in the air. "I'll sell it for you. Not for five hundred, though. Three hundred feels like the right price point to start. Two ninety-five."

"Whatever you think," I said. "It's a much more compelling prospect than trying to lose twenty pounds."

"You just had a baby," she said, looking me up and down. "You look great."

"Thank you," I said, running my hand along the pudge hanging over my jeans, the pudge that wouldn't budge. "I'll just say thank you."

"You know," she said, arranging the bikini top on the shelf and folding the ties over, "self-loathing is the evil curse of the twenties. I see that now that I'm thirty."

"You'd really be willing to hang it up?"

"Definitely. Like I said, I love it. I'll put my money where my mouth is. And how about I get ten percent if it sells?"

"At least that, you designed it, after all," I said. "Thank you."

"No, thank *you*," she said with exaggerated politeness.

She helped me pick more colors—a bright teal, a gorgeous spectrum of oranges and reds and a purple and green that went strangely well together—exactly the colors I'd imagined in my head, only better.

"I can see how you'd get obsessed with yarn," I said. "Some of them are so beautiful, and they're so different, how they're made, how they hold dye. Even if you make something in one color, there's so much to look at with the variations."

"It can get addictive," Carmen agreed. "I have women who come in here and buy tons of yarn, you know, for later projects, but then they don't do anything with it. They just have to own it."

Ian started to squirm around in the sack, so I undid the clips and pulled him out.

"So how's it going?" Carmen asked. "Do you like being a mother?"

"My dad once told me the best way to answer a question you didn't know how to answer was to compliment the question," I said. "Interesting question."

"You're right, what was I thinking, asking that?" She pushed Ian's sock, which was close to falling off, over his ankle. "Can I hold him?"

"Sure." She took him, gripping his bum. "God, what an angel," she said. "Such a yum. He's got the perfect-shaped little baby face. Like a Gerber baby. I'll bet everyone says that, right?" She brushed her cheek against his head. "How's your boyfriend?"

"Not so good," I admitted. I rolled my eyes and she made a sad face. I'm not crying in front of her, I told myself. I'm not. It was important that she thought I was tough and could handle things. "Anyway, thank you again," I said pointedly. "Thanks for offering to sell it for me."

"Fingers crossed," she said.

41.

The weekend rolled around and Dad pushed me to go out. "You deserve a break," he said. "I'll watch the kid." So I called Donna to hang out. Donna went to Barnard. She was more of a quasi-friend—she was really closer to Vanessa—but I called her because I couldn't think of anyone else who was still in the city other than Will.

I got Ian ready for bed, praying he wouldn't poo since I didn't think Dad could handle it. I pumped milk with the machine Mom had given me for the first time, the repetitive sucking noises sending me into a trance. "Ya homesick, ya homesick," it chanted over and over. Ian was fed and cleaned up and when I left, he and Dad were lying on the floor under Ian's mobile, jingling the terry-cloth hearts.

"We won't wait up for you," Dad said.

Donna lived in a ground-floor apartment on 104th and Amsterdam. A girl wearing magenta tights and motorcycle boots that fit her calves like gloves answered the door. Her hair was impossibly thick and messy—some of it had to be extensions—and she had on a plaid miniskirt with some sort of rainbow sweatshirt material squeezed around her midriff, clashing flawlessly with the skirt.

Before she could say anything, a guy yelled to her from inside.

"Cloudia!" he said, then something about a *"bacio."*

Cloudia, whom I guessed was Claudia to mere Americans, couldn't be bothered with introductions. I thought, This girl knows how to dress in a way I never will. I took comfort in the knowledge that I could recognize, understand and accept that fact as I watched her backside swing toward an emaciated guy in leather pants.

Donna was on the phone in the kitchen. It was weird to see her living here, actually inhabiting Manhattan. When we were in high school, she was a tourist, with her black leggings–black sneakers combo and her iPod wires always hanging off her, helping her bide her endless hours on the R train from Queens. But ah, how things had changed.

"Oh, please," she repeated into the phone. "Oh, please." Her eyes crinkled with a self-confidence I'd always found off-putting. I imagined it came from growing up with the kind of family who were very clear and straightforward about how they loved her. A lot of kids from Forest Hills had that.

Eventually she hung up.

"How are you?" She reached out from halfway across the room for a hug.

"I'm good, really good," I said, my enthusiasm nowhere near hers.

"Come," she said, grabbing a tray with a bottle of wine

and some glasses. "Ginny's in my room." Ginny was Donna's best friend from high school.

"Ginny's here?"

"She just transferred to Barnard in the beginning of January. You didn't know?"

"No, I didn't," I said.

"Claudia, come have some wine," Donna called to the living room, where Claudia was playfully straddling Emaciato.

"Your roommate?" I whispered, though it was obvious. I couldn't think of anything to say. Ginny was sitting on the radiator in Donna's room, hunched over in an attempt to blow smoke out the window.

"Hey, Thea, how's mothahood?"

"Hey, Ginny," I said. Ginny's big, stiff, blue-black Queens shag remained intact in spite of the wind blowing in. I looked at her and felt the instant affection I'd always felt toward her. Why weren't we better friends? If we'd spotted each other on the street now, we would have just waved and stayed talking on our cell phones.

"Donna, I am not living in this dump, I will tell you right now," Ginny said, laughing her husky laugh. "You've got termites or something, I'm telling you. You see this dust?" She pointed a magenta pinky nail toward the windowsill.

"I'm trying to get Ginny to move in with me," Donna explained. Claudia slinked in, poured two glasses of wine and left without a word.

"My mothah won't have it," Ginny said. "Not when she sees this." It was an interesting comment, given that Ginny's mother worked in the garment industry and barely noticed Ginny was alive—at least, that was what Donna used to say. Donna's family was Ginny's surrogate family. That was the lore.

211

We went to a Columbia fraternity party. Part of me wondered if I'd see Will there, but I knew there was very little chance of him showing up at a party like this. It wasn't exclusive enough for him. They played music from the eighties and there were guys in big plaid shirts with the sleeves cut off and greased-back hair, jumping and fist-popping like I remember people doing at Mom's club. It reminded me of Mom sticking shoulder pads into her black silk blazer and going to work.

I ended up getting rip-roaring drunk, sitting bored at a cafeteria table where Donna and Ginny glommed onto some guys from Long Island. Later on I found this guy Florian and made out with him in the stairwell while people trudged by us, their rainy shoes stepping on our coats.

For a while it was nice to kiss someone new, to erase Will from my lips. Florian had a rich, spicy smell that I attributed to his being Greek, and he wanted me to come back to his room, pulling my face toward his in a wonderful need-you, need-sex way. But I played coy. The truth was, I thought of Ian and that little spot under his chin I loved to kiss, his God-spot, and what if Florian was an ax murderer and killed me while we were doing it, leaving Ian motherless. Donna and the cheesy guys ended up going to a club in the West Twenties. I bullied the cab driver into letting five of us ride, thinking I might go too, but I ended up bagging and was home by one, and even that felt too late.

42.

"How was the night?" Dad came out of the kitchen with a plate of cheese. He'd been at work all day, working on a deal, which he rarely did on Sundays anymore. "How's your friend Donna?"

"Okay." I eyed the cheese and thought of Mom with a plate of Brie resting on her chest, how she'd dig at it and keep it lying around on her bed all night. Dad always precut his cheese and put a predetermined, matching number of crackers—in this case, six—on his plate. Then he would sit down purposefully to eat, as though it were an eating "session."

"How's she liking Barnard?" He swiveled in his chair. The only thing Dad knew about Donna was that she went to Barnard.

"She didn't say," I answered, relishing the first few moments of an Ian-free room. He'd finally gone to sleep after a never-ending stream of hungover hours I'd spent feeding, changing and entertaining him and trying not to call Will. As much as I wanted to talk to him, I didn't know where he was with the adoption thing—how much he was going to push it— and I was afraid to find out.

"What did you guys do?" he asked, a chipper lilt in his voice. I didn't know why he thought seeing Donna would make me feel good about things.

"Not much, Dad, we just went out. Hung out." I picked up a *New Yorker* and leafed through it, trying to find the movie reviews. "The whole college thing makes people very smug, doesn't it?" I asked. "Is everybody just so damned happy with themselves? Their schools? Their jobs?"

"What do you mean, smug?" Dad asked, watching me carefully.

"Just, you know, just very, very pleased with their little lives. Donna's doing some integrative studies thing. She thinks this somehow makes her very, very special. Her prof this, her prof that. She's reading St. Augustine. So what?"

"Is she enjoying it?" Dad asked, inserting a stack gingerly in his mouth.

"Yes, she's enjoying it," I said. What an asshole, I thought.

"Sometimes smugness, if I understand what you're getting at, is just another way of dealing with anxiety."

"Huh?" It occurred to me that I'd never complained about my friends to him. I'd preferred to let him think we were so-phisticates; any dirty laundry was too cool to be leaked to out-siders.

"Most people have a lot of anxiety, Thea," he said. "Even when things are going well."

"What does that have to do with it?" I asked. "I'm just say-ing she's being annoying. Her GPA and how it's the highest in her seminar, blah blah."

"Maybe she doesn't want it to end," he said, sweeping crumbs to one side of his plate.

"Doesn't want what to end?"

"Whatever success she's experiencing at the moment." He picked up another cracker and held it pensively in front of his mouth.

"What, is something up at work?" I asked.

"No, it's okay." He leaned back. "Not great. It's been a tough year. I'm only down thirty percent, better than some, but I've still got lots of layoffs."

"Are you going to get the ax?"

"Who knows?" He sighed, setting the plate on the ottoman. "I'm sure I'm on someone's list."

"You're being very cool about it," I said.

"Not cool, just resigned, maybe. Now, how about that salad? I've got some Parma ham and I've boiled some eggs to throw in." He got up and went to the kitchen with his plate.

"Great," I said, stretching my sore, hungover muscles on the couch.

"In the meantime, it's no fun having to fire a bunch of people. A lot of them have kids Ian's age."

"Do you call them into your office"—I lowered my voice, trying to imitate him—"Look, I have some bad news. . . ."

"It's not a game, Thea," he said, turning around from the kitchen counter to glare at me.

"I didn't say it was. It's just that you never seem to be . . ."

"To be what?"

"I don't know, too engaged in what people think anyway."

"What kind of thing is that to say?" His back was to me again and he was making big sweeping motions with his hands, tossing the salad.

"Well, why don't you have any friends? How come you're alone so much?"

"Am I alone? I wouldn't describe it that way."

"Besides us, I mean, and work."

"You take up more of my life than you realize." He pulled the plastic string on a bottle of olive oil and the wrapper popped off. I had a guilty pang that came in a rush. What was that supposed to mean? Were we really that much of a burden? Then I immediately resented him for pinning all his social failures on *us*.

"Look, Thea," he said. "Don't take this the wrong way, but

I'm not that interested in what a twenty-five-year-old kid start-ing out has to say. Why does he need to get up on the table and do the Macarena, or whatever."

"What are you talking about?" I asked.

He peeled an egg and dumped the shells into the garbage. "Why does he need to make an impact that way? Moreover, why does he need to tell me, to *explain* to me, that that's what he does at parties? Why is this a defining feature for him? One he needs to tell people about? Tell *me* about?" He shook the new olive oil into the bowl.

"What's your point?" I asked. "That you don't care?"

He made a shooing motion with his hand as he carried out the bowl on two plates. "I don't know what the point is, maybe I *am* intrigued by these people, these young guys who come in so eager and giddy, with their elephantine egos, their inflated, fragile sense of self." He shook his head and sat down at the table. I dragged myself to the chair in front of him. "Maybe I'm even fond of them. From afar, ideally." He rubbed his hands together. "Salad du chef."

We chewed in silence.

"Maybe we should go wake up Ian," Dad said. "He'll cheer me up."

"Wake him and die," I said. My phone rang and I reached for it on the table.

"Thea, please, don't answer the phone at the dinner table." He scowled. "You don't see me doing that."

I hit the green button. "Your bikini?" I recognized Carmen's slightly scratchy voice. "It sold in less than an hour. I remem-ber looking at my watch. It was, like, forty-seven minutes after you left."

"No way," I said quietly.

"I think she was Brazilian, I'm not kidding. I was going to

216

call you right after, but I had to catch a train to Wellfleet for a family thing and I ran out of juice. I just got back. Anyway, you should make more. How long did it take you to make that one?"

"A while," I admitted. "But I think I can ramp it up."

"Well, why don't you do, like, two or three more and bring them in. You have the yarn, right?"

"Yup," I said. Dad was glaring at me, but I put my hand up, gesturing, Wait till you hear this.

I hung up, my heart racing, some weird baroque music sounding in my brain. I felt like a window had opened up in my head again, cool air blowing through it, the same way I felt in Carmen's shop when I was first there with Vanessa.

"So something really exciting just happened." I looked at Dad, picking up my fork.

"What's that, Thea?"

"I sold a bikini."

"Bikini?" Dad focused on stabbing his last lettuce leaf.

"Vanessa taught me how to crochet, and I made this bikini, just like one I had when I was a kid—there's a picture of me at the beach on Charter, Nana made it. Anyway, this woman Carmen helped me, a lot, actually, and then she sold it in her shop. That's what she called to tell me."

"I didn't realize you made swimsuits," he said, standing up with his plate. He either wasn't listening or was really dense.

"She sold it for three hundred bucks," I called after him as he headed to the kitchen. He turned toward me and paused at the mention of money.

"That's great," he said. "That's terrific, Thea." He continued to the kitchen, looking befuddled and slightly worried, as though my earning three hundred dollars were potentially illegal. "Some more salad?"

43.

My life and Ian's in the shitter, I drowned myself in crochet. I brought it with me everywhere—on the subway to Ian's doctor; to coffee with Mom, where it calmed me as she told me things were heating up with Alex the married guy; to the park, looping and twirling while Ian stared at the branches over us. I'd grab it whenever Ian slept, and when he woke up, I'd do just a few more stitches. Sometimes I'd push it, listening as his sharp cries changed to long, low growls. Just a few more stitches. I'd pick him up and he'd scream into my ear, showing me how mad he was, and I'd mash his cheek against mine and beg forgiveness.

It had taken two days to finish the first teal and royal-blue zigzagged bikini. I crocheted from six a.m. Thursday until two a.m. Friday, stopping only to put Ian on the boob for ten minutes a side. When he wasn't nursing, he lay next to me in a nest of blankets I constructed to help him sleep. On Friday I started again at nine a.m. and went until midnight. By midnight my eyeballs were swollen and frozen in their sockets and my index finger felt like a burnt twig. But Saturday morning I started right in on the second one.

The second bikini had the hardest design—a red, orange and yellow sunburst pattern. It took me almost five days of nonstop crocheting to finish it, and I was feeling so good about it, I thought for sure Will would call before I finished to say he hadn't been thinking straight. He didn't.

The third bikini's pattern was almost identical to the bikini I had when I was six, and as I cast on the first few chains of green, I pulled out the original photo of me, in glorious red, white and blue, that I'd kept in an envelope. I looked at my Mona Lisa–smiling face in the photo and remembered how miserable I was after that fight Mom and Dad had had in the middle of the night, and how hard it had been to smile for my grandmother, who was snapping photo after photo of me on the beach. How long after that had they gotten divorced? Six long years. I did the first row and all the slipknots, remembering the day I found out.

"You know, I was thinking," Mom had said, standing in my doorway, "last night when I picked you up from Kyra's and you were running down the hallway to the elevator . . . your pants are too short. Your ankles are starting to show again." She'd sat on my bed and examined a chicken pox scab healing on my cheek. "When did I take you to that horrible place for jeans? September, when school started. And already they're getting too short."

"I don't want new ones," I'd said. She always started an argument with me as I was just waking up.

"Sweetheart, you look like Twiggy."

"Who?"

"Never mind. Let's just get you a couple more pairs and you can at least alternate. Wherever you want. Your choice. We'll get some breakfast first."

"Daddy too?" I'd asked.

"He's got errands," she'd said. "Just us."

I don't remember what I had. It was gray and windy and there were puffed-up plastic bags in the tree outside our booth window. Mom brought the paper and she read it while we fought about letting me go to some movie that she didn't want me to see. Then we went to an army-navy store, where I got a pair of black corduroys.

"How about we go look for dresses for Aunt Cecilia's wedding?" she'd offered. Her face was bright but tense, the way some people looked after snorting cocaine.

"It's not till July," I'd said. A strange, open-ended feeling had started taking over the day.

"We don't need to buy," she'd said. "Just look and think."

So we went to Barneys. We walked around the second floor and Mom picked up sleeves of black jackets and long-sleeved shirts and dropped them. She tried on a pair of brown suede boots.

"Let's get a coffee, shall we?" she'd asked. "Are you hungry again? I love the café next door. Let's go."

It was starting to fill up for lunch and we sat down at the last free table.

"Aren't we lucky," she'd said, straightening her place mat.

It was one of the few times in my life I remember her sitting still. She held the menu up to her face and read it for a long time. Then she put it down.

"Thea, there's something I need to speak with you about."

"What?"

"It's about your father and me."

She called him "your father" instead of "Daddy" and I knew right away. She went back to calling him Daddy again after they got divorced. She still calls him Daddy and he still calls her Mom when they're with me.

When we got home to our lobby, Dad was talking to Tom, the doorman. He was standing with a suitcase between his legs, the same way he stood when he waited for the elevator. He turned around and looked at me, all of a sudden a stranger.

As I started to cry, Mom asked Tom if the mail had come, and Dad hugged me, not saying anything. I thought about how good everything had been since he'd stopped drinking. How he'd helped me do my homework and made popcorn in the lobster pot and did crosswords under the black lamp. Every single night he was Dad instead of the sleepy-eyed, drunk imposter who'd come home late from work and fling his arms around in the air whenever he said anything. But for some reason that I couldn't for the life of me figure out, the fact that he'd finally quit made no difference to Mom.

"Where are you going?" I'd asked.

"I'll be close by," he'd answered, and as I looked at his face, I thought I could see disappointment as big as mine.

Ian stirred and scrunched his face next to me, burrowing his head into my leg. I put down the crochet hook and picked him up as he opened his eyes. The questions that had plagued me since I'd left Florence's crowded the air around his head: Did he know Will was gone? Did he miss him? Would I be able to love him enough to make up for not having a dad? I kissed him and held him, letting his warm cheek sink into my neck. It was all I could do.

44.

I took my new green-and-purple-squared bikini with me to the moms' group I'd read an ad for on Craigslist, thinking it would facilitate hanging back, not getting caught in the fray.

Ian and I were the first to arrive at the restaurant, which somehow confirmed that I had no friends. I sat down in the middle of a long, narrow farm table as Ann and Hilary, the preexisting friends who'd started the group, came in together with their babies. They saw me and parked their strollers by the door.

"Are you Thea?" Hilary shook my hand overly hard, jutting out her Sigourney Weaver jaw.

I nodded, getting up. Ian was in the sack, his head nestled against my chest.

"Don't, you're in kangaroo mode." She smiled, nodding at Ian.

"Thea, this is Ann. Leah and Kate should be here any minute."

"Hi, Thea," Ann said in a nasal voice. She grabbed the menu. "Eggs, I want eggs," she said. Her baby reached for the brown sugar packets.

"If I have another coffee, my head's going to explode," Hilary explained. Her baby stood on the floor in a jean jacket, leaning on her, swatting her legs. "He's just standing, as of yesterday."

Hilary was an associate at a law firm and had taken a year off, but she'd just hired a nanny because she was "going back." She was having trouble relinquishing control to the nanny.

"I feel like she can't do it I like I can," she said, banging her empty latte cup on the table. She glanced at me crocheting away. I tried to catch her eye every so often to not seem rude. "We're working on it."

"You know what will make your life so much easier when you're working?" Ann asked urgently, licking her thumb and sticking it on the table to sop up the spilled sugar from the packet.

Hilary and Ann started in about a meal delivery service. I watched them, wondering, How did I used to make friends?

How did I make friends with Chris Fontana from Staten Island, who I had nothing in common with other than pre-calc? We laughed about Mr. Kushman's shoes and made fun of the way he rolled his *l*'s, as in *l-l-l-evel*. We'd write notes back and forth—"What did you do last night?" "Went to the mall with my mother, she picked out something for her date with the butt doctor." And then all of a sudden you knew each other, you could ask specific questions—"How was the date with the butt doctor?" "Sucky, poor Mom," and so on. It was easier then, I thought, watching as Kate, too pretty for me, arrived in boho-chic perfection, a binky-sucking boy slung on her hip.

"Thea, you're the new girl," she said, holding her free hand away from me. "I won't shake," she said apologetically. "He's got something."

"No problem," I said, nodding earnestly, then smiling at the baby. He turned his head as far away from me as it would go, and I decided I hated making small talk with other people's children. My knees bumped up against the table as I watched her saunter around to the other side, to a seat next to Hilary. Kate had a nice, direct way about her, and she was wearing a cute embroidered-leather belt. But there were pots of jam and menus, nestled between hunks of bread, blocking our way, and I just felt too tired.

I loitered at the table after they all left, pulling my hook and yarn out of the bag, annoying the waiters seating lunch customers. I ordered another coffee and crocheted until my fingers were white-knuckled and sore, my arms aching from holding the whole thing over Ian's sleeping body. I slipped the last loop off the hook just as someone placed my check squarely in front of me. It was Friday—exactly two weeks since I'd started. I was done and ready to haul my new stash to Stash.

My phone rang as we got outside.

"Hi," Will said.

I leaned my shoulder against the traffic-light post on the corner, the ticking noise from inside it reverberating through me. I couldn't speak. It had been almost three weeks since I'd left Florence's. Cars clunked over a manhole in the street. I wished I could sit down someplace quiet where I could hear him better.

"How are you? How's Ian?" He sounded distant. All business.

"He's fine." Everything I looked at took on a surreal quality. I had no idea how I felt or how to "be" with him.

"Thea, I'm sorry I haven't called. I needed to think."

"About what?" I mumbled.

"Listen, I want to talk to you about something and I want you to really think about it. Do you want to meet someplace?"

"What is it?" I asked.

"Maybe we should meet."

"Just tell me, Will," I said. "I don't want to wait."

"I talked to someone at an adoption agency. They were incredibly understanding and . . ."

The light had turned green, but I stayed put. "No," I said.

"You can't just say no without talking about it first."

"Yes, I can."

"Well, I want to talk about it."

"There's nothing to talk about. If you don't want to be a part of it, that's fine," I said. "There's nothing to talk about beyond that."

"Thea, please . . ."

I hung up the phone and crossed the street. The first thought that went through my head was that I was going to have to change my cell phone number. I caught our reflections in the window of a sushi place, my puffy black down jacket, Ian in his checked hat, broadcasting whited-out loneliness in the flat winter sun.

After that, Will became the enemy. I wondered how far he was willing to go. Would he plant drugs on me? Would he lie about me? What was he capable of? I walked around to the front of the stroller. It was almost as if Ian's whole body broke into a smile as he looked at me. If anyone took you away from me, I don't know how I could keep living, I thought. How could Will even consider it? How could he know me and know how I felt about Ian, even when it was tough and I was in a bad mood—how could Will even begin to think about doing what he was doing?

"Just go on with your life," Vanessa said when I called her right afterward. "He's powerless and he knows it."

"I'm so scared, Vanessa," I said. I'd gone one block while I was on the phone with her, staring the whole way at the whirly pattern of Ian's knit hat. When I got to the next corner, it hit me how quickly things changed. How sharply and un-waveringly betrayal could sink in.

45.

Ian kicked in his stroller the next day, knocking a box of matzo off a shelf. It was starting to dawn on me that he really didn't like food shopping.

My hand was in a plastic bag, about to grab some lettuce, when Carmen called.

"They're gone," she said. "All three. Sold today."

"No way," I said, debagging my hand.

"Saturday is always my best day, but this is nuts. I think you've got something, Thea. People looove them."

I spotted Dad standing by a refrigerator, pointing to a bottle of juice in a strangely shaped bottle, gauging my interest, the Saturday crowd jostling past him to get at the roast chickens. I shrugged at him, my heart racing.

"They're just unique," Carmen continued. "I don't like that word, but that's what they are. The cut . . . I admit I tried the teal one on. It just lay on the hips so nicely. Even on *my* hips. If I could buy one, I would."

"I'll make you one," I said.

"The last one to sell was the fiery red and orange. The customer even asked if there were other colors, and when I said there weren't, she bought it anyway. That says something to me."

"What sold first?"

"The teal one, of course. Then the purple and green."

"Wow, Carmen, I can't believe it."

"Nine hundred clams, baby, believe it! So what next? You need to make more. A lot more. I could put you in touch with these women I know in Brooklyn, they're seamstresses who do everything—knit, crochet, whatever. Maybe you could work something out with them. Do you have any money you could . . . you know, start something with?"

"I might," I answered.

"Well, I could hook you up with them," she said. "They do great work. Let me know. In the meantime, congratulations! Come by and I'll give you a check."

My first thought was to call Will and say, *"See? I actually did something. You thought it was stupid and you were wrong. You're wrong about everything."*

226

I found Dad on the line, pursing his lips at a woman in front of him who was digging into the bowels of her wallet for change.

"So guess what!" I asked, almost ramming the stroller into the checkout station.

"What's that, Thea," he asked, placing two artichokes on the belt.

"All three bikinis sold today. I dropped them off at Stash yesterday and they all sold today."

"You don't say." Dad smiled, distracted. He pulled a credit card out of his wallet and gave it to the cashier, who nodded and motioned for him to swipe it.

"Carmen said she could hook me up with some women in Brooklyn who could help me make, you know, more of them than I could alone."

"Who's Carmen?" he asked, swiping his card in the black groove.

"The woman at the knitting store I told you about, remember?"

"Vaguely," he said. The cashier motioned for him to do it again, which he did, but it was the wrong way. I grabbed it out of his hand and turned it around.

"She said these women could help me make more than I could just by myself."

"What is it, like a sweatshop?" he asked. He looked at the cashier, annoyed. "Do I have to sign?"

"No, not a *sweatshop,*" I said quickly as the cashier shook her head at him, shooing us down the line. "Do sweatshops even exist anymore?" I hung one of the bags on the stroller and we pushed through the big green doors.

"Are you kidding?" He laughed, looking at me sideways.

"There are laws in this country, right?" I asked.

"Well, how many workers do they employ? How much do they make an hour?"

"I don't know, Dad."

"Well, that's something you'd want to research."

We headed west on Broome Street, past the soot-stained cast-iron buildings and I wondered how I could bring myself to ask him to help me again, when he was already helping me out so much. The truth was, I hated asking him for anything because it made me feel guilty. Especially since I'd gotten pregnant and was now living with him. What was more, the idea of asking him for things always reminded me of when I was little and he, bombed out of his mind in the middle of a Saturday, took me to the toy store on Charter Island. We'd wheeled a shopping cart around the store as we piled stuff in—a Barbie makeup head, Barbie outfits, games and more games, a red soccer ball. Bright orange, see-through plastic water guns with extra-long barrels. A badminton set and extra birdies.

"What about a skateboard?" he'd asked.

"I have one in the city."

"Yes, but did you bring it?" He'd plopped a red plastic skateboard onto the heap. Its wheels were too small, but the thrill plodded on.

At the register I'd waited to hear "Thea, we've overdone it—put this one back, why don't you." But it never came. I watched as everything went into shopping bags, excited beyond containment at my luck. But after Mom and Dad split, the scene that replayed in my head was of me cashing in on all the crap that had been going on between them; I got a Barbie makeup head because Dad was on the verge of a nervous breakdown. Then, when I got older, I'd just sneak or take what I wanted instead of asking, like when I snuck off to Europe.

As we crossed Sixth Avenue, I told myself that I'd bring it up again at dinner, hating the fact that after all he'd done, I still needed his help. But when we got home, he went into the kitchen and threw himself into making dinner, grunting at me when I asked him where the Diet Coke was as he whisked together a marinade for the steaks and cut up paper-thin slices of garlic to grill them with.

"Table twenty-four enjoying their jar course, I see." Dad walked slowly out of the kitchen with our plates and utensils in one hand, steak sauce in the other. He'd nicknamed the high chair "table twenty-four" and he called Ian the Machiavelli party. It was after nine o'clock when we finally sat down, and by that time I was too undone from starvation and accumulated-over-the-day depression about Will to have a productive conversation about anything. And then, with Dad's impeccable sense of timing, he threw me a curveball.

"So listen, Thea, I spoke to Tom Davidson this afternoon. His office needs someone while his assistant is on maternity leave."

"What's his office?" I asked, pulling my napkin out of its ring.

"What do they do, you mean?" He threw so much pepper on his steak that the top was almost black. "Pullman Capital. It's a midsize private equity firm. They do some derivatives work for us. What's wrong?"

"Nothing," I said, wiping Ian's mouth.

"Thea, I think this could be a good thing," he said, cutting his steak methodically into small bites. "You could do this until you're ready to go to NYU. It would be a good thing to have on your resume."

"Despite the fact that I have no intention of going into

finance," I said. I'd been with him all afternoon. When had he spoken to Tom Davidson? Had he pulled this idea out of his hat because he thought I was getting too caught up in my little bikini dreams? Resentment rushed over me. He wanted me to do something and it didn't matter whether I wanted to do it or not; if I loved him or, more importantly, if I wanted his love, I had to do it.

"What about Ian?" I asked.

Dad leaned forward on his elbows, in serious mode. "Bonnie Whelan gave me the name of an agency that places domestic help. She found her nanny through them and she's been with them for years. Apparently there's only one agency you want. That should be your plan this week. To find a nanny."

"You mean an agency? Like St. Mary's?" I asked.

"No," Dad grunted, shaking his head. "These women are professionals. They do this for a living."

"Remember Bridget?" I said, rubbing it in. My parents had funny luck with babysitters. They'd gotten them all through a Catholic agency next to the church down the street. There was Elishka, the nudist; Patty, the pyromaniac; and Bridget, who took me with her to O'Neal's Pub to meet her boyfriend. She sat on his lap, letting him stick his tongue through her hoop earring, while I hid in the booth with them, seeing how many times I could tie her incredibly long gum-wrapper chain around my neck. The bartender gave me a ginger ale with about seventy maraschino cherries in it. When we got home, Dad was standing in the living room with two cops.

I thought for sure he'd at least smile at the memory. He sat there waiting, his shoulders slumped, for my enthusiastic response.

"Do I have to go there?" I asked.

"No. You call them up and they send over a few people to interview."

"All at once?"

"One by one," he said, rolling his tongue across his teeth. "Is this how you're going to be?"

"What do you mean?"

"You're behaving helplessly."

"I am not," I said, prying Ian out of his high chair. "I'm trying to figure it out. It's not that easy to just stick him with someone. He's pretty attached. Or maybe it's me who's attached to him." I squeezed Ian's soft, springy foot and thought of Will again with a weird combination of fear and missing him. I stopped myself from imagining for the millionth time that someone was at the door, ready to lift Ian out of my arms. I wanted to kill Will for making me feel so vulnerable. But if I killed Will, they would definitely take Ian away.

"A little separation will be good for both of you," Dad said in a way that hinted he thought Ian would be a wimp if he was attached to me. He crunched into a green bean, sat back and crossed his arms. It started dawning on me that he was going to force the job issue. "Your mom loved working, remember?"

I remembered and was suddenly homesick for her.

"What?" Dad asked. "What is it?"

"I kind of want to pursue this bikini thing," I said meekly. "I think I could really make something happen with it."

"Thea, it sounds like a little more than you can chew at the moment," Dad said impatiently, throwing more pepper on his steak.

"Well, I'd rather do that than private equity," I said, laying Ian on a blanket on the couch.

There was a long silence, then Dad said evenly, in a way I knew there was absolutely no room for argument: "I think we should give this opportunity at Pullman a chance."

"When does it start, this opportunity?" I asked.

"As soon as possible," he said, sauntering victoriously into the kitchen. "But I bought you a week because I knew the nanny would need taking care of."

"You bought me a week? Is that like buying me a vowel?" I followed him, dumping my half-full plate in the garbage.

"It's an exciting place," he said. "See where it goes. That's all I'm thinking. You can't sit home with Ian. I won't have it. Eventually you'll start college, and this is a perfect way to bide your time until you do. It will help give you options in the workforce after you graduate."

"Workforce. It sounds like a branch of the military." I took his plate and yanked open the dishwasher as he made a beeline for his room.

46.

Joy was from the Philippines. It struck me about halfway through my conversation with her, when she told me that she loved "working" with babies, that I was in the middle of a job interview. That she was there to get hired.

"So you're currently working for another family?" I asked.

"Yes." Joy smiled. "Two girls. One is ten, the other, seven." She folded her hands primly on her knees, anticipating questions. "They're in school now. Mom Melissa doesn't need a full-time nanny anymore. Just part-time." The tone of her voice seemed sad, and I felt bad for her. She had so little control over it, kids getting older.

Adelle came, followed by Yvonne an hour later. Adelle had three grown kids. Yvonne from the Farrell Agency said she was "seasoned." I thought she seemed seasoned too, by the way she reached for Ian right away and made a big deal about him, his long eyelashes, his dimpled chin, but his eyes kept darting toward me.

Monica was from Barbados. When I opened the door, she glided in with a beautiful scarf tied tightly around her head, which made me wonder about her hair. She was getting a degree in criminology at night and wanted to be a detective. She looked me in the eye more consistently than I could look anyone in the eye, and she walked with a fun swing to her butt. She had long legs and a formidable presence. She looked like she'd be alert and on-the-ball enough to prevent Will from running with Ian out of a park.

I barely remembered how she was with Ian, just that her smile seemed real, and that she had the air of someone who was doing worthwhile things with her time. I told Dad when he came home that night, and he was overly proud of me for making the decision so quickly. "Your mother was always amazed at what good child care was available in the city," he said, which forced me to consider whether Monica might actually be an ax murderer.

He smiled at me from the foyer, slipping his shoes off and lining them up under the red silk chair. Ian was lying on a mat by the dining room window, reaching for a drape near his hand by the floor.

"Ian, don't," we both said at the same time, and Ian turned

toward me with a sweetly defiant look on his face that was so Will it made my whole body ache.

"I appreciate what you're trying to do, Dad, I really do," I said, grabbing my coat from the red chair and hanging it in the closet. "But this bikini thing could be interesting. Don't you think?"

Bikini thing. I realized how silly it sounded, especially to someone like him. He paused and looked at me, then walked purposefully to the fridge and pulled out a bottle of Pellegrino, giving me the impression that he was mulling it over. He struggled to twist the bottle, sticking it between his knees, but it wouldn't budge. He grabbed a dish towel and after more struggling he opened it, then downed it straight from the bottle. "Aaaaah," he said. At that point it was clear he'd forgotten what I'd asked, and I was once again too tired and disheartened to bring it up again.

47.

Monica arrived on my first morning at work and pulled a beaten-up *Goodnight Moon* out of her purse after I handed Ian to her. I wondered if she thought we didn't have enough books in the house, and if she was going to read him *Goodnight Moon* because she wanted him to nap all day. I headed to the subway, thinking about Will colluding with Monica to steal Ian, traveling with him for miles, across borders. How would I get him back? I imagined my legs moving through water, or running in slow motion in the air like in a dream. I wondered if I'd ever hear from Will again.

Pullman Capital was in a tall, narrow building on Sixth Avenue, or Avenue of the Americas, depending on your mood. When I got to reception, the guy behind the desk phoned someone named Sue and motioned for me to take a seat on a black leather couch. After a couple of minutes I picked up the front section of the *Times,* just to peruse the headlines, because I hated getting interrupted in the middle of a story, like I always do in a doctor's office. A few more minutes went by and I caved and started at the back with an obituary about a children's book illustrator, which made me wonder when I should start reading to Ian. I finished the article and still no sign of Sue. Hopefully this is what the job will be like, I thought. Hopefully they'll just install me in some cubicle and forget about me and I'll be free to crochet under the desk. I'd take my six hundred dollars a week after taxes and save it toward a production deal with the women in Brooklyn. If they left me alone, I could actually ramp up production to two or three bikinis a week, sell those and prove to Dad how lucrative it could be. But I was interrupted.

"Thea Galehouse?" A boxy woman in a black pantsuit and glasses with beaded croakies stood by the reception desk.

"Hi, yes, that's me, nice to meet you." I stood up, straightening my too-tight Gap pencil skirt.

"Nice to meet you, I'm Sue. So follow me. We're going to need you to help out in client services, if that's okay." Sue pushed through both glass doors, giving us a wide berth, and led me to a room with a bunch of long, wide tables, the same size as the lunch tables at school, pushed into a large U. She launched into a synopsis of the meaning of Pullman Capital and explained, in incredibly unspecific terms, what I'd be doing there. Every second or third seat had a computer screen, and some of the screens had men sitting in front of them, but most did not.

"Why don't you have a seat here and make yourself comfortable," said Sue, exiting the room in long strides across the carpet. "You can hang up your coat in that closet, and Malcolm will be with you soon."

Now I had nothing to read. I noticed that my spot at the U didn't have a phone. I hoped I had cell reception but wasn't optimistic because the room was windowless. What if Monica needed to reach me? A guy next to me was enunciating something into his phone, and at first I couldn't figure out why I was having trouble understanding him—I thought maybe it was another language—but then I realized he had a speech impediment that made him lose all of his *s* sounds. Each time he said "Seabrook," it sounded like "Heabrook." He also talked very fast and it made me sure that only those who had an intimate relationship with him could understand what the hell he was saying. I prayed he wasn't my boss because I would definitely offend him.

He was, of course.

"You're Hea? Nie to meet you," he said, wheeling over to me. "I'm Malcolm. Terrific you're here."

"Hi," I said. It looked like his tongue was missing. I was immediately, painfully conscious of trying to act normal in front of his disability, positive he could tell. But he was gallant. Later on, someone alluded to the fact that he'd had cancer in his jaw.

"I'd like you to tart, if you would, with organi-ing hom of our pre-entation folder," he said.

I nodded, relieved I understood.

"We have heven department at Pullman Cap, each of which is repre-hented in the folder. You'll find a page for each of the heven loaded on and in-hide that con-hole over there."

I spun my chair toward the console in the corner. The job would require getting up and down a lot.

"Come." He got up and motioned me to the presentation station.

Together we put a folder together, taking a packet from each pile and sliding it in.

"Not the moht eck-hiting thing, but we need them deh-perately," he said, throwing his arms dramatically in the air.

"No problem." I smiled, wondering how many folders I'd have to put together before I could work on the bikini under the desk.

"Fabulouh," he said, exiting the room.

I wondered if I could cheat and bring seven little stacks back to my chair and stuff them into folders from there. Surely Malcolm didn't expect me to stand at that console all day. I'd do five or six standing up, get my bearings, and then bring it over to the desk, where I'd do twenty or so, and then I'd crochet three or four rows on my lap under the desk.

I opened drawers, looking for an empty one to hold my bag. Someone snickered behind me.

I turned around and saw a guy with jaw-length, shiny black hair slumped in his chair, his shirttail hanging out. "We'll need ten thousand of those today," he joked with a pronounced English accent, flicking back his hair. "And they all need to be FedExed. We'll get you the list."

I shot him a dirty look.

"What's your name?" he asked, grinning.

"Thea. What's yours?"

"Daniel," he said. "Good luck. You'll be at it for decades. Careful of paper cuts. Nice top, by the way."

"Thank you," I said, trying not to appear embarrassed or antagonized.

"Paisley always makes me think of the Beatles," he said.

"It's my mother's," I said as I glanced at the door, half expecting Malcolm to appear and shush us.

"She must be very chic," he said, flipping the pages of a huge loose-leaf binder.

I'd never heard a boy say "chic."

"She's into clothes," I said, pulling my sore, blistery heel out of the black flat I hadn't worn in months.

"Into clothes?" he drawled in a cheesy American accent, flicking his hair out of his face yet again.

"She enjoys shopping for and purchasing women's wear. She's a fashionista. That better?"

I got up and went to the stacks at the console. Men, no women, came into the room throughout the morning, mostly to check the computer screens or to buzz someone on the intercom, and then they'd leave. I sat and stuffed, listening to Daniel on the phone—he was talking to someone named Elle who was having a party and wanted him to bring a bottle of Pernod, and to someone named Cass, who I took to be his girl-friend in London.

"Fly here this weekend, babe," he kept saying. "Study for it on the flight. I can't bear it, darling . . . you know I can't . . . I've got no money." At twelve-thirty he let out a loud yawn. "Thea, let's trot out. I'll take you to meet Mr. Spaghetti."

I went with him down Fifty-Sixth Street to a guy standing in front of a takeout place with a platter of tomato bruschettas.

"So I have this mental picture of you in my head," Daniel said, taking a bruschetta off Mr. Spaghetti's tray and spilling it down his chin as he ate it. "Tell me if I'm right. You had a breakdown during your, what do you call it here? Sophomore year, so you've dropped out to take some time to collect yourself, to 'find yourself' as you Americans say, and since someone owed Daddy a favor, you're now biding your time in the hallowed hallways of Pullman Capital. Am I right, darling?"

"Why do English people call everyone darling?" I asked, popping a bruschetta into my mouth as we stepped into the takeout place and onto the long line. I was tempted to just tell him my True Hollywood Story but wasn't ready to part with the idea of free-and-easy Thea yet.

As we paid, he motioned to the cashier, saying, "See that woman? She's mad for me." The receptionist in the front hall of Pullman was also mad for him. On the way back he let me listen to a dance track on his iPod, made by a guy from some club in Dubai or St. Bart's. "I like my music long," he said, and something about the way he thumped his head back and forth reminded me of a turtle. He told me he was living in the East Thirties for six months, on some kind of break from Oxford.

We got back to our desks and ate. He pointed a breadstick in my direction.

"No, thank you," I said. He smiled over some secret little joke to himself and turned back to his desk.

48.

Ian finally started sleeping through the night—really sleeping—from seven or eight p.m. until seven in the morning, after I let him cry for fifteen million hours over the course of two days, like the book said. It worked. As the weeks went by, we fell into a routine: Woke up at seven and messed around on our favorite spots—my bed, the floor in our bedroom, under the mobile. Dad would feed Ian while I jumped in the shower before Monica showed up at eight. When Ian was around five months old, Dad got very into making some recipe he'd concocted with watered-down oatmeal and mashed-up bananas. He would make a big bowl for breakfast and share it with him. "I forgot how much I love bananas," he said almost every morning, alternating a big spoon into his mouth, a baby spoon into Ian's.

Mom took me to a media-elite Italian place for lunch one Friday after I'd been at Pullman for a couple of months. We sat down at a tiny two-top and dove into a bowl of olives as Mom spied on the people next to us, trying to listen in. She looked back at me and I swore I saw a trace of a wince.

"Did I tell you we are finally, finally, closing on that Astor Place apartment tomorrow?" she asked, tossing a pit into a zebra-striped wooden bowl. "I never thought it would happen. The buyer made endless demands—replace all the windows, redo the floors—it was ridiculous and I never thought it would happen, but it finally is. My first closing. I'm really pleased." An undercurrent of spite trailed under her voice, like I hadn't been involved enough throughout the transaction, the whole undertaking.

"Maybe you've found your calling," I said. "Remember when I looked at all those places with Daddy? We could have used someone good, someone who's good at figuring out what people want."

"It's fun, but it's a lot of work." She browsed the menu. "I'm craving pasta. Isn't that strange?"

I pulled the hook out of my bag. It was becoming almost

like a compulsion, the crocheting; I couldn't figure out if it was helping me engage or disengage. I just felt compelled to do it.

"What is that?" she asked, peeking out from behind her menu.

"It's a bikini. You like it?"

"I have to first come to terms with this ludicrously domestic picture in front of me," she said, blinking dramatically. "First you get yourself knocked up, now you're knitting."

"I'm crocheting. You've seen me do it before. Vanessa taught me, remember?"

"Whatever," she said, setting her menu down. "Knitting, crocheting, they're all dowager sports." She scraped her chair out and crossed her legs. "I'm convinced sometimes you must be someone else's daughter. But then I remember . . ." She frowned and made horns on the top of her head. "Evelyn Galehouse . . ."

"Chill out, Mom," I said, tucking the yarn into the crook of the banquette. "It's not a big deal. Just because you don't do it."

"It's more than I don't do it. I'm unnerved to see you doing it. It's so . . . retro in a not pleasant or inviting way."

"Well, what if I told you I'm making money from it?"

"How?"

"I'm selling bikinis for three hundred bucks a pop at this knitting store," I said. "You'd like it, it's trendy, not crafty. This woman Carmen, the owner, she's been selling them and she wants to hook me up with some women in Brooklyn who can help me."

"Who is Carmen?" she asked suspiciously, as though I were utterly incapable of conducting business.

"She owns the knitting store on Charlton Street. Vanessa took me."

"Of course she did," Mom said, rolling her eyes.

"She thinks I should try and not mass-produce them but work something out, like a production deal, and sell them to small boutiques."

"Do you notice that I clench my jaw?" she asked. A large plate of pasta with mushrooms arrived in front of her and she passed a bite over to me, dripping oil across my plate of ravioli.

"You're changing the subject," I said.

"This awful dental assistant who did my cleaning last week at Dr. Church's," she continued, ignoring me. "She asked me if I ground my teeth. Just from her asking it, it was like she made it true. I'm a tooth grinder. A jaw clencher." She took a pocket mirror out of her bag and examined her mouth. "I hate it when someone insinuates something and then somehow you start believing it. Daddy used to do that."

"What do you mean?" I asked, letting the buttery ravioli melt in my mouth.

"Oh, he was so critical. Every little thing. And it always came in question form." She hissed the "sss" in "question." It hit me how pissed she was, still. "Do you think your bangs are a little long, honey? I can't see your pretty eyes." She looked at me and closed her lips. "Anyway, never mind. How's it going over there? How's the old codg adjusting to modern parenting?"

"He's trying," I said, cutting my ravioli in fours in an attempt to eat it slowly. "He's home by seven most nights now."

"Unbelievable," she said, shaking her head. "Maybe he's finally getting his head in the right place."

242

"Hey, I just thought of something," I said. "Doesn't your friend Christine work at *Bazaar*? Maybe you could call her and tell her about the bikinis and she could do a little write-up about them."

She picked up the lemon wedge hanging on the rim of her Diet Coke and bit it, her red lipstick staining the rind. "You're really thinking about this."

"I am," I said.

She plunked the lemon into the glass. "I haven't spoken to her in ages, but I'll see what I can do. Can I see it?"

I wiped my hands, picked the bikini off the banquette and handed it over. This one was off-white with a turquoise and gold zigzag running vertically down the side of each hip.

"Where on earth did you learn to do this?" she asked, stretching the bottom out.

"I've told you before," I said. "Vanessa taught me."

She handed it back. "I'll see if I can track down Christine." She took a slice of baguette out of the basket and swished it around her plate. "So where is Will these days?"

"He's still at Florence's, I guess—I haven't heard from him in a few weeks." I forked the last quarter-ravioli and put on a brave face. "In a way it's easier without him."

"Sure," Mom said, laying down her fork. "One agenda. But is it over?"

"What? No," I said too loudly. I felt sick from the butter and oil. First he turns on me, then he disappears. I didn't know what I was more angry over—the fact that he so badly betrayed me with the adoption bullshit, or the fact that he'd then just dropped it, and dropped out of our lives. And the worst of it was the unavoidable reality that I still loved him.

49.

Daniel cast his wide-set, hazel eyes on the woven leather bag that I'd filched from Mom a while ago.

"Tell me, sweet Thea," he said, flicking his hair. "Why do American girls carry such big bags? Where I'm from, girls don't try to carry the world around with them like you do. What do you have in there?"

My phone rang before I could answer him. It was Mrs. Weston.

She'd called the house and gotten my number from Monica.

"I hope I'm not bothering you." Her voice sounded higher-pitched and more whispery than I'd remembered.

"You're not at all," I said. "How are you?"

"I'm well, thanks," she said, sounding nervous. "I'm having some trouble with my mom, but aside from that."

"Oh no," I said.

"She's just had a hard time, you know, losing my brother. She's not herself. She's suddenly afraid to go outdoors, afraid her freckles will burn, she's sort of spiraling."

"I'm sorry," I said.

"Yes, well, she's in Calabasas, in California, so hard to manage from afar." She cleared her throat. "Thea, I don't want to keep you. I'm sorry this is so hard for Will. I'm sorry that you probably feel let down."

"Yeah, well." I could barely get the words out.

"Well, I'm glad you're moving forward. You've found a job, that's wonderful."

"Yeah," I said, "Dad's idea."

"In any event, Thea, we still want to help you in any way we can with Ian. That still holds true, needless to say."

"Thanks," I said, wondering what Will had told them. Had he just said we'd broken up? Had he told them he wanted to give Ian up? "Would you like to spend some time with him? He's with the nanny while I'm here, at work. You can see him anytime you like."

"I'd like that. I have her number now. I'll call her to set up some dates, if that's all right with you."

"That would be great," I said, hoping that spending time with Ian would effectively wipe out any talk of adoption.

"Is he eating solid food yet?"

"He is," I said authoritatively. "He loves to eat."

"I want to bake him something yummy," she said. "Something with mushy apples."

"I'm sure he'd love whatever you make," I said.

There was an awkward pause as I couldn't think of anything else to say, but then Mrs. Weston responded, her voice somber and serious. "You're going to make this work for you, Thea," she said. "I can tell you are already. You're a strong person. I admire you."

"Thank you," I mumbled, not sure what to make of her attempt at a pep talk, another version of her famous "Be positive," wondering why she had ever scared and intimidated me so much. Was it just because I was so desperately in love with her son? Did he have that much power over me that he could transfer it to other people? The idea that I could have forged some kind of relationship with her if Will hadn't busted everything up hurled me into a black hole.

I hung up. Daniel was zoning into his computer screen. I was enjoying a harmless flirty thing with him to pass the time and didn't want him to hear. There was an empty, closet-sized room down the hall with a phone in it that no one ever used. I went to the room and dialed Will's cell phone. He'd see the number and not know it was me and pick up. It was three o'clock on a Thursday and his last class ended at one-forty. It had been over a month since we'd spoken.

"I haven't heard from you," I said when I heard his voice.

"I know," he said. He sounded totally caught off guard. "How's Ian?"

"Ian's fine," I said. "But why do you even get to know that?"

Silence.

"What's going on?" I asked.

"I'm sorry."

"Sorry for what?" I was scared of what he was going to say.

"Just sorry."

I held my breath. "You know I'm not giving him up, right? I'm never giving him up."

"I know." He sighed.

I ran my fingers over the back of the linty-wool chair, relief washing over me in the dark room. Outside the glass door, a man with red hair deposited a large plate of black-and-white cookies on top of a file cabinet. He glanced at me disapprovingly and turned back down the hallway.

"So you're going to leave it alone, the adoption thing," I said.

"I don't have a choice, do I?" There was resentment bordering on nastiness coming out of him. I wanted to take those cookies, break each of them at the exact mark where black met white, hurl them at the ceiling and shatter all of the hot dog–shaped fluorescent lights onto everyone. I was working so hard and I was doing a good job.

"You know what, Will? I'm a good mother," I said. "The fact that I even have to say it, to justify myself to you, it makes me sick. You make me sick, Will. You make me sick."

My throat felt jammed. I slammed the phone down and banged the desk like a two-year-old, stinging my hand. After I got it together, I went out and made my twelfth green tea of the day and brought one to Daniel.

"I'm so bored," he said, leaning so far back in his chair he was almost lying down.

"It's boring here," I said, my voice hollow. "You'll get no argument from me."

"Good, because I couldn't bear to have you cross with me." He slumped and wriggled, one pod of a headset in his ear, the other traversing his flat, almost concave, chest. "You look blue. Come to the supply closet and I'll cheer you up." He looked up at me and winked. "It locks."

"I thought you were gay," I said.

"Now, that's a cheap shot, Thea." He blew into his tea. "Surely you can do better than that."

I glanced at the door and looked at my watch. 4:20. I'm going to do something stupid, I told myself. I'm going to do something stupid. "You're sure?" I asked as I followed him, feeling achy and already full of unruly remorse.

He turned a metal lock near the floor. "Alone at last," he said as he backed me into a corner shelf, kissing me so hard I could feel his teeth behind his lips.

"You kiss like a dog," I said.

"I do?" he asked. "Well, you have a lovely mouth. Your lips are so smooth and thin and pained. Such a slant to those pained lips." We crammed ourselves down onto the minuscule floor space, and I thought about something Will said once, how I always kept my eyes open.

"Do you have . . ." I asked, half hoping he didn't.

"As luck would have it." He smiled, reached into his trouser pocket and pulled out a condom.

A poster of a smiling Asian girl with doughnuts flying around her head stared back at me from the wall. I was imagining how great it would be if Will could just be brave, like me, and throw doubt to the wind in the name of love, as Daniel tore the edge of the condom wrapper with his teeth. The closet was black with my disappointment. Daniel moved around on top of me, his black hair hanging down, kissing my cheeks and forehead.

"Forget it," I said, wrestling out from under him and standing up. "I can't do this, sorry."

"You're joking," he said, still on the floor.

"I'm not," I said. "Sorry." I opened the door. It felt like we'd been in there forever, but when I got to the table stacked with marketing packets, the clock said 4:35. Daniel appeared and immediately got on the phone, ignoring me, and when it was time to go, I grabbed my bag and my coat and left without looking at him.

Someone shoved the revolving door downstairs, speeding it up and ejecting me onto the granite-flecked sidewalk. I turned the corner and passed a hot dog vendor, who smiled at me from under his baseball cap. I looked down at the black garbage bag hanging off his cart. I hadn't done it. That was good. But I wondered if it was possible to feel any emptier.

50.

When I got home, Monica walked toward me holding Ian in front of her. He was facing me, flailing his arms.

"Someone's happy to see you," she said.

"Hi, boo," I said, kissing him under his chin. I took him and he looked at me and smiled, quickly squirming around, wanting to get down. Monica left for school, and Ian and I headed into our room so I could lie down and figure out our next move. Ian didn't want to go, but I put him down on the rug next to my bed anyway. I stared up at the ceiling and saw the mean queen take shape within the shadows and light from outside. As Ian groped my sheet, I looked down at him and noticed a triangle-shaped bruise on the lower part of his cheek. It hadn't been there when I'd left that morning. I reached into my bag and texted Monica: *Did I. have a spill?*

Something started brewing as I waited for her to respond, the same rage that had been percolating all day, but now more distilled, honed. Monica was not taking as good care of Ian as I could. Monica was probably texting some friend as Ian pulled himself up the coffee table and then fell back down, banging his cheek.

I don't know how much time went by before I heard a key in the door. When I heard it, I had a split-second moment of thinking it was Ian's mother, finally coming home; that she'd give me my money and send me on my way.

Dad was on the phone telling someone he'd "circle back" to them after "the due diligence." I wondered how he could stand doing what he did all day. I got up slowly and brought Ian out to the living room, feeling voraciously hungry. Dad was in the kitchen, rinsing a cucumber, a bag of spinach on the counter.

"I don't want spinach salad," I said, getting a glass out of the cabinet and letting it slam shut.

"I wouldn't dream of making you spinach salad," he said offhandedly. "I was going to sauté it in some garlic."

"What's that?" I pointed to a cucumber on the cutting board.

"I believe it's a cucumber," he said, holding it up and turning it around, examining. "I was just going to slice it up to dip in some hummus. That all right?"

"I'm starving," I said. I filled the glass with water, letting it fill up too quickly to overflowing. My lonely life settled onto me like soot.

"Ian has a giant bruise on his face," I said, ripping off a paper towel. "I texted Monica because I want to know what the hell happened, but she hasn't responded."

He put the knife he'd been cutting the cucumber with down and went out to the living room to look at Ian's face.

"I don't see it," he said.

I stormed out of the kitchen. "Right there," I said, pointing. "How can you not see that? It's getting darker by the minute."

"Oh, that," he said, straightening up. "It doesn't look too bad. Just a little nick."

"No, well, I've got news for you," I said, my brain starting to tighten. "He's not safe! He's not safe, Dad, and you don't give a shit!" As I said it, I wondered what I was actually screaming about. I didn't want to watch Ian all day. I liked being away from home, escaping, even if it had to be at Pullman. I picked up a square plastic block Ian had chucked under the couch, understanding deep down that my emotional turmoil was much vaster and murkier than I realized, and that only pissed me off more.

Dad held his hands up and went back to the kitchen. "You're blowing this way out of proportion. Whatever happened, it's a small bruise. Given what happened with his leg, you must realize that accidents happen. To everyone. Including you." He pointed his finger at me.

"Now *you're* going to start with the irresponsible Thea bullshit?" I said.

"I didn't mean it as an attack," he answered, his voice growing tighter and more monotonous as he went back toward the kitchen. "Just be careful."

"I am careful!" I screamed, making him fumble and almost drop the cucumber. "I'm nothing but careful. Why is nothing I do ever good enough for you?"

He started to say something, then turned stonily back to the cutting board. Then he looked up again, gritting his teeth.

"C'mon, Dad, out with it!" I yelled, shaking. "What else? Anything else? Let's hear it. You think I'm a complete screw-up. Trust me, you don't have to say it."

"Thea, I suggest you collect yourself," he said, pointing the knife at me. "I certainly didn't come home early to hear this."

"Who asked you to come home early? You think I want to spend every freaking night with you? Please, go find a client who wants to have dinner, for once. Please!"

He looked at me, his mouth tightening into a little ball, which only spurred me on.

"I wish I could be anywhere *but* here, believe me."

"Great." He thrust his arm out at the door. "Then go."

I shoved past him and grabbed Ian off the living room

floor. He was wearing a onesie with blue stars on it. I'd have to get Ian dressed. We both looked at Ian. My whole life with Dad rose in my throat, our awkward, silent dinners, all the empty time I spent alone at his apartment when I was younger and he was at work, flipping through the pages of his photography books while I waited for him to get home, just so that I could say goodnight and finally go to bed—how I always, always waited up to say goodnight just to make it feel like there was a purpose to me sleeping over.

Dad stood frozen in the kitchen, the knife at his hip.

"Mom was right," I said. "What the hell was I thinking?"

51.

I had the key but I rang, which felt weird. Mom opened the door in her black silk bathrobe. She leaned forward, gripping the half-open door, and kissed me, smelling like sugary grapes.

"Sorry I didn't call," I said, hoisting Ian higher on my hip. "Dad and I had a fight."

"You did?" she whispered. "Alex is here."

"The married guy?" I asked, disgusted. She nodded. There were mascara smudges under her eyes, but the smudges somehow accentuated them. She looked pretty.

"I won't keep you." I threw our bag onto a dining room chair. "We just need to crash here." There were stacks of glossy real estate brochures held together in thick strips of white paper covering the table.

"What happened?" she asked, tying her bathrobe tighter.

"I don't even know. It was stupid." Ian wriggled to get down. Part of me expected her to pull up a chair and devour any gory details.

"You'll work it out," she said quickly. She glanced down the hall at her door, then turned and headed to the kitchen.

"He doesn't want to come out and say hi?" I asked, following her with Ian. "Meet your grandson?"

"Now's probably not the time for that," she said, looking skittishly at Ian. "Where's he going to sleep?"

"Don't worry, I'll rig something up." As I said it, it dawned on me: Ian had never been there.

"Okay, well, it's getting late. You guys should get some sleep." She looked nervous, like she wanted us to clear the area.

"Do you have any food?"

"Take a look." She opened the fridge, letting it hang ajar, and darted out of the kitchen before I could ask her to take Ian while I scavenged.

Ian had just started sitting up. I put him down on the kitchen floor with a toy and found a takeout container of brown rice. I dumped some soy sauce in and ate ravenously, spilling out dry rice clumps onto the floor. Ian spotted some rice near him on the floor and reached for it, but instead fell back on his head, his feet sweeping into the air. There was a long, deep pause before he screamed. His pipes had really developed and he seemed much louder, all of a sudden, than he used to be. I wondered about the neighbors, the Chesleys, next door with their stupid dachshund. I scarfed a few more bites and chucked the container into the trash, then grabbed Ian and scooted down the hallway to my bedroom.

Everything looked the same: my bed neatly made with my

white duvet and little lace pillow squarely in the middle of my two bigger pillows. How long had it been since I'd been there? I pulled Ian's blanket out and lay it on the floor. He fussed but grew quieter once I found the pacifier and shoved it into his mouth. I took his clothes off and put on a clean onesie, counting out loud with a stretchy mouth to keep him distracted. I took off my clothes down to my underwear and tank top, picked up Ian and jammed his head down on my shoulder as I walked him around singing "Twinkle, Twinkle." He was asleep within a minute, like he'd breathed in a magical rose in a fairy tale. I turned off as many lights as I could and pulled the covers down, figuring I'd put Ian between me and the wall. I did and he stayed miraculously asleep. I got my hook out of the bag and sat down at my desk, but I couldn't bring my hands to move. I looked around the dark room, at the line drawing of the Eiffel Tower above my bed and the stack of old jeans on the floor in the closet. There was something really sad about being there, as though time was passing and things were changing too quickly. I got into bed.

In the middle of the night I woke up in a panic, wondering if there was a chance that the fight with Dad would make him go down to the deli and buy a couple of six-packs, drink those, go down again for two more six-packs, drink those and pass out. The idea of him drinking again was almost as scary as the idea of him dying. I fell back to sleep, but then Ian woke up crying. I picked him up and walked around in the dark, squeezing his body across my chest, biting the inside of my cheeks, worried he was going to wake Mom and the cheater. He went on and on, calming down, then starting back up. He kept looking at the door, wanting to go, I think. At one point Mom peeked in.

"What's the matter with him?" she whispered.

"I don't know," I said, nudging the door closed. "He'll be all right. Go back to sleep."

In the morning I woke to the sound of drilling outside on the street and the sound of Mom's voice, telling someone on the phone, "Cancel it. I don't need it."

Ian was sleeping soundly after finally falling back at six. I pulled the duvet over his little shoulders, put my teddy next to him and snuck out, covered in a heavy, almost painful blanket of fatigue. When he woke up, he'd need to eat. There was a mango in the straw basket on the kitchen counter. I picked it up and squeezed, wondering if Ian could gum it down. Mom appeared, showered and with her hair combed back off her face.

"Did you get *any* sleep? she asked.

I shrugged. "He doesn't usually do that anymore. He's been really good at night."

"Guess I got lucky," she said. "Alex slept through it—how, I don't know. I think all men sleep like the dead."

"I think it's being in a new place," I said, cutting the mango into tiny pieces. "Is he still here?"

"He snuck out earlier."

"Of course he did," I said.

"He's not so bad, Thea." She swiped a piece of mango and popped it into her mouth.

"How would I know, right?" I asked. Ian woke up as I was plating the mango. I put the plate down on the dining table and went to my room. He was wedged into the crack by the wall, trying to roll onto his back. "Good morning, shuggi-buggi," I said. "I have mango." He looked up and around, wondering where the hell we were now.

"So what happened with Daddy?" Mom asked, eyeing me as I sat down with Ian.

"What are you looking at?" I asked.

"Nothing," she said innocently. "Did you see the flyers?"

"What flyers?" I asked, only then registering the piles of flyers covering the table. I picked up a stack and, with my free hand, slid the white sleeve down to the bottom so I could see what it was: a quadrant of photos, backlit and shot with a wide angle, of our apartment. HUGE, TRADITIONAL WHITE-BOX LOFT—TWO-BEDROOM IN THE HEART OF CHELSEA, read the banner across the front.

"Two million dollars?" was the first thing that came out of my mouth.

"That's what we valued it at," she said, standing yoga-ready straight, obviously proud.

"Wow," I said. I picked up a piece of slippery mango with my fingers and found Ian's lips. "Do you think you could have talked to me about it?"

"Oh, it's nothing, really," she said, sitting down on the living room rug in front of us. "I just thought I'd cast the net, see what little fishies I caught." She looked at Ian, watched him pick a piece of mango up by himself. "He's so sort of self-sufficient now, isn't he?"

"Mom, where would you even go?" I asked.

She lay down and flexed her red-toenailed feet. "I don't know," she said. "Maybe Gramercy or Tribeca. It's time for me to downsize."

My phone rang. It was Dad. "Look, Thea, I'm sorry about last night."

I put Ian on the floor next to Mom and scurried back to my room, ignoring his cries. "Why did you ask us to come and stay with you when it's clear you don't want us there?" I asked.

"Of course I want you here." His voice was a confused muddle. "What makes you think I don't want you here?"

"You just seem like you'd rather be alone."

"That's not true."

"Dad, you grunt. I ask you a question when you're cooking and you grunt."

He sighed.

"And I can't wait till nine o'clock to eat," I said. I smiled in spite of myself. "I just can't."

"Then have a snack, for Christ's sake."

"I can't. You make it impossible to set foot in the kitchen. It's a no-fly zone when you're in there. Face it. If you don't want us there, I don't want to do that to you."

"I do want you here." He said it so quietly I could hardly hear him. "I do. Can you come back? Before I go to work? I'll wait for you."

Back in the living room, Ian was lying on the rug, swatting at a playing card Mom was dangling in front of his face.

"I've forgiven him for last night," Mom said. "That was Daddy?"

"He wants us to go back," I said, stabbing a piece of mango.

Mom lay down on the rug, swaying her knees from side to side, the morning light delineating the deep smile lines around her mouth, her "parentheses" as she referred to them. "You two'll work it out," she said, yawning.

"Wait, I'm not done talking about this," I said, waving the flyer. "I think this is weird, just selling this place out from under me, without even *discussing* it first."

"Thea, I *told* you, it's just to see if someone bites."

"And if they do?"

"Then who knows." She tickled Ian's belly and he laughed, rolling onto her arm. "You've got such a cute little giggle, who knew?"

I asked her why she didn't seem that interested in hanging out with Ian.

"Of course I'm interested," she said. "I see him."

"You haven't seen him in at least a month."

"I haven't?" she asked, overly surprised.

"Yeah," I said. "I don't get it. He's your grandson."

She grimaced. "Don't remind me, please."

"But don't you want to see him growing? He changes every day. He's so bright-eyed. How could you not want to see him?"

"Of course I want to see him," she said, playing peekaboo with Ian. "Maybe I've been a little distracted with this real estate thing. I have four listings now. And I think I'm about to get another one."

"That's great," I said.

"Don't be so defensive," she said.

"What?" I implored. "It is. I mean it. I miss you, though."

"Well, I'm *around,* Thee." She rolled her eyes. "It's not like I'm not here if you need me."

"If you don't like seeing him, if he just reminds you of how I'm a failure, just say it. You can tell me, you know. That's kind of what it feels like. It's what everyone seems to be feeling these days."

"It's nothing like that," she said quickly. "I'm proud of you. You're making your own way. With any luck you'll end up in better shape than the Vanessas of the world. Maybe this will show you early on that it doesn't come easy. We can hope, right?"

258

She covered her face with her hands and said, "Huzzah!" when she took them away. Ian watched, delighted, waiting for her to do it again, and she smiled at him, but her eyes darted around the room restlessly. I'd seen that restless look so many times in my life and it occurred to me, maybe she'd gotten restless with *Dad*. Maybe, after all the fury around getting him to stop drinking, and after all the crazy anger she had about Bill Mindorff getting him to stop and not us and how Dad cared too much about work and making money, maybe all of that was just an excuse. Maybe she just hadn't loved him anymore.

She straightened her legs in front of her on the floor and stretched while Ian stared at her, awaiting her next move. "Anyway, Daddy always said I wasn't a baby person. And he might be right. I think I'm better when they speak."

52.

Dad opened the door and shooed us inside, as if he were pulling us into shelter from a tornado. "I worried about you two all night. Where did you go? Where did you sleep?"

"Mom's," I said, putting Ian down on the living room floor with the pack of playing cards Mom had given us. It seemed like I was always plopping him on the ground, like a sack of potatoes.

He looked at me intently. "Well, I'm glad you're back." He shifted his glasses up to the bridge of his nose. "I think we both could have handled things last night a bit better, don't you? I think we *both* have some apologizing to do."

"I guess so," I mumbled. Inside my head I was saying to myself, *Come on, be an adult. Apologize.* But I couldn't get the words out. Ian flung the cards all over the rug, and Dad and I watched as he tried to bend them back into the pack.

"Thea, you've got to bear with me," he said, leaning against the living room wall. "Your mind works at this clip. So like your mother. I didn't mean that, exactly. Christ, I don't know what I mean. Just that it's hard with you sometimes."

"What's hard?" I asked. "I'm doing everything you want me to do."

He shook his head vigorously, as though trying to clear his head of my voice and gather his thoughts. "You've got to stick with it, kiddo."

"Anyway, that doesn't matter," I said, kneeling on the floor. "Last night doesn't matter. What matters is, I have to make this work for me. I can't go crazy. I can't lie down and die. I'm his mother, and I love him and I'm a good mom, no matter what anyone says. But I have to dig myself out of this hole."

"You're in a hole?"

I laughed. "Isn't it obvious?"

"Well, I don't like to hear you say that."

"You can take it," I said.

He started to say something, but his eyes fixed on a *Newsweek* on the coffee table. For a second I thought he was actually starting to skim an article the magazine was open to. But then he looked up. "I don't understand how we got here, Thea," he said, searching my face. "I try and figure out how we all got here." His eyes crumpled into something I hadn't seen before and he hid his face behind his big knuckles, like I was the sun and he was shielding his eyes from me. He retreated with his hands like that till he reached the hallway, then turned around and went to his room.

"Ddddsss," Ian said from the floor, sprinkling spit down his chin. I reached over and wiped it with my sleeve, the living room weirdly silent and empty. After a few minutes Dad came down the hall with his suit jacket on and the features of his face in their usual placid formation. "Okay, well, I should get going." He paused in front of us on the floor, tugging his shirt sleeve.

"Dad, you know what?" I blurted out. "It's not the end of the world, what happened last night."

"I know it isn't." A quick, almost embarrassed smile flashed across his face, but his eyes stayed fixed on me; it was like an understanding passed between us that we both, in some hazy way, had been thinking of Mom and the old fights.

"You're really not enjoying that job, are you?" he asked.

"Uh, no," I said. "But enjoying it's not the point, is it?"

"Well, it's not meant to be torture." He laughed stiffly. "I just want you to get a glimpse. It's not always patently obvious to people what path they should pursue, based on their talents or skill sets or what have you."

"It's patently obvious that I don't want a career in private equity," I said. "It's patently obvious to me that I want to sell crocheted bikinis. And maybe crocheted skirts. It may sound silly or frivolous to you, but it's not."

"Let me ask you this, Thea," he said, clearing his throat. "How long does it take to make one swimsuit?"

"One bikini?" I said, standing up and taking my jacket off. "A couple of days. I'm getting really fast."

"And theoretically, how many orders would you expect to receive?"

"I'm not sure," I said. "But those three that just sold, and that first one I made, they all sold very quickly."

"How much do you think you could sell them for?"

"They each sold for three hundred," I said. "Remember, I told you?"

He brushed the shoulders of his suit jacket. "So if you made, say, ten a month, to be safe, that's well under three thousand dollars, given store commissions. Pre-tax."

"Yes, but there are those women in Brooklyn who could help."

"How many could they make?" he asked. He took a drink from a glass of water sitting on the stereo console, probably left there the night before.

"I don't know, fifty a month?"

"They'd make fifty," he said evenly.

"I'm not sure of the numbers yet, but that's what I was thinking."

"All of this is irrelevant since we're not clear on the numbers," he said, picking his briefcase up from the chair in the hallway. "But the point is, how much do you want to make on every swimsuit? You'd have to figure out how much you could sell the swimsuits for and then how much you can afford to make them for. Depending on how many stores have interest in your swimsuits and whether you could get someone to make them for as little money as possible or whether—"

"I don't have those answers yet," I interrupted, his repetition of the word *swimsuit* making me crazy. "Is this how you are with your clients? Someone comes in with a great idea and you just . . . shove it right up their asses?"

"You might say that." He smiled, fiddling with the lock on his briefcase. "That's what they pay me for." He opened the door and looked back. "You going to be home tonight?"

262

I nodded, thinking, How could it be any clearer: we had nowhere else to go.

When Monica arrived, I jumped in the shower, got dressed and kissed Ian goodbye. Monica had left her phone at our apartment, on top of the fridge, so she'd never gotten my text asking about Ian's bruise, which was barely visible at that point, so I decided to let it go. I got to work and Daniel ignored me, giggling into his headset. I couldn't believe I'd almost had sex with him. Malcolm didn't make an appearance all morning, and when I finally asked Daniel, he murmured something about his being in Canada.

Sue from Human Resources came by and said I could leave early if I wanted to, so I neatened the pile of forty files I'd just put together and left at three. I let Monica go and took Ian to the park in Union Square, where I pushed him in a swing for the first time. As I pushed him, his body flopped backward and forward inside the black rubber swing, and he had a sort of anxious look in his eyes and a tightness in his lips that made him look alarmingly like Dad. A bunch of little kids ran around with big sand-filled balloons, and the whooshing sound surrounded me as they punched them into the air. I remembered Dad, spouting his wisdom about my bikinis that morning, and thought, Maybe he wasn't critiquing my bikini dreams for pure sport or to make me feel like shit. Maybe he *was* trying, in his that's-what-they-pay-him-for, tutorial way, to help me.

53.

Mrs. Weston called me at work a month later.

"Will mentioned to me that it's your birthday Sunday. I thought I'd offer my services if you want to spend the day celebrating."

Even though I hated Will and thought he was the world's biggest traitor, wimp and asshole rolled into one, I took comfort in the fact that he had remembered my birthday.

"Thank you, Mrs. Weston," I said. Spend the day celebrating. I pictured myself leading a parade of drunken revelers down Broadway, waving silk streamers and banging oversized kettle drums.

Vanessa took a bus from Vassar on the big day and met me for lunch at a bistro in Soho we used to go to late night during our dancing days.

"I haven't been here since before I met Will," I said as I dove into the dark-wood banquette.

"Amazing, isn't it?" Vanessa chirped. The waiter sloshed water into our glasses.

"Am I a total loser, Vanessa? Living with Dad? Ian? Is it all just too much loserness?"

"You're only a loser if you feel like one." She opened her bag and pulled out a box wrapped in polka-dotted paper. "Do you feel like a loser?"

"Sometimes yes, sometimes no," I said, waving the box away.

"Well, I'm in the same boat. Vassar has a small amount of loser-stink on it. But it's okay."

"You sound like Mom," I said, putting on her voice. "School is for bloody wankers. . . ."

Vanessa laughed. "Remember how pissed she used to get at you when you said the word *wanker*?"

"But she could say it whenever she wanted." I nodded.

"God, I love this bread," Vanessa said, unfolding the cloth napkin that covered it. "Remember how much of it we used to . . . just . . . basket after basket?"

I picked up my present and opened it. It was for Ian: a stiff little black dog with a red leather collar.

"I thought it was adorable," she said, chewing.

I put the dog on the table, facing her. "You know you're a grown-up when you don't even care if presents aren't for you," I said. "Means I'm a good mom, right?"

"That's right," she said, flashing me a wink.

"He loves that other dog you gave him, by the way," I said, remembering how much I resented it when she first gave it to me at my makeshift shower. "He holds it to his chin by its ear, and the other day he made me take it outside with him. It's his favorite."

"I knew it would be when I saw it," she said gravely. "I had a feeling."

After lunch we walked around Soho, checking out clothes we couldn't afford as she told me about a preppie guy from Michigan she was obsessed with. It was a relief to hear her drone on and on, like a radio broadcast, about how he wasn't her type, about his ruddy cheeks and short, square body and his hands, blistered from playing lacrosse. It was a relief to be taken out of my dull, slightly worrisome existence. I asked her to stay over and she pretended to be tempted but then mentioned a party that night at school she "was supposed" to go to.

"You need to come visit soon," she said, sounding offended as she kissed me on the cheeks. "I can't believe you haven't yet. Give the boy a kiss for me, okay? From his auntie Ness?"

Vanessa got in the cab to Port Authority and I went to pick Ian up at Starbucks, the meeting spot Mrs. Weston had established in the two or three times she'd come to get him. She was always very accommodating about coming down to me from the Upper West Side, but she'd made it clear that she didn't want to pick him up at Dad's. She'd established the meeting spot right away—"Isn't there a Starbucks near you on Thirteenth Street?" she'd said, which made me think she'd figured it out before she called. I was a few minutes early, so I bought a massive cookie with M&M'S in it and sat down in a dirty velvet chair.

"Happy birthday, Mommy," I muttered to myself. The espresso machines screeched as I picked the M&M'S out of the cookie and thought about the fact that I didn't have any friends other than Vanessa. I would have to work on that. Even Vanessa was in a different place, as nice as it was to see her smiling, confident face.

She'd looked different. Her eyes seemed by turns more jaded and more excited, as though school had somehow intensified her reactions to the world. Was that what college did to people? Or maybe she'd always been like that and I'd just noticed it now. There were things that seemed new about her. Like the way she fired off texts with lightning speed instead of slowly hunting and pecking like she used to. And I hadn't seen her twirl her hair behind her shoulder once the whole day. It was an age-old habit of hers. I was trying to remember when I'd last seen her do it when the door swung open and Ian rolled in, asleep in his navy-blue sack. He was being pushed by Will.

I stood up. Will's head did a slow pivot across the line at the register, the tables, the corners. His hair was shorter and he was wearing a gray coat with tattered, unraveling cuffs, which I'd never seen. When he spotted me, a nervous smile crossed his face and quickly vanished, just like smiles appeared and vanished on his mother. He headed to the back in long, purposeful strides. I'd forgotten how tall he was. My legs were shaking.

"Hey," he said. We stood in front of each other for the first time since I'd left.

"Do you see him a lot?" I asked, my words rushing out as if we'd been midconversation. "When your mom gets him, do you see him then?"

"Sometimes, yeah," he said, crossing his arms. "That's okay, isn't it?"

"It would have been nice to know, that's all," I said. I put my hand on the stroller, starting to make a move.

"Can you stay a minute?" he asked.

"What for?"

"Just to talk."

"What about?"

"Come on, Thea," he said, forcing a smile.

"Come on, what? What is there to say?"

He tapped the velvet chair across from the one I'd been sitting in and then grasped my shoulder. "Sit."

I sat on the arm of the chair, staring at the door. I hated him, and at the same time I also wanted to crawl into the dark cave of his coat and spew and sputter my misery out.

"I just"—Will sat down and leaned forward—"I want to try and explain to you what happened. I still don't have a handle on it."

"Go ahead," I said.

"Look, Thea, I just, it was too much. I felt trapped."

"I didn't trap you," I said.

"I'm not saying it was right. I agreed to everything that went down, I know it. But that's how I felt."

He turned his head to the counter, where a crowd of people stood waiting for their drinks. "And when Ian was hurt, it sent me over the edge. I don't know how else to explain it. I panicked."

"It's one thing to panic," I snapped. "It's another to threaten and torture me."

"I know," he said quickly.

"How could you do that to me?" I asked. He leaned over and held me in a tight, awkward hug as I felt myself dissolve into sobs. I looked at Ian over his shoulder and allowed myself to feel it for the first time—how scared I'd been.

"I wish I could be as brave as you are," Will murmured. "You're so brave and you're a really good mother. I know you are. What I did was unforgivable." He pulled away and sank back into the velvet chair. "Thea, I feel like a failure on so many levels, I don't know where to begin."

A mom waiting by the bathroom opened up a bottle of juice, making the lid pop, and handed it down to her daughter. I didn't know what to say to Will. It seemed like there was nothing to say.

Will eyed the mangled cookie on the table. "Why didn't you just buy some M&M'S?" he asked, smiling weakly at me. "Happy birthday, by the way. Mom says you have a job."

I nodded. "Ian has a nanny." I couldn't help smiling. It sounded ridiculous.

"So did you know I'm thinking of getting my eye fixed?" he said.

"Fixed?" I asked. "How?"

"There's this thing they can do with a laser. I still won't be able to see out of it, but I'll be able to move it. It'll follow the other one."

"Wow," I said. We're so young, still, I thought. There's still so much to fix.

"Wow, what?"

"I think I might miss it."

"You'd miss my lazy, wandering eyeball?" He sat back and his good eye crinkled with something that I recognized for the first time in a clear, straightforward way. Will loved me. Despite what was going on, despite the fact that we couldn't be together. I had a flash of the way I often used to feel when I was with him, without even knowing it—rudderless and lonely—and I realized something: That was *me*, my emptiness, my cauldron of crazy, bottomless need, it wasn't him. Will *loved* me.

The kids behind the counter were starting the closing process, running water in the sinks, talking earnestly about whatever, laughing. We watched Ian sleep for a long time without saying anything, a storm of pride and desolation ripping through me before the fumes from the floor cleaner chased us out.

54.

"Ian, watch!" Dad calls from down the beach on Charter Island, where Ian is hobbling around, knee-deep in the water. Ian is two now. Even though his arms are immersed in the murky water as he digs for rocks, I can see how the crescents of fat around his wrists are dissolving into defined strokes of arms and hands.

Dad skips a rock seven times, almost all the way out to the raft. Ian looks up, too late.

"Yay!" Ian shouts, even though he missed it. A flock of geese sits on the water, out by the diving board at the end of the bluff. One by one they circle out from behind the rocky pier, forming a wide, moving arc.

"They're like dancers on a stage," Dad says, moving behind Ian and holding him by the shoulders to keep him from falling backward. "See that, Ian?"

I stand behind them on the beach, trying not to get my feet wet, fishing my camera out of my bag. I pull it out and turn it on, flipping back to the shot of Will and Ian I took a few days ago on the rocks in Central Park. Ian was trying to climb, but Will was smiling at the camera with his thumb in the belt loop of Ian's jeans. The confident father. We meet every weekend now, the three of us, and usually spend the day—but never the night—together, and at the end Will walks us to Dad's and gives us long, lingering hugs outside the building before he heads down the street.

"Can you take one of us?" I ask, handing Dad the camera and kneeling down next to Ian, who is bent over trying to dig a rock half his size out of the sand. Dad walks backward, in the water.

"Ian! Hoo hoo!" Dad calls.

I squint into the sun, just like I did on the same beach when I was six and Nana took that picture of me in the red, white and blue bikini. Sometimes when Dad and I fight, about the usual things—how I leave those plastic milk tabs lying around that always get tangled up in the garbage disposal, how I'm not taking any steps to enroll at NYU even *part-time*—I'll catch a flash of the same confused look on his face that he had sometimes with Mom, and I remember how angry and lost he seemed when I was younger, like he was kind of wrecked. Men are very fragile, it turns out. It's hard to bounce back from rejection. Once I understood that about him, it got easier for us.

I'm still working at Pullman. I graduated from the internship to a salaried position with benefits. Even though it is still mostly paper-pushing, I have my own desk. It actually makes me proud to flash my medical insurance card with my own name on it.

A few weeks ago Mom's friend Christine at *Bazaar* finally came through after Mom kept bugging her for me. In the June issue, next to a small photo of a model sitting on a beach ball in my all-time favorite red, white and blue bikini, Christine wrote that "Galehouse's designs" were "unique in their modesty," and that she could imagine them kicking off a "fresh, slutty-conservative trend in swimwear." I'd tacked up a website right before the article ran, and two weeks later I had 312 orders. Mom then took it upon herself to get in touch with her old friend Graham, who used to bartend at Fiona's and who's now a buyer for Barneys. That's when I sat Dad down in front of my laptop and we did the math.

"Ninety-three thousand, six hundred dollars," he said coolly. But I saw that jump-start his eyes did when he was discussing anything that involved a profit. It wasn't hard to miss.

"So what about helping me?" I'd asked matter-of-factly. This time, I was not the drunken slut crashing my rental car into gas stations in Europe, or even the little girl with the too-big shopping cart at the toy store. I was a mother who wanted to support her kid doing something she loved. This time I was channeling Ian. Ian Galehouse Weston, my albatross, my savior. I had to go after what I wanted, or neither of us would stand a chance. "I can't crochet three hundred bikinis all by myself. Can we please go to Brooklyn and meet these people?"

Dad shifted in his chair, clicking the tip of a pen up and down. "Okay," he'd finally said.

The shop was in a one-story, tan brick building in Red Hook. Carmen and I got there first and went up a flight of stairs, into a dim room with a square table in the middle of it. The table was covered with brown paper, with streaks of masking tape running along the sides and bottom, and five women were sitting around it. They all had long, black hair, and all but one had it tied back in low ponytails.

"Thea, this is Dalma, Lydia, Elizabeth, Josie and—I'm sorry I've forgotten your name," Carmen said. "You're new, aren't you?"

The woman nodded and smiled. "I'm Jade."

"Josie and Jade," Carmen said. "So this is Thea and she has designed a beautiful bikini, which everyone wants to buy."

Dad walked in as they said, "Ahh, bikini," giggling, in unison.

"What's so funny?" he asked.

"This is my father," I said to Carmen.

Carmen shook his hand vigorously. "Nice to meet you." She waved her arms around the room. "Yeah, so we're trying to set Thea up with a . . . production situation."

Dad glanced at me skittishly, nervous about what he was getting into. "Right," he said. "And are these the women who would be helping?"

Carmen nodded. "They're wonderful. Very skilled and very meticulous. I love their work."

"How does it go, then?" Dad said. "They get orders from designers and fulfill them within a certain time frame?"

As if on cue, a man with his hair combed over in a short-sleeved button-down shirt stepped out of a door in the narrow corridor at the end of the room. He walked up to us and introduced himself.

"I'm Mr. Silva," he said. "We charge by the hour. If the order is a large one, sometimes by the piece."

"Or the two-piece." Dad smiled at me. "Get it?"

One of the women was sliding the bikini onto a white plastic mannequin.

"It's so nice," the woman said. The others nodded enthusiastically, then dipped their heads back to their needles.

"It *is* nice, Thea," Dad said, surprised. "There's a pretty cut to them. I was expecting them to look more . . . showy."

"That's the whole point," I said.

"She's got a very specific sensibility," Carmen interjected. "She knew exactly how she wanted them to look."

"Hmmm . . ." he said, turning to Mr. Silva. "Well, how do we do this? Is there some sort of contract?"

"You tell me what you want and I write something up for you," Mr. Silva said.

Dad looked at him and rubbed his mouth. I could tell he was put off by Mr. Silva's vagueness. "Well, you need to make three hundred," he said, turning to me. "Is that right, Thea?"

I nodded. "Three hundred and twelve, so far, but I can do the twelve."

"We have to factor in shipping costs." Dad put his hand on my shoulder and paused, watching the women.

"And work out some kind of wholesale deal for the yarn," I said.

"I can help you with that," Carmen said quickly.

"And are you . . . looking for anything?" Dad asked Carmen.

"Me?" she asked, putting her fist to her chest. "Oh, no, I'm just helping her out."

It hadn't occurred to me that Carmen would want a cut. "Thank you," I said. "Really, thank you."

Carmen smiled at me and put her hand on my back. "You deserve it, kiddo."

"I have no idea what the margins are in the garment business." Dad frowned at the floor. "Mr. Silva, what if we offered you twenty thousand dollars to do the work?"

Mr. Silva looked away, smiling passively. "Three hundred pieces?" he said, gesturing at the women. "Twenty-five."

Dad looked at me. "When do you need them by?"

"Two weeks?" I said. "Is that a reasonable amount of time or will you have to hire more women?"

"We'll see how it goes," Mr. Silva said.

"Shall we put something in writing, then, to that effect?" Dad said. "I can write you a check today."

I heard a garbage truck groan outside as Dad started to follow Mr. Silva. "This will all be in addition to your work at Pullman," he said sternly. "And you're going back to school someday."

I nodded as he turned down the hall. Carmen winked at me and shot me a subtle high five.

"I'm going to make Dad proud," I said.

Now I watch as Dad turns the camera horizontally, then vertically, then horizontally again, my eyes almost tearing from the setting sun, trying to hold Ian still as he fends off a patch of seaweed coming toward him. I wonder if we'll just go on together like this forever, until Dad's an old man and I'm a spinster, long forgotten by Will, and Ian's a punk in the park. About a year after we split, Will and I started talking on the phone, late at night, when the rest of the world was shut down and far away, the way we used to when we first met. I learned some new things, mainly just *how* afraid he was of failing. I tried not to think about the irony of it: he was so afraid of failing and yet he'd failed *us* so completely. But as time went on, I realized that part of being a healthy, well-adjusted adult meant not holding on to stuff that made you so angry you couldn't see straight. There was no point.

Will is coming back to us someday, I think, as Dad finally clicks the shutter. He is, and if he doesn't, more power to me for believing that he will. Once I'm hooked, I don't let go. So sue me. I'm not holding my breath—I've got things to do, a luxury crocheted-accessories business to build. Department store contracts to win.

I splash seaweed out of Ian's way and let him throw about fifty more rocks into the water until it starts to get dark. "We should get back to the house," I say, imagining all the things I wanted to do once Ian went to sleep, like think about designs for a collection of crocheted skirts. "It's getting late."

Dad wades onto the beach and rolls down his khakis. I pick Ian up and we climb the steep steps and cross the street into the parking lot, where Dad helps me strap Ian into the seat on the back of my bike.

"So I'll see you two at home," he says. He is running into town to pick up a pizza. A car drives by, too fast for Dad's liking, stirring up the sandy pavement.

"Slow down!" he yells after the car, taking a few indignant steps out into the street. "Jesus!" he mutters, turning back to me. "Should I get a salad?"

"Only if you want," I say. "It's too hard to think about salad when there's a pizza staring you in the face." He smiles, the creases on his forehead relaxing, revealing little white lines. "You're a little sunburned," I say.

"Am I?" he asks, wiping sand away from Ian's mouth and tightening his strap. He heads to his car as I start to pedal out of the parking lot, getting ready for the hill that leads to our house. Dad passes, waving his arm at us out the window, and I have a strange thought—the weird, hard-to-connect possibility that Dad loves me in the same, dumbstruck way that I love Ian. When we reach the top of the hill, Dad's blinker fires shots of red into the dusk as he turns the corner. His car stretches farther ahead of us, his blinker still on, a flickering, distant star, here now but not forever.